Hooked

Political Interest is the strongest predictor of "good citizenship," and yet we hardly know anything about it. For the first time in over three decades, here we have a study explaining what political interest is, where it comes from, and why it matters. Providing the most thorough description available of political interest in four Western democracies over many decades, the book analyzes large household panel data sets, rarely used in political science, to explain how interest develops in people's lives. The book's analytical approach pushes applied social scientists to consider how we can use panel data to better understand political behavior. It does so in a way that doesn't gloss over complexities, but explains them in accessible language. Advanced statistical methods are presented informally, accompanied by graphical illustrations that require no prior knowledge to understand the methods used.

MARKUS PRIOR is Professor of Politics and Public Affairs at Princeton University. He is the author of *Post-Broadcast Democracy* (Cambridge University Press, 2007), which won the 2009 Goldsmith Book Prize and the 2010 Doris Graber Award for the "best book on political communication in the last 10 years." Prior's work has appeared in numerous journals including *American Political Science Review*, the *American Journal of Political Science*, and the *Journal of Politics*.

Hooked

How Politics Captures People's Interest

MARKUS PRIOR
Princeton University

CAMBRIDGE
UNIVERSITY PRESS

University Printing House, Cambridge CB2 8BS, United Kingdom

One Liberty Plaza, 20th Floor, New York, NY 10006, USA

477 Williamstown Road, Port Melbourne, VIC 3207, Australia

314–321, 3rd Floor, Plot 3, Splendor Forum, Jasola District Centre, New Delhi – 110025, India

79 Anson Road, #06–04/06, Singapore 079906

Cambridge University Press is part of the University of Cambridge.

It furthers the University's mission by disseminating knowledge in the pursuit of education, learning, and research at the highest international levels of excellence.

www.cambridge.org
Information on this title: www.cambridge.org/9781108420679
DOI: 10.1017/9781108355001

© Markus Prior 2019

First published 2019

Printed and bound in Great Britain by Clays Ltd, Elcograf S.p.A.

A catalogue record for this publication is available from the British Library.

Library of Congress Cataloging-in-Publication Data
NAMES: Prior, Markus, 1974– author.
TITLE: Hooked : how politics captures people's interest / Markus Prior.
DESCRIPTION: New York, NY : Cambridge University Press, 2019. |
    Includes bibliographical references.
IDENTIFIERS: LCCN 2018010105 | ISBN 9781108420679 (hardback) |
    ISBN 9781108430746 (pbk.)
SUBJECTS: LCSH: Political psychology. | Political participation–Psychological aspects. |
    Democracy–Psychological aspects.
CLASSIFICATION: LCC JA74.5 .P694 2018 | DDC 324.01/9–dc23
    LC record available at https://lccn.loc.gov/2018010105

ISBN 978-1-108-42067-9 Hardback
ISBN 978-1-108-43074-6 Paperback

For Purcell

Contents

Figures

Tables

Acknowledgments

One of the hardest things for me is knowing when to stop. When Kinder tells you to "finish the damn thing!" and your editor's reaction to the possibly last remaining chapters is, "mercy, it's comprehensive," it might be time. When colleagues ask you about progress with that tender air of not wanting to push you further into psychological distress, it might be time. When friends stop asking altogether – out of empathy or because they don't think they could possibly be correct that you're still working on *that* thing – it might be time.

But Kinder also urged Zaller to take a bottle of vodka into the woods to do more work on the last chapter of *Nature and Origins*. Maybe Kinder just went easy on me because he felt guilty about possibly having made Zaller the author of the greatest unpublished book in social science. (Yes, different book. Same Zaller, though.) And often, there is good reason to keep at it, to march (crawl) toward learning more, to not give up when there's still a chance of getting it right, just a little more right.

Also, so much stuff out there would have benefited from a little more time and another bottle of vodka.

I did learn from the masters. In those professional-impressionable years after I was hired at Princeton, Larry Bartels, Tali Mendelberg, and Marty Gilens all took many years to finish their respective book projects. But who's counting now, after three magisterial volumes that changed how we think about inequality, representation, and, oh wait, men being unable to shut up. If the outcome is only half as good in my case as in theirs, I'll be fortunate to have followed their lead.

Over the years, I have benefited from the advice and support of many people. Larry has been an intellectual inspiration, a role model, and a quiet, patient mentor. He offered much advice early in the project; in recent years, I have often regretted that I couldn't just walk down one flight of stairs to ask him more questions. Tali and Marty have provided many reactions and suggestions on this project, but above and beyond, they are fantastic and generous colleagues. Doug Arnold read several versions of the manuscript and offered helpful feedback. I greatly value his professional support and friendship. And it's hard to have a conversation with Chuck Cameron that's not thought-provoking, or a meal not pleasantly excessive.

Lori Bougher worked with me on this project for almost four years. She knows many of the large, complex, and challenging datasets used in this book better than I do and made it possible to get so much out of them. I thank Princeton for supporting her position and Lori for her skillful, thorough work. Ask her about the measurement of education in European household panels sometime!

Gaurav Sood helped me with this project when he was postdoc at Princeton. I benefited from discussion of my work and theirs with my graduate students Katie McCabe and Kabir Khanna and with CSDP fellows Vin Arceneaux, Talia Stroud, and Sean Westwood as part of our occasional discussion group meetings.

Skip Lupia and Nick Valentino organized a book manuscript workshop for me in Ann Arbor. The two of them and Jamie Druckman read the entire manuscript and provided very detailed, tremendously helpful written comments. For discussion and suggestions at the workshop, I also thank Ted Brader, Vince Hutchings, Stuart Soroka, Rocio Titiunik, Hakeem Jefferson, Alison Beatty, Erin Cikanek, Chris Skovron, Fabian Neuner, and Dan Hiaeshutter-Rice.

Some of the analysis in this book relies on techniques developed in econometrics thirty years ago and thoroughly out of fashion in modern political science research, for justifiable reasons I only appreciated slowly. Many political methodologists took hours out of their days to help me understand the methods I was hoping to use and address my often somewhat confused questions: Chris Achen, Neal Beck, Matt Blackman, Josh Clinton, Simon Jackman, Shigeo Hirano, Kosuke Imai, Suzie Linn, Luke Keele, In Song Kim, Michal Kolesár, James Lo, Scott Lynch, Marc Meredith, Xun Pang, Kris Ramsey, Jas Sekhon, Rocio Titiunik, and Greg Wawro.

For feedback and comments on early versions of the book manuscript, conference papers that would become the manuscript, and research I presented at different venues, I am thankful to Erik Amnå, Eva Anduiza, Adam Berinsky, André Blais, John Bullock, David Campbell, Michael Delli Carpini, Claes deVreese, Eugénie Dostie-Goulet, Andy Guess, Jacque Eccles, Peter Enns, Ryan Enos, Connie Flanagan, Aina Gallego, Jane Green, Eitan Hersh, Sunshine Hillygus, John Holbein, Cindy Kam, Joe Kahne, Young Mie Kim, Casey Klofstad, Martin Kroh, Adam Levine, Brett Levy, Dave Lewis, Aaron Martin, Irene Martín, Sara McLanahan, Cecilia Mo, Russ Neuman, Maria Petrova, Silvia Russo, Dhavan Shah, Danielle Shani, Håkan Stattin, Laura Stoker, Dietlind Stolle, Jesper Strömbäck, Josh Tucker, Ariel White, Chris Wlezien, Alexander Wuttke, and John Zaller.

Audience reactions helped me when I presented this work at the Department of Political Science at the University of Southern California, the Working Group in Political Psychology and Behavior at Harvard University, the College of Communication at University of Texas, Austin, the conference for Panel Data Users in Lausanne, the Institute for Political Economy and Governance in Barcelona, the Amsterdam School of Communication Research, the Department of Political Science at Lavall University, the Centre for the Study of Democratic Citizenship at McGill University, the Department of Political Science at Columbia, the Department of Government at Cornell, the Department of Political Science at the University of Michigan, the School of Communication at Northwestern University, the Institute for Social Research at the University of Michigan, Örebro University, the Juan March Institute, the Universidad Autónoma de Madrid, the Universitat Autònoma de Barcelona, and the MIT American Politics Speaker Series.

Princeton University has generously supported time for research on this book. So did the Shorenstein Center on Media, Politics and Public Policy at Harvard's Kennedy School where I spent a semester as a Joan Shorenstein Fellow in 2016 and the Center for the Study of Democratic Institutions at Vanderbilt University in 2014. I would like to thank Helene Wood at Princeton for her assistance over all the years I've been there.

This book draws on a lot of secondary data. Many principal investigators devoted their time and effort to collecting those data. Many funding agencies paid for the data collection. I am grateful to all of them, but this book would simply not exist without the household panel surveys conducted in Britain, Germany, and Switzerland. It is inspiring to see governments use considerable public funds to allow projects of this scope and quality.

Robert Dreesen, my editor at Cambridge, provided detailed advice on how to make the book more readable. I couldn't make it into a page-turner, but his interest and effort inspired me and significantly improved this book. For their work on the design and production of this book, I thank Josh Penney, Ishwarya Mathavan, Chris Bond, and Liz Connor.

Why Political Interest Matters and How to Understand Its Origins

You are interested in politics. Chances are you regularly vote and follow the news and know something about the major legislative proposals debated in Congress or Parliament. You may well have contributed some of your time and energy to making self-governance work, perhaps volunteering with a community group, serving on the school board, or helping raise money for a political cause. You are not alone. Many other people are politically interested. They might not all pick up this book, but they read political history and *Politico* and inside accounts of election campaigns; they'll read *The Atlantic* and *The Economist*, and biographies of presidents and prime ministers. Largely owing to their political interest, devoting hours and hours to reading and hearing and talking about politics is a treat for them, not a burden.

Yet here's what people who read books like this one often forget: Not everyone lives this way. Our interest in politics makes us different from many other people. There are people who have no interest whatsoever in politics, and there are many more with varying degrees of moderate interest. On a five-point scale used by the American National Election Study in 2008, about 10 percent of Americans reported being "extremely interested ... in politics," and another 25 percent "very interested." But close to 10 percent are "not interested at all" and about 20 percent are only "slightly interested." And they don't read, watch, or hear much about politics.

At first glance, this variation in political interest seems no more remarkable than variation in taste for wine, country music, or modern art. In all of these domains – and many others – interest ranges from low to high, with plenty of shades of gray in between. Yet even if interest in politics resembles the psychological experience of interest in art or music, the consequences for our societal well-being are profoundly different: Only political interest comes with a membership in the self-governing class.

The self-governing class[1] is the segment of the population that contributes to collective decisions about how we run our country. Membership is not formal, and contributions vary. Some people only cast a vote now and then, without much information about their choice. Others may not even vote, but collect and share information that influences those who do. Some people study politics exhaustively just to make their own best decision. Still others give much time and effort to building coalitions and organizing collective action. Together, through their political decisions and actions, they decide how a country addresses challenges and moves forward.

Political interest is not required to join the self-governing class. Some learn about politics or get involved out of a civic duty. Others just say yes when asked. Some receive a salary for their contributions to governance or feel that political involvement is necessary to preserve their fortune. Likewise, political interest does not guarantee membership. Structural features of the political system and the constraints of individual lives can make it difficult, sometimes even impossible, for politically interested people to become politically involved. But for the most part, the obstacles in modern democratic systems are not powerful enough to deny membership in the self-governing class. As research reviewed later in this chapter demonstrates, people who join in self-governance, in ways big or small, alone or with others, not only turn out to be more interested in politics but are often involved precisely because they are more interested.

This book's central puzzle arises directly from the established link between political interest and political involvement. If the boundaries of the self-governing class are defined not by property requirements, professional qualifications, or reasoning skills, but by the extent of people's interest in politics, then where does this political interest come from?

It's tricky, yet the reason for trying to solve this puzzle could not be clearer: Imagine that we understood how to raise political interest among the third of Americans who are "slightly interested" or "not interested at all." According to existing research, many would join the self-governing class because their raised interest would lead them to see what's at stake in the next election, learn something about the candidates and parties on the ballot, and cast a vote. The third of Americans with middling levels of interest may already dabble in self-governance once in a while, perhaps voting in the loudest presidential elections or occasionally peeking at a headline. Yet make them "extremely interested in politics," or at least "very interested," and they might read beyond the first paragraph, consider their political decisions more thoroughly, and vote even in state and local

---

[1] I owe this phrase to Ted Brader, who used it at a manuscript workshop for this book and does not remember if he heard it somewhere or came up with it himself.

elections with less of a roar. Some might even go from supporting a representative to representing others. To be sure, greater political interest would not make everyone a model citizen. Some people's opinions may become stronger but not wiser. And higher political interest alone is not enough to break down remaining structural barriers to political participation or afford everyone the time to get involved. But on balance, greater political interest promises greater civic engagement and more effective self-governance.

So, how does political interest develop? We don't know. We do not even know if political interest has the stability of a personal trait or the volatility of a regularly updated assessment of the political environment. Psychologists and educators have found ways to motivate individuals to tackle a specified task – but politics is more than a task, and political interest is different from persistence in the face of adversity. In this book, I build on ideas from psychology to derive and test a theory of political interest.

The very nature of how interest forms and blossoms presents a formidable challenge for research, however. Analytically speaking, the trouble with you, me, and the other politically interested folks is this: Our interest in politics rarely dips from its high levels. It was not the bill considered by the legislature last month or yesterday's cover story about rivalries between cabinet members that got us interested. We've been at this for a long time. Reports and analyses and historical accounts of politics don't create our political interest; they feed it.

Hence, one reason why you and I are not particularly helpful here is that we cannot easily point to a particular root cause of our political interest. Because, as this study will show, most of us have been interested for a very long time and there are not too many adults whose political interest changes markedly, even over long periods. We thus have limited material to work with in figuring out what triggered these changes. It's a challenge worth accepting, though, because its promise is a greater understanding of how political interest develops and how we might increase it among those who lack it. Doing that might help make our democratic system work better. Before we spend more time chasing the vision of greater political interest, however, I owe you two explanations: What exactly does it mean to be interested in politics? And, how sure can we be that raising political interest would expand the self-governing class and increase its capacity?

WHAT IS "POLITICAL INTEREST"?

There are two basic types of interest, both of which you have surely experienced (although perhaps not with respect to politics). When something around you catches your attention, intrigues you right then and there, and makes you feel (possibly without thinking it), "Hmm, this is interesting" – that's one type of interest. The other type is the sense that leads you to say "I am interested in X," even when X is not around at the moment. Instead, you expect that engaging with X in the future will be a gratifying experience.

The first type is a feeling of curiosity and discovery. It is an emotional reaction triggered by something around us and involves a momentary sense of wanting or liking the object that prompted it. Psychologists call this type of interest *situational* interest. It can be over very quickly, either because the emotion wears off or because the object that triggered it disappears from our environment.

The second type, *dispositional* interest, is a more lasting sentiment that can sustain itself even when the initial environmental stimulus has disappeared. In the absence of the triggering object, there must be something inside us that makes us go back, either to the same object or an object like it, because we expect that doing so will be rewarding. Dispositional interest arises from situational interest, but most experiences of situational interest never develop into a predisposition that endures in the absence of the environmental trigger.

Applied to the political domain, political interest starts with situational interest when something in the environment related to politics triggers an affective reaction. Dispositional political interest entails an expectation that engaging with political content again in the future will turn out to be gratifying. Chapter 2 will flesh out this definition of political interest and describe the general psychological model of interest on which it is based.

For a proper understanding of representative democracy, the distinction between situational or dispositional interest is significant, so determining empirically to what extent political interest is dispositional will take up a good portion of Part I of this book. If few people ever develop dispositional interest, attention to politics would be driven mostly by a long series of environmental triggers that might get people to see this or support that. The key to self-governance would be to ensure constant political stimulation in the hopes of continuously generating situational political interest. The hoopla of political campaigns and the breathless pace of the media's horserace coverage look like they operate on the assumption of mostly situational interest. If, on the other hand, interest in politics is to a considerable extent dispositional, self-governance does not require constant stimulation because people develop a demand for politics that is sustained even when the hoopla dies down. People become involved in politics because they want politics, not because politics wants them.

A fundamental property of interest is already obvious: It is an internal disposition, clearly distinct from a behavior. Participation, in contrast, is a behavior. Just as participation can occur in the absence of political interest, it is possible to be interested in politics without participating in it. Barriers to participation may not be barriers to becoming politically interested. Resource constraints, for example, impose limits on political participation, but in principle should not affect interest. People may be too busy to follow politics or volunteer (Brady et al. 1995; Verba et al. 1995), but even someone without a minute to spare for these activities can still be highly interested.[2]

Political interest is also different from political sophistication, a cognitive concept that encompasses knowledge and understanding of politics. Political sophistication is at least in part the result of political learning, another behavior. It is possible to be knowledgeable about politics without finding it interesting. Likewise, a politically interested person does not necessarily have a clear and well-informed grasp of politics.[3]

Political interest, political participation, and political sophistication are sometimes conflated and treated as one. They are typically considered as facets of "good citizenship." And, as the next section will show, they are strongly related empirically. But in order to understand this amalgam of motivational, behavioral, and cognitive political engagement, it is important to distinguish the three concepts and examine their causal connections because their close interrelations are neither inevitable nor immune to contextual variation. What makes political interest important as a separate concept is the claim that it drives the other two.

WHY POLITICAL INTEREST MATTERS

A half-century of research on public opinion, political psychology, and political behavior has made it an article of faith that politically interested individuals are, in a variety of ways, more politically involved than people who lack interest. Political interest stands out in past research as a strong, often the strongest, predictor of political engagement. For Bennett (1998, 539), "[w]ithout question, the most important reason for young Americans' lack of exposure to political reporting in the media is indifference to public affairs." Analyzing the impact of political interest on political sophistication, Luskin

---

[2] Past studies of political involvement have often used summary scales of involvement in which political interest is one component along with self-reported behaviors (e.g., Verba and Nie 1972; van Deth 1990; Nie et al. 1996; Zukin et al. 2006). This practice makes it impossible to distinguish the roles of motivation and behavior. Lupia and Philpot (2005, 1122) equate high political interest with "spend[ing] considerable time focusing on politically oriented tasks and materials." Operationally, Lupia and Philpot (2005, 1132) treat political interest not as a behavior, but as an intention to engage in political behaviors (learning about politics, talking with others about it, and voting). This is closer to the definition of political interest as a predisposition. It still infers interest from its correlates, however.

[3] Political interest also differs from Zaller's (1992) concept of "political awareness ... [which] refers to the extent to which an individual pays attention to politics *and* understands what he or she has encountered ... Political awareness denotes intellectual or cognitive engagement with public affairs as against emotional or affective engagement or no engagement at all" (21, emphasis in original). Zaller contrasts political awareness and political interest, mentioning "people who describe themselves as highly interested in politics, which I take as a form of affective involvement" (43). The characterization of political interest as purely affective is not consistent with psychological work on interest.

(1990, 344, 348) concludes "that interest has a huge effect" and that "[b]y far the most influential variable, unsurprisingly, is interest." In Shani's (2009a, 152) reading of the literature, "The importance of citizens' political interest for explaining democratic politics can hardly be overrated. Virtually every scholar who has studied people's political knowledge, political participation, and many other political phenomena has noted the central role of the motivation to engage in politics." Politics looks very different to politically interested people.

Politically interested people are more likely to seek out information about politics (Prior 2007; Geer et al. 2014). All that reading, watching, and listening makes a difference for the quality of political decision-making. Many studies have shown politically interested people to be more knowledgeable about politics (e.g., Berelson et al. 1954, 31; Atkin et al. 1976; Bennett 1986, 130, 137; Luskin 1990; Verba et al. 1995, 348 fn.29; Delli Carpini and Keeter 1996; Jennings 1996; Westle 2006; Prior and Lupia 2008; Prior 2014).[4] They are also more likely to hold political opinions, identify with a political party, and prefer one candidate over another for president (Lazarsfeld et al. 1948 [1944], 41; Zuckerman et al. 2007; Sides and Vavreck 2013, 106). Yet having opinions and candidate preferences is not necessarily indicative of good decision-making. It could, after all, follow a rush to judgment or a failure to consider counter-arguments. But politically interested people are also more internally consistent in their political thinking (Berelson et al. 1954, 26–7; Baldassarri and Gelman 2008), and more likely to make political decisions in accordance with their preferences. Kohler (2005), for example, finds that the impact of changes in occupational status on party preference in Germany is conditioned by political interest. Former workers who become self-employed or start to employ other people change their party affiliation to the conservative, pro-business side (CDU/CSU) only if they are politically interested. Likewise, it takes high political interest for individuals who experience the opposite transition to change their affiliation to the labor-friendly Social Democratic Party.

The association between political interest and political participation, too, is empirically strong. Politically interested people are much more likely to report having voted (e.g., Lazarsfeld et al. 1948 [1944], 45–6; Berelson et al. 1954, 31; Bennett 1986, 130, 142; Powell 1986; Verba et al. 1995). They also report many more other forms of participation, such as attending political meetings, donating money to campaigns, and engaging in socially-motivated boycotts of consumer products (Bennett 1986, 130, 146–50; Verba et al. 1995; Gaiser and Rijke 2000; Campbell 2006, ch.6; Quintelier and van Deth 2014). The main reason for these associations is probably that interest motivates behavior, but the political environment is also more inviting of politically interested people. They are more likely to be the target of mobilization (Enos et al. 2014; Hersh

---

[4] This is consistent with research in educational psychology, which has repeatedly shown interest to help comprehension, learning, and depth of information processing (for reviews, see Schraw and Lehman 2001; Hidi and Renninger 2006).

2015), and attempts to encourage political participation often have significantly greater effects on individuals who are politically interested to begin with (Brady et al. 1999; Finkel 2002).

Much of the research on interest and participation is based on respondents' reports of their participation. If all evidence came from self-reports, we should be concerned that greater political interest might only make people good at pretending to be politically involved. Part of the relationship between political interest and reported political involvement is indeed spurious because it reflects correlated measurement error. Politically interested respondents are more likely to report that they voted when in fact they abstained (Ansolabehere and Hersh 2012). Overreporting of news exposure may also be more pronounced among the politically interested (Prior 2009b). But this does not mean that strong correlations between interest and involvement are measurement artifacts. For one, political interest is still the strongest correlate of turnout when data on turnout come from official records (Bennett 1986, 130, 144; Clarke et al. 2004, 252–61; Ansolabehere and Hersh 2012). Moreover, some elements of political involvement can be measured well in surveys. The ability to accurately answer knowledge questions is higher among more politically interested respondents, and this is not a quantity that can be overreported. In fact, Prior and Lupia (2008, 175) find that a monetary incentive for answering knowledge questions correctly has a particularly strong effect on more interested respondents, suggesting that "traditional survey procedures fail to motivate moderately and (to a lesser extent) strongly interested citizens to try as hard as they can when answering political knowledge questions. Hence, past survey-based studies have likely underestimated the effect of political interest on political knowledge."[5]

Another reason for skepticism is more serious. Research linking political interest and citizenship outcomes often rests on the association between these

---

[5] Prior and Lupia (2008) also show that lack of ability is *not* the main obstacle to a more informed electorate. When survey respondents are given a full day to answer political knowledge questions, the politically uninterested among them reveal considerable learning skills. Politically very interested people still answer significantly more questions correctly, but the difference is only half as big as the equivalent difference when respondents must answer immediately:

> Many people who are intrinsically motivated to follow politics acquire political information regularly and regardless of whether a decision is impending. They are knowledgeable when we ask them fact-based questions on surveys. Others who do not enjoy politics as much are less likely to carry such information in their declarative memories. When survey interviewers contact them without warning and the survey rushes along apace, these people do not perform well. But it would be a mistake to assume that such observations are sufficient to infer a general lack of capability. (Prior and Lupia 2008, 179)

Judging by the behavior of less interested respondents, the de facto impediment to learning for them is not that they are incapable of finding political information, but that they are not usually motivated to do so. Political interest brings that natural inclination to learn about politics even if you could look up information later.

variables measured in the same survey. That makes it difficult to establish that political interest is indeed the cause. Both political interest and the citizenship outcome are in place at the time of measurement, and there is no straightforward way to determine which came first. Elements of citizenship may have influenced political interest. Or an unmeasured third variable influenced both political interest and citizenship outcomes.

Studies that aim to break up this simultaneity are not as frequent. Butler and De La O (2011) note that residents of different linguistic regions in Switzerland tend to follow media coverage from neighboring countries that share their language. Because an election in a neighboring country raises political interest only among those Swiss who speak the language of the country, they can plausibly break the chicken-and-egg challenge by assuming that elections in neighboring countries cannot be influenced by political interest of Swiss people (and, in technical terms, can thus serve as valid instruments for political interest). Butler and De La O's results show substantial effects of interest on participation.

Verba et al. (1995, 352–3) also use an instrumental variables technique to reduce simultaneity concerns. When they instrument political interest in the same interview that also gauged political participation with political interest measured in a screener interview about a year earlier, the coefficient for political interest predicting political participation doubles, while the associations with partisan attachment and political information, equally instrumented, remain unchanged. (It should be noted that the estimates remain biased if participation, measured but not necessarily performed at a later time, already caused political interest in the screener.) In estimating reciprocal causation between political interest and political sophistication (a multi-faceted measure of what people know about politics), Luskin (1990) makes the assumption that age and parental political interest cause interest, but not sophistication. His analysis supports a large effect of interest on sophistication.[6]

Measuring political interest some time before measuring the purported effects of interest also adds plausibility to the case for interest as a causal factor (although it cannot rule out alternatives completely). Blais and St-Vincent (2011) use data from a two-wave panel and find that the association between political interest and turnout is somewhat weaker but still statistically significant when political interest measured in the pre-election wave replaces political interest measured in the same post-election interview as turnout. Political interest is also related to future political learning (Dimitrova et al. 2011) and change in the self-reported frequency of political discussion (Eveland et al. 2005).[7] I add a similar demonstration in Chapter 4, showing that turnout

---

[6] Luskin's analysis requires some strong assumptions (that parental interest does not affect sophistication directly, for example, and that news exposure cannot raise interest).

[7] All of these findings involve intervals between measurements of under half a year. Measuring the supposed cause and effect at different points removes distortions from some types of measurement

and political knowledge at election time are predicted by both political interest early in the campaign and gains in interest over the course of the campaign.

Collectively, these findings justify a large bet that an increase in political interest would be followed by an increase in the kinds of civic behaviors and ways of political reasoning that are commonly associated with good citizenship. Political interest is typically the most powerful predictor of political behaviors that make democracy work. More politically interested citizens know more about politics, think more systematically about their political decisions, vote at higher rates, and participate more in the political process in other ways. The evidence for a strong association between political interest and these outcomes is overwhelming, and evidence demonstrating causal impact, while sparser, exists as well.

For some outcomes, such as learning of factually correct information and the quality of decision-making, normative desirability is unambiguous. Other outcomes linked to political interest, such as opinionation, turnout, or protest, are not unequivocally desirable, but are normally seen as indicators of a healthy democracy. The prospect of higher turnout rates among uninformed individuals may spark concerns about unintended side effects of raising interest. But past research suggests that greater interest would not selectively increase one outcome alone, but instead raise a whole bundle of them, such as turnout rates and political knowledge and the quality of decision-making. Based on the existing research, it is thus reasonable to assume that a person gaining political interest would, as a consequence, become more politically involved in a variety of ways. If a substantial number of people became more interested, collective political decision-making and the public's capacity for self-governance would likely improve.[8]

---

error. For example, in the same interview, a respondent who reported high political interest may inflate subsequent reports of participation because it would look inconsistent or feel awkward to concede not having voted or volunteered. If the two questions appear in different interviews, these consistency pressures are likely much lower. Political interest is also related to future self-reports of news exposure (e.g., Atkin et al. 1976; Strömbäck and Shehata 2010; Boulianne 2011).

[8] The exclusive focus in this review on political interest as a cause of political involvement and participation does not imply that political interest is the only cause, or even the only internal disposition that leads to engagement. Some individuals do not find politics particularly interesting, but turn out to vote due to a sense of civic duty (Campbell 2006; Blais and Achen 2011). Cognitive mechanisms (such as political efficacy or civic duty) and identity (such as identification with a political party) could have effects through political interest or directly on political participation. A sense of efficacy could raise political interest by strengthening the expectation that reengaging with the domain of politics will be rewarding (see Chapter 2), but it could also lead to political participation independently of political interest. Similarly, civic duty can strengthen political interest by linking the domain of politics to role definition and self-concept, but it could also lead people to participate who are not interested in politics. Party identification could make politics seem important and interesting but could also invite people to mechanically turn out for their side.

THE ORIGINS OF POLITICAL INTEREST

Despite the widely accepted role of political interest as a pivotal precursor to normatively desirable behavior, social scientists have devoted little attention to studying its roots. Early survey research suggested that political interest was an important factor in encouraging electoral participation. Causes of political interest were less obvious, however. In their pioneering study of the 1940 presidential election, Lazarsfeld et al. (1948 [1944], 46–7) concluded that

three-quarters of the non-voters stayed away from the polls deliberately because they were thoroughly unconcerned with the election... Only a small number of people were kept from the polls by a last minute emergency. The possibility that the deliberate non-voters could have been made more interested during the campaign is slight; their decision not to vote was too persistent. A long range program of civic education would be needed to draw such people into the orbit of political life, and further studies are needed to unearth the specific nature of their lack of interest.

Much existing research has examined the external factors that encourage or thwart political participation, the "last minute emergency" that keeps people from voting or the structural features that do so more systematically by imposing costs on casting a vote or learning about one's options. A corollary to this line of research are studies of voter mobilization and other external forces that reduce the cost of participating. The impact of these external factors is smaller than the large differences in participation between politically interested and politically uninterested citizens. In fact, Get-out-the-vote efforts are finely targeted toward moderately interested individuals right at the cusp of turning out, precisely because these are the individuals for whom external encouragement has a chance of affecting behavior (e.g., Hersh 2015). Likewise, high costs of voting – imposed by advance registration, new identification requirements, or extended distance to the polling place – are bound to lower turnout among citizens who, without those additional hurdles, would have just enough internal motivation to make their way to the polls and complete a form or two.

The purpose of this book is not to question the relevance of external encouragements and deterrents to political participation, only to give the underlying internal motivation its due. It may turn out that the difficulty of raising participation by raising political interest justifies the large amount of resources devoted to marginal changes in behavior through external mobilization. Or, the former just takes longer, and patience and effort could be rewarded with stronger impact.

More than half a century after Lazarsfeld and colleagues conducted their pioneering work, we are, mostly, still waiting for those "further studies"

Mobilization by campaigns and encouragement through interpersonal networks can get less interested people to vote, volunteer, or donate money (although GOTV efforts tend to target individuals with a high ex-ante probability of turning out; see Enos et al. 2014; Hersh 2015). Political interest alone is not enough to become involved; people must also have some time and resources (Verba et al. 1995).

explaining why some people lack political interest. Not too long ago, the Standing Committee on Civic Education and Engagement of the American Political Science Association called this research gap "perplexing" (Macedo 2005, 35). In a delightful parallel, an eminent psychologist diagnosed at about the same time as Lazarsfeld et al. that "one of our greatest defects is our lack of a consistent or adequate theory of interest" (Allport 1946, 341). Three quarters of a century later, "this situation has not yet changed," according to two leading educational psychologists (Renninger and Hidi 2011, 168), although the next chapter will show that psychologists have made some progress.

You may think that you already know what causes political interest to develop because you have read a lot about why people vote and participate in politics. But there are several reasons why the turnout literature may not be a good guide for our intuitions about political interest formation. Conceptually, the two are quite different, one a behavior, the other a sentiment inside a person. Some theoretical arguments about participation – for example, that it takes at least minimal resources to go cast a vote, or time to participate, or money to give money – simply do not apply to political interest. And methodologically, the bulk of research on participation comes from cross-sectional studies, which suffer from many of the same problems I work hard to avoid in this book, or get-out-the-vote experiments, which focus on testing short-term forces. When I pay careful attention to these considerations, the kinds of stories we might have told based on the participation literature and the analysis of cross-sectional data often fail to receive much empirical support.

PLAN OF THE BOOK

Just a few pages in, a handful of stark observations has raised big questions about political interest. You and I delve into news coverage, political analysis, and history because it feeds our political interest. In opinion surveys, we would likely report being "extremely interested in politics." Although just words, these words take on broad political significance because people who say them reliably engage in many behaviors that characterize good citizenship and strengthen self-governance.

One big question, thus, is how much of a difference the precise words make in the measurement of political interest. Part I of this book examines how political interest can be measured and what, exactly, we pick up when we ask people how interested they are in politics. Chapter 2 investigates what else people say about politics who tell us that they are interested in it. Chapter 3 describes past studies that examine the extent to which measurement context affects political interest reports. And both Chapters 3 and 4 review the large number of survey questions that have been used to gauge respondents' political interest. Questions about interest in related domains, such as "politics," "public affairs," or "government," but also "local," "national," and "international" politics, all correlate very highly. Even interest in election campaigns is quite similar to interest in politics generally. The precise way in which people are asked about their political interest turns out to make little difference.

A second big question concerns the stability of our tendency to follow politics. Would you have picked up this book a year ago? Will your political interest lead you to devour the next political biography? Does political interest routinely develop from situational to dispositional, as psychologists tell us it can? There are a number of ways to find out. Several chapters in Part I chart political interest over periods of time, from months to decades, to determine if political events leave a mark on a nation's collective interest. Part II addresses the question from a different perspective: Do the same people report similar levels of political interest when they are asked repeatedly over time? In either analysis, some empirical answers would dispel the notion of a self-governing class constituted of politically interested individuals. If events mattered a great deal, so that political interest dropped considerably in the absence of continuous situational stimulation, the image of a "class" of people exerting ongoing influence on policy and governance would be misleading. Likewise, if the same individuals vacillated between reporting high political interest one year, low interest the next, the beneficial effects of interest on citizenship would still be real, but the capacity for self-governance would lie with a system that draws in enough people at important points in time, not with a set of citizens whose political interest provides a stable civic foundation.

The third big question arises from the empirical answers to the second one. To a remarkable extent, it does indeed turn out that political interest is dispositional and does not ebb and flow much with the political currents. The self-governing class is in fact a class in the sense that people who join usually remain for a long time. But how do they get there? Early in life, the concept of "politics" has yet to become meaningful. Young children do not have a sense of whether politics is interesting to them until they acquire some idea of what it entails. The psychological model of interest strongly suggests that the roots of political interest lie in adolescence or childhood. Much of Part II examines when political consciousness develops and how quickly it leads to a dispositional political interest.

Part III aims to go beyond describing when dispositional political interest forms to understanding why and under what conditions it is most likely to develop. Is the self-governing class an elite club because education and material resources have a big impact on who develops political interest, or does it counteract resource inequality by opening underprivileged citizens a way to political influence? Does it draw predominantly from the segment of the population that views the political system positively, or can negative assessments also generate political interest and thus provide the self-governing class with a capacity to recognize, and perhaps even address, deficiency of the system? The chapters in Part III analyze the effects of education (Chapter 10), parents (Chapter 11), material resources and well-being (Chapter 12), specific experiences with politics (Chapter 13), and political attitudes and identities (Chapter 14).

The Data

This book draws on a large ensemble of data. Because folk wisdom has it that political interest is an important element of political psychology and political behavior, most public opinion surveys include a question gauging respondents' political interest. Some include more than one, perhaps based on the intuition that people's cognitive and affective predisposition to engage with politics could not possibly be captured by one item. But in the absence of deliberate analysis, we cannot be sure if that amounts to measuring the same thing twice or two different components of political involvement.

In Chapters 3 and 4, I gratefully use this abundance of survey questions touching on facets of political interest to address the questions of measurement and dimensionality. The analysis will draw on recent election surveys in the United States and Germany, countries for which particularly thorough and diverse measures of political interest are available. For a detailed picture of aggregate political interest over decades, not just years, Chapter 5 draws on a variety of surveys that repeat the same political interest question on a (more or less) regular basis. At this point, the book adds two more countries, Great Britain and Switzerland.

The most important data sources for this book, introduced in Chapter 5, are three European household panel surveys. The German Socio-Economic Panel Study (GSOEP), the British Household Panel Survey (BHPS), and the Swiss Household Panel (SHP) all conduct annual interviews with large samples of panelists. These data collections are true blockbuster material:

They are high-quality national probability surveys.
They include all members of the sampled households above the eligibility age.
They conduct annual interviews with each eligible household member.
They do so for as long as household members are willing to participate.
They interview household members as young as 11 (in the BHPS), 14 (SHP), and 16 (GSOEP).
They periodically add refreshment samples to start new panels.
And (almost) every year, they ask panelists how interested they are in politics.

The longest-running study, the GSOEP, started in 1984, offering up to 29 measurements of political interest for its panelists. (At the time this sentence appears between book covers, several more waves of data will be available.) In total, the three household panels provide data from over 130,000 panelists who, together, reported their political interest more than 800,000 times.

This treasure trove of panel data will be employed to greatest effect in Parts II and III of the book. In Chapter 6, for example, it adds considerable statistical leverage to distinguishing the effect of aging on political interest from static differences between birth cohorts. The household panels are indispensable for assessing the stability of political interest at the individual level, an endeavor I began in earlier work (Prior 2010) and continue here in Chapter 7. In Part III, I draw on the household panel data to estimate the effects of other variables on political interest. It is there that panel data offer their chief analytical advantages. These advantages – the Big Benefits of panel data, as I call them – come with added responsibilities, however: careful and aware application of statistical tools.

The Toolkit

This book has two tracks. One track is substantive, providing an explanation of political interest and its origins. The second track focuses not on what we know, but *how* we know. It describes the analytical and statistical tools we require to understand individual-level change that potentially unfolds over long periods of time. I include this second track primarily for two reasons. First, it offers transparency, a hallmark of scientific inquiry. Second, it highlights both the magnificence of the main data source, the household panel data, and the new analytic challenges that emerge even with the luxury of these formidable data.

Following the second track in this book does not require sophisticated knowledge of statistical methods. Parts I and II present a series of analyses that help to understand what political interest is and describe its movement over time, both among individuals as they age and in developed democracies as time passes. These analyses give attention to measurement details, sampling issues, and the complex nature of the underlying panel data, but they are mostly presented graphically.

Part III asks more challenging analytical questions and therefore demands more careful thinking about cause and effect. But even there, dynamic relationships between political interest and other variables will be presented graphically as much as possible. Graphs are an intuitive way to check the plausibility of causal effects. If a change in the purported causal factor is not followed by a change in the dependent variable, a causal effect is unlikely. And if both variables do change, the temporal order of the changes can be informative.

There are three principal advantages panel data offer over observational cross-sectional data: The ability to focus on changes, not levels; the ability to detect temporal variation in causal impact; and greater leverage in distinguishing cause and effect by exploiting the timing of their respective changes. The first two of these Big Benefits are straightforward and unambiguous. The third one often depends on critical assumptions that cannot be directly verified. They are weaker than the assumptions necessary to identify causal effects using cross-sectional observational data, but stronger than the assumptions experimental designs require. Especially for potential causes of political interest that defy random assignment, the third Big Benefit is thus of great practical value, but the intricacy of its assumptions imposes more methodological, and occasionally technical, development.

To convey the basic principles of panel estimators and explain appropriate techniques for statistical inference, Chapter 9, the first chapter in Part III, lays out the challenges to causal inference and the ways in which I try to address them. Chapter 9 offers a guide to panel analysis, applied to the study of political interest. Although I cover advanced panel methods at a conceptual level in that chapter, it is written for a reader without technical knowledge of panel estimation and moves many econometric details to a chapter appendix. Without the luxury of experiments, estimation details are important and sometimes critical. In the absence of randomization of the purported causal factors, explaining change with observational data requires careful attention to a more complex analytical foundation. To relegate that foundation entirely to appendices would give the wrong impression that the choice of estimator and the validity of underlying assumptions are obvious and incontestable. Sometimes they are. When they are not, Chapter 9 gives you a conceptual understanding to appreciate the sources of ambiguity that qualify some of my conclusions.

* * *

If anything, the need to understand the origins of political interest is mounting because its effects appear to be growing. In my previous work, I found that people's preference for news and political information, a characteristic quite like political interest, has become a more powerful predictor of their political involvement now that new technologies offer vastly more content (Prior 2005, 2007). Most of the time, people now watch, read, or listen to their preferred media content, not content that the media environment imposes on them (as it did when three or four broadcast channels constituted the total of television and a newspaper from another state was hard to come by). People who are not interested in politics and public affairs can easily avoid news exposure. And you probably need no reminding that those who like news and politics, conversely, can find an almost endless supply of political information. The consequence is greater inequality in news exposure, political knowledge, and turnout.

The goal of this book is to make headway on the puzzle of political interest's unknown origins. Political interest is not the only intrinsic motivation that leads to political involvement, and other motivations may sometimes compensate for its scarcity. But the consistency, scope, and magnitude of its effects on political behavior easily justify this study's focus on a single variable that stands out so clearly. Many scholars include measures of political interest as control variables in their analyses without explaining why. There appears to be an often unstated recognition that politically interested people are different, think differently about politics, and behave differently. But what exactly do we control for when we include political interest as an independent variable?

PART I

DESCRIBING POLITICAL INTEREST

2

The Psychology of Political Interest

Many of us understand intuitively what it means to be "interested" in something. Asked to report their interest in politics, very few survey respondents say they "don't know" or refuse to answer the question. To state interest in something expresses a complex sentiment, however. It involves both feeling and thinking, multiple phases of development, and a prediction about uncertain future gratifications.

Long ago, Lane (1959, 133) defined interest as "a sense that giving attention to some phenomenon is rewarding." Politics is the "phenomenon" examined in this book. Modern psychology vouches that interest is content-specific, by which Hidi and Renninger (2006, 112) mean specific to "particular classes of objects, events, or ideas," and most current models and theories agree with them (see Renninger and Hidi 2011). Later chapters will investigate the extent to which people have varying interest in different kinds of political "objects, events, or ideas"; but what exactly are the "rewards" that Lane talks about?

Researchers largely agree that interest "has both cognitive and affective components... [and] a physiological/neurological basis" (Renninger and Hidi 2011, 169; also Sansone and Smith 2000, 345). That sounds like an unhelpful answer because it seems to say that interest is a little bit of everything. But rewards can indeed take different forms. The most straightforward reward is pleasure. Yet the reward might be the avoidance of something bad, so the emotions involved in the formation of interest are not always positive. For example, a feeling of anxiety or not knowing enough about politics can spark political interest. Possible rewards in this case may be reassurance that anxiety is unwarranted or a better sense of how the anxiety-inducing phenomenon can be handled.

The way to unlock this confusing diversity of rewards is to realize that interest has different phases and that different types of rewards operate in different phases of interest development. Lane's definition sidesteps this complication. By "a sense," does he refer to the momentary feeling while we give attention to something? Or a more calculated expectation that giving attention to something in the future may be rewarding? At its most fundamental, this is the distinction between *situational* and *dispositional* interest: "Situational interest refers to focused attention and the affective reaction that is triggered in the moment by environmental stimuli, ... whereas individual [dispositional] interest refers to a person's relatively enduring predisposition to reengage particular content over time as well as to the immediate psychological state when this predisposition has been activated" (Hidi and Renninger 2006, 113).[1] Hence, interest involves both impulsive reaction and continuing judgment, both feelings and thoughts.

This chapter explains the psychology of interest and constructs a roadmap that will guide the analysis of political interest in the rest of the book. The chapter concludes by compiling the full list of hypotheses, including those mentioned along the way here or sketched in the previous chapter, and notes where in the book they will be examined.

EMOTIONS AND SITUATIONAL POLITICAL INTEREST

Early in the process of interest formation, physiological responses and the emotions we experience "in the moment" dominate what we perceive as interest. Psychologists see interest as a discrete emotion, and "healthy people in a safe and comfortable environment experience interest far more of the time than any other emotion" (Izard and Ackerman 2000, 257). Situational interest typically involves heightened arousal and an affective reaction to the object that triggered it. Silvia (2005, 89) refers to situational interest as "an emotion associated with curiosity, exploration, and information seeking." The experience of situational interest appears to be grounded in physiological activity related to wanting and/or liking (e.g., Izard and Ackerman 2000; Litman 2005). At a later stage, expectations about the future rewards of "reengag[ing] particular content" accommodate cognitive elements. The transition from situational to dispositional political interest is complex, yet it is useful to start by illustrating the basic point that political interest involves emotions.

Survey data provide strong evidence that political interest has an affective component. As part of a panel study by AP-Yahoo conducted in 2008 and 2009, respondents were asked whether a series of words, including "interested," "excited," and "bored," described how they "feel about the upcoming presidential election." Figure 2.1 graphs the relationships between these reported feelings about the election and responses to a question about political interest: "How much interest do you have in following news about the

---

[1] Hidi and Renninger use the term "individual interest" for the same concept that that Krapp (2002), Litman (2010), and Robison (2017) refer to as "dispositional interest."

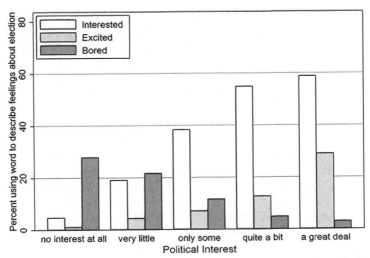

FIGURE 2.1 Political Interest and Feelings about the 2008 U.S. Presidential Election

Note: 2008–9 AP-Yahoo Panel. Data in Figure 2.1 combine the initial sample and the refreshment samples in waves 3 and 9, so all responses come from the first time an individual was interviewed.

campaign for president?" (The Online Supplementary Materials contain more information about this and all other surveys mentioned in this chapter.)

Almost 60 percent of respondents who say they have "a great deal" of interest in following presidential campaign news also use the word "interested" to describe their feelings toward the election. Among those with "no interest at all," only a handful do, and the intermediate categories show a linear increase. The association between the stated feeling of interest in the presidential election and reported interest in following campaign news is quite close.

Affective elements of political interest include excitement and absence of boredom about an upcoming election. Figure 2.1 shows an approximately linear relationship between the measure of political interest and feelings of excitement about the election. While a minority of respondents overall feel excited about the election, the inclination to do so is clearly related to political interest. The relationship with feelings of boredom is almost exactly reversed. Politically interested people are less likely to be "bored" by an election. Politics being boring also stands out in a different study as the reason German students give to explain their lack of political interest in an open-ended question (Ingrisch 1997, 151–6).

It is possible for negative emotions, such as anxiety, to serve as an initial physiological trigger for situational interest. Hidi (2000, 312) gives the example of a student uninterested in science who watches a TV show about the gravitational pull of black holes: "Fascinated and somewhat frightened, the student's interest is triggered." To be interested in something, it is not necessary to enjoy it or think of it as pleasant, and "many studies find interest in unpleasant events" (Silvia 2005, 98; see, e.g., Stattin et al. 2017). Litman (2005; Litman et al. 2005) contrasts curiosity in anticipation of a pleasant experience with curiosity motivated by a "feeling-of-deprivation" caused by emotions (e.g., anxiety) or attitudes (e.g., an obligation to do something).[2]

As anticipated by the general psychology, political interest can develop despite a negative affective reaction to politics. Respondents in the AP-Yahoo study were also asked about negative emotional reactions to the 2008 election. People who reported feeling "angry" or "frustrated" about the election were not, on average, less interested in the campaign than people who did not report those feelings.[3] Bennett (1986, 171) reports that American respondents who felt "delighted" or "pleased" in 1972 about "what our national government is doing" expressed only slightly higher political interest than those who felt "unhappy" or "terrible." Martin (2008) finds a link between political interest and the number of negative news stories that appeared in the newspaper an individual reports reading.

Semi-structured interviews with young people (ages 18–24) have also shown that interest in politics does not always coincide with positive evaluations of the political process (Snell 2010). Even though some respondents displayed "apparent interest and knowledge, they described themselves as disliking or even hating politics" (Snell 2010, 276). Illustrating a central tenet of the general psychological model, political interest is more likely to be linked to positive affect, but also occurs in the presence of frustrations with the domain of politics.

DISPOSITIONAL POLITICAL INTEREST: ROOM FOR COGNITION

As noted, there is more to political interest than emotional reactions "in the moment," especially when it grows into dispositional political interest. Multiphase models of interest development (Krapp 2002; Hidi and Renninger 2006) explain how an initial situational interest can develop into an "emerging" and subsequently a "well-developed" dispositional interest. For a triggering interest to develop further, it has to be sustained internally. At the transition from a situational to a dispositional interest, the environmental trigger is usually replaced by an internal spur to reengage with the content domain as dispositional interest is "typically but not exclusively self-generated" (Hidi and Renninger 2006, 115). Continued availability of content in the domain of

---

[2] In political science, Marcus and colleagues (Marcus and MacKuen 1993; Marcus et al. 2000) have argued that anxiety triggers information seeking (see also Valentino et al. 2008).

[3] Political interest was also strongly related to respondents saying the presidential election made them feel "hopeful." Use of the words "overwhelmed," "helpless," and "proud" was unrelated to interest.

situational interest is helpful in facilitating the development of dispositional interest, but sustained situational interest also builds up willingness to seek out content, even if that requires effort. Situational interest is, in other words, a bit like a take-it-or-leave-it offer made to us by our environment. Dispositional interest, on the other hand, adds more of our own thinking and anticipation to the immediate emotional reaction sparked by the environmental trigger.

Survey data confirm that political interest is related to both positive affect and cognitive appreciation of the political domain. Figure 2.2 shows the relationship between political interest and agreement that "following politics is fun" (affect) and that "I like complex political issues even if they require my full attention" (a combination of affect and positive cognitive evaluation). Two different measures of political interest are available in the survey, both related to appraisals of politics in very similar ways. Political interest correlates strongly with the assessment that politics is "fun." The correlation with the second assessment, which also emphasizes that politics can be complex and demanding, generates an even stronger relationship, suggesting that political interest also has cognitive elements. In Ingrisch's (1997, 152–5) study of young Germans, wanting to know what is going on in Germany or the world substantially outnumbered all other open-ended explanations for political interest.

It would be wrong to think of early situational interest as involving only emotions, and cognition (thinking) taking over entirely when dispositional interest develops. Even situational interest likely requires cognitive elements, if only to link the feeling of interest to its purported environmental trigger. Interest as a purely emotional phenomenon may (briefly) occur before any cognition (Izard and Ackerman 2000), but without a (subjective) understanding of its trigger it is difficult to interpret. Silvia's (2005, 2006, 2008) "emotion-attribution theory of interest development" elaborates how even short-term, momentary feelings of interest include cognitive elements as people attribute their emotional states to a particular cause.

The transition from situational to dispositional interest does not necessarily involve more cognition than some interpretation of the feeling of interest and a tally that tracks ensuing experiences with the supposed trigger of interest. Situational interest can develop into enduring dispositional interest simply through physiological reactions of liking and expectation of future hedonic experience. In Silvia's theory, people use their initial attribution to form expectations about future emotions which guide future behavior and may develop into an enduring, repeatedly confirmed expectation: "Happiness cultivates attachments to things, places, and experiences that have proved rewarding in the past" (Silvia 2008, 59).

Psychology links interest and curiosity. Izard and Ackerman (2000) describe interest as a discrete emotion, but with variation across people in the threshold at which it is activated. This variation gives rise to individual-level differences in

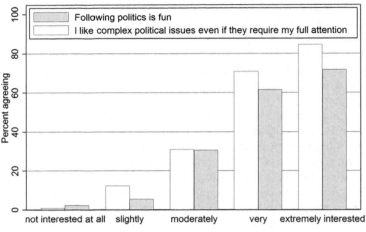

Interest in Information about Government and Politics

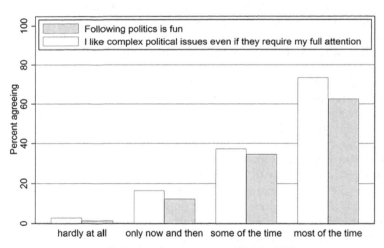

Following Government and Public Affairs

FIGURE 2.2 Affective and Cognitive Elements of Political Interest in the United States
Note: Knowledge Networks survey, March and April of 2008. Left graph: "Generally speaking, how interested are you in information about what's going on in government and politics?" Right graph: "Some people seem to follow what's going on in government and public affairs most of the time, whether there's an election going on or not. Others aren't that interested. Would you say you follow what's going on in government and public affairs most of the time, some of the time, only now and then, or hardly at all?"

the chance of experiencing situational interest. Curious people are particularly likely to find things interesting. Curiosity is similar to the openness trait of the commonly-used Big Five personality structure. Openness is assessed asking people about their appreciation of new ideas and artistic experiences and correlates strongly with scales measuring curiosity (Kashdan et al. 2004; Litman 2005, 799).

Curiosity and a personality open to new experiences might put people into a larger number of "situations" that have the potential to trigger an initial situational interest. Curiosity and openness to experience cannot explain why someone would develop interest in politics as opposed to other content, but they could encourage political interest simply by increasing the chance that people experience situational interest in something – which could be politics for some people. Openness is thus not a sufficient condition for political interest development, but may be conducive to it nonetheless. I test this **Curiosity Hypothesis** in Chapter 8.

PATHWAYS TO DISPOSITIONAL POLITICAL INTEREST

Even though dispositional interest could form simply through repeatedly confirmed emotional reactions to the same stimulus, other processes may also be at play. The greater role for cognitive mechanisms in the transition from situational to dispositional interest opens additional pathways to enduring interest because it allows more considerations about the interest domain to affect the predisposition to reengage. For the purposes of this study, this complexity is helpful because it draws connections to other elements of political psychology.[4]

Interest in particular content tends to be heightened when the content has value to us, is comprehensible and manageable to us, and relates to who we are. More generally, what we think about the content can affect how interesting we find it.

Subjective Value, Self-Interest, and Importance

We may develop interest in politics because politics has value to us. Different psychological models generate this expectation, and political science has also long been fascinated by notions of self-interest and instrumental reasons for engaging with politics. The precise meaning of "value" varies in these different research traditions. Psychologists tend to define value broadly. Eccles and Wigfield (2002, 122), for example, contend that value goes beyond material self-interest and also derives from perceptions of social roles, feedback from others, and self-concepts, so that "values are linked to more stable self-schema and identity constructs, and choice is not necessarily the result of conscious

---

[4] The underlying models tend to come out of educational psychology, so they need some translating into the realm of politics where goals are less likely to be externally imposed than in an educational setting and where success is more ambiguous than in educational tests or professional advancement.

rational decision-making processes." According to a common argument, content and behaviors have value to an individual if they help accomplish his or her goals (e.g., Sansone and Smith 2000; Eccles and Wigfield 2002; Eccles 2009).[5] In Silvia's model of interest (2005, 99), "appraisals of goal congruence" facilitate the formation of enduring interests.

Understanding value in a material sense would narrow the argument to a claim about self-interest commonly made in economics and often hard to demonstrate empirically in political science (e.g., Sears and Funk 1991). A canonical example for material self-interest as a motivation to behave differently is the senior citizen who knows a lot about government-provided retirement benefits because she depends on them for her livelihood (e.g., Campbell 2003; Henderson 2014). Objective conditions put her into an "issue public" (Converse 1964). If this kind of instrumental political interest is common, we should see specific domains of politics stand out as disproportionately interesting to some individuals. According to the strong version of the instrumental interest argument, material self-interest generates only strictly domain-specific interest without raising general political interest.[6] In Chapter 3, I test this hypothesis by analyzing whether people who are interested in one policy area or domain of politics are also interested in other areas. But because we rarely measure interest in a large number of specific policy domains, my analysis will remain somewhat ambiguous.

According to a weaker version of instrumental interest, self-interest is the starting point for the generation of more general political interest (so the senior

---

[5] Some of this work does not focus on interest specifically. The Expectancy Value Model of Motivated Behavioral Choice (e.g., Eccles and Wigfield 2002; Eccles 2009)aims to explain people's actions. The subjective value of a behavior and the expected chance of succeeding at the behavior both influence whether people engage in the behavior. Both variables are themselves a function of other processes. Subjective value depends in part on whether the behavior it generates is interesting to the individual, on the cost of the behavior, and on the extent to which the behavior helps an individual achieve her goals. Eccles' model thus draws on the concept of interest as an independent variable and has little to say about its origins. The model becomes helpful for present purposes if the outcome is defined to include not only specific behaviors, but also the propensity to "reengage particular content," that is, dispositional interest.

[6] Examining motivations for information seeking, Atkin (1973, 205) distinguished "non-instrumental" reasons for exposure to information when exposure produces instant gratification due to its consumption value and "information seeking for utilitarian purposes ... as a means toward solving [a] practical problem." Such distinctions can be blurry, as when Atkin considers "personal interest in the subject matter" (205) and "intrinsic uncertainty" (237) non-instrumental, but reduction of "extrinsic uncertainty" (237) and monitoring count among the utilitarian motivations.

The distinction between "intrinsic" and "extrinsic" motivation is sometimes connected to the concept of interest. Sansone and Smith (2000, 343) define "individuals to be intrinsically motivated when their behavior is motivated by the actual, anticipated, or sought experience of interest." Interest is inherently intrinsic but may be caused by extrinsic motivations such as the requirement to take a civics course. Hidi (2000, 315) argues vehemently against the term "intrinsic interest" because it "sets up an expectation of extrinsic interest." However, not only is such a concept an oxymoron but nobody in the literature has actually referred to extrinsic interest."

citizen receiving retirement benefits ends up interested not only in retirement policy, but in many other aspects of government and public affairs). Examples of this process will be examined in Part III of the book, by checking whether life events that make individuals members of certain issue publics also raise their general political interest.

Using a broad measure of "value," Figure 2.3 illustrates the plausibility of the connection between value and interest in the political domain by plotting the relationship between political interest of German citizens and the importance of the outcome of an approaching election "to [them] personally." The association is linear, strong, and almost identical for two different elections, in 2009 and 2013. The large majority of the most interested respondents consider the election outcome very important. The least interested predominantly rated the election outcome as "fairly unimportant" or "completely unimportant." (Drawing on a slightly differently worded question, Blais (2016) reports a similar relationship for samples in five different countries.)

Broadly construed instrumentality is also evident in the explanations German students provide for their own political interest. One group in Ingrisch's (1997) study gave the reasons for their interest in response to an open-ended prompt. A second group was then asked to say how much of each of those reasons applied to them. The explanation that "it is about our future" was the second-most frequent open-ended response and the most endorsed statement. "It is about one's own life" was in the top four. These statements may reflect the instrumental importance of politics in a system of self-governance. Yet students rarely gave narrowly instrumental reasons. The need to be politically interested for school or to talk with friends was mentioned by only a handful of students and represented the two least-endorsed reasons for political interest.

In short, people may develop interest in politics because they think politics is important and has value to them. This pathway to interest has a stronger cognitive component than the straightforward hedonic path. Analyses later in the book will examine the extent to which this path is based on manifest self-interest and limited to specific political issues, not politics generally.

Expectation of Success, Efficacy, and Ability

We tend to be more interested in things that we are good at – or at least think we are good at. Expectation of success is a second pathway to interest. For reengagement with political content, success is much more subjective than in educational settings, but the hard-to-verify sense of understanding politics can still affect political interest. The expected chance of success as a cognitive element appears in many models of motivation. Bandura's (1997) work on self-efficacy shows a link between beliefs in the ability to accomplish a task and the motivation to achieve it. Silvia's (2006) model of interest emphasizes coping potential, a similar concept, as one of the dimensions on which a situation or object is cognitively appraised. Even if an object or a situation is appraised as

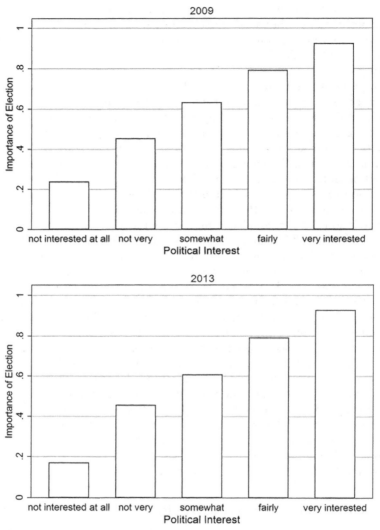

FIGURE 2.3 Campaign Interest and Personal Importance of Election in Germany
Note: German Longitudinal Election Study 2009 and 2013, pre-election in-person interviews. Interest question: "Und wie stark interessiert Sie speziell der gerade laufende Wahlkampf zur bevorstehenden Bundestagswahl – sehr stark, ziemlich stark, mittelmäßig, weniger stark oder überhaupt nicht?" ("And how interested are you in particular in the current campaign for the forthcoming federal election? Very interested, fairly interested, somewhat interested, not very interested, or not interested at all?") Outcome importance question: "Wie wichtig ist es Ihnen persönlich, wie die kommende Bundestagswahl ausgeht? Sehr wichtig, ziemlich wichtig, mittelmäßig, weniger wichtig oder überhaupt nicht wichtig?" ("How important are the results of the forthcoming federal election to you personally? Very important, fairly important, neither/nor, fairly unimportant, or completely unimportant?") Graphs use the 5-point response scale transformed to range between 0 and 1.

new and/or complex, people may not perceive it as interesting if they believe that they lack the ability or resources to understand it.

Existing research on political interest, typically regarded as illustrating measurement concerns, provides direct evidence for this connection between political efficacy and political interest. According to a repeatedly replicated finding (Bishop et al. 1984b, 1982; Bishop 1987; Schwarz and Schuman 1997; Lasorsa 2003, 2009), political interest reports are lower when a series of difficult political knowledge questions precede the interest question, especially among respondents who were unable to answer the knowledge questions correctly (Lasorsa 2009; Robison 2015). This result is very consistent with the definition of political interest as reflecting an expectation of future rewards from engaging with the political domain. An individual may experience reduced interest in politics because failure to answer a series of political knowledge questions lowers his expectation that he can achieve a gratifying outcome by reengaging in the political domain. The lower interest reports among the least knowledgeable respondents are a compelling illustration of self-efficacy and coping potential as predictors of interest (Bandura 1997; Eccles and Wigfield 2002; Silvia 2006). Experimentally manipulating beliefs about government responsiveness, Robison (2017) provides similar evidence that political interest is affected by external efficacy, the belief that one's political views will be taken into account.[7]

Randomly lowering efficacy (at least temporarily) through difficult knowledge questions is a neat way to break the mutually reinforcing relationship between political interest and efficacy. In observational data, especially the annually spaced reinterviews that constitute my main data source, it is challenging to disentangle the two variables. I will briefly examine the **Efficacy Hypothesis** directly in Chapter 14.

Our sense that we are good at something usually does not come out of nowhere. We tend to feel efficacious about tasks and domains in which we are knowledgeable and well trained. In the political domain, internal and external political efficacy are higher among people with knowledge about politics, but also among more educated people and those with higher general cognitive ability (e.g., Pasek et al. 2008). General ability, in other words, may facilitate the formation of political interest because it instills a sense of efficacy across the board, including in the political domain. This idea motivates both the **Cognitive Ability Hypothesis**, which I test in Chapter 8, and the **Education Hypothesis**, the subject of Chapter 10.

---

[7] In Ingrisch's (1997) study of young Germans, explanations related to efficacy (politicians do not keep their promises or do not care about young people; young people's actions won't make a difference) are the top three reasons for lack of political interest when they are presented in a list and participants are asked if they agree. Yet few students volunteered these types of reasons when the question was open-ended. About one in eight gave their own lack of political understanding as reason for disinterest, the second-most volunteered explanation (after finding politics boring.)

The possibility of a connection between general ability and domain-specific political interest is supported by research in developmental psychology on the mastery of tasks across different domains, such as the ability to be successful academically, professionally, and in one's private life, as parent or partner (Roisman et al. 2004; Masten et al. 2005). As young people grow older, they have to acquire new skills to master new sets of tasks because "developmental tasks follow a course through life of waxing and waning salience and organization" (Roisman et al. 2004, 125). These tasks are typically related temporally because they occur at successive developmental stages, but they fall in different developmental domains. Eventual mastery of particular developmental tasks is not as strongly predicted by early experiences in the same domain as it is by mastery of tasks in other, developmentally earlier domains. In one longitudinal sample, work competence of adults was strongly predicted by their academic and social competence 10 years earlier, but not by their work competence as adolescents (Roisman et al. 2004). Mastering an early developmental task can be helpful at a later developmental stage in a different domain: "Success in transactions related to major expected tasks of development emerges gradually, scaffolded by prior success in other domains of life as well as current contextual supports" (Roisman et al. 2004, 124). Getting along with others in adolescence or early adulthood, for instance, helps people develop work-related competence later.

This research is relevant here because one of the domains in this "developmental cascade" (Masten et al. 2005) is civic life. Academic and social competences manifest during adolescence explain civic engagement later in life, and they do so *better* than initial forays into civic life: Once early competence measures are accounted for, youth involvement (including extracurricular activities) no longer predicts civic engagement of young adults (Obradović and Masten 2007). The authors conclude that "young adults who have been successfully negotiating previous and concurrent salient developmental tasks are found to be more predisposed to successfully fulfill citizenship responsibilities in young adulthood" (Obradović and Masten 2007, 14). This link between different developmental domains is important because it suggests that origins of political interest could lie outside the domain of politics.

It is not easy to come up with a good reason why material resources should affect political interest once education or general cognitive abilities have been accounted for. Political scientists have often treated education as one component of socioeconomic resources. According to the resource model (e.g., Verba et al. 1995), skills learned in education are resources just like income or occupational status that increase political participation by reducing its cost. Yet, while this argument offers an explanation for the link between material resources and participation, it does not involve political interest. The psychology of interest suggests no obvious role for resources either. My **Resource Hypothesis** is thus a null hypothesis: Material resources do not explain political interest. I examine it empirically in Chapter 12.

Identity and Political Attitudes[8]

Subjective value and expectations of success as antecedents of interest open the door for many other variables to play a role in the development of dispositional political interest. We may value politics because it is a central element of how we define ourselves. Eccles (2009; Eccles and Wigfield 2002) explicitly includes "self-schema and identity constructs" as predictors of subjective value, which in turn affect behavior and perhaps predispositions for future behaviors. A salient political identity may also affect political interest by instilling efficacy and an increased resolve to cope with the complexities and demands of politics.[9]

In Chapter 14, I examine the possibility that one of the most widely studied political identities, identification with a political party, affects political interest development. According to the **Partisan Identity Hypothesis**, initially uninterested individuals who identify with a political party develop political interest because their partisan identities raise the subjective value of the political domain or make it less intimidating. Other reasons for identifying with politics, such as having strong political opinions, may have similar effects.

These types of influences need not be limited to identities. Political attitudes and opinions about the political system could also affect how much value we see in reengagement with politics and how easily we can cope with content in the political domain. Unlike for political identities, the direction of the expected effect on political interest is more ambiguous for attitudes toward the political system, such as trust in government or satisfaction with democracy. As Bennett (1986, 7) points out, people could lack interest in a political system that they consider sound and fair, but also boring in its predictability. Or they could lack interest for essentially the opposite reason, a belief that the system is broken und unjust beyond repair. It is also conceivable that trust in, and satisfaction

---

[8] Although identities and attitudes can be involved in the formation of political interest, political interest is not itself an identity or an attitude. Political interest has affective and cognitive processes and is, at least in the case of dispositional political interest, subject to causal influence from identities and attitudes.

[9] Even the findings by Obradović and Masten (2007) that early non-political competences predict later political engagement could be an effect of political identities or attitudes, not, as the authors believe, general abilities. To explain the development of civic engagement as a product of adaptive success in non-political domains, the authors make the strong assumption "that civic engagement is an important domain for young adult adaptation" (3), in part because there is a "universal expectation that young adults carry out citizenship duties" (15). This assumption follows the general belief that "developmental task expectations in societies may result from the implicit recognition within a given culture of when it is important to achieve what kind of adaptive behavior in order to progress successfully through life in that society" (Masten et al. 2005, 744). But it is by no means certain that development of political interest is a widely shared developmental goal akin to the outcome variables typically analyzed in the cascade model such as professional success or good parenting. If only some young adults hold developmental goals related to civic engagement, it may be this variation, conceptually closer to subjective value (Eccles and Wigfield 2002) and goal congruence (Silvia 2006), that explains the empirical results.

with, the political system reduces the importance of engaging with the political domain because it generates a sense that little is at stake. The psychological model of interest thus generates plausible alternative predictions for the System Support Hypothesis, which I assess empirically in Chapter 14.

AGE AND THE DEVELOPMENT OF DISPOSITIONAL POLITICAL INTEREST

Even if many people end up with dispositional political interest, the psychology is clear that development begins with situational interest. The development of political interest can start at different times in life for different people. In order to report political interest, people must have at least a basic level of political consciousness, a rudimentary awareness of politics as a domain of potential interest. (It is conceivable that situational political interest is triggered even before people become aware that politics is in fact the domain of their interest. A "predisposition to reengage with particular content," however, would seem to require some awareness of the domain.) Chapter 6 discusses research aimed at pinning down when children become conscious of politics.

It also follows from the psychological account of interest development that after young people first encounter and notice politics, their political interest should still be more situational, and therefore less stable, for some time in childhood or adolescence. This Stabilization Hypothesis resembles the "impressionable years" hypothesis in political socialization research (e.g., Sears and Levy 2003), which predicts initial malleability of political attitudes followed by increasing stability. Chapter 7 tests this hypothesis and provides empirical evidence about the relationship between age and stability of political interest.

If political interest is malleable early because situational political interest still dominates in adolescence, potential triggers of situational interest may have disproportionate influence. According to the "Event-Driven Socialization" Hypothesis (Sears and Valentino 1997), elections and other politically relevant events have larger effects on young people because their dispositional political interest has not yet fully formed to maintain interest independent of their political environment. I test this hypothesis in Chapter 6 by allowing elections and other events to have different effects, depending on the age of the individual. Part III of the book examines other influences that operate particularly among young people, including education and parental influence.

CUMULATIVE EXPERIENCE WITH POLITICS AND POLITICAL INTEREST

At the heart of the psychological model of interest formation is the transition from situational to dispositional interest. The anticipation of positive affect and the operation of cognitive mechanisms are part of the explanation for when this transition succeeds – and when it does not, so that short-lived situational interest does not develop into a predisposition. Less clear is how people might encounter the political domain with its potential to trigger situational interest in the first place. Two key principles that are not part of the psychological model help generate additional expectations for the development of dispositional political interest.

First, the accumulation of political experiences – of finding oneself in situations with the potential to trigger situational political interest – should increase certainty about the expected rewards. To use a statistical analogy, the reliability of dispositional political interest should rise with the number of past political experiences. As reliability of interest grows, it becomes less likely that new experiences will change dispositional political interest. Even if a political encounter fails to trigger situational interest for once, this experience is unlikely to be powerful enough to overrule reliable dispositional interest that is the result of many previous experiences. Reliable interest is less likely to be updated. Early experiences should thus have disproportionate influence on young people who do not yet have a sense if politics is interesting to them. Accumulating experiences strengthens and stabilizes people's evaluations, unless they dramatically contradict existing impressions.[10]

This notion of reliability of dispositional interest is not part of the psychological model. It not only amends the conceptualization of what it means to be dispositionally interested in politics, it also leads to an important distinction between lack of interest due to absence of political experience and reliable disinterest. Initially, individuals without experience with the domain of politics are both unlikely to be politically interested and unlikely to have a strong predisposition to find politics uninteresting. Some people may never figure out if politics is interesting to them because the appeal of other domains limits their political experiences. Examining young people's own explanations of their lack of political engagement, Zukin et al. (2006, 93) find that "young people have not so much dropped out as they have never tuned in ... the members of the youngest cohort have not rejected the political system so much as they are indifferent to it." If, on the other hand, people's situational political interest has been triggered repeatedly without evolving into dispositional political interest, their assessment of the domain as uninteresting should become more reliable.

---

[10] The updating process has some basic characteristics of a Bayesian learning model. In political science, these models have been developed predominantly to account for people's party identification and vote choice (Achen 1992, 2002; Bartels 1993; Gerber and Green 1998). As citizens encounter more information about parties and candidates, they update their "benefit differential" (Achen 1992), the difference in benefits they expect, based on past experience, to receive from each party if it were in power. In the absence of major changes in the positions or records of the parties, change in party evaluations becomes less likely as people's familiarity with the parties grows. The first pieces of information about the parties are therefore often most powerful in modifying people's party identification. A similar mechanism could guide updates of political interest.

The first principle of cumulative political experience generates the hypothesis that reliability of political interest increases with political encounters. I cannot test it directly, however, because both reliability and the tally of people's experiences with politics are unobserved. Assuming that reliability manifests itself in stability and that the number of political experiences is approximately proportional to a person's age, the first principle reiterates the Stabilization Hypothesis, albeit derived differently than from the psychological model.

Anyone with an inkling, reliable or not, that politics is not interesting can avoid much of it. The second principle of accumulating political experiences relates to this selectivity in many political encounters. Based on their first tentative assessment of politics as interesting, young people may either become motivated to seek out more of it in the future or conclude that politics is not their idea of fun. Exposure to politics often follows deliberate choices, such as signing up for extracurricular activities, watching a news program, or joining a political discussion. These choices can be mistakes, and politics may prove unappealing or relatively less rewarding than other domains. But for people who have formed initial evaluations of politics as interesting or not, a kind of (partial) path dependence develops. Experiences with politics can prod someone to update his or her assessment of politics, but these experiences are often a consequence of prior assessments. Selective exposure to politics can reinforce interest, but it often begs the question why people would select political experiences in the first place. As expectations about rewards become more certain, and dispositional political interest more reliable, it should increasingly influence the chance of future political encounters, and thus the chance of experiencing situational political interest. But even people who have not deliberately concluded that politics is uninteresting can be selective in their exposure to politics. All it takes is for some other activity to be reliably appealing so that political exposure is never their first choice.

It is no surprise that selectivity is less central in the psychological model.[11] Educational psychologists typically conduct their research with the goal of understanding structural learning situations that give instructors considerable opportunity to create triggers of situational interest in pre-specified curricular domains. Lack of interest reduces educational outcomes, like learning and comprehension. But the barrier to exiting the learning situation altogether, by dropping out of class or even out of school, is very high. This is significantly different for encounters with politics. The primary purpose is not learning, and there is no barrier to exit.

The two principles combine to explain why a potentially interest-provoking encounter with politics might not in fact change political interest. Individuals

[11] The notion of selectivity is recognized in other areas of developmental psychology. Caspi et al. (2005, 470) discuss the "corresponsive principle," according to which "the most likely effect of life experience on personality development is to deepen the characteristics that lead people to those experiences in the first place."

with dispositional political interest will tend to seek out such encounters, but will rarely update their assessment of politics as interesting, both because one more encounter gets less weight than it would for an uninterested person and because they selected into the encounter for the very reason that they expected it to be rewarding. Individuals who lack dispositional political interest, on the other hand, will not seek out such encounters and perhaps even avoid them. As a result, they miss the chance to be inspired, motivated, or convinced that politics is actually interesting. Lack of dispositional political interest lowers future chances of experiencing situational political interest. The greater the opportunity to select into (or out of) an encounter, the lower the potential for the encounter to change political interest.

According to a strong version of the **Selectivity Hypothesis**, selective encounters with politics will thus have no effect on political interest. Joining a political party, for example, is a voluntary political experience that is hardly ever inadvertent. Tracking political interest among people who join political parties should thus not reveal much change. This version of the hypothesis is extreme because even for the most selective, consciously chosen political experiences we do not usually observe the chooser's motivation. A politically uninterested person may decide to join a party because she hopes to address a problem by organizing a collective response. Selectivity is still present, but it is not selectivity based on her political interest. Without observing the precise selection mechanism, a weaker, more realistic (and vaguer) version of the Selectivity Hypothesis would thus only predict relatively small effects on political interest of political encounters that are *typically* highly selective.

Not all political experiences are, or can be, selected. Even if people have already formed reliable disinterest in "politics," they sometimes experience politics whether they like it or not. Children's interactions with their politically engaged parents or required civics courses in high school are examples of experiences that are not the result of selection based on the expectation that they might be interesting. These experiences defy selectivity because they are, to some extent, unavoidable.

National elections or other salient political events also fall in this category. A highly attention-getting political environment reaches deep into the population and generates widespread exposure. The greater the interestingness of the environment, the less likely exposure to politics will be selective. Its impact, however, is likely mediated by an individual's propensity to tune out political events. The interestingness of the environment is an exogenous variable, but the resulting exposure is not.

Other experiences may be avoidable, but people do not anticipate their political relevance ahead of time and thus encounter politics despite low political interest. This can happen when people select into politics, but for reasons that have nothing to do with it. Examples include joining a non-political organization that deals with civic issues and marrying a politically interested person. These expectations are summarized by the **Inadvertent Political**

Encounters Hypothesis. Experiences with politics that are either inadvertent or unavoidable have high potential to raise situational political interest.

WHY POLITICAL INTEREST? THE VANILLA PROBLEM

Children of politically interested parents may be more likely to encounter politics and thus develop a more reliable assessment of the political domain. But what is the theoretical framework to predict whether they will come away from these encounters with high or low political interest? The same question arises for other encounters with politics. Psychological research provides helpful starting points to understand what "interest" in politics is and how it can form. Yet, as some educational psychologists have acknowledged (e.g., Krapp 2002), why people develop interest in a particular content domain has remained rather elusive.[12]

Verba et al. (1995, 527) contend that "political interest is, unlike an individual's preference for chocolate or vanilla, not simply a matter of taste." Political interest may not involve the biological mechanisms that create a sensation of taste when we put vanilla in our mouth. Leaving biology aside, however, the psychology of interest describes processes that resemble taste formation. At its core, interest is about the initial affective reaction, often just a diffuse emotion of liking and enjoyment. Psychologists know that it happens, but not why it happens for particular content. When it comes to situational interest developing into dispositional interest, there are a number of cognitive processes that make enduring political interest more likely. But they are not necessary conditions for the formation of dispositional interest, which can also develop simply because people want to repeat the initially enjoyable experience. That part of interest, at least, sounds very much like taste.

There are some theoretical approaches that yield directional hypotheses. According to social learning theory (Bandura 1969), a child, at least initially, models her parents and adopts their attitudes and values. This theoretical perspective has been used in political socialization research that examines the "transmission" of attitudes and identities from parent to child (e.g., Jennings et al. 2009). These social learning models generate a directional prediction, that political interest of the child will develop to resemble political interest of the parents. I will test this **Parental Influence Hypothesis** in Chapter 11, but its plausibility is limited to (young) children. It is less compelling to argue that wives might model their husbands and adopt their political interest. And if

---

[12] The relationship between personality traits and political involvement suffers from a similar indeterminacy. Gerber et al. (2011, 274) speculate that "[t[he relationship between Openness to Experience and participation may be explained by the fact that those high on this trait respond favorably to opportunities to hear new ideas and experience new things – opportunities that abound in the political arena." That may well be true, but plenty of other "arenas" also offer those opportunities without involving politics.

someone ends up at a meeting that centers on political matters, she does not simply model other participants and adjust her political interest to their levels.

UNDERSTANDING POLITICAL INTEREST: ROADMAP AND HYPOTHESES

This chapter has begun to answer some basic questions about the meaning of political interest, but its larger purpose was to draw the roadmap for the rest of the analysis. Table 2.1 summarizes the hypotheses derived in this chapter about the meaning and origins of political interest. The table charts the three-part structure of the book and lists the places in the book where each hypothesis will be examined empirically.

The pieces of the puzzle addressed in the remaining chapters of Part I concern the measurement of political interest, its dimensionality, and the critical distinction between situational and dispositional political interest. While the empirical examples presented in this chapter fit the psychological model, they raise the question of what it means for political interest to be content-specific or specific to "particular classes of objects, events, or ideas" (Hidi and Renninger 2006, 112). The first example (in Figure 2.1) used interest "in following news about the campaign for president," the second (in Figure 2.2) interest "in information about what's going on in government and politics" and "follow[ing] what's going on in government and public affairs." Do these survey items measure interest in one "class" of ideas? Or do people have differing interest in "news," "information," and "politics" or in "the campaign" compared to "government and public affairs"? I address this question in the next two chapters by comparing a variety of different survey questions used to gauge political interest.

Key to the psychological model is the distinction between situational and dispositional political interest. Situational interest is largely caused by the environment, whereas dispositional interest describes an enduring sentiment that persists even in the absence of situational triggers. Which of the two types of interest do researchers measure when they ask individuals to report their interest in politics? Psychological theory suggests that parsing the way interest was measured can not necessarily resolve this question because the same measurement instrument could pick up both types of interest. Instead, measurement context and the relationship between repeated measures of political interest must be considered to understand how common dispositional political interest is in the population. For example, to the extent that political interest is a developed predisposition to reengage with the political domain, it should not depend a whole lot on the presence of interest-generating political events, such as an impending election. Events could well provide the spark that lights situational political interest, but a core property of dispositional interest is that it sustains in the absence of continued situational stimulation. I assess this

TABLE 2.1 *Testing the Psychological Model of Political Interest: Hypotheses and Research Questions*

I. What Is Political Interest?	Chapter
Cognition & affect hypothesis: Political interest has both cognitive and affective elements	2
Valence hypothesis: Political interest correlates positively with positive affect toward politics; political interest does not correlate negatively with negative affect	2
Importance hypothesis: Perceived importance of politics and political interest are positively related	2
Efficacy hypothesis: A sense of political efficacy raises political interest	2,14
Research Question: How many content **dimensions** does political interest have?	3,4
(Strong) **Instrumentality hypothesis:** People are (only) interested in domains of politics associated with instrumental value to them	3,12
Research Question: Is political interest **dispositional**?	4,5,7
Research Question: Can **events** trigger **situational** political interest?	4,5,6

II. When Does Political Interest Change?	
Aging hypothesis: Aging raises political interest	6
Stabilization hypothesis: The individual-level stability of political interest increases with age	6
Event-driven socialization hypothesis: Events have a stronger effect on political interest among young people	7
Curiosity hypothesis: Political interest is higher and/or develops faster among people with an open personality	8
Cognitive ability hypothesis: Political interest is higher and/or develops faster among people with high cognitive ability	8

III. What Changes Political Interest?	
Education hypothesis: Education raises political interest	10
Resource hypothesis: Material resources are not causally related to political interest	12
Partisan identity hypothesis: Identification with a political party raises political interest	14
System support hypothesis: Trust in government and satisfaction with democracy increase political interest	14
Selectivity hypothesis: Selective encounters with politics (e.g., involvement in a civic organization, politically relevant employment) have no effect on political interest	13

III. What Changes Political Interest?	
Inadvertent political encounters hypothesis: Experiences with politics have the greatest potential to raise political interest when they cannot be avoided or are inadvertent	10
Parental influence hypothesis: Parents' political interest affects political interest of their children	11

question empirically by tracking changes in reported political interest over the course of election years (in Chapter 4) and over much longer periods of time (in Chapters 5 and 6). Individual-level stability of political interest reports provides a second piece of evidence to ascertain dispositional interest. If people report the same or very similar levels of political interest whenever they are asked, their answers are likely to reflect dispositional, not situational, interest (see Chapter 7).

After Part I establishes that survey-based reports of political interest reflect dispositional interest in one broadly construed domain, the rest of the book is devoted to understanding why some people develop stronger dispositional interest in politics than others.

3

Measuring Political Interest

In one of the earliest election surveys, Lazarsfeld et al. (1948 [1944], 40–1) described the predictive power of political interest and noted that

> the respondent's self-rating was the best index we had of his interest. The question was "Would you say you have a great deal of interest in the coming election, a moderate interest, a mild interest, or no interest at all?" And his answer was more closely related to his involvement in the political scene than any other test we could make. So we took his word for it.
>
> This is actually not as naïve as it may sound. It is not surprising that people's self-rating on interest stands up well under a series of tests of consistency and validity. For being interested is a clearly recognizable experience, as anyone knows who has ever been unable to put down a detective story or been bored to tears at a cocktail party. Given any two activities, we can frequently tell at once which is the more interesting for us.

The intuition by Lazarsfeld and his colleagues that interest is a subjective sense best measured by asking people how interested they are has been confirmed by research on the psychology of interest. Relying on research participants' self-reports of political interest presumes that they have the ability to discern their own interest and are willing to report it faithfully. Precisely because interest is subjective, assessing one's own current level is easier than recalling past behaviors or gauging the probability of future action. Social desirability pressure does not turn out to be the obstacle in the measurement of political interest that it can be for some other concepts.

With some assurance that people can report their own interest, the next question is, interest in *what*? Here, the psychological model of interest begs the question. Defining dispositional interest as a "predisposition to reengage ... particular classes of objects, events, or ideas" (Hidi and Renninger 2006, 112–13) does not clarify the dimensionality of political interest. The number of "classes of objects, events, or ideas" in politics is potentially very high, but people may not distinguish their interest in different aspects of politics. To move forward, it is important to appreciate what people mean by "politics" and how survey questions about political interest map onto those meanings.

Popular understanding of "politics" tends to involve notions of government and parties as well as conflict about policy and principles (e.g., Walsh 2004; Fitzgerald 2013). The subjects of Walsh's study associate "politics" with "elections, debates involving Democrats and Republicans, and occasionally elected officials carrying out their duties" (p. 38). Many survey questions designed to gauge political interest do focus on these ideas, but there is almost bewildering variation in the precise wording of the interest domain. Some survey questions simply ask about interest "in politics." Others refer to the interest domain as "government" or "public affairs," while yet others ask about information or news regarding politics, government, or public affairs.

Analysis in this chapter justifies a considerable simplification of the measurement task: Political interest is close to a one-dimensional construct. We can safely disregard minor differences in question wording and have a solid measure of general political interest that can be tracked over time and used as a valid dependent variable to understand how political interest develops. Specifically, this chapter examines whether respondents meaningfully distinguish among different domains of interest such as "politics," "government," and "public affairs;" and give different answers when they are asked "how interested" they are in politics, "how much attention" they pay to it, and "how closely they follow" it. We can also consider if people have clearly distinguishable levels of interest in different policy areas, such as "environmental issues," "political issues within your local community," and "international politics." Last, there are the differences in the way a domain is presented: Does it matter if the question asks about interest in "politics," "news about politics," or "information about politics"? (Interest in elections, another subdomain Walsh finds central to the common understanding of politics, will be covered in the next chapter.)

Each one of these analyses indicates that politics is a general, broadly defined domain, so a single question about it can tap much of the variation in political interest. It is important to understand the dimensionality of political interest because it guides measurement of political interest and because it begins to resolve a theoretical question from Chapter 2: the extent to which political interest is driven by material self-interest. If, as the **Strong Instrumentality Hypothesis** holds, people care only about the aspects of politics that promise them material gain, we should see many people interested in only a few policy areas or domains of politics, making political interest many-dimensional. Instead, politics, policy, and government are primarily understood as one general domain.

TAKING THEM AT THEIR WORD?

Measuring an internal state (or trait) such as political interest poses a challenge: How do we know that a respondent's reported political interest corresponds to her actual political interest? At least until brain science allows us to observe internal states directly and distinguish specific motivations, it is impossible to validate political interest reports against independent benchmarks. This section compiles evidence suggesting that people's reports of their interest do in fact correspond to their actual interest.

I've been a strong critic of self-reported media exposure measures (Prior 2009a, 2009b, 2012, 2013), yet I'm less concerned about self-reported political interest. People's reported exposure to news and political debates often differs dramatically from independent assessments that do not rely on self-reports. The main explanation for the low validity of these self-reported behaviors is task difficulty: It is simply too difficult to recall all instances of relevant media exposure in the referenced time period, so respondents estimate their exposure and in doing so employ misleading estimation rules (Burton and Blair 1991; Prior 2009b). There are no such difficulties in ascertaining one's political interest: Psychology explicitly defines interest as a subjective state or predisposition. The expectation regarding future rewards that are one basis for this predisposition need not be accurate or objectively verifiable. In fact, it is a feature of interest that expectations sometimes turn out to be wrong, leading to updated predispositions. Absent the main obstacle to reporting media exposure accurately, task difficulty, it is not unreasonable to expect self-reports of political interest to be much more accurate than self-reports of media exposure.

Social desirability could be a greater threat to accurate reporting of political interest than task difficulty. Survey respondents may be reluctant to report low interest (regardless of domain) if the image of being interested in *something* is appealing to them. Specific to interest in politics, they may feel pressure to conform to civic norms and reduce this pressure by reporting greater political interest than they actually feel. There are only a few tests of these hypotheses. Blais et al. (2014) compare political interest reports in two experimental conditions. When interest in several different domains is assessed (including "sports" and "arts & culture"), political interest reports are not statistically different from reports of political interest in isolation. Survey respondents, that is, do not raise their political interest reports simply because there is no other way to present themselves as interested individuals.

Shani (2009a) offers another test. She takes advantage of a question-wording experiment in the American National Election Study (ANES) that successfully removed some social desirability pressure from self-reports of turnout. If, Shani argues, political interest self-reports are also affected by social desirability bias, then the version of the turnout question that lowered desirability should be less strongly correlated with political interest reports. If anything, the opposite was true, which "should dismiss the concern that the proposed measures of political interest are polluted with social desirability effects" (Shani 2009a, 152). According to one test applying a list experiment, self-reported news exposure is not affected by social desirability pressures (Prior 2009b). If people do not report "watch[ing] a news program on television yesterday" out of social desirability, then they might not feel compelled to exaggerate their political interest either.

Measurement error introduced by the survey context represents another potential threat. I already discussed in Chapter 2 the finding that political interest reports are lower when a series of difficult political knowledge questions precede the interest question, especially among respondents who were unable to answer the knowledge questions correctly (Bishop et al. 1984b, 1982; Bishop 1987; Schwarz and Schuman 1997; Lasorsa 2003, 2009; Robison 2015). This result is sometimes seen as cause for doubting the validity of political interest or people's ability to accurately report it. But, as I explained in Chapter 2, this finding is precisely what the psychology of interest would predict: Efficacy is a key predictor of interest, so a demonstration of respondents' lack of political knowledge should reduce reports of political interest. The proper conclusion to draw from this result is not that political interest has low validity, but that survey researchers should be careful to avoid manipulating efficacy in the run-up of an interest question.

The household panel surveys that make up the most critical empirical foundation for much of this book use the same question order in most years, include few political questions, and do not include measures of political knowledge. Hence, context effects should be small. The Data Appendix provides details on question context for the household panels, and Chapter 5 returns to this point when their data are first used. In the context of charting long-term trends in political interest, Chapter 5 will also discuss and use Shani's (2009b) corrections for context effects in the ANES time series of political interest.

In sum, existing evidence lessens concerns about the misreporting of political interest due to task difficulty or social desirability. The much-documented impact of political interest on behaviors associated with good citizenship (see Chapter 1) provides another justification of using people's own reports as a valid measure of interest. Survey-based measures of political interest predict political behaviors even when measurement of those behaviors cannot be affected by related types of errors (e.g., tests of factual political knowledge not subject to social desirability bias or turnout based on official records not subject to recall error).

Lastly, statistical procedures can correct for some forms of measurement error. The analysis of different political interest questions that follows in this chapter and the next will implement such corrections. Panel analyses later in the book will be able control for the effect of time-constant confounders and uniform context effects. To the extent that the experience of social desirability pressure during political interest reports results from a stable trait, it will therefore not distort those analyses. Variation in survey context that affects all respondents in a given survey will be absorbed by period effects.

INTEREST IN POLITICS, GOVERNMENT, AND PUBLIC AFFAIRS

During the 2008 election cycle, the American National Election Study (ANES) alone used five different questions to gauge general political interest, scattered around different parts of its data collections. Table 3.1 lists them along with other questions and instances of the same questions used in other large surveys. This variety is confusing, but it offers a good opportunity to determine if small, seemingly arbitrary differences in question wording affect what it is that respondents reveal to us.

The first four questions ask respondents about the same domain, general politics, but in slightly different ways. Two of them use the term "interest," while the other two refer to "attention." The first question asks about interest "in politics," the other three about interest in (or attention to) "politics and government." Finally, the second and third questions mention "information," while the other two do not specify a dimension of general politics. If political interest is a nuanced, multi-dimensional concept, we should expect these differences in wording to generate different response distributions. People might be interested in politics, but not in "what's going on in government." They might find some aspects of politics and government interesting, but not "information." And they might make a distinction between their interest and their attention. This section examines to what extent different questions generate the same general answer.

The different questions might also produce different answers because they were not asked at exactly the same time. The recruitment survey for the ANES Panel started in late September of 2007 and concluded in January of 2008. The ANES later added a second cohort to the panel using the same recruitment procedures (and the same interest question). This survey was in the field in the summer of 2008 (late May to early September), a few weeks after a Knowledge Networks (KN) survey (see Prior 2014). Interviewing for the ANES Time Series pre-election wave started in early September and continued until just before the election. The post-election wave, which repeated the interest question and included both attention questions, began the day after the election and remained in the field until the end of December.

Despite these differences between the questions, their response distributions in Figure 3.1 are remarkably similar. Between 5 and 15 percent of respondents select the top category. For example, 10 percent of the population is "extremely interested ... in politics," 12–15 percent are "extremely interested ... in information about what's going on in government and politics," and 7 percent pay attention "extremely closely ... to information about what's going on in government and politics." The range in the middle categories is somewhat larger. Fewer than 30 percent are "very interested ... in politics," compared to around 40 percent "very interested ... in information about what's going on in government and politics." The range is equally low for the lowest category

Item Name	Question Wording	Response Options	Source
Interest in Politics (Int Pol)	How interested are you in politics?	not interested at all, slightly interested, moderately interested, very interested, extremely interested	ANES 2008–9 Panel Study (recruitment); also: GLES (Ch.4)
Interest in Information about Politics (Int Info)	How interested are you in information about what's going on in government and politics?	not interested at all, slightly interested, moderately interested, very interested, extremely interested	ANES Times Series (2008 pre, 2004 post), 2006 Pilot, 2008–9 Panel Study
	Generally speaking, how interested are you in information about what's going on in government and politics?	not interested at all, slightly interested, moderately interested, very interested, extremely interested	KN 2008
Attention to Information about Politics (Att Info)	How closely do you pay attention to information about what's going on in government and politics?	not closely at all, slightly closely, moderately closely, very closely, extremely closely	ANES Times Series (2008 post), 2006 Pilot
Attention to Public Affairs (Att Gov)	How often do you pay attention to what's going on in government and politics?	never, once in a while, about half the time, most of the time, all the time	ANES Times Series (2008 post), 2006 Pilot
Follow Public Affairs (Fol Gov)	Some people seem to follow what's going on in government and public affairs most of the time, whether there's an election going on or not. Others aren't that interested. Would you say you follow what's going on in government and public affairs..."	most of the time, some of the time, only now and then, hardly at all	ANES Times Series (2008 post, 2004 post), 2006 Pilot; KN 2008; NAES 2004, 2008; *also:* Pew (Ch. 5)

Note: ANES refers to American National Election Study, NAES to National Annenberg Election Survey, GLES to German Longitudinal Election Study. The 2008–9 ANES panel recruitment survey and the 2006 ANES Pilot were conducted by phone. Pre- and post-election waves of the ANES Time Series study use in-person interviewing. Field dates for the 2008–9 ANES Panel recruitment interviews were Sep 26, 2007–Jan 27, 2008 (period 1) and May 28–Sep 9, 2008 (period 2). The pre-election wave of the 2008 ANES Time Series survey was conducted Sep 2–Nov 3, 2008, and the post-election wave Nov 5–Dec 30, 2008. KN refers to Knowledge Networks, which conducted an online survey with a probability sample of Americans in March and April of 2008. For more information about surveys, see Book Appendix B.

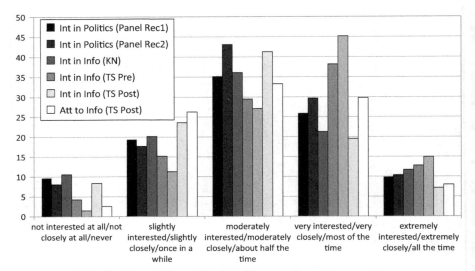

FIGURE 3.1 Distributions of General Political Interest Responses, 2008
Note: Figure includes respondents who did not complete the ANES post-election interview. Limiting the comparison to respondents who answered the respective interest questions in both waves does not change the result.

(9 percentage points) and only slightly larger for the second-lowest and middle categories (14–15 points). Only the second-highest category exhibits somewhat greater range (25 points).

Some of the differences in Figure 3.1 reflect measurement error. Some intuition for its magnitude comes from comparing the difference between questions in Figure 3.1 to the impact of simply reversing the response options for otherwise identical questions. The 2008 ANES Time Series survey and the 2008 KN survey randomly varied the order in which response options were read (or shown) to respondents for the four questions from these surveys. Figure 3.1 plots responses for respondents who heard (or saw) the lowest interest level first and the highest interest level last. (The Panel Recruitment survey only used this order. Response order is thus constant for all distributions in Figure 3.1.) When response options were presented from highest to lowest, the share of respondents selecting the highest category increased for all questions (by 8, 6, 5, and 3 percentage points, respectively) and the second-highest category dropped (by 6, 6, 5, and 7 points). Asking about general political interest in different ways does not make much more of a difference than changing the response order for the same question.

The last question in Table 3.1 is the most commonly used political interest question in America. It makes explicit the distinction between general political interest and interest in a particular election or episode. It also has the advantage of historical comparability, having been included in the ANES since 1964. But for the purpose of distinguishing concepts, its wording is unhelpful. It conflates a behavior – following "what's going on in government and public affairs" – and a motivation – political interest. And the response options refer to the behavior, not the motivation.

The question was included in the 2008 ANES Time Series post-election survey and the spring 2008 KN Survey. According to the 2008 ANES, 26 percent of Americans followed government and public affairs "most of the time," 38 percent "some of the time," 25 percent "only now and then," and 12 percent "hardly at all." The respective percentages in the KN survey were similar at 31, 36, 19, and 14.[1]

Since the *Follow Public Affairs* question, unlike the items shown in Figure 3.1, uses only four response categories, it is difficult to compare their distributions. Furthermore, similar distributions are not sufficient to conclude that the different questions measure similar constructs. Correlations between different questions provide more direct evidence of the extent to which they pick up the same construct. Since the questions come from a variety of surveys, it is not possible to calculate one comprehensive correlation matrix. Instead, the following analysis draws on a patchwork of correlations between any pair of questions included in the same survey.

To understand if interest in politics, following politics, and attention to politics constitute three clearly separable dimensions of political motivation or one underlying tendency, Figure 3.2 examines the correlations between the different questions listed in Table 3.1. Each marker in the plot represents a correlation between a pair of questions. Correlations are graphed as a function of the time interval between measurements. The size of the markers is proportional to the number of observations. Triangles denote correlations between different measures of political interest. For example, *Interest in Politics* and *Interest in Information about Politics* were included in the recruitment survey for the 2008–9 ANES Panel and the first panel wave, respectively. The correlation was .70 for the first cohort (in early 2008) and .66 for the second cohort (in the third quarter of 2008). About 3 months passed between the two measurement occasions, so Figure 3.2 places these correlations just left of the 100-day mark.

Correlations between different political interest questions in Figure 3.2 are tightly clustered around .6 to .7. The absolute magnitude of correlations is difficult to interpret, however. A value of 1.0 would indicate a perfect correlation, but measurement error necessarily attenuates correlations between any two survey items. Correlations around .7 are generally taken to indicate strong similarity between questions measured with error, and even a correlation of .6

---

[1] These estimates average forward- and reverse-coding because response order effects on this question were not statistically significant in either survey.

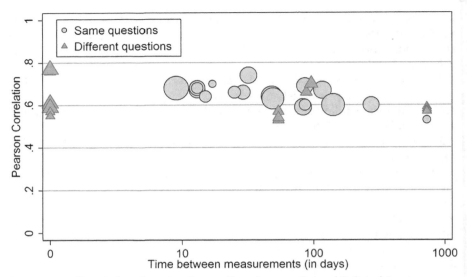

FIGURE 3.2 Correlations between Survey Questions on General Political Interest
Note: Details on each correlation plotted in this figure appear in the Online Supplementary Material, Table OL3.1. With the exception of the 2006 ANES Pilot Study, which has a very low N, correlations are between questions with the same ordering of response options.

is still high. But there are more precise ways to gauge how strong correlations would be in the absence of random measurement error.

First, comparing correlations between different questions to correlations between the same questions asked repeatedly over time provides clues. If correlations between the same question are not much higher than correlations between different questions, different questions appear to measure roughly the same underlying concept. If, in other words, the correlation between two identical questions is only .6 or .7, then a correlation of .6 or .7 *between different questions* looks like a strong association. Analyses along this line indicate that the different questions used to measure political interest capture essentially the same underlying concept. Question wording and conceptual nuances make little difference. Correlations between the same political interest questions asked repeatedly over time, shown by the circles in Figure 3.2, are not noticeably higher than correlations between different questions asked within similar measurement intervals. For example, in the first two panel waves they completed, both cohorts of ANES panelists twice answered the *Interest in Information about Politics* question. Their answers, separated by between 2 and 7 weeks, were correlated at .74 (cohort 1) and .66 (cohort 2). Correlations between repeated responses to the same interest questions are thus barely different from comparable correlations between different interest questions (the .70 and .66 values reported earlier). As the interval between the responses to the same questions was considerably shorter, this result suggests that the domain of interest ("politics" versus "information about what's going on in government and politics") matters little in this case.

Second, the decline in correlations as a function of the measurement interval yields insight about the correlation we would obtain in the absence of measurement error. The correlations in Figure 3.2 reflect a mix of true differences between two variables and measurement error. The decay of the observed correlation as the interval between measurements increases provides a sense of the relative magnitude of true difference and measurement error (Heise 1969; Wiley and Wiley 1970). If the true correlation between two measurements of *Follow Public Affairs* within 3 weeks was indeed .67 (the weighted average of the observed correlations), the correlation should be about .45 (= $.67^2$) over 6 weeks and about .20 (= $.67^4$) over 12 weeks. Yet, we still observe correlations of about .63 for three panels with intervals of about 12 weeks (or 84 days). This pattern of very modest decay in observed correlations as intervals increase is consistent with considerable measurement error.[2] If the error is random, the true three-month correlation would have to be about .98 to approximate the observed decay.[3]

With sufficient data, it is possible to statistically remove measurement error to gauge the true correlations between different interest questions. The statistical correction rests on the following logic: Two different questions asked in the same survey (at Time A) share measurement error (for example, because the respondent's mood or the survey context affects both answers in a similar way, because the same interviewer asks both questions, or because a processing glitch results in the same type of error for the entire survey) which

---

[2] It is important for this argument that the difference in intervals can be treated as random. Some National Annenberg Election Survey (NAES) panel studies shown in Figure 3.2 are broken up to provide estimates for several intervals (see Table OL3.1). There are good reasons to assume that this does not introduce systematic error. In the 2008 survey, the interval is approximately random because all reinterviews were conducted within 5 days after Election Day. In the 2004 survey, it is approximately random because the reinterview schedule also followed a rolling cross-section (RCS) design and contact with drawn numbers was attempted for up to 14 days in both panel waves. Reinterview dates for the 2000 Election panel have no random component, but were conducted within 4 weeks of Election Day, so intervals greater than 4 weeks are approximately random based on the RCS design of the first interview. In the 2000 Debate panel, the long interval is generated approximately randomly by including respondents first interviewed before the conventions in the reinterview sample for the third debate. For more information about the NAES surveys, see Chapter 4 and Online Supplementary Material.

[3] If this is about right, then the question has a reliability of about .68, which means that just over half of its variance is noise. If that is true, then observed correlations between different measures of general political interest in Figure 3.2 are considerably attenuated. Using Heise, the true correlation between 3 weeks and 12 weeks is the observed correlation between Time 1 and Time 3 (12-week interval) divided by the observed correlation between Time 1 and Time 2 (3-week interval), which is .63/.67 = .94. If this is the "true" correlation over 9 weeks, π_{23}, then the "true" correlation between Time 1 and Time 2, π_{12}, is $.94^{1/3}$ = .98. Reliability can then be calculated as $\pi_{12}\pi_{23}/\pi_{13}$.

attenuates the correlation between the two. If the respondent answered at least one of the questions at another time (Time B), we can use her answers from that interview and the average relationship between answers to the same question at Time A and Time B to predict answers at Time A. (The Time B answer is used as an instrument.) This prediction does not use respondent-specific information collected at Time A – and is therefore not affected by measurement error induced at Time A. The correlation between this prediction and other questions asked at Time A thus no longer share measurement error. To the extent that measurement error at Time A is unrelated to measurement error at Time B (because the respondent's mood, the survey context, and the interviewer are all different), the distorting effect of measurement error on the correlation is removed.[4] This is referred to as a disattenuated correlation.

The 2008–9 ANES Panel presents one opportunity to apply this correction. Random measurement error is removed from the *Interest in Information about Politics* question in Wave 1 by using respondents' answers to the same question in Wave 2 as an instrument. Regressing *Interest in Politics* from the recruitment survey on this instrumented *Interest in Information about Politics* shows a very strong relationship of .87, compared to .71 without instrumenting. Applying the same method to the second cohort, the relationship is .92, compared to .75 without instruments.[5] In the 2008 ANES Times Series, it is possible to instrument pre-election *Interest in Information about Politics* with post-election responses. Regressing post-election *Follow Public Affairs* on the instrumented variable yields a regression coefficient of .99, thus indicating an almost 1-to-1 relationship between the two variables.[6] When corrections for measurement error are possible, disattenuated correlations come very close to their theoretical maximum of 1.0.

All of these analyses indicate that interest in politics generally appears to be well approximated as a one-dimensional concept. Reports of interest in "politics," "information about government and politics," and "public affairs and government" have very similar response distributions and are highly correlated with each other. Questions about interest in, attention to, or following "what's going on" in this domain yield responses so strongly related to each other that

---

[4] Measurement error correlated across waves weakens this correction. In an analysis of measurement error in political interest, I found some significant correlations between measurement errors in different waves, but the magnitude of these correlations was small (Prior 2010).

[5] The second cohort was asked *Interest in Politics* for the first time in wave 9. Standardizing variables first to make the regression coefficients more comparable to the correlation coefficients in Figure 3.2 generates a strengthening to .84 from .69 without instruments for cohort 1 and to .83 from .68 for cohort 2.

[6] Because of split-half randomization patterns in the pre- and post-election surveys, this estimation requires an out-of-sample prediction for respondents who answered *Interest in Politics* only in the pre-election survey based on the instrumenting regression estimated for respondents who answered *Interest in Politics* in both waves.

one underlying dimension captures most of the differences between people. (After comparing different political interest questions in the 2006 ANES Pilot Study, Shani (2009a) reaches a similar conclusion. She finds no evidence that interest in political information is more closely related to political learning than other measures of interest.)

INTEREST IN DIFFERENT DOMAINS OF POLITICS

Separate questions in the same survey about different levels of government or different issue domains can reveal to what extent the population splinters into "issue publics" (Converse 1964). Blais and St-Vincent (2011) measured political interest in Canada using four 11-point scales that cover interest in "international politics," "federal politics," "provincial politics," and "local politics." Cronbach's alpha for the 4-item scale is .90, providing strong support for one dominant dimension of political interest. The Eurobarometer survey 60.1 conducted in 2003 leads to the same conclusion.[7] Respondents were asked about their interest in "politics and economics" in their own country, "politics and economics in other countries of the European Union," and "politics and economics in the rest of the world." The question then asked about interest in "arts and culture," "music," "sport," and "lifestyles." Like political interest, interest in these other domains was assessed for the same three geographically-defined areas. Data show a clear clustering of responses by domain, not geographical area: Across all 15 countries (n = 16,082), the correlation between the three political interest questions was .75, compared to an average correlation of only .32 between interest questions that share the same geographical realm.[8]

Verba et al. (1995, 553) asked separate questions about interest in national and local politics (in the United States). The two are correlated at .54. Stattin et al. (2017) asked their sample of 13-to-18-year-olds how interested they were in politics and "in what is going on in society." The correlation was .62. Campbell and Winters (2008) compare general political interest and interest in reading newspaper articles about five different topics (in Britain). In their factor analysis, the first factor, capturing general interest, interest in partisan politics, and interest in foreign policy, accounts for 40 percent of the total variance. A second factor, picking up interest in domestic policy issues, explains another 19 percent of variance. Both factors are correlated at .40, however, suggesting that even interest in domestic policy is bundled with interest in other domains. And because these analyses do not account for measurement error,

---

[7] Fieldwork for Eurobarometer 60.1 was conducted from October 1 to November 7, 2003 using address-based multi-stage probability sampling and face-to-face interviewing with randomly chosen household members aged 15 years or older.

[8] In Great Britain (*n* = 1,055) and Germany (*n* = 2,039), two of the countries examined in detail later in the book, the respective values were .56 and .75 between political items, and .32 and .30 within geographical realms.

they likely understate how closely interest in different policy domains is interrelated.

Perhaps the most thorough analysis of interest in different domains is made possible by the 2008–9 surveys conducted in 38 countries by the International Civic and Citizenship Education Study (ICCS).[9] Asking students "How interested are you in the following issues?," the ICCS survey covered seven domains of interest: "political issues within your local community," "political issues in your country," "social issues in your country," "politics in other countries," "international politics," "environmental issues," and, in European countries, "European politics." Response options were "very interested," "quite interested," "not very interested," and "not interested at all." Across 26 European countries (n = 80,242), a principal component analysis provides strong evidence that the seven interest questions form a one-dimensional construct.[10]

In sum, a good number of people express interest in specific political issues, but those who do tend to also find other aspects of politics interesting. People are sometimes particularly knowledgeable or personally concerned about specific policy areas (e.g., Hutchings 2001; Han 2009; Henderson 2014). Yet, as a first approximation, interest in different political domains and levels of government is so strongly related that one common factor is enough to pick up the preponderance of variation in political interest. Political interest is typically quite general, extending to a variety of aspects related to politics, policy, and governance.

POLITICAL INTEREST VERSUS INTEREST IN NEWS

For the purposes of measuring political interest, it does not appear to matter much if the question refers to "interest in" politics, "interest in information about" politics, "attention to" politics, or "attention to information about" politics. All of these phrases pick up about the same underlying sentiment. As news is people's main source of information about politics, this raises the question if political interest is even the same thing as interest in news.

Not quite. All of the survey questions that gauge political interest still define the domain of interest in political terms. "News" is broader. There is sports news, celebrity news, and, more generally, "soft" news (e.g., Baum 2003). "News" varies in the amount of political and public affairs coverage. Some

---

[9] The population for the ICCS surveys, eighth graders, differs from other surveys examined in this chapter. ICCS used a stratified two-stage probability sampling design. In each country, the first stage sampled schools with probability of inclusion proportionate to school size. Within each school, one class was randomly selected in the second stage.

[10] The first factor, with an eigenvalue of 4.1, explains 59 percent of the total variance. The second factor has an eigenvalue of .8, clearly below the conventional cutoff of one. In England (n = 2,713) and Switzerland (n = 2,861), the first dimension explains 65 and 55 percent of the total variance, respectively. Cronbach's alpha for the seven items is .88 (Europe), .91 (England), and .86 (Switzerland). (Germany did not participate in this ICCS study.)

news formats feature little or no such coverage. Political interest should thus correlate with interest in news only to the extent that the news format in question covers politics and public affairs.

Evidence for this proposition comes from a survey I conducted in 2002 and 2003 that asked respondents which types of news they liked and disliked (see Prior 2003). They were shown the following list of news formats and asked to select the one they liked most:

Reading daily newspapers
Reading current affairs magazines (such as *TIME* or *Newsweek*)
Watching Local News on TV
Watching National News on TV
Watching Late Night or Daytime Talk Shows (such as *Letterman* or *Oprah*)
Watching "Infotainment" programs (such as *Hardcopy* or *Etonite*)
Listening to the news on the radio
Getting news from Internet sites

The question was repeated three more times, and respondents were then asked to mark any of the remaining formats that they disliked.

Figure 3.3 shows news preferences (calculated as the percentage disliking a format subtracted from the percentage including it in their top 3) by level of political interest[11] for the four news formats that were most clearly related to political interest. The more politically interested the person, the more likely she is to prefer national TV news and daily newspapers, two formats that routinely cover politics at considerable length. Watching "Late Night or Daytime Talk Shows (such as *Letterman* or *Oprah*)" and "Infotainment programs (such as *Hardcopy* or *Etonite*)" follow the opposite pattern. They typically include little coverage of politics and public affairs, and more politically interested people are more likely to "dislike" these formats. The wider spread of the bars in Figure 3.3 at high levels of political interest illustrates that the news preferences of the most politically interested individuals are most sensitive to the amount of political coverage offered by different types of news.[12]

---

[11] Political interest was measured earlier, as part of Knowledge Networks' political profile, using the following question: "In general, how interested are you in politics and public affairs? Very interested, somewhat interested, slightly interested, or not at all interested"

[12] Preferences for some news formats were unrelated to political interest. "Listening to the news on the radio" and "getting news from Internet sites" were least likely to appear among both preferred and disliked sources, probably because the description is very vague. "Reading current affairs magazines (such as *TIME* or *Newsweek*)" was the fourth-most preferred format, but also disliked by some politically interested respondents. I expected a stronger correlation with political interest, but these magazines do include apolitical coverage, and the term "current affairs magazines" may have reinforced this impression. Lastly, local TV news was universally popular.

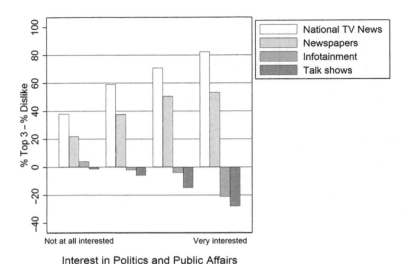

FIGURE 3.3 Political Interest and Preference for News Formats (KN 2002–3)

If political interest is roughly equivalent to interest in a specific subset of news – news about politics – it follows that less politically interested people should enjoy news more than politics because news includes apolitical content they like better than politics. For a test of this idea, I return to the 2008 KN survey that asked respondents if "following politics is fun" and whether they liked "complex political issues." A second, randomly chosen, half of respondents were instead asked if "following news is fun" and whether they liked "complex news stories." Figure 3.4 shows the impact of this wording difference for the relationship with political interest (measured by an additive index of the *Interest in Information about Politics* and *Follow Public Affairs* questions).

Except for the most politically interested people, "news" is indeed more popular than "politics." People with low political interest are essentially unanimous in rejecting that "following politics is fun," but perhaps a fifth of them still agree that "following news is fun." Likewise, those with little political interest clearly do not like "complex political issues," but a quarter of them say they "like complex news stories." They have (limited) interest in news, just not the kind that covers politics. For politically interested people, on the other hand, it makes no difference whether the question asks about news or politics. When they hear the term "news," they think of news about politics and public affairs, and so the two terms describe very similar domains for them. Political interest, in short, is interest in particular content, not interest in a particular delivery of that content.

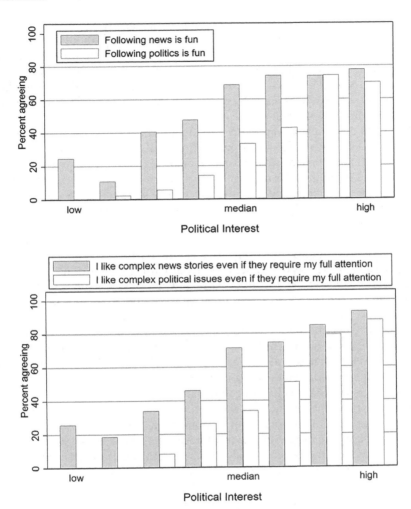

FIGURE 3.4 "News" versus "Politics" (KN 2008)

CONCLUSION

The evidence in this chapter demonstrates that people who express interest in one area of politics are typically also interested in other political areas. Survey questions appear to measure the same kind of interest regardless of whether they ask about "politics," "information about government and politics," "public affairs and government," "social issues in your country," or "environmental issues." Questions about politics at different levels, from "local politics" to "international politics," were also strongly correlated. When the survey design permits statistical procedures to remove the distorting impact of random measurement error, correlations between interest reports about seemingly different domains of politics are remarkably close to 1.0 – the statistical equivalent of measuring the same thing twice. This conclusion matches the results of Delli Carpini and Keeter's (1996, 175) analysis of political knowledge across different types of issues which leads them to infer that "most of those interested in politics are broadly interested."

Not only do people group many subdomains of politics together when they offer their assessment of political interest, they also delineate limits of what is political. In the Eurobarometer survey analyzed in this chapter, interest in "politics and economics" is notably different from interest in "arts and culture" or "lifestyles." An experiment in my own survey showed that people meaningfully distinguish "news" and "politics," so they do not report interest in politics when the news format they prefer rarely covers politics.

Despite the large number of different interest questions examined in this chapter, some domains were not covered. In particular, interest in specific policy areas is rarely asked in surveys. Even with the important exception of policy areas covered by the International Civic and Citizenship Education Study, the evidence is not sufficient to completely rule out that individuals have idiosyncratic interests in domains that promise material gain or that issue publics exist. But the strong correlations between different interest questions, the emergence of a dominant first dimension in factor analyses, and the associations between single-item measures of general political interest and many relevant outcomes all demonstrate that understanding general political interest means understanding much about political interest.

The household panel studies that represent the empirical backbone of this project all ask a similar version of the question, "How interested are you in politics?" Thanks to the analyses in this chapter, we now know that results presented later in the book would not have been much different if the panel studies had instead worded their question slightly differently, referenced "information" or "news" about politics, or asked instead about "government and public affairs" or any number of alternative descriptions of politics.

This chapter has examined all kinds of survey questions gauging interest in various aspects of politics. But there was one notable omission: Questions about campaigns and elections did not appear. Campaigns and elections are the main focus of the next chapter, both as a specific domain of interest and as a possible situational stimulus that might trigger interest. How the public's interest responds to impending elections provides important clues about the extent to which political interest is dispositional.

4

The Impact of Elections

Is political interest an enduring predisposition or largely a temporary reaction to a political stimulus? If you just tell me your level of political interest once, I cannot tell. If you say that you are interested in politics, the psychological model of interest implies that you have either just encountered a political stimulus that triggered your interest by causing an emotional reaction, perhaps positive such as liking the stimulus and wanting more of it, or negative because it made you anxious. Or, you reported an interest in politics that has been sustained after it was triggered earlier, perhaps much earlier. In that second scenario, it is possible that you also just have experienced a political stimulus, but you would have reported high interest even if nothing political had occurred in your environment recently. This is the difference between situational and dispositional interest. Both types of interest lead you to give the same answer in response to a question about your political interest, but they have very different implications for the operation of a democratic system. Situational political interest leaves citizens dependent on events, reacting again and again to short-term forces. Dispositional political interest creates conditions for people to monitor their representatives and act politically in a more continuous and independent fashion, even in quiet times.

One way to distinguish between situational and dispositional interest is to track political interest over time as environmental stimuli come and go. According to the psychological model, environmental stimuli trigger situational political interest. The extent to which situational political interest evolves into dispositional interest is an empirical question. It is a mark of dispositional interest that it endures even in the absence of situational triggers. If political interest changes little despite an ebb and flow of political stimuli, we are likely looking at dispositional political interest. This chapter tracks political interest before, during, and after one of the greatest political stimuli, U.S. presidential elections. It also presents data for election campaigns in Germany which are shorter and, some would say, sweeter.

Analysis of interest during election campaigns generates another question about the dimensionality of political interest: Does interest in campaigns differ from the general kind of political interest that I analyzed in the previous chapter? The question of dimensionality is different than in the previous chapter because interest in specific campaigns and elections is meaningful only for a limited time. After comparing trends in general and campaign-specific interest, the chapter ends by juxtaposing their impacts on learning during the campaign and turnout in order to determine which of the two is more relevant for political outcomes.

Results support the conclusion that political interest is largely dispositional. Campaign-specific interest responds a little more to an approaching election because it seems to capture situational interest to a greater extent. All told, however, campaign-specific interest is not much different than general political interest.

Most data in this chapter again come from U.S. election studies conducted in 2008, a year in which several different research organizations, most prominently the American National Election Study (ANES), fielded large, longitudinal surveys including interest questions. The rolling cross-sectional studies conducted by the National Annenberg Election Survey (NAES) in 2000, 2004, and 2008 provide useful comparisons. The 2009 and 2013 German Longitudinal Election Studies, which included several different survey components, provide comparable data from a different country.

GENERAL POLITICAL INTEREST IN ELECTION YEARS

In the weeks before an election, campaigns dominate the political agenda and saturate news coverage. If the focus on candidates and competition makes politics more interesting to many people, it would be more difficult to conceive of general political interest as a disposition. A limited response to the higher overall volume of political discourse, on the other hand, would support political interest as a trait-like predisposition that primarily depends on mostly stable predictors and an enduring image of politics, not short-term fluctuations in how and how much it is covered.

For several political interest questions introduced in Chapter 3, response distributions can be compared at two points in time, one closer to Election Day than the other. Does interest increase as the election approaches? The *Interest in Politics* question included in the two independent recruitment surveys for the 2008–9 ANES Panel shows barely any change between the last quarter of 2007 and the late summer of 2008: The share of "extremely interested" Americans remained at 10 percent, the share of "very interested" increased by 4 points, and "moderately interested" dropped by 1 point. Between

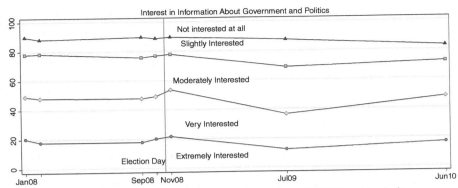

FIGURE 4.1 Political Interest Distribution in the 2008–9 ANES Panel Including 2010 Recontact

the pre-election interviews for the 2008 ANES Times Series in the fall and the reinterviews in November and December, *Interest in Information about Politics* rose marginally with a 2-percentage-point increase in "extremely interested" Americans and a 7-point rise of "very interested" people. The *Follow Public Affairs* question also generated very similar distributions in the ANES Time Series post-election wave and my KN survey conducted in the spring of 2008 (even though the two surveys employ different sampling methods and interview modes).

The 2008–9 ANES Panel provides a more extended look at change in political interest in the months before and after the 2008 presidential election. Starting in the first panel wave after recruitment, panelists were asked the *Interest in Information about Politics* question repeatedly. Figure 4.1 shows responses from 727 panelists who answered the interest question each of the seven times it was included in 2008 and 2010. The graph (like similar ones that follow) cumulatively stacks the percentages at different levels of interest so they add up to 100 percent. Across the four interviews before the election, starting in January 2008 and ending in October, the distribution changes minimally. The small late rise in the share of "extremely interested" panelists extends to the first post-election wave in November 2008. In that wave, the share of "extremely interested" panelists is 4 points higher than at its pre-election minimum, and the "very interested" category adds 3 points. This increase in interest, which closely matches the magnitudes in the ANES Time Series study, is substantively small. The election does nothing to raise the share of people who are "slightly interested" or "not interested at all." The 7-point increase may understate the election impact if the Obama-Clinton rivalry and the competitive Republican nomination campaign elevated interest throughout 2008. There is a hint of evidence for this possibility in the drop between the post-election wave and the next interviews in July 2009. The top two categories lose a combined 18 percentage points in this period and the share of panelists who are no more than "slightly interested" rises by 10 points. By June 2010, however, interest has recovered roughly to election-year levels.

One concern about the data in Figure 4.1 is the possibility of panel effects: Perhaps panelists who completed so many interviews differ from the rest of the population. Examining interest among panelists who eventually left the panel and treating the second recruitment cohort as a refreshment sample yields evidence for only minor panel effects and maintains the finding that election-year change was rare in 2008 (see Online Supplementary Material, Figure OL4.1.) A different research design, the rolling cross-section, offers an alternative way to answer the same question. In a rolling cross-section, new random samples of respondents to be contacted are released every day, so aggregate trends can be tracked without reinterviewing any of the respondents, avoiding panel effects altogether. The National Annenberg Election Survey (NAES) conducted rolling cross-sections in 2000, 2004, and 2008. The 2008 survey did not include any question in the general interest domain, but in 2000 and 2004, the NAES used the same *Follow Public Affairs* question as the ANES. Figure 4.2 graphs responses to this question over the two election years.

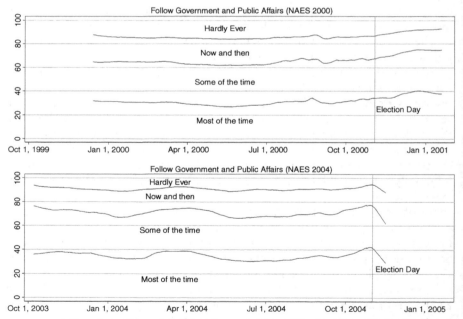

FIGURE 4.2 Trends in General Political Interest during Election Years, United States, NAES 2000 and 2004

Note: A small fraction of respondents, under 1 percent, answered "Don't Know" to political interest questions. They are coded as the minimum level of interest.

Political interest, as measured by the *Follow Public Affairs* question, exhibits only minor variation over the course of the 2000 and 2004 election years. The 2000 trend is almost exactly flat before Election Day, save for a small bump around the time of the Democratic convention in mid-August. In 2004, the share of Americans who say they "follow what's going on in government and public affairs most of the time" rises by around 10 points in the month before the election. Magnitude and timing of this rise are similar to what is evident in the ANES 2008–9 Panel in Figure 4.1. The clearest difference between 2000 and 2004 occurs after the election. In 2004, interest levels dropped back to typical election-year levels within a week or two after Election Day. The protracted resolution of the 2000 election, which culminated in the Supreme Court's *Bush v Gore* decision announced on December 12, 2000, appears to have maintained and even slightly raised election-year interest levels.

The very limited response of political interest to approaching elections is not confined to the United States. The German Longitudinal Election Study (GLES) carried out a rolling cross-section design before the 2009 and 2013 federal elections in Germany.[1] The GLES included the *Interest in Politics* question also employed by the ANES 2008–9 Panel Study recruitment survey, adding "in general terms" as a prefix. The distribution of responses over time is graphed in Figure 4.3. In the final days of the 2009 campaign, the share of Germans who are at least "fairly interested" ticks up by a few points. In 2013, political interest barely increased. Much like Figures 4.1 and 4.2 for U.S. campaigns, Figure 4.3 does not reveal a great deal of change in political interest as Election Day approached.[2]

In all, general political interest thus appears to be dispositional, a largely chronic predisposition that does not respond much to short-term bursts of political coverage and campaign hoopla. Elections lead only a few people, often fewer than 10 percent, to express greater interest in politics, government, and public affairs. This empirical finding is consistent across different longitudinal designs (panel and repeated cross-section), election years, and two countries (United States, Germany).

---

[1] In 2009, CDU/CSU and FDP won a combined 48.4 percent of the vote (and ended up forming a governing coalition). In 2013, the FDP narrowly missed the electoral threshold, forcing the CDU/CSU to enter a grand coalition with the SPD.

[2] The GLES RCS is a phone survey. GLES also conducted independent in-person cross-sectional surveys before and after the election (with field periods of 6–7 weeks). Political interest is lower in the in-person studies ("very interested" by 9 points in 2009 and 1 point in 2013, "fairly interested" by 3 points in 2009 and 6 points in 2013), suggesting significantly larger sampling effects than in the United States data. In both years, the difference between pre- and post-election in-person estimates of political interest is small, however.

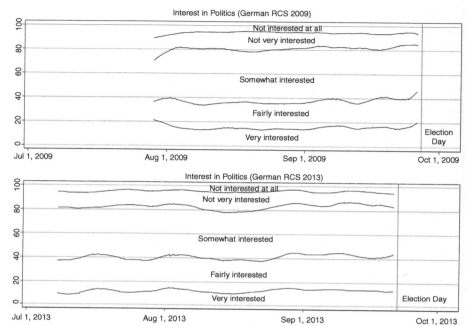

FIGURE 4.3 General Political Interest in Germany before the Elections of 2009 and 2013, GLES

Note: Wording: "Einmal ganz allgemein gesprochen: Wie stark interessieren Sie sich für Politik – sehr stark, ziemlich stark, mittelmäßig, weniger stark oder überhaupt nicht?" ["Generally speaking, how interested are you in politics – very interested, fairly interested, somewhat interested, not very interested, or not interested at all?"]

CAMPAIGN-SPECIFIC INTEREST

Many surveys include questions gauging respondents' interest in campaigns specifically. Table 4.1 shows several questions used in 2008. Since 1952, the ANES has commonly included the *Interest in Campaigns* question, often in both pre- and post-election surveys. In the pre-election interviews of the 2008 ANES Time Series study, 44 percent said they were "very much interested," and another 41 percent "somewhat interested." The 2008 National Annenberg Election Survey (NAES) carried the *Follow Presidential Campaign* question. In the subset of NAES interviews conducted during the ANES pre-election field period (Sep 2–Nov 3), 45 percent reported following the campaign "very closely," and another 40 percent "somewhat closely" – almost precisely the same percentages as the two top categories of the ANES *Interest in Campaigns* question.

Figure 4.4 compares answers to the NAES *Follow Presidential Campaign* question with yet another question, asked in the AP-Yahoo 2008 Panel Study about *Interest in Campaign News*. AP-Yahoo fielded three refreshment samples

TABLE 4.1 *Campaign-Specific Interest Questions Referenced in This Chapter*

Item Name	Question Wording	Response Options	Source
Interest in Campaigns (Camp Int)	Some people don't pay much attention to political campaigns. How about you? Would you say that you have been very much interested, somewhat interested, or not much interested in the political campaigns so far this year?	very much interested, somewhat interested, not much interested	ANES 2008 Times Series (pre & post), NAES 2000
	How interested are you in particular in the current campaign for the forthcoming federal election?	very interested, fairly interested, somewhat interested, not very interested, not interested at all	GLES 2009, 2013
Follow Presidential Campaign (Follow Pres Camp)	How closely are you following the 2008 presidential campaign?	very closely, somewhat closely, not too closely, not closely at all	NAES 2004, 2008
Interest in Campaign News (Int Camp News)	How much interest do you have in following news about the campaign for president?	a great deal, quite a bit, only some, very little, no interest at all	AP-Yahoo 2008 Panel Study
Interest in Presidential Campaign (Pres Camp Int)	Would you say you have been very much interested, somewhat interested, or not much interested in the presidential campaign so far this year?	very much interested, somewhat interested, not much interested	NAES 2000, 2004
Attention to Campaign News (Camp Att, *old version*)	In general, how much attention did you pay to news about the campaign for President?	a great deal, quite a bit, some, very little, none	ANES 2008 Times Series (post)
Attention to Campaign News (Camp Att, *new version*)	In general, how much attention did you pay to news about the campaign for President?	a great deal, a lot, a moderate amount, a little, none at all	ANES 2008 Times Series (post)

Note: ANES refers to American National Election Study, NAES to National Annenberg Election Survey, GLES to German Longitudinal Election Study. For more information about surveys, see Online Supplementary Materials.

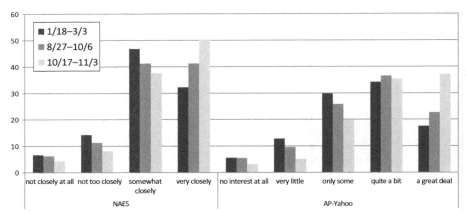

FIGURE 4.4 Campaign Interest in 2008 over Three Periods, NAES and AP-Yahoo
Note: NAES wording: "How closely are you following the 2008 presidential campaign?"
AP-Yahoo wording: "How much interest do you have in following news about the campaign for president?"

during the time that the NAES conducted its interviews. Figure 4.4 shows responses to the AP-Yahoo question for these three samples (on the right) and NAES response distributions for the same time periods (on the left).

Even though one question asks about "interest . . . in following news about the campaign" and allows five response options, while the other asks about "how closely" respondents "are following" the campaign and offers four (different) options, their response distributions are remarkably similar in several regards. The shares of respondents selecting the two bottom categories are almost identical across both questions and changes are almost identical over the three time periods. While the top categories receive a greater share of responses in the NAES question with only four options, the change over the three time periods is also very similar. In fact, if the "quite a bit" responses in the AP-Yahoo question are allocated in equal proportion to "only some" and "a great deal," the distributions of the two different questions become essentially indistinguishable from one another in each of the three time periods.

The similarities between different questions about campaign interest are highly suggestive. For one difference, a precise test is possible, thanks to a randomized experiment conducted as part of the NAES 2000, which carried the traditional ANES *Interest in Campaigns* question (without the first two sentences.) Another, randomly chosen sample of respondents was instead asked a slightly altered version about "the presidential campaign so far this year." As Figure 4.5 shows, it makes virtually no difference whether the question refers to "the presidential campaign" or "political campaigns" more generally. Interest in the presidential campaign was possibly a few points

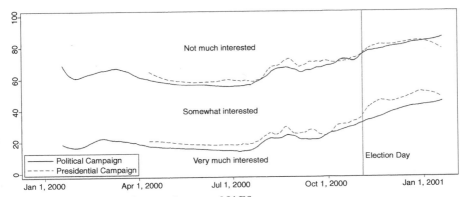

FIGURE 4.5 Campaign Interest in 2000, NAES

higher than interest in campaigns generally, but the difference is small and the time trends in the two series are nearly identical. Campaign interest rises during the fall, but the largest difference occurs after Election Day, when uncertainty about the presidential election outcome remained while other campaigns had ended.

Different ways of asking about campaign interest yield very similar aggregate response distributions. To assess if different questions also agree on the ordering of individuals' interest levels, I examine correlations between questions. Details of this analysis, which use the same techniques to correct for measurement error as in Chapter 3, are in the chapter appendix. Results indicate that different ways of asking about campaign interest measure roughly the same underlying variable. It makes very little difference whether a question asks about presidential campaigns or campaigns more generally, about campaigns or news about campaigns, about interest, attention, and following campaigns – questions reviewed here all seem to pick up a general tendency to find campaigns interesting and report close attention to them. Campaign interest, like general political interest, can be treated as a one-dimensional construct without sacrificing much nuance.

CAMPAIGN INTEREST IN ELECTION YEARS

It is difficult to consider interest questions that refer to specific campaigns or elections as measuring dispositional interest. Campaign interest may therefore be inherently more situational than general political interest. To assess this expectation, this section plots campaign interest over time. Figure 4.5 already showed that interest in the 2000 campaign increased around the conventions, remained at that higher level, and increased slightly more in the days before the

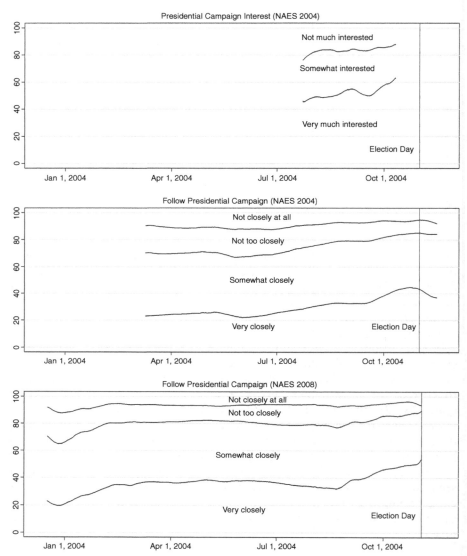

FIGURE 4.6 Campaign Interest in 2004 and 2008, NAES

election. The share of "very interested" people rose from around 15 percent in the summer of 2000 to over 30 percent by Election Day.

Figure 4.6 plots all campaign interest questions included in the 2004 and 2008 NAES rolling cross-sectional surveys. The 2004 NAES included the *Interest in Presidential Campaign* item for only a few weeks, but used the *Follow*

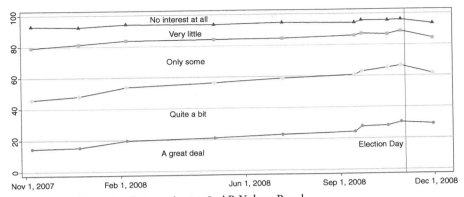

FIGURE 4.7 Campaign Interest in 2008, AP-Yahoo Panel
Note: Graph uses responses by panelists from baseline and refreshment samples and applies cross-sectional weights provided with the data. As data consist of a mix of panel reinterviews and fresh cross-sectional cases, panel effects could possibly affect the trends.

Presidential Campaign[3] question the entire year. In the period in which the two questions are available, their distributions suggest parallel trends, both indicating an accelerating rise in campaign interest in late September. Judging by the *Follow Presidential Campaign* trend, this rise continued until close to Election Day. Between the summer and the end of the 2004 campaign, the percentage who report following the campaign "very closely" increased by about 20 points. These estimates are consistent with the 2004 ANES Time Series study. Between the pre-election survey (conducted in September and October) and the post-election survey, there is an 11-point rise in "very much interested" respondents on the *Interest in Campaigns* measure. Given that the rise in NAES *Follow Presidential Campaign* began before September and reversed even before Election Day, the magnitude of the increase in the two measures is very similar.

The bottom graph in Figure 4.6 shows the *Follow Presidential Campaign* measure over the course of 2008. The trend closely mirrors the same variable in 2004, revealing a similar 20-point rise in people following the campaign "very closely" that starts in late August. The 2008 ANES Time Series, which again misses the early part of the rise, shows a 12-point increase in "very much interested" respondents between pre- and post-election waves. Lastly, the *Interest in Campaign News* question in the AP-Yahoo Panel Study plotted in Figure 4.7 reveals a rise of about 10 points in the share of respondents with "a great deal of interest" in the last two months of the campaign.

A relatively small increase in campaign interest of 10–15 points may in fact be typical. The first survey-based election study (Lazarsfeld et al. 1948 [1944],

---

[3] The wording was almost identical to the 2008 NAES version: "How closely are you following the campaign for president?" After Election Day, wording changed to "How closely did you follow the campaign for president over the past year?"

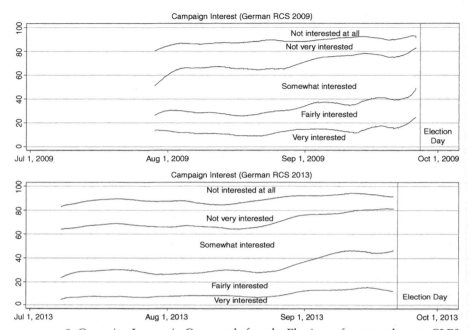

FIGURE 4.8 Campaign Interest in Germany before the Elections of 2009 and 2013, GLES

77), conducted in Erie County, Ohio in 1940, found a 10 percent rise in campaign interest between May and October.[4] The GLES rolling cross-sections show an increase of about 15 points in the months before both the 2009 and 2013 federal elections in Germany (Figure 4.8).

Politics and Campaigns: One or Two Dimensions?

Elections increase campaign interest somewhat more than general political interest, in the aggregate, but the difference is not large. This section examines whether this similarity is a coincidence, or if survey questions about general and campaign-specific interest measure one dominant dimension of interest – and that's why these two variables move together. Do people differentiate between the campaign-specific domain of electoral competition, campaigning, and candidate focus and the domain of general politics that more explicitly includes governing, lawmaking, and public administration? Or is campaign interest just another indicator of general interest that is dormant most of the time and becomes activated by impending elections?

To find out, this section analyzes correlations between measures of the two domains, general and campaign-specific interest. As previously discussed, even

---

[4] In the 1948 Elmira study, campaign interest rose barely at all between June and October of 1948 (Berelson et al. 1954, 28). It is possible that the first measurement occurred too late to pick up the entire increase associated with the election.

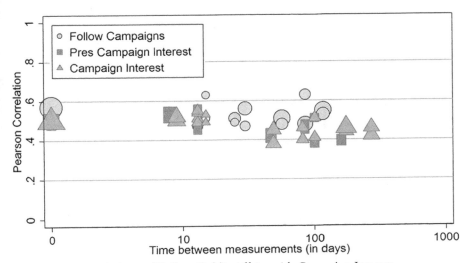

FIGURE 4.9 Correlations of *Follow Public Affairs* with Campaign Interest Questions, NAES

very strong associations will not show up as perfect correlations when indicators are measured with error, so the analysis again attempts to correct for measurement error. Figure 4.9 displays correlations between the *Follow Public Affairs* measure of general political interest and three separate measures of campaign interest. When included in the same survey (but not in immediate succession), *Follow Public Affairs* has a correlation of .57 with *Follow Presidential Campaign* and .50 with *Interest in (Presidential) Campaigns*. These estimates are based on tens of thousands of interviews, conducted as part of the NAES RCS components in 2000 and 2004. (The magnitude of their markers, on the left of Figure 4.9, is reduced by a factor of 10 to keep them from filling most of the graph.) Breaking up the full RCS into different periods of the election year reveals very little variation in these contemporaneous correlations over time, except for a drop of about .05 after Election Day (see Online Supplementary Material, Table OL4.2.)

Correlations in Figure 4.9 with intervals greater than zero come from the 2000 and 2004 NAES panel studies. They show minor declines as the interval between panel waves increases. As discussed in Chapter 3, this pattern is indicative of two variables that are closely related but measured with error.[5] Heise

---

[5] Data from the 2008 ANES Time Series study lead to similar conclusions as the NAES data. The advantage of the ANES study is that it included seven different interest measures (two of which were included in pre- and post-election waves). The disadvantage is that not all questions were answered by all respondents due to several randomization designs. Hence, it is not possible to generate the full correlation matrix between all measures. Based on the correlations that can be calculated (shown in Online Supplementary Material, Table OL4.3), the relationship between measures within one domain (general political interest or campaign interest) is, on average, .65 for contemporaneous relationships (based only on the post-election survey) and .53 for over-time (pre/post) relationships. The corresponding between-domain correlations are .54 and .52,

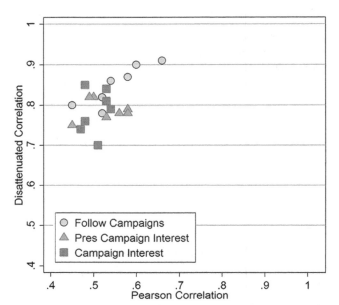

FIGURE 4.10 Correlations of General and Campaign-Specific Interest, Observed and Disattenuated, NAES

Note: Graph plots correlations between *Follow Public Affairs* and different campaign interest questions. Horizontal axis shows observed Pearson correlations, vertical axis disattenuated correlations corrected for random measurement error.

adjustments to the observed correlations reveal implied true correlations of .94 to 1.01 for the association between *Follow Public Affairs* and *Follow Presidential Campaign*, and .98 to 1.02 for the association between *Follow Public Affairs* and *Interest in (Presidential) Campaigns.*[6] The NAES panel studies also offer opportunities to remove measurement error using the instrumental variables approach applied in Chapter 3. Figure 4.10 plots the observed against the disattenuated contemporaneous correlations.[7] When measurement error is removed, correlations increase by two to three decimal points to between .7 and .9.

respectively. The magnitudes of the correlations are highly similar to the NAES estimates. If anything, the association between general and campaign-specific political interest is even stronger in the ANES data. In the German GLES, the correlations between the 5-point scales of general and campaign-specific interest depend on the sample. In the in-person pre-election surveys, correlations are high at .72 (in 2009) and .74 (in 2013). In the phone RCS interviews before the election, the same questions are less strongly correlated at .55 (2009) and .56 (2013). In the GLES, campaign-specific interest immediately follows the general interest question.

[6] These ranges are for true correlations with a 10-day interval.

[7] Because both variables are included in both waves, disattenuated correlations are calculated through a pair of instrumental-variables regressions. Regressing Variable A on Variable B, instrumented with its value from the reinterview, yields one regression coefficient. Regressing Variable B on the instrumented Variable A provides a second coefficient. Taking the square root of the product of the two coefficients translates the regression coefficients into the metric of a correlation coefficient.

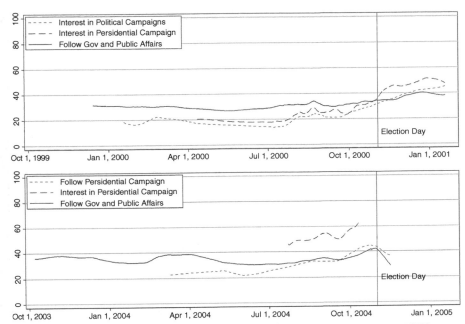

FIGURE 4.11 Comparing General Political Interest and Campaign Interest, NAES 2000 and 2004

Note: For each variable, graphs show the daily percentage of the sample selecting the highest interest response and apply lowess smoothing.

Patterns of correlations between general political interest and campaign-specific interest indicate close similarity. Some correlations even approach 1.0, suggesting that both types of questions measure the same concept. The average correlation when random measurement error is removed is closer to .8 to .9, so it is best to think of them as tightly related. Even if general and campaign interest capture close to the same thing, this chapter has already shown that the latter is somewhat more strongly affected by elections. Figures 4.11 (for the U.S.) and 4.12 (for Germany) illustrate the magnitude of this difference by plotting the share of respondents with high general and campaign-specific interest in the same graphs. All four graphs show essentially the same pattern: As Election Day approaches, campaign interest rises modestly and eventually reaches the almost flat general interest trend. This "catching up" of campaign interest is particularly compelling for the German data and the 2004 NAES *Follow Presidential Campaign* item because they use the same number of response options to measure both types of interest (and in the German case even the same wording of response options). As the correlation between general and campaign-specific interest does *not* change as the election approaches, the "catching up" of campaign interest appears to indicate its activation rather than a strengthening link with general interest. Campaign-specific interest may really only become a meaningful sentiment close to the election. In order to examine this possibility more directly, the following

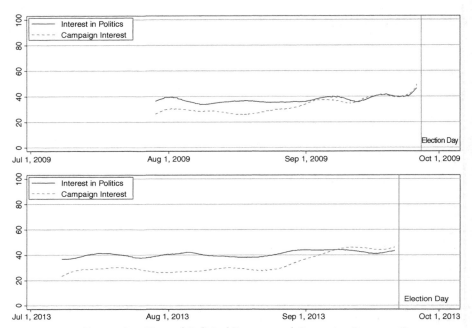

FIGURE 4.12 Comparing General Political Interest and Campaign Interest, Germany 2009 and 2013
Note: For each variable, graphs apply lowess smoothing to the daily percentage of the sample who report being "very interested" or "fairly interested."

analysis compares the extent to which general and campaign-specific interest, measured at different points during the campaign, predict subsequent outcomes.

In the post-election reinterviews, the NAES panel studies in 2000 and 2004 asked respondents whether they had voted and measured political knowledge using a long battery of questions about the presidential candidates' biographies and their positions on many policy issues.[8] The reinterviews also measured, again, respondents' general and campaign-specific interest. These data make it possible to compare how well campaign-specific and general interest measured months before the election and changes in interest between interviews predict turnout reports and political knowledge after the election.[9] If only an approaching election serves to activate campaign interest, it should have relatively little predictive power earlier in the campaign. After this activation has occurred,

[8] The knowledge scales are composed of 26 items (in 2000) and 14 items (in 2004) and rescaled to the 0–1 interval. Questions are listed in the Online Supplementary Material.

[9] Other data sources used in this chapter do not permit this kind of analysis: The AP-Yahoo Panel did not measure general political interest. The 2008–9 ANES Panel did not measure campaign interest. The ANES TS 2008 includes measures of both, but in separate subsamples. The GLES RCS surveys include both measures in repeated interviews for the same individuals, but there is too little variance on turnout (95 percent report voting) and surveys include no knowledge questions.

TABLE 4.2 *The Relationship between General Political Interest and Campaign Interest on Political Outcomes*

2000		July/Aug	Sept	Oct/Nov
Turnout				
	Fol Gov	1.4 (.2)**	1.3 (.3)**	1.3 (.2)**
	d(Fol Gov)	.4 (.2)*	.4 (.3)	.4 (.2)*
	Camp Int	.8 (.4)**	.5 (.3)	1.0 (.2)**
	d(Camp Int)	.7 (.4)**	.4 (.2)	.3 (.2)
	N	1,676	1,018	1,353
	Pseudo R²	.18	.12	.17
Pol. Knowledge				
	Fol Gov	.27 (.04)**	.31 (.05)**	.25 (.04)**
	d(Fol Gov)	.20 (.04)**	.12 (.04)**	.11 (.04)**
	Camp Int	.11 (.03)**	.04 (.04)	.11 (.04)**
	d(Camp Int)	.09 (.03)**	.09 (.04)*	.04 (.03)
	N	816	502	655
	R²	.26	.28	.24

2004		July/Aug	Sept	Oct/Nov
Turnout				
	Fol Gov	2.2 (.3)**	1.4 (.4)**	1.6 (.4)**
	d(Fol Gov)	1.6 (.3)**	1.1 (.4)**	.7 (.4)*
	Follow Camp	.4 (.4)	.5 (.5)	1.6 (.4)**
	d(Follow Camp)	.1 (.4)	-.3 (.4)	.6 (.4)
	N	1,159	792	921
	Pseudo R²	.23	.14	.26
Pol. Knowledge				
	Fol Gov	.35 (.04)**	.24 (.05)**	.24 (.05)**
	d(Fol Gov)	.21 (.04)**	.17 (.05)**	.26 (.05)**
	Follow Camp	.23 (.05)**	.13 (.06)*	.30 (.06)**
	d(Follow Camp)	.13 (.04)**	.00 (.06)	.14 (.05)**
	N	1,146	790	911
	R²	.37	.20	.29

** $p < .01$, * $p < .05$
Note: NAES panel data. Cell entries are probit (for turnout) or OLS (for knowledge) coefficients with standard errors in parentheses. Models also include an intercept and the number of days between first and second interview.

campaign interest should explain outcomes such as turnout and political learning after the influence of general political interest has been accounted for – but only to the extent that it constitutes a genuine second interest dimension.

Table 4.2 reports the results of regressions that predict post-election outcomes for three groups of NAES panelists: those first interviewed in July/

August, in September, and in October/November. For each interest question, regressions include two components, the level of interest at the first interview and the change between the first and second interview.

No matter when the first interview took place, general political interest at the time and the change between then and the post-election interview are significantly, and often strongly, related to self-reported turnout and political knowledge after the election. This is not always the case for campaign-specific interest. Before October, campaign interest effects are weaker and occasionally not statistically significant. The results for different years and outcomes have in common that the coefficients for campaign interest become larger as the election approaches, whereas the coefficients for general interest start large and become somewhat smaller. General political interest strongly predicts post-election outcomes months before campaign-specific interest becomes meaningful and retains much of its impact in the final campaign month.

Using only information collected in July or August (and thus only the levels of interest, not the change score), the general interest component alone explains 15 percent of the variance in post-election knowledge in 2000 and 25 percent in 2004. Adding campaign interest measured in July or August raises the variance explained by only 1 and 5 points, respectively. Even for interviews conducted in October and early November, general interest alone explains 19 and 23 percent of the variance in 2000 and 2004, respectively. Adding the campaign-specific component increases the explained variance by only 3 points in 2000 and not at all in 2004. These results rule out that campaign-specific interest is uniquely important in generating campaign-specific knowledge (about candidates and their proposals, in this case). Although campaign-specific interest makes an independent contribution to predicting subsequent candidate knowledge, the contribution is small and general political interest is sufficient to account for the bulk of the interest-knowledge link.

In sum, activation of campaign interest as an independent motivational force late in the campaign is very limited in scope. Approaching elections raise general political interest a little and campaign-specific interest a little more. Even late in the campaign, general interest alone is almost as predictive of self-reported turnout and post-election knowledge as the two types of interest together. These findings indicate that it is not particularly important to differentiate an election-specific domain of political interest from a more general domain that also includes government and public affairs outside of the campaign context. Interest in campaigns and interest in politics are very similar sentiments.

CONCLUSION

This chapter has provided the first evidence that political interest is, to a large extent, an enduring predisposition, rather than a temporary reaction to a situational trigger. Despite billions of dollars of campaign spending on U.S. elections and a news media that covers campaigns with singular abandon, political interest hardly increases as Election Day approaches. As the opening of this chapter illustrated, a single measurement of political interest cannot distinguish situational from dispositional interest. The analysis in this chapter has shown that if we ask new samples of people over time how politically interested they are, the breakdown of responses remains very similar.

It would be premature, however, to declare political interest largely dispositional based on this evidence alone. First, it might take events other than elections to detect temporary bumps due to elevated situational interest. In the next chapter, I track political interest over much longer periods of time and check if other events introduce more aggregate change. Second, nearly constant aggregate political interest does not rule out individual-level instability – which would call into question the diagnosis of an enduring predisposition. To determine if individuals, as opposed to populations in the aggregate, have stable levels of interest, it is necessary to talk to the same people repeatedly. I move to examine this kind of individual-level stability in Chapters 6 and 7.

Campaign-specific interest appears slightly more situational than general political interest. It increases by a small but measurable amount as an election approaches, whereas general political interest usually remains almost constant. Further analysis suggests, however, that this does not indicate the activation of a genuinely independent motivational force late in the campaign. Even late in a campaign, campaign-specific interest does not add much to predictions of self-reported turnout and post-election knowledge based on general political interest. Interest in campaigns and interest in politics are very similar sentiments. The main reason for their modestly different trends before an election may simply be that a question about interest "in the campaign" is difficult to answer when the general election is still several months away (and, in the United States, primaries have not yet produced nominees). Campaign interest is different from the domains examined in Chapter 3 because its domain – approaching elections and ongoing campaigns – is not continuously meaningful. Consequently, a major part of what campaign interest picks up is not a separate dimension of political interest, but a highly correlated dimension that involves a lot of uncertainty early in a campaign.

The key point here is not that political interest is precisely one dimensional, but rather one dimension is sufficient to capture most of the variation; the rest of this book would not be too different if other political interest questions had been examined. An approaching election may raise campaign-specific interest in a few people who find lawmaking and governing quite boring, but this is a minor departure from a dominant general appraisal of politics. This finding resembles Delli Carpini and Keeter's (1996) prescription for measuring political knowledge: Although some people are political specialists who know a disproportionate amount about a specific political issue, a few general questions can provide an excellent approximation of people's overall political knowledge. Likewise, if the goal is to characterize the vast majority of people, most of the time, one survey question about their general interest in politics does remarkably well.

Appendix to Chapter 4

COMPARING ASSOCIATIONS BETWEEN DIFFERENT MEASURES
OF CAMPAIGN INTEREST

Figure A4.1 displays the correlations between the same and different questions about campaign interest. Compared to correlations within the general interest domain, correlations in Figure A4.1 are somewhat lower, but this is largely a function of the lower number of response options: All campaign interest questions, except for the *Follow Presidential Campaign* question, have only three response options, which generates considerable measurement error.[10] For this reason, the graph uses separate markers (squares) for correlations of *Follow Presidential Campaign* over time. Indeed, over time correlations of *Follow Presidential Campaign* do not drop as the measurement interval increases, suggesting high underlying stability over the course of a campaign.

Correlations of the three-point *Interest in Presidential Campaign* and *Interest in Campaigns* measures are remarkably strong over short periods of time, especially given their limited number of response options. The observed correlations drop by more than two decimal points as the interval between measurements increases. It is important to note that this drop suggests only slightly greater true fluctuation in campaign interest over the course of an election year than in general political interest or *Follow Presidential Campaign*, because much of the observed attenuation over 20 weeks would be expected for a stable variable measured with considerable error. Applying the same calculations as

---

[10] Randomization of response order can illustrate measurement error. In the reverse coding condition in the 2008 ANES Time Series post-election interview, not a single respondent reported being "not much interested" when that option was read first. When respondents heard the "not much interested" option last, 9 percent selected it. No such response order effect occurred in the pre-election wave.

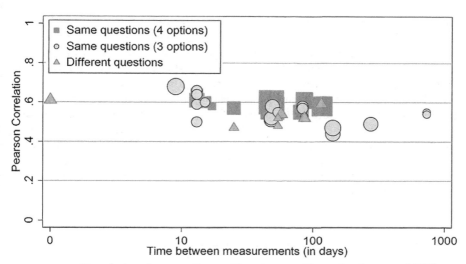

FIGURE A4.1 Correlations between Survey Questions on Campaign Interest, ANES and NAES

Note: See Online Supplementary Material, Table OL4.1 for details.

before for general interest, the observed correlations over 12 weeks (.57) or about 20 weeks (.44) imply "true" correlations of .95–.97 and reliabilities of .70–.71. These values are almost identical to the comparable values for *Follow Public Affairs* presented earlier, suggesting considerable (relative) stability in *Interest in (Presidential) Campaigns* combined with minor short-term variation induced by campaign events.

The correlations between different measures of campaign interest, shown by the triangles in Figure A4.1, appear to be heavily attenuated by measurement error as well. There is no sign that the correlations weaken as the interval between measurements increases from three weeks to four months. The most likely explanation for this pattern is a strong association between two variables measured with considerable error. The difference between *Follow Presidential Campaign* and *Interest in (Presidential) Campaigns* is lower reliability in the latter, not lower stability. Lower reliability would explain why correlations between the two are not closer to one even for short intervals. This interpretation is backed up by the finding that the observed correlations between different questions are very similar to the correlations of each variable with itself for comparable measurement intervals.

The data also present a few opportunities to calculate disattenuated correlations by removing measurement error through instrumenting (as previously described). In the 2004 NAES Election Panel, *Follow Presidential Campaign* in the reinterview can instrument *Follow Presidential Campaign* in the pre-election interview. Regressing *Interest in Presidential Campaign* on this instrumented measure yields a regression coefficient of 1.05. For the 2004 NAES Debates Panel, the same method yields a coefficient of .93. Removing attenuation through measurement error brings the contemporaneous association between different questions about campaign interest very close to a 1-to-1 relationship.[11] This approach also corrects one of the lowest correlations in Figure A4.1, the .48 correlation between *Interest in Campaigns* (before the election) and *Attention to Campaign News* (after the election), which comes from the 2008 ANES Times Series study and corresponds to a modest regression coefficient of .33 (when both variables are scaled 0–1). Again, measurement error appears to hide a stronger association: Instrumenting pre-election *Interest in Campaigns* with its post-election values boosts the regression coefficient to .73.[12]

---

[11] Because of randomization patterns, the instrumenting equation requires out-of-sample predictions in the 2004 NAES panels.

[12] Due to randomization patterns, this analysis is only possible for the old version of Interest in Campaign News using in-sample 2SLS.

5

Sixty Years of Political Interest

If you could take an overnight train through the last sixty years of history, and your sleeper car shook every time something caught people's interest in politics, how well would you sleep? Pretty well, it turns out. The fall of the Berlin Wall would make you sit up, and the data do reveal some noticeable bumps during several U.S. presidential election years. A few years halfway through the 1970s stand out in the United States, perhaps as a reaction to Watergate. The 2003 Iraq war also made a minor mark. In Germany, the end of the cold war is impossible to miss.

But that is about it. These exceptions aside, aggregate political interest is essentially constant over time. This chapter thus reaches a rather different conclusion than Putnam (2000, 36) in his influential work. There has been no "slow slump in interest in politics and current events" in the United States, or, for that matter, in Britain, Germany, or Switzerland.

It is not that the previous half century lacked noteworthy events. For political junkies, recent history is lined with memorable, fascinating, and shocking episodes: the military interventions in Korea and Vietnam, the Cuban Missile Crisis, the assassinations of John F. Kennedy, Martin Luther King, and Robert F. Kennedy, major civil rights legislation and urban unrest of the mid-1960s, Watergate, the fall of Saigon, the Iran hostage crisis, Ronald Reagan's election, Iran-Contra, the military response to Iraq's invasion of Kuwait, the impeachment of Bill Clinton, 9/11, Barack Obama's election, and the Great Recession of 2008. A European perspective would add several events for the years since 1980, the start of the earliest data series for one of the European countries analyzed here: Margaret Thatcher, the nuclear disarmament movements of the early 1980s, Mikhail Gorbachev and the beginnings of "glasnost," the fall of the Berlin Wall and the collapse of the Soviet Union, the Maastricht Treaty establishing the European Union, NATO intervention in former Yugoslavia, the landslide election of Tony Blair, and the introduction of the Euro currency.

Yet what is noteworthy to a political junkie does not necessarily reach much of the population – or reaches it without triggering their political interest. In the various time series tracking political interest, it is remarkably difficult to spot reactions to most of these events. Graph after graph shows mostly horizontal bands of near-constant levels of political interest over time. This repetitiveness is important because the finding that most elections and newsworthy events do not affect aggregate political interest contradicts conventional wisdom. The most likely explanation for this surprising pattern: Political interest is largely dispositional. To the extent that political interest is an enduring predisposition to reengage with the political domain, it should not depend much on the presence of interest-generating political events.

This chapter presents a concise summary of the public's interest over recent decades. It offers the most comprehensive analysis of political interest trends in the United States to date, drawing on five different series of interest questions that overlap the last 60 years. It also shows trends over several decades for Great Britain, Germany, and Switzerland, each using at least two data sources. The main purpose of the chapter is to examine aggregate levels of political interest at the country level to understand if the civic foundation afforded by interested population segments is driven by events and thus characterized by major bumps, or if it is closer to a "chronic" feature that countries can draw on even in times of relative political quiet. Following last chapter's examination of the short-term interest foundation, mainly in election years, this chapter expands the view from years to decades.

To analyze systematically the extent to which political interest is dispositional without compiling debatable lists of discrete historical events, this chapter develops a set of country-specific measures that track the environment's potential to trigger political interest, a concept I call "interestingness" of the environment. Elections can make the political environment temporarily more interesting and sometimes do trigger situational political interest. But they are not the only potential triggers. I use the amount of media coverage and changes in economic conditions to gauge interestingness more systematically.

This chapter introduces the British, German, and Swiss household panel surveys that have measured political interest over many years and will form the empirical basis for understanding individual-level development of political interest in the rest of the book. These data require an explanation of the advantages and challenges involved in using panel data. Benchmark comparisons reveal hardly any evidence for concern about the most common challenges, panel attrition and panel conditioning.

POLITICAL INTEREST IN FOUR WESTERN DEMOCRACIES

The time series presented in this chapter depict general political interest in the United States, Britain, Germany, and Switzerland. Most of the questions use similar versions of the "How interested are you in politics?" wording, while two U.S. series asked the *Follow Public Affairs* question until recently.[1] It is possible to depict aggregate political interest longitudinally with repeated cross-sectional surveys alone. That is, in fact, how this chapter will proceed for political interest in the United States. For other countries, especially Switzerland, availability of cross-sectional data is more limited, so panel data could contribute noticeably to the characterization of aggregate trends. Yet, while panel data offer indispensable advantages for the kinds of analyses conducted later in this book, when used for aggregate description they demand attention to a precaution that cross-sectional data avoid: When repeated waves of panel surveys are used to explore time trends, it is important to attend to the possibility that change occurred because some people were interviewed in some waves but not others, and because the repeated participation on the panel changed people. These two effects, panel attrition and panel conditioning, can reduce the representativeness of all but the first panel wave relative to what a new cross-sectional sample would offer. Fortunately, the household panel studies do in fact occasionally draw fresh samples, so it is possible to use precisely this kind of comparison to verify that older panel samples are not losing their representativeness. For each country, at least one additional, entirely cross-sectional, survey is also available as a benchmark.

United States

Beginning with Gallup polls in the 1950s, time series of political interest in the United States are available for more than a half-century, collected by Gallup, the American National Election Study (ANES), Roper, *Newsweek*, and *Times Mirror*/Pew. ANES and *Times Mirror*/Pew use the *Follow Public Affairs* question. The other three ask respondents how much interest they have in "politics" (Gallup, *Newsweek*) or "current events and what's happening in the world today" (Roper). Figures 5.1 and 5.2 show the distributions of the longest series, by Gallup, ANES, and Roper, all based on in-person interviews, with response options shown verbatim in the graphs. (More information about all survey series is available in the Online Supplementary Materials.)

The ANES has measured political interest at 2- or 4-year intervals over close to 50 years. Some of the other series provide shorter but more closely spaced spurts of measurements. Gallup, for example, asked about political interest in eight separate surveys in September and October of 1952. The range of estimates for this period in Figure 5.1 is a combination of sampling error and a small (2–3 point) increase as the 1952 presidential election approached. The largely unchanging levels of aggregate political interest and the absence of a

---

[1] The data in this chapter describe the voting-age population in order to preserve the focus on the population studied in the previous chapter over shorter periods of time. Unless otherwise noted, analyses in this chapter also maintain the same treatment of residential status as in Chapters 3 and 4 by including residents regardless of citizenship.

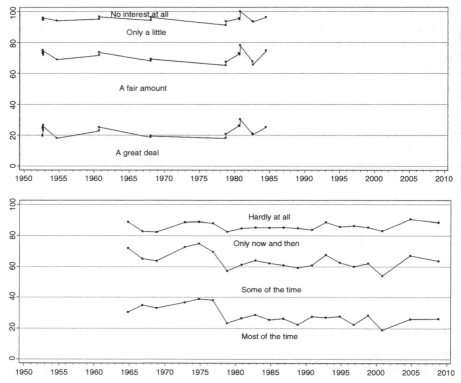

FIGURE 5.1 Trends in General Political Interest, United States (top: Gallup, bottom: ANES)

Note: Question wording, Gallup: "Generally speaking, how much interest would you say that you have in politics – a great deal, an average amount, only a little, or no interest at all?" ANES: See Chapter 3.

trend are well illustrated by the Roper series in Figure 5.2, which offers several different measurements per year for over a decade. Nothing happened between 1974 and the late 1980s to keep around 15 percent of respondents from expressing "not very much interest."

The only noticeable departure from essentially constant aggregate interest in the Gallup and Roper data occurs in 1980. In the Gallup data, three polls conducted in the fall, the last of them days before Election Day, show an increase in political interest of about 10 points. As in the Roper series, 1980 stands out with an increase of about 15 points in the share of respondents who "have been taking a good deal of interest in current events." Roper data add nuance to this conclusion by locating the beginning of this increase in early January of 1980, in the first measurement after hundreds of Americans were taken hostage in Iran in late November of 1979. Interest leveled off

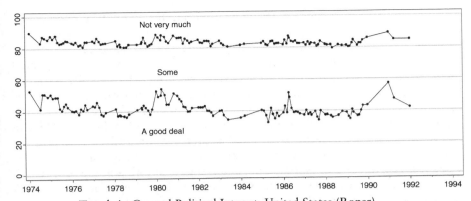

FIGURE 5.2 Trends in General Political Interest, United States (Roper)
Note: Question wording: "Would you say that you have recently been taking a good deal of interest in current events and what's happening in the world today, some interest, or not very much interest?"

over the summer and spiked again in the weeks leading up to and following Ronald Reagan's election as president. Both Roper and ANES show slightly higher interest in 1974, perhaps related to Watergate and the resignation of President Nixon.

The Roper series shows a second noticeable uptick, in early 1991. The start of Operation Dessert Storm, the military campaign in response to Iraq's invasion of Kuweit the previous summer, falls within the field period of that survey and constitutes the most likely explantion for elevated interest. By the time of the next Roper survey, in the second quarter of 1991, Dessert Storm was over and interest had already begun to subside again. In January of 1992, interest is down all the way to its long-term average.

There is one curious difference between the ANES and the other two series. According to the ANES, political interest dropped considerably between 1976 and 1978 and did not recover, but neither Roper nor Gallup reveal even a hint of this drop. Roper, which measured political interest about two dozen times in this time period, is particularly well suited to raise doubts about the ANES trend. But Gallup, too, shows about the same level of interest in two polls in 1968 as in another pair of polls a decade later. It turns out that the 1978 ANES is precisely the year in which the survey context changed considerably because several difficult knowledge questions were added just before the measurement of political interest. This change in the ANES survey prompted the investigations by Bishop et al. (1984b, 1984a) and others (Schwarz and Schuman 1997; Lasorsa 2003, 2009) which consistently demonstrated that the inclusion of the knowledge items can explain a large portion of the drop in reported political interest in the ANES. Following the argument in Chapter 2, this context effect is entirely consistent with the psychological model of interest.

But for the ANES to properly measure long-term trends in political interest, it is necessary to adjust for this effect.[2]

Polls from *Newsweek* and Pew help isolate the impact of events at the beginning of the millennium (Figure 5.3). The 2000 election campaign did little to raise political interest, a conclusion confirmed by the NAES rolling cross-section in Chapter 4 and the ANES estimates for that year as well. It was the prolonged resolution, culminating in the Supreme Court's *Bush v Gore* decision, that had a small positive impact on interest *after* Election Day. In Figure 5.3, political interest is a touch higher even in early 2002, possibly reflecting the 9/11 attacks and the military engagement in Afghanistan. Interest dropped by a few points before rising again slightly starting in the second half of 2003 and leading up to the close 2004 presidential election. The rise in 2004 appears in all series (both series in Figure 5.3, the ANES in Figure 5.1, and the NAES 2004 rolling cross-section in Figure 4.2). The series do not fully agree on the magnitude, but the increase was in the 10–15 point range. To this consensus, the *Newsweek* series adds the suggestion that the rise in political interest began with the U.S. intervention in Iraq in 2003. Interest reverts to its long-run levels after the 2004 election.

The 2008 presidential election, perhaps paired with the financial crisis in the fall of that year, raised interest again, but the data here and in Chapter 4 suggest that the 2008 effect did not quite reach the magnitude of 2004.[3] There is a noticeable absence of data around the 2012 election. Only Pew data cover 2016. They show a gradual rise of interest over the long nomination period. Interest peaked during the primaries and dropped slightly by late summer 2016, the latest available survey.[4]

Bearing in mind that estimates vary slightly from poll to poll simply because of sampling error, the first-order summary of Figures 5.1, 5.2, and 5.3 is a set of parallel horizontal bands with little fluctuation over time in the proportion of interest responses. Some big events and a few elections break this pattern, but only temporarily. To illustrate the continuity of aggregate political interest

---

[2] Shani (2009b, ch.3) developed adjustments to the full *Follow Public Affairs* ANES time series that correct not only for the placement of the knowledge questions but also several other differences in survey administration, including how many days after an election the survey is administered and whether the survey had a pre-election wave. Adjusting for these differences simultaneously, Shani estimates the impact of the tough knowledge questions to be about 4 points, considerably smaller than the largest experimental findings. (Figure OL5.1 in the Online Supplementary Materials shows the unadjusted and adjusted series.) The post-1976 drop is less steep, but still present. Judging by the Roper data, Shani's adjustment may be conservative.

[3] A lot was made during the 2008 U.S. elections of the supposed mobilization of young voters. Young Americans did appear to have been more energized, but their energy was already in place in 2004. Estimated turnout among 18-to-29 year-olds was 51 percent in 2008, 2 points higher than in 2004 and 11 points higher than in 2000 (Kirby and Kawashima-Ginsberg 2009).

[4] Figure 5.3 also shows a number of polls from the second half of the 1980s. They were conducted by Gallup and, starting in 1990, Princeton Survey Research Associates, for *Times Mirror*. These surveys also use the *Follow Public Affairs* question, but were conducted as in-person interviews.

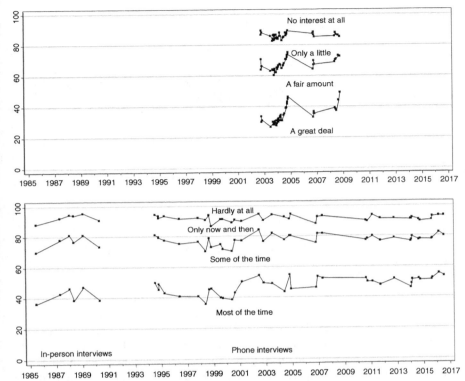

FIGURE 5.3 Trends in General Political Interest, United States (*Newsweek*, *Times Mirror*/Pew)

Note: Question wording: "Generally speaking, how much interest would you say you have in politics... a lot of interest, some interest, only a little interest, or no interest at all?" (*Newsweek*, top graph), "Some people seem to follow what's going on in government and public affairs most of the time, whether there's an election or not. Others aren't that interested. Would you say you follow what's going on in government and public affairs most of the time, some of the time, only now and then, or hardly at all?" (*Times Mirror*/Pew, bottom graph). In 2010, Pew dropped the two opening sentences from the question. Their August 2010 survey compared both wordings in a split-half design. The frequency distributions are statistically indistinguishable (N = 3,490).

more clearly, Figure 5.4 plots all time series in one graph after transforming political interest reports to the 0–100 interval so that the lowest response option is coded as "0" and the maximum as "100." To make the shorter three series with many polls in quick succession easier to see, the graph plots individual

They, too, support the conclusion that political interest is largely constant in the aggregate (with perhaps a small bump around the 1988 presidential election).

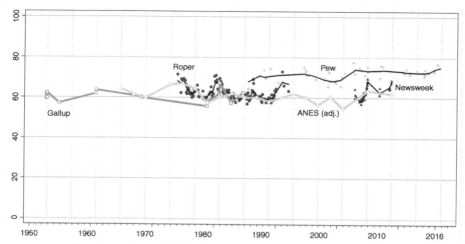

FIGURE 5.4 Trends in General Political Interest, United States (All Series)
Note: Vertical lines mark elections.

estimates and mildly smoothed lowess trends. Vertical lines mark the dates of presidential elections and will be discussed latter in the end of chapter.

Neither the occasional bump caused by an election or a particularly note-worthy event nor methodological questions[5] can distract from the main con-clusion: Stitching together a timeline of political interest in the United States over almost 60 years produces something very close to a flat line. This finding differs markedly from Putnam's (2000, 36) verdict of a "slow slump in interest in politics and current events." Putnam reaches this conclusion based on the same Roper data displayed in Figure 5.2, but takes them as evidence that "the

---

[5] Figure 5.4 raises one more methodological question. The longer Pew series and the ANES use the same question (*Follow Public Affairs*) and show roughly the same time trend, but, as noted by Robison (2015), the Pew means are about 10 points higher. There is some suggestion that this difference might be explained by survey mode. In 1987 and 1988, Gallup used the same interest question in two phone surveys it conducted for *Times Mirror* amid the usual in-person surveys graphed in Figure 5.3. Both yielded higher interest reports: A phone survey in October 1987 pro-duced a mean of 75, compared to 70 in April of 1987 and 69 in January of 1988 in face-to-face surveys. And the mean of 82 in a September 1988 phone poll significantly exceeds the mean of 75 in a January 1989 face-to-face survey. (The second comparison may be distorted by the 1988 presidential election.) But the mode hypothesis finds no support in the 2000 ANES, which was conducted by phone for a random subset of respondents but yields indistinguishable esti-mates for the same interest question. (Graphs in this chapter showing ANES estimates exclude the phone interviews to keep mode constant.) And the 2004 NAES, conducted by phone (see Figure 4.2), produced estimates very close to the in-person ANES that year, and about ten points lower than Pew's phone poll. Interview mode thus does not seem to explain why Pew's estimates are consistently higher. While their level is unexpectedly high, their strong aggregate stability is very much in line with the other time series.

tide of the public's interest in current events gradually ebbed by roughly 20 percent over this quarter century." It is hard to look at Figure 5.2 and see any gradual ebbing.[6] The more comprehensive data sources summarized in Figure 5.4 make clear, moreover, that the slightly higher levels of interest at the start of the Roper series were a temporary high, not a stage in a long-running downward trend.

Political interest is not perfectly constant in the aggregate, but the bumps are rare, small, and temporary, about 10 points on a 0–100 scale at most. Elections that noticeably increase political interest are the exception, not the rule – only 1980, 2004, 2008, and 2016 made (a small) difference. Watergate, or something else in the mid-1970s that had its peak impact in 1974, and the 2003 Iraq war also made a minor mark.

Germany

Cross-sectional data on political interest in Germany come from the Allgemeine Bevölkerungsumfrage der Sozialwissenschaften (ALLBUS) and European Social Survey (ESS). Figure 5.5 displays them together with estimates from five independent German Socio-Economic Panel Study (GSOEP) samples, which began, respectively, in 1984, 1998, 2000, 2006, and 2011. To make population definitions comparable, only citizens aged 18 years and older are included. The top graph in Figure 5.5 uses only cross-sectional estimates for unified Germany (i.e., after 1990) and panel samples started after reunification. The bottom graph in Figure 5.5 goes back before the fall of the Berlin Wall. It shows the 1984 GSOEP sample of the West German population and adds the pre-1991

Response rate differences are probably not the cause either. The Pew Research Center has conducted several experiments to evaluate the impact of lower response rates. In 1997, 2003, and 2012, they boosted response rates for random halves of their samples through advance letters, additional callbacks, and longer field periods. These efforts succeeded in raising response rates from 36 to 61 percent in 1997, from 25 to 50 percent in 2003, and from 9 to 22 percent in 2012 (Pew Research Center 2012). Although no political interest question was included in any of these surveys, related items showed no systematic differences. On the closest proxy for political interest – "And how much do you enjoy keeping up with political news about campaigns and elections – a lot, some, not much, or not at all?," asked in 2012 – there is a small but significant difference in the opposite direction of what would be expected if hard-to-reach respondents were less politically interested: 27 percent of respondents in the high-effort condition reported enjoying keeping up with political news "a lot," compared to 23 percent under typical conditions (Pew Research Center 2012). Self-reported news exposure, included in 1997 and 2003, did not differ between the two half samples (Keeter et al. 2006). Response rates have declined considerably over the period examined here. If less politically interested individuals were increasingly missed by surveys, the downward trend in response rates would distort the estimated trend in political interest. These experimental studies do not justify such a concern, however.

6 Putnam (2000, 36, 448) mentions a second series for roughly the same time span that "steadily slumped," but he does not report the data and they come from the DDB Needham Life Style surveys, which use non-probability opt-in sampling.

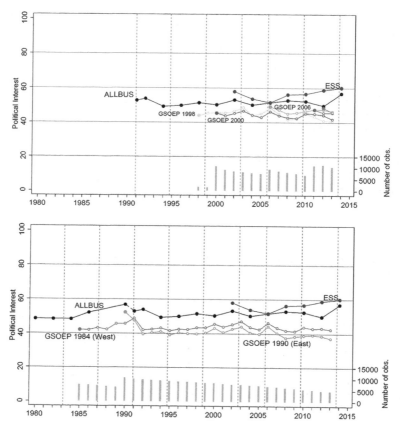

FIGURE 5.5 Political Interest over Time in Unified Germany (top) and East/West Samples (bottom)

Note: Vertical lines mark elections. Filled circles indicate cross-sectional estimates or first wave of each panel. Hollow circles indicate estimates from later panel waves. The first interview of the 1984 GSOEP sample (Sample A) did not ask about political interest. Estimates for 1985, when the political interest question was first included, are thus subject to panel effects. The bars show the number of observations for GSOEP estimates. Because ALLBUS initially included only citizens, all estimates are based on citizens only. Until 1990, the population is West German citizens (including West Berlin). Question wording: ALLBUS: "Nun zu etwas ganz anderem. Wie stark interessieren Sie sich für Politik? Sehr stark, stark, mittel, wenig, oder überhaupt nicht?" (Now for something entirely different. How strongly interested in politics are you? Very strongly, strongly, somewhat, just a little, or not at all?); ESS: "Wie sehr interessieren Sie sich für Politik? Sind Sie sehr interessiert, ziemlich interessiert, wenig interessiert, oder überhaupt nicht interessiert?" "How interested in politics are you? Very interested, fairly interested, little interested, or not at all interested?); GSOEP: "Einmal ganz allgemein gesprochen: Wie stark interessieren Sie sich für Politik? Sehr stark, stark, nicht so stark, oder überhaupt nicht?" (Generally speaking, how strongly interested are you in politics: Very strongly, strongly, not so strongly, or not at all?)

ALLBUS estimates for West Germany. (ALLBUS updated its population definition to include the former East Germany in 1991.) The graph also plots
political interest among Germans who lived in the East in the summer of
1990, just before reunification in October. This is the population for the
1990 GSOEP sample of East Germans. Vertical lines mark election dates.

The years around reunification in 1990 exhibit the greatest fluctuation in
aggregate political interest in Germany. Political interest in Germany peaked
during the period of reunification. After the post-reunification drop in the mid-
1990s, none of the three data sources suggests much of a time trend. Ups and
downs are small enough to be nothing more than sampling variation and
measurement error.[7]

Even the fall of the Berlin Wall and reunification produced a change of only
about 10 percentage points among West Germans, and the change was temporary. The two series for West Germany both show an increase in political
interest in 1989–90. In 1990, in their first panel interviews, East Germans
expressed the highest level of political interest measured by the GSOEP in its
almost thirty years. Within two years, however, their interest dropped by more
than ten points and fell slightly below the level of West Germans in the 1984
panel. For the next twenty years, the two different populations move in parallel
with just a few minor ups and downs (following the same trend as the samples
of unified Germany in the top graph).[8]

The use of panel data raises the possibility of panel effects. The first year of
each panel sample cannot be affected by panel effects, however, and is thus
representative of the sampled population in the same way as the cross-sectional
estimates. All estimates not subject to panel effects are shown by large filled
circles. The smaller, hollow circles show estimates from later panel waves. The
bars at the bottom of the graph show the number of observations on which the
GSOEP estimates are based.[9]

---

[7] There may have been another, smaller drop around 2004–5, but GSOEP and ESS do not quite
agree on the timing of this drop, and ALLBUS is essentially flat in this period. The GSOEP also
shows a slight bump around 2006 that is not evident in the other two survey series. (The
ALLBUS survey shows a noticeable increase between 2012 and 2014 that is not evident in the
ESS for the same years or in the GSOEP between 2012 and 2013. The ESS field dates overlap
with the ALLBUS but are shifted later by several months. The ALLBUS increase is thus most
likely a temporary blip or measurement error.)

[8] A weighted average of the 1984 and 1990 GSOEP samples approximates a sample of unified
Germany. The share of Germans who live in the former East German parts of the country is
about 20 percent today (and was a point or two higher just after reunification). East German
respondents make up about 40 percent of the combined 1984 and 1990 samples (a ratio that
hardly varies over time). To the extent that patterns and explanations for political interest are
different in the former East Germany, combining the two samples without frequency weights
thus mischaracterizes the average effects for Germany as a whole.

[9] Household panels use precisely specified follow-up rules to guide the tracking of initial panel
members and the addition of new ones to their sample. The population being represented in the
first wave is individuals (above a certain age) living in private households. In subsequent waves,

There are two ways to gauge the magnitude of panel effects. First, estimates from an ongoing panel can be compared to the first wave of a refreshment sample, which is not subject to panel effects. Second, panel estimates can be compared to the cross-sectional times series. It is very difficult in the top graph of Figure 5.5 to visually differentiate the four different GSOEP samples. Interest estimates from the first wave of newly started panels tend to sit on top of estimates from the continuing earlier samples. The first estimates from the 2006 GSOEP sample is a few points higher than the 2006 estimate of the large refreshment sample started in 2000. And the first measure from the new 2011 sample is slightly higher than continuing samples. The direction of these differences is not consistent with standard panel effects, however, according to which long-running panels would become *more* interested or involved through disproportionate attrition among less interested panelists or rising interest as a result of serving on a panel. Either way, the magnitude of these differences is very small. The GSOEP also moves over time in much the same way as the ALLBUS and, with the exception of the 2006 data point, the ESS. Figure 5.5 raises little concern about panel or context effects.[10]

Great Britain

The cross-sectional data estimates of political interest in Britain are from the British Social Attitudes Survey (BSA) and ESS. The British Household Panel Study (BHPS) began interviewing in 1991 with a probability sample of British households. In 1999, additional samples were drawn in Scotland and Wales. They amount to refreshment samples for Scotland and Wales, but not Britain as

original sample members are being reinterviewed even if they have left their original household (unless they have moved abroad). Their children and other individuals who become members of their households also join the sample. New household members become part of the sample either when they move into an eligible household or when an original panel respondent moves into their household. All of the households in this sample contain at least one member of an originally selected household (or a child born to an originally selected panelist). When all originally selected panelists leave a household, other members who were not initially part of the panel are no longer included in the sample I use in this book (see Book Appendix A). With these rules, the sample follows the population of individuals living in private households over time, that is, with generational and mobility-related replacement. In the absence of panel effects, estimates from later waves of these household panel studies should thus closely resemble estimates from fresh national probability samples.

[10] The position of the political interest question in the GSOEP survey instrument changed occasionally, but it was usually preceded by non-political items about health and well-being or social transfers. The possibility for context effects may be different in 1987, when questions about social injustice appeared before the interest question, in 1997, when it was preceded by attitudes toward social responsibility, and in 2010, when it followed a question about turnout. (Online Supplementary Materials provide details on question context for all three household panels.) Estimates for these years in Figure 5.5 do not stand out, however, so context effects are likely quite minimal.

a whole.[11] Figure 5.6 therefore shows political interest trends separately for England (top graph), Scotland (middle graph), and Wales (bottom graph). The Understanding Society (USoc) study, which started in 2009 (see Book Appendix A for details), constitutes a large refreshment sample for all three parts of Britain. BHPS panelists were integrated into USoc, but only reinterviewed in its second wave in 2010.[12]

Political interest trends are highly similar in England, Scotland, and Wales. In England, the new USoc sample started in 2009 constitutes a very large refreshment sample. Its estimates are difficult to see in Figure 5.6 because they are almost identical to the estimates for continuing BHPS panelists, even though the latter have at that point served on the panel for up to two decades. This is very strong evidence against panel effects in the BHPS. One external benchmark, the ESS, shows essentially the same mild up-and-down pattern. The second cross-sectional benchmark, the BSA, increasingly diverges from the BHPS. Political interest in the BSA and among BHPS panelists starts at comparable levels in the early 1990s and declines slightly through the decade (although this decline occurs a few years later in the BSA). Yet, by the mid-2000s, the BSA estimates are noticeably higher. This divergence is in the opposite direction of typical panel effects, and the USoc refreshment sample revealed not a hint of panel effects, so this difference to one of the cross-sectional benchmarks may have other causes.[13]

For the period before the booster samples for Scotland and Wales were added to the BHPS in 1999, trends for those two countries are based on a very small number of cases. BSA and ESS also have few respondents in Scotland and Wales. The number of BSA and ESS interviews in Scotland is 100–300 and 160–220 per year, respectively, and even lower for Wales (50–200 in the BSA,

---

[11] Starting in 1999, the joint sample therefore includes an oversample of Scottish and Welsh households. Before 1999, Wales and Scotland made up 5 and 9 percent of the full sample, respectively, which is very close to the proportions in the population. The 1999 sample additions boosted Welsh households to 21 percent of the joint sample and Scottish households to 23 percent. In the joint BHPS/USoc sample, these proportions decline again to 9 and 11 percent, respectively.

[12] Except for continuing BHPS panelists, USoc uses a two-year field period (see Book Appendix A). The USoc data points shown in Figure 5.6 pool the nominal and the following year (that is, data for the USoc estimate for 2009 was collected in 2009 and 2010, and so on). The difference between early and late interviews in a wave is always less than 2 points.

[13] Although turnout is not a proxy for political interest, it is noteworthy that it declined considerably in 1997 (71 percent in England, compared to 78 percent in 1992) and 2001 (59 percent) before recovering slightly (61 percent in 2005 and 66 percent in 2010). Butler and Kavanagh (1997, 299) write that "[i]t seems clear that the 1997 general election excited less interest than any other in living memory." Four years later, "low turnout was far from unexpected. Not only had turnout been lower in 1997 than at any election since 1929, but local and European elections held between 1998 and 2000 had also seen new record low levels of turnout" (Butler and Kavanagh 2002, 307). For what it is worth, the BHPS political interest trend fits the turnout pattern better than does the BSA trend and mirrors the 2001–5 turnout trough more closely.

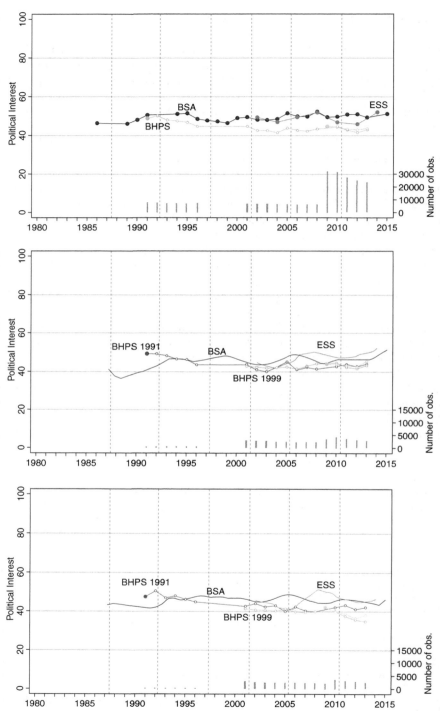

FIGURE 5.6 Political Interest over Time in England (top), Scotland (middle), and Wales (bottom)

90–160 in the ESS). Hence, Figure 5.6 shows smoothed averages instead of point estimates for the cross-sectional benchmarks. There is no evidence for panel effects in Scotland and Wales when the refreshment samples for those two countries are compared to the original 1991 sample[14] or when the 1999 refreshment sample is compared to the new USoc cases. In Wales, political interest drops in 2010–12 according to both refreshment samples. This drop is not evident among original BHPS panelists, suggesting a possible instance of panel effects. At that point, the original BHPS trend is based only about 250 respondents per year, so sampling error may also explain this divergence. Overall, mean levels of political interest in England, Scotland, and Wales are nearly indistinguishable, although Wales may have seen a unique late drop of 3–4 points.

With considerable reassurance that measurement artifacts[15] are not wreaking havoc in Figure 5.6, the summary of aggregate political interest trends in Britain is simple: It changed very little over the last thirty years. There is a slight increase in the early 1990s, perhaps triggered by the fall of the Iron Curtain, or the fall of the Iron Lady. But the change is minimal at about 5 points over several years. Political interest declined again by an equally small amount in the 1990s, the early years of the BHPS, and has not trended up or down since then.

Switzerland

For Switzerland, Figure 5.7 shows cross-sectional estimates from the ESS and panel data from the Swiss Household Panel (SHP), which started in 1999 and added refreshment samples in 2004 and 2014. The ESS series is almost precisely flat, whereas political interest first rises by a few points in the SHP and then falls, possibly below starting levels. The two lowest estimates, in 2011 and

---

FIGURE 5.6 (*cont.*) *Note*: Vertical lines mark elections. Question wording: BSA: "How much interest do you generally have in what is going on in politics... a great deal, quite a lot, some, not very much, or none at all?"; ESS: "How interested would you say you are in politics – are you very interested, quite interested, hardly interested, or not at all interested?" BHPS/USoc: "How interested would you say you are in politics? Would you say you are very interested, fairly interested, not very interested, or not at all interested?"

---

[14] 1999 values are not full circles because the 1999 refreshment samples were asked about political interest only beginning in 2001.
[15] Survey context for the political interest question in the BHPS and USoc fits one of two patterns. In most years, the political interest question follows items about turnout and vote choice. In 1991, 1993, 1994, and 1996, as well as in all USoc waves, a set of branching questions about party identification precede the interest question. Figure 5.6 provides no suggestion that this variation in context affected the measurement of political interest.

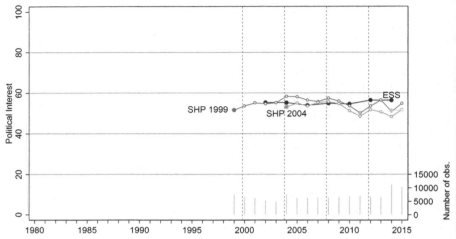

FIGURE 5.7 Political Interest over Time in Switzerland

Note: Vertical lines mark elections. The first interview of the 2013 SHP sample did not ask about political interest. Estimates for 2014, when the political interest question was first included for this sample, are thus subject to panel effects. ESS wording: "Wie stark interessieren Sie sich für Politik? Würden Sie sagen, Sie sind sehr interessiert, ziemlich interessiert, kaum interessiert, oder überhaupt nicht interessiert?" (How strongly interested in politics are you? Would you say you are very strongly interested, pretty interested, hardly interested, or not at all interested?); SHP wording: "Wie stark interessieren Sie sich ganz allgemein für Politik, wenn o "gar nicht" und 10 "sehr stark" bedeutet?" (Generally, how interested are you in politics, if o means "not at all interested" and 10 "very interested"?)

2014, are likely explained by methodological artifacts, however, so the decline is less than it seems in the figure.[16]

Signs of panel effects are more evident in the SHP than in the other two household panel studies, but they are not present throughout and their magnitude is still quite small. The initial estimates from the first two SHP samples match the ESS estimates very closely: The first ESS estimate in 2002 is essentially the same as the SHP estimate for that year, the fourth panel wave of the original sample. The 2004 ESS estimate is very close to

[16] In all years except 2011 and 2014, the political interest question appeared in the SHP after a series of questions about associational membership (1999–2009) or volunteering (2010, 2012, 2013, 2015). In 2011 and 2014, the preceding questions asked respondents to evaluate the justifiability of various acts of cheating and lying. In light of the literature on context effects discussed in Chapter 2, this is exactly the kind of variation in context that could lead to measurement artifacts. The drops in observed political interest in 2011 and 2014 are suspiciously consistent with panelists admitting slightly lower interest in politics after having just expressed their moral outrage about cheating and lying.

the initial estimate of the 2004 SHP refreshment sample. Comparison of the 2004 refreshment sample and the original 1999 sample yields evidence for a panel effect: The two samples are about 5 points apart (and the 1999 panelists differ by about the same amount from the ESS). The effect is in the expected direction: The continuing members of the 1999 panel expressed greater interest than the panelists newly recruited for the 2004 refreshment sample and the cross-sectional ESS respondents. In subsequent years, the two SHP samples move closer together again, however. By 2010, the original SHP sample matches the ESS estimates again. The 2013 SHP refreshment sample is also very close to the longer-running SHP panels. It is now the ESS that looks like the outlier.

To sum up, aggregate political interest in four Western democracies reveals a few unsurprising ups and downs. The fall of the Berlin Wall and reunification raised political interest in Germany for a few years. The 2003 Iraq war, followed by the close presidential election of 2004, increased interest in the United States. So did the elections in 1980 and, to a lesser extent, in 2008 and 2016. More surprising is how short this list is. Given how many big events – the tumultuous sixties in the U.S., the end of the Kohl era in Germany, Tony Blair in Britain, 9/11 anywhere – leave essentially no mark at all, the dominant finding is the remarkable continuity of aggregate political interest. The only caveat to this conclusion is the order in which it proceeds: Plot aggregate interest, then see if movement over time fits events we remember.

THE IMPACT OF ELECTIONS ON POLITICAL INTEREST

It is common to think of politics as following a rhythm imposed by the electoral calendar. When an election approaches, the spectacle of the campaign and the possibility of political change draw in more and more people, exposing them to more political information, raising their political awareness, prompting them to think harder about the competing options – and stoking their political interest. Yet, as far as the last effect is concerned, the empirical evidence is much less impressive than the image of the electoral cycle suggests.

Chapter 4 uncovered only modest increases in political interest over the course of election years in the United States. The 2004 and 2008 U.S. presidential elections did raise interest by around 10 points, but the more extended polling time series presented in this chapter reveal those two elections to be exceptions. Data going back to the 1952 contest add only 1980 to the list of election bumps. The ANES is only in the field in election years, but a comparison of midterm years and years with presidential elections confirms the general conclusion. Despite national campaigning, more media coverage, and more political advertising, the average level of interest in presidential election years is about the same (61.1) as in midterm years (60.7).

The evidence is even weaker in Britain, Germany, and Switzerland. Were it not for the vertical lines marking elections, anyone without knowledge of election dates would have a hard time guessing from the graphs in this chapter in which years those countries went to the polls. Of the five elections in Britain during the period covered in Figure 5.6, the election of 2005 is the only one plausibly associated with an increase in political interest – a tiny blip of about 2.5 points.[17] In Germany, the largest election effect is a 4-point increase, the second largest is 2 points, and the other three are barely positive. Due to the GSOEP field dates, these estimates can only pick up effects that last about three months, but the barely evident election effects are consistent with the rolling cross-sectional surveys analyzed in Chapter 4.[18] Switzerland is the least diagnostic case because power-sharing between parties reduces the prospect for election-induced political change, and frequent referenda and initiatives, occurring in non-election years as well, have an unusually important role in determining policy. For what it is worth, election effects on political interest using the SHP are in fact negative.[19]

---

[17] Unlike most election studies, which are conducted only in election years, the household panel studies and the British Social Attitudes Survey, fielded year after year at about the same time, are well-suited to pick up the surge in political interest in election years. The 2005 election was held in May. Most interviews for the BSA were conducted between June and September in both 2004 and 2005. Political interest in 2005, just following the parliamentary election, was 2.8 points higher than a year earlier. Interviewing for the BHPS starts later in the year. For the 2004 and 2005 waves, almost all interviews were conducted between September and December. In the 2005 wave, between four and seven months after the 2005 election, political interest was 2.1 points higher than in the 2004 wave. The same before/after comparisons for the elections in April 1992, June 2001, and May 2010 are all smaller: 1.4 points in 1992 (BHPS), -.3 points in 2001 (BSA), and -.2 in 2010 (BSA). (The distribution of interview dates was very similar to 2005.) The BSA was also in the field around the first election of Tony Blair in May 1997, arguably the biggest (albeit anticipated) upheaval in British electoral politics in recent decades. One would not know it from political interest levels in Britain: 47.9 in May/June 1996, 47.4 in January to March 1997, and 47.7 in April to August 1998.

[18] The GSOEP was in the field before and after the German federal elections of January 1987, October 1994, September 1998, 2002, 2005, and 2009. (The impact of the 1990 election cannot be differentiated from reunification in the same year.) GSOEP interviewing begins in January and 90 percent of interviews are usually conducted by May or June. For elections from 1994 to 2009, GSOEP can thus measure the change in interest between the first half of an election year (before the start of campaigning) and the first half of the year after the election. These changes were -1.7 (1994–5), .3 (1998–9), 1.6 (2002–3), 4.2 (2005–6), and 2.3 (2009–10). Because the 1987 election occurred in January, the appropriate comparison is between the 1986 and 1987 waves. Even though the 1987 wave began in the month of the election, political interest was only 1.2 points higher in 1987.

[19] Elections occurred in late October of 2003, 2007, and 2011. The SHP conducts about 90 percent of its interviews between September and December, just when elections would be stimulating interest. According to Figure 5.7, however, political interest in all three election years was actually lower than a year later and no different than in the year before the election. In fact, 1999 and 2011 have the lowest annual political interest averages in the SHP, more than 4 points lower than the average of the remaining years. Both were election years. (The other two election years, 2003 and 2007, were about average.)

These minimal effects are not inconsistent with previous research. There is little evidence that political events such as national elections have large stimulating effects on political interest. Strömbäck and Johansson (2007) examine annual surveys conducted in Sweden and find only a small difference in political interest between years with and without elections. Van Ingen and van der Meer (2016) find no increase in a panel study ahead of the 2010 Dutch election. In the ESS, there is little association between timing of the interview and political interest, but as interview timing is not random, this result is difficult to evaluate (Solvak 2009). Butler and De La O (2011) take advantage of the different linguistic regions of Switzerland whose residents tend to follow media coverage from neighboring countries that share their language. An election in a neighboring country raises political interest only among those Swiss who speak the language of the country. The magnitude of this effect declines with the time between election and interest report. The difference between an election half a year and a full year before the interview, the closest range of foreign elections in their data, translates into about 4 points of additional interest on a transformed 0–100 scale.[20]

There is little evidence that close elections in particular stimulate political interest. Under proportional representation, the closeness of elections at the national level should be most relevant. The 1992 British election saw a close race narrowly won by John Major, while 1997 and 2001 were landslides. Yet, the year-to-year changes in political interest were barely different from zero in all cases. Similarly, the closest election in Germany, in 2002, raised interest by less than two points. Close races at the state or district level should matter more for presidential and congressional elections in the United States. Lipsitz (2011, 76, 105) examines the relationship between political interest and competitiveness of congressional elections in the United States. For both House and Senate elections, she finds no significant differences in political interest between safe districts and toss-up districts (or states).[21]

Measuring Interestingness

Not every election is equally interesting, and elections are not the only events that might stir political interest. The occurrence of other, less predictable events with political relevance also affects interestingness, the extent to which the political environment in a country might trigger situational interest. The Online Supplementary Materials include a detailed explanation of how I gauge the

[20] Butler and De La O (2011) include a measure of the months since the last election in a neighboring country, but not for months until the next election. A cluster of the elections they examine occurred about four years before respondents were interviewed, which would suggest that the next election was fast approaching at this time. Yet these respondents tend to report relatively low interest.

[21] Pacheco (2008) finds closeness of contemporaneous local and state elections to be unrelated to turnout reports, but her study cannot address if this relationship is mediated by political interest.

interestingness of the political and economic environment and plots of all time series. To avoid circularity in the relationship between interestingness and interest, the former is measured in ways that leave little room for the political interest of a country's population to affect the determination of interestingness of the country's environment. The judgments of journalists who work for publications outside a country provide the input for measurement of interestingness in the country. Two measures draw on media coverage to distinguish global and country-specific political events. I also use economic data as indicators of interestingness.

Metrics of interestingness pick up several key events of the period that were not elections: the fall of the Berlin Wall and German reunification, the U.S.-led military intervention in Iraq in early 1991, the terrorist attacks of September 11, 2001 and the ensuing war against the Taliban in Afghanistan, the start of the 2003 Iraq war, and the 2008 financial crisis (mixed with the election of Barack Obama as U.S. president). They also identify the two arguably most eventful German elections in this period, the end of the Kohl-era in 1998 and the surprise reelection of Gerhard Schröder as chancellor in 2002. In Great Britain, the 2010 election, which unexpectedly produced a coalition government, attracted a fair amount of coverage and remained newsworthy for the rest of the year. Metrics of economic interestingness clearly mark the 2008 financial crisis.

There is no clear correspondence between political interest and key events, however. The fall of the Berlin Wall is reflected in the media-based measures of interestingness and likely raised political interest in Germany between 1989 and 1991 (see Figure 5.5). The media data for Germany also show a combination of national and global events in the first half of 2003 (the Iraq war, which the German government opposed after extended debate) that correspond to slightly higher political interest that year. But there are many counterexamples: 9/11 and the 2008 financial crisis seem not to have affected political interest. There is no obvious change in interestingness to explain the slight bump in political interest in 2006. And the first half of the 1990s shows frequent NYT coverage, but no movement in political interest (and no drop when coverage subsides in the second half of the decade). Political events in Britain and Switzerland are not obviously related to aggregate interest in those countries.

Sustained periods of economic growth in Germany in 2005–07 and 2010–11 correspond to somewhat higher political interest. But market crashes, like the one in 1987, have no apparent effect. In Britain and Switzerland, political interest seems largely unconnected from the economy, at least in a casual comparison of trends.

While this heuristic assessment of the link between interestingness and interest suggests that events have very limited impact on interest, the individual-level analysis of the household panels that begins in the next chapter will provide a more precise answer by systemically estimating the impact of variation in interestingness in the days and weeks leading up to panelists' interviews.

CONCLUSION

Whereas the previous chapter focused on the months before and just after elections, this chapter expanded the time horizon and instead examined political interest over several decades. Without the labeling of time units, this difference would be difficult to appreciate: The two sets of plots look nearly the same, revealing largely unchanging levels of interest over time. Among the daily and weekly measurements of political interest in Chapter 4, it could be difficult to discern campaign events or noticeable upticks as elections approach. And among the yearly measurements in this chapter, it is often even harder to pick out election years.

Aggregate political interest is of moderate magnitude and very stable over decades. While differences in question wording make country comparisons imprecise, political interest levels are typically quite close to the scale midpoint and remarkably similar in Britain, Germany, Switzerland, and the United States. Highly stable aggregate political interest is evident not only for the countries examined here, but also in several other European countries during the same time period (Martín 2005; Kroh 2006; Zuckerman et al. 2007, 39; Howe 2010, ch.3).

The analysis in this chapter ultimately raised few concerns about panel effects. Although differences between panelists and cross-sectional cases emerged in several places, the magnitude of these differences was no more than a couple of points. More importantly, the direction of these differences was not uniform across the three countries. Only in Switzerland was panel tenure associated with marginally higher interest levels relative to new cases, and that was true for only one of two refreshment samples. Nonetheless, the next chapter will continue to look for panel effects, this time as a function of age.

Plotting political interest trends for different countries in separate graphs and looking closely at sample averages without considering sampling error emphasizes small differences. There are a few in this chapter. Around reunification, in particular, Germans temporarily showed greater interest in politics. And in the United States, the 1980 presidential election and the combination of the Iraq War and 2004 election stimulated interest. Yet, widening the lens to compare averages across countries and country trends over several decades shows remarkable continuity and strong similarities.

From Part I to Part II

This chapter concludes Part I of the book. Corroborating the psychological model of interest, the analysis so far has shown political interest to have both affective and cognitive components and to exist even in the presence of negative assessments of politics. Cognitive facilitators of interest, including the importance of the domain of interest and a sense of efficacy, influence how much interest in politics people express. As far as measurement is concerned, political interest is close to a one-dimensional construct and can properly be assessed by any of a number of different survey questions, including a straightforward question asking individuals how interested they are "in politics."

Political interest serves an important democratic function because it leads people to learn about politics, develop more informed and deeply reasoned opinions, and support the system of self-governance by participating in politics more reliably. Previous research, summarized in the opening chapter, has documented these consequences of political interest in considerable detail, and I demonstrated them yet again in a basic analysis in Chapter 4. Although it does not necessarily have only beneficial effects, the vast majority of empirical results indicates that political interest strengthens citizenship and serves as a civic foundation.

As measured by mean levels of political interest or the share of the population with high political interest, this civic foundation is of moderate strength in the United States and several Western European democracies, often around 50 on the 0–100 scales I use throughout this study, as many people in each country and each year report little or no political interest. Equally important, it is also very steady over time. Political interest creates a chronic civic foundation on which a country can draw consistently because it is not much affected by ups and downs in interestingness of the political or economic environment. The steady nature of aggregate political interest constrains the potential for elections to create temporary peaks and thereby limits the quality of collective decision-making and the widespread representativeness of election outcomes. But chronic if middling political interest also has important advantages: Polities can ill afford to turn off accountability outside of election season because the democratic benefits of citizens' monitoring their elected representatives are bound to be greater when it occurs in a regular and sustained way.

A chronic civic foundation is an aggregate property of a country that arises through the political interest of its citizens. It is tempting to take nearly unchanging aggregate interest as evidence for widespread dispositional political interest among individual citizens, the enduring predisposition that, according to psychological models, develops out of situational interest and becomes self-sustaining so it does not require constant situational triggers to persist. Although I have argued repeatedly that constant political interest in the aggregate is consistent with dispositional interest, it is at best a necessary condition. Spurts of situational interest in different parts of the population over time could also produce constant aggregate interest levels. To be certain that political interest is dispositional, it is necessary to understand its development and examine its stability at the individual level. Part II of the book takes on this task. It will add younger people to the analysis for the simple reason that politics does not start when people turn 18. The psychological model of interest strongly suggests that the roots of political interest lie in adolescence or even childhood.

THE DEVELOPMENT OF POLITICAL INTEREST

6

Political Interest over the Life Course:
The Population Average

You are likely to find politics more interesting than the kid who just walked by, at least if you are both typical for your age. A wealth of research has shown that older people have greater interest in politics. When we hear statistics like this, our mind often jumps to the conclusion that age is the cause of the interest difference – you've been around longer than that kid and your extra years built up extra interest. But that is not the only logical explanation. It is also possible that you are part of an unusually interested birth cohort: Even when you were the kid's age, you were already more interested in politics. Politics was more captivating when you were younger than it is for kids now, so the political environment triggered situational interest more often, which developed into greater, more widespread dispositional interest among you and your generational peers.

This distinction between aging effect and cohort effect comes across as a somewhat arcane conceptual point, but it holds the key to the kid's future. Or at least his future political interest. If aging (or things that happen to many of us as we age) causes political interest to develop, we can expect the kid's interest to rise, perhaps to catch up with yours after we account for other differences between the two of you. If, on the other hand, cohort effects are the source of the current interest difference between you and him, he is doomed to remain less interested for the rest of his life, and his generation with him. And hence we would expect the civic foundation of the country to slowly decline as members of the kid's generation increasingly outnumber yours.

Those are the stakes of the current chapter. To understand which it is – cohort or aging – we have to go on a detective's chase for clues because the empirical challenge is not as straightforward as it may seem.

In fact, there is a third possibility why people of different ages can have different levels of political interest. If you and the kid had reported your interest at different times – maybe you were asked just before a big election, and he was asked last summer when politics was on vacation – variation in the "interesting-ness" of politics might account for the difference in your interest reports. In short, interest can differ between two people of different ages because one of the two was born earlier (cohort effect), because the environment was more stimu-lating during one of the measurements (period effect), or because one of the two has lived longer (aging, or lifecycle effect). Only the last effect implies that people will become more interested as they get older. The effect of *aging* on interest is not the same thing as the relationship between *age* and interest. The main purpose of this chapter is to test the **Aging Hypothesis**, according to which people develop political interest as they get older.

There is a payoff for going on the painstaking analytical chase in this chapter. It turns out the relationship between aging and political interest is considerably less steep than the relationship between age and political interest. Much of the association with age among adults is in fact explained by cohort effects: Individuals who were born in the 1940s and came of age in the tumultuous 1960s are the most interested cohort in all three countries – and they just happen to be older than most other panelists in the datasets. Evidence for aging effects is evident only before people reach their thirties. These empir-ical regularities – remarkably similar in Britain, Germany, and Switzerland once we peel away the methodological confounders – would remain hidden without a deliberate approach to distinguish aging, period, and cohort effects.

Aging effects concentrated in adolescence and early adulthood are consistent with the **Impressionable Years Hypothesis**. Because (some) young people are just starting to develop an enduring dispositional interest, the interestingness of the environment may still play a bigger role for them in triggering situational interest. Even if elections and events do not make much of a difference for political interest in the electorate as a whole, as the previous chapter began to suggest, their impact on young people's interest could still be disproportionate. The second half of this chapter offers a test of this hypothesis.

In order to understand the role of age and aging, this chapter must first address a fundamental question about political interest: At what age do young people first experience an awareness of politics that permits the formation of interest? It may be possible to experience situational political interest even in the absence of such awareness, but for situational interest to develop into dispositional interest, individuals need to attribute their spontaneous affective reaction to the political nature of the situational trigger (following Silvia 2005, 2006). In order to reengage with a domain, individuals have to identify it as political (following Hidi and Renninger 2006) – and thus have some sense of what politics is.

POLITICAL INTEREST AMONG YOUNG PEOPLE

People are not born with a notion of "politics" (or its more specific elements, such as "government," "the public," "laws," and "politician.") Only a person with at least a basic idea of "politics" can assess it as interesting or not interesting. Starting with the earliest work on political socialization, scholars have tried to determine when children develop "political consciousness" (Easton and Dennis 1969). Many studies show beginnings of this development in children's late pre-teen years, a time most children spend in elementary school. At this age, young people rapidly learn about key political actors and some political functions:

> It is in childhood that a member, born into a system and, therefore, without previous political conceptions at all, first learns how to cognize or "see," certain parts of the political world, how to feel about them, how to evaluate them, and how to identify and react to representative symbols of this world, such as "government," "party," "Washington," and "Uncle Sam." (Easton and Dennis 1969, 87)

Analyzing a survey of white children between 7 and 13 years old (2nd and 8th grade) in eight U.S. metropolitan regions, Hess and Torney (1967) and Easton and Dennis (1969) found that political consciousness developed in elementary school. As measured by their stated certainty of what "government" means and a sense that Congress, not the president, "makes the laws," students have some understanding of "government" as early as 4th grade. Moore, Lare, and Wagner (1985) add detailed evidence about the development between kindergarten and the conclusion of 4th grade (age 5–10) by measuring children's political understanding annually over this five-year period in the 1970s in a sample of about 250 children in California. Van Deth et al. (2007) interviewed roughly 800 children before and after their first year of elementary schooling in a mid-size German city. These studies confirm Easton and Dennis's conclusion that most children have some political consciousness at the end of elementary school.

The earliest objects of political consciousness are the president and police officers among American children (Hess and Torney 1967; Easton and Dennis 1969; Moore et al. 1985) and the chancellor and mayors in Germany (van Deth et al. 2007). Haug (2013) instructed German children between 4 and 10 years of age to draw a picture of themselves, their lives, and their hopes and fears "as a grown-up." About a quarter of the 230 drawings were classified as related to politics, most frequently to themes of war and peace or the environment. Older children were more likely to include references to political themes.

Only a few kindergartners or first-graders have any understanding of political processes, however. To elementary school children, "the government is a man who lives in Washington, while Congress is a lot of men who help the President" (Hess and Torney 1967, 32). About ten percent in Moore et al.'s (1985, 49–51) study had some sense of what an election is, how the president is selected or who makes a law. More children at this age believed that "the policeman," God or Jesus make the laws. Asked who "is the boss of the country" or "who does the most to run the country," about forty percent of kindergartners named God, Jesus, George Washington or Abraham Lincoln. Few of the German first-graders had any sense of what a democracy is or what politicians do. A third of them responded that "the king" makes most decisions, even though the other two response options were chancellor and mayor (van Deth et al. 2007). None of the American children had even a basic understanding of the Watergate scandal, which dominated the news at the time these children were in kindergarten (Moore et al. 1985).

By 4th grade, mentions of God, Jesus, or a long-dead president are almost entirely gone and "more than 90 percent of our sample understood such regime-related matters as what courts are, what judges do, what an election is, and that we do not have a king in the United States" (Moore et al. 1985, 92; for similar findings, see Atkin and Gantz 1978). Some dimensions of political consciousness, in particular questions of resource allocation and partisan competition, only develop later. With barely a handful of exceptions, fourth graders in Moore et al.'s study could not yet explain what a party was or how Republicans and Democrats differed. Easton and Dennis (1969) found that children were aware of other institutions than the presidency and developed more detailed conceptions of their roles by about 8th grade (for similar findings for German youths, see Ingrisch 1997).

Easton and Dennis (1969), Moore et al. (1985) and Van Deth et al. (2007) do not discuss children's political interest, so their work does not tell us much about children's motivation for politics. Focus groups of 193 British youths between the ages of 14 and 24 conducted in the late 1990s showed that most young people have a concept in mind when they are asked about "politics," even when they do not find it interesting. Only a few participants

claimed that the word "politics" brought nothing to mind, and, in some instances, that they had never heard the word before... A second, and much more common response, was to associate politics with traditional party politics in Britain and the Prime Minister, Parliament, government, politicians and political parties were mentioned. Politics was framed in these terms by young people of different ages, almost irrespective of their level of interest in politics. (White et al. 2000, 23)

The least interested participants appeared to have little idea about politicians' behavior or the role of parliament. But their responses did not lack all political relevance. Asked for their opinions about politicians, "those who lacked interest in politics mainly expressed views about the current and former prime ministers, Tony Blair, John Major, and Margaret Thatcher or party leaders such as William Hague, Paddy Ashdown and Neil Kinnock" (31).

In sum, various studies show clearly and consistently that children have a basic understanding of "politics" at the end of elementary school, around age ten. This opens up the possibility to form evaluations of politics as interesting or not. Especially in elementary school, survey responses still reveal an idealized view of the president, so it is entirely possible, even likely, that initial political interest is subject to change when children develop more realistic perspectives later. But few young teenagers draw a complete blank when it comes to "politics."

POLITICAL INTEREST AND AGE

It is firmly established that older people are more politically interested (e.g., Lazarsfeld et al. 1948 [1944], 44; Berelson et al. 1954, 25; Bennett 1986, 73–6; Bennett and Rademacher 1997; Putnam 2000, 253; Zukin et al. 2006, 82; Howe 2010; Neundorf et al. 2013). This empirical pattern is evident in the household panel studies introduced in the previous chapter. While the previous chapter used only participants who were at least 18 years old, these studies also interview younger household members. The youngest SHP panelists are 14. The youngest panelists in the GSOEP and the adult portion of the BHPS are 16 years old.[1] At this age, almost all respondents give a substantive answer to the political interest question.[2] Figure 6.1 plots interest levels among these young panelists along with older age groups.[3] They confirm the positive relationship between age and political interest. In all three countries and in all years, the youngest respondents express the least political interest. This positive association between age and interest suggests that the near-constant aggregate political interest[4] is the result of people getting more interested as they age while at the same time young people enter the population with lower levels of interest.

---

[1] The BHPS youth sample cannot be directly compared because it employs a modified political interest question. It is examined later in this chapter.

[2] In the three household panels, including the BHPS youth sample, "don't know" responses or refusals to report political interest are exceedingly rare: 4 cases out of 9,939 in the BHPS youth sample of 11- to 15-year-olds; 9 cases out of 10,445 in the BHPS adult samples at age 16 or 17; 17 of 5,225 responses from panelists between ages 14 and 17 in the SHP; and 59 of 10,798 responses from 16- or 17-year-olds in the GSOEP.

[3] Analyses from this point on are based on a rolling core sample of citizens (see Book Appendix A). Analyses will drop residents who do not have citizenship and also exclude panelists who were born outside the country (in the GSOEP) or moved to the country after 1950 (in the BHPS). As a group, individuals who immigrated as adults have noticeably lower interest levels (Prior 2010, 751–2; Müssig and Worbs 2012) and different age trajectories. As the goal of the analysis shifts to understanding the individual origins of political interest, the task is simplified by focusing on individuals who grew up in the same society. Chapter 8 provides additional details.

[4] The absence of a time trend among young people in Germany initially looks inconsistent with the results of a *Shell Jugendstudie*, a series of cross-sectional surveys of young Germans funded by Shell Germany. In their 2010 installment, Albert et al. (2010, 131) report decidedly higher political interest levels in 1984 and 1991 than in more recent years. The drop in interest among youth between 15 and 24 years of age is from 57 percent expressing interest in 1991 to only 34 percent in 2002. The two subsequent surveys in 2006 and 2010 show only a modest recovery. Rather than an actual decline, the empirical pattern most likely reflects changes in question wording and use of convenience samples. The political interest question changed from "Interessierst Du Dich für Politik?" (Are you interested in politics?) with two response options (yes/no) until 1996 to "Nun zu etwas anderem: Interessieren Sie sich ganz allgemein für Politik?" (Now for something different: Generally speaking, are you interested in politics?) with four response options ("Würden Sie sagen Sie sind stark interessiert, interessiert, wenig interessiert, gar nicht interessiert?" in 2002–10; Would you say you are strongly interested, interested, weakly interested, not at all interested?) Interviewers selected respondents on the basis of demographic quotas and were permitted to recruit friends: "Die konkrete Auswahl der vorab exakt definierten Zielpersonen wurde den Interviewerinnen und Interviewern überlassen. Sie konnten ihre

Even the two most notable instances of aggregate change, the period around reunification in Germany and the smaller, more gradual drop in Britain in the early 1990s, are evident in all age groups. This is also true for the post-reunification trend among East Germans alone. In 1990, just before reunification, East Germans of all age groups are more interested than their Western counterparts. Over the following two years, their interest drops by roughly the same extent in all age groups so that by 1992, they are about the same as among West Germans. These results are remarkably consistent with Ingrisch's (1997) longitudinal analysis of youths in East and West Germany in 1990–2: She also finds significantly higher political interest among students in the East in 1990, but can no longer distinguish interest levels in 1991–2.

The three graphs in Figure 6.2 plot political interest responses by age for each country. Because the samples become small at high ages, responses by the oldest one percent of participants are excluded, leading to a maximum age of 84 in Switzerland, and of 85 in Britain and Germany. In all three countries, political interest increases with age until well into adulthood before it stabilizes, a pattern that has appeared in other analyses of political interest (Bennett 1986, 98; Zukin et al. 2006, 82). "Not so strongly interested" is the most frequent answer in the GSOEP, accounting for more than half of all responses in some age groups. In the BHPS, "fairly interested" and "not very interested" are more common than the scale endpoints. In the SHP, which offered 11 response categories, "0," "5," and "8" are more common than other responses.

The BHPS plot in Figure 6.2a includes data from the youth questionnaire for household members between 11 and 15 years of age, which was introduced in 1994. It shows the unfortunate change in the number of response options between the youth and the adult interviews. In the youth survey for respondents under the age of 16, around 70 percent say that they are "not interested." The adult interview then gives them the option to differentiate between "not very interested" and "not at all interested." Starting in people's late teens, the share of "fairly" or at least "not very" interested panelists increases noticeably. But this increase in interest is not yet evident among young teens: Between 11 and 15, political interest does not change much according to the BHPS.

Does Growing Older Raise Political Interest?

It is important to note that Figure 6.2 does not tell us much yet about how individuals' political interest changes. The most intuitive explanation is a lifecycle effect – people developing greater political interest as they grow

---

Interviewpartner in ihrem persönlichen Bekanntenkreis, im Rahmen von Institutionen oder innerhalb von typischen Jugendtreffpunkten oder Ähnlichem anwerben" (Albert et al. 2010, 366–7). (The specific selection of target persons defined precisely in advance was left to the interviewers. They were permitted to recruit their interviewees among personal acquaintances, in organizations, or at typical youth meeting spots.)

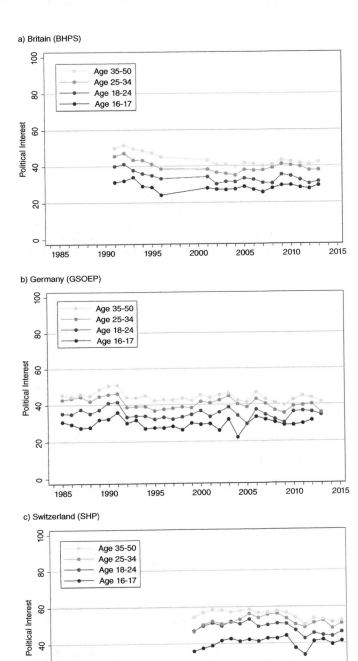

FIGURE 6.1 Political Interest in Different Age Groups

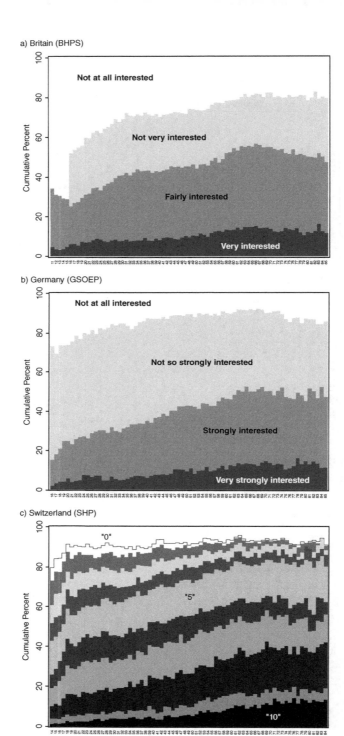

FIGURE 6.2 Distribution of Political Interest by Age
Note: Graphs show the weighted distribution of responses to the political interest
question in each panel study for the rolling core samples. GSOEP data uses the 1984,

older. But it is possible to obtain the patterns in Figure 6.2 without lifecycle effects. Instead, if interest were constant over the lifecycle, but younger people started out less interested, cohort differences could produce an increase in average interest at older age. And there is a third possibility, but the results in Chapter 5 effectively rule it out: Period effects could lead to a positive aggregate relationship between age and interest if respondents all became more interested during the later panel waves. The pattern in Figure 6.2 could thus reflect any combination of lifecycle, cohort, and period effects, not necessarily the exclusive impact of aging on political interest.

More systematic analysis of the household panel data can distinguish life-cycle effects from cohort differences and period effects. Comparing panelists who were the same age when they were interviewed, but born in different decades, helps estimate cohort and period effects. For example, the German SOEP includes 35-year old panelists born in 1950 (in the 1985 wave) and 35-year old panelists born in 1970 (in the 2005 wave). If these two sets of panelists report different interest levels, age cannot be the reason, but their different birth cohorts or the different time of the interview could. Comparing interest levels in the same interview year for respondents of different ages helps identify lifecycle and cohort effects. Finally, comparing panelists born in the same year but interviewed at different times holds constant cohort difference to reveal lifecycle and period effects. An analysis that carries out all of these comparisons simultaneously is known as an age-period-cohort (APC) analysis.

Three analytical elements are key to isolating the effect of aging on political interest. Even though none of the panel studies followed any individual for more than thirty years, I estimate a full age trajectory by splicing together the many incomplete pieces of the full age trajectory that individual panelists provide. Integrating observations over subsets of the life span into an average trajectory over the full age range is known as a "cohort-sequential" or "accelerated cohort" design (Preacher et al. 2008, 42) because the age range is greater than the length of the study. Second, instead of trying to estimate the common change of political interest that all panelists experience in a given year, I use the measures of interestingness introduced in Chapter 5 to estimate the common effect of events that occurred within a certain period before the survey interview. This move makes the APC analysis a lot easier technically and is in fact closer to the idea that the environment can trigger situational political interest. Third, and most importantly, I do *not* estimate the effect of aging by comparing two different individuals' *levels* of political interest and then drawing inferences from the

---

FIGURE 6.2 (*cont.*) 1990, 1998, 2000, and 2006 samples (A, C, E, F, H). BHPS includes the original 1991 sample, the Wales and Scotland extensions added in 1999, and Understanding Society (USOC), which continues the BHPS and adds a large new sample (see Book Appendix A). SHP uses 1999, 2004, and 2013 samples.

fact that one is older than the other. Instead, I compare the same individual at different times, so the estimate is based on *change* in political interest. This approach has the decided advantage of removing any other constant differences between people from the comparison that could otherwise bias estimates of how much aging matters for political interest.

Conceptually, the most pertinent reason why the association between age and interest may not reflect the effect of aging alone is cohort differences. The data in Figure 6.2 combine the political interest reports from different birth cohorts. For example, the youngest original respondents in the GSOEP were observed in 1984 at the age of 16. By the time of the 2013 panel wave, they had reached their forties. They thus provide information for the portion of the age-interest relationship between 16 and 45 years of age. Other respondents were in their mid-twenties when they joined the GSOEP panel in 1984. These respondents provide information for a different, but overlapping age range, the range between the ages of, say, 26 and 55. Combining the political interest reports of these two groups into a joint trajectory of political interest for people between 16 and 55 is justified only if these two groups (cohorts) actually follow the same trajectory. Although we do not know how political interest in the second group developed before the panelists turned 26 (i.e., before 1984) and we do not (yet) know how political interest in the first group evolved when its members entered their fifties, the overlap between the two trajectory pieces allows us to assess the validity of representing both groups by one trajectory. We observed members of both groups between the ages of 26 and 45, but members of the first group were born in 1968 or 1969, while members of the second group were born in 1958 or 1959. It is only appropriate to treat the combined trajectories of different cohorts as the impact of aging on interest if birth cohort makes no difference for the age trajectory or its effect is separated out.

Each of the three analytical elements corresponds to specific parts of the estimation process. The following pages explain the conceptual benefits of these elements and demonstrate how they lead to different substantive conclusions about aging effects than a naïve approach that tries to draw inferences from plots of raw data such as Figure 6.2. Full technical details appear in the appendix to this chapter, but I show the model here to provide a succinct summary of the analytical task and add precision to the conceptual discussion:

$$PI_{it} = \pi^{AGE}_{it} + \mathbf{x}^{N}_{t} + \pi^{BC}_{i} + \pi^{S}_{i} + \alpha_{i} + \varepsilon_{it} \qquad (6.1)$$

The dependent variable is a panelist's interest report in a specific panel wave. The variable thus gets two subscripts because it designates a response by individual i at time t. The first three variables on the right-hand side capture the three elements of the APC model: aging effects, period effects, and cohort effects. Of the three, only the age term has two subscripts because age differs between individuals and changes for the same individual over time. x^N_t captures period effects (by proxy, as explained momentarily), and only has a t subscript because it soaks up the common influences at any point in time that do not vary from individual to individual. Cohort effects (BC_i) only have an i subscript because birth cohort (or year of birth) is a constant for each panelist, so it is the same at every t.

The fourth term (s_i) is a bit player. It indicates to which sample a panelist belongs (the original panel or a refreshment or extension sample.) It should not affect political interest, and analysis of this variable in indeed shows that it hardly does (see Online Supplementary Materials for details).[5]

The two remaining terms are not observed but very important. Including α_i allows each panelist to have his or her own long-run average political interest. With only a subscript for individuals, this term varies between people, but not over time. It amounts to a separate intercept for each panelist. This is a big help in estimating the effect of aging on political interest. Without α_i, the model would treat all political interest reports identically regardless of whether they were made by the same panelist. After accounting for the other variables in the model, all of the remaining interest differences between two observations from different panelists would then be attributed to age, even though other unmeasured characteristics that differ between panelists might explain them. This would still be a valid description of the age-interest relationship, but age differences could reflect mechanisms other than getting older. With α_i in the model, the other variables seek to explain variation in the deviations from each individual's average political interest, not their absolute levels of interest.

It turns out to be most convenient not to estimate the α_i's for each panelist. Instead, they can be removed by transforming the model. One possible transformation is to "demean" the model – to subtract the subject mean of each variable in the model. This eliminates α_i because α_i equals its subject mean and is thus subtracted from itself. The same is true for all other constant terms in the model, including cohort and sample indicators. After the transformation, the model is based entirely on within-subject variation, differences in the measurement for the same panelist at different measurement occasions. As the same panelist gets older, how much does her political interest change

---

[5] Refreshment samples help distinguish lifecycle, cohort, and period effects because they further break up collinearity between the three. But they also introduce panel effects as another potential source of variation. If, after accounting for the fact that panelists in the refreshment samples were, on average, born later than panelists in the original sample, different samples yield different conclusions about the growth of political interest; panel conditioning or panel attrition might be the cause. Chapter 5 demonstrated very minor panel effects for yearly averages of political interest, so the focus for this chapter's analysis was on differences in the relationship with age.

relative to her average over her full tenure on the panel (after accounting for differences generatey variation in interestingness of the environment)? Whether or not other panelists of different ages have higher or lower interest no longer affects the estimation. The transformation thus isolates the effect of aging on political interest. The Chapter Appendix describes these important estimation steps in detail.

Including individual intercepts α_i in the model is one of the three analytical steps that get us from raw data to an estimate of aging effects. The other two steps are more easily explained. The age term in the model varies over individuals and time. With α_i accounted for, it looks for a relationship between age and individuals' deviations from their average political interest. Panelists provide information about such deviations for different stretches of time. No individual provides more than 30 years' worth of deviations, but the model can estimate the aging effect over the full lifecycle (starting at the age when panelists are first interviewed). The household panel studies make it possible to estimate this effect without arbitrary functional assumptions about its shape. The studies' samples are so sizable and the panels so long that they provide enough data to enter age as a series of dummies (π^{AGE}_{it}) and still obtain very precise estimates.

The last critical analytical step is to address the well-known identification problem of age-period-cohort analyses (Mason et al. 1973; Glenn 1976) that arises because the three variables are perfectly collinear: Subtracting birth year from interview year equals age. When the three variables enter as sets of dummies, dropping one dummy each for age, birth year, and interview year fails to identify the model.[6] The forthcoming analysis breaks up this collinearity by replacing year effects with the substantively more relevant measures of interestingness of the political environment introduced in the previous chapter. x^N_t contains several different measures of interestingness: closeness to the next election, time since the last election, recent national and global news events, recent announcement of economic growth, and recent stock market variation. The rationale for holding constant period effects is to account for influences that affect political interest simultaneously for all panelists regardless of their age or birth cohort. These influences are not the general difference between this year and last year, but the difference between the proximity to events that possibly triggered situational interest. Replacing year dummies with measures of (proximity to) potentially interesting events is thus both methodologically necessary and theoretically justified.

Figure 6.3 shows the results of estimating model 6.1 using different estimators. Employing different estimators visualizes how peeling off different

---

[6] Omitting a second dummy for one of the components technically identifies the model, but the choice of which values to omit has arbitrary implications for the results (Hall et al. 2007; Yang and Land 2013).

confounders from the relationship between *age and political interest* eventually reveals the relationship between *aging and political interest*. Graphs use (very mild) local mean smoothing of predicted values and show 95-percent confidence intervals around the estimated age-interest relationships. (Equivalent graphs showing estimates for each age dummy and their confidence intervals are available in the Online Supplementary Material, Figure OL6.1.) Figure 6.3 removes the influence of sample effects and interestingness of the environment by setting sample and interestingness to the same value for all panelists.[7] As before, political interest responses are transformed to a 0–100 scale. Responses from the BHPS youth interviews are included, using a splicing approach described in the Online Supplementary Materials.

The darkest lines in Figure 6.3 are based on a naïve model that ignores the panel nature of the data entirely. It adjusts for differences in interestingness of the environment at different interview times, but does nothing to distinguish the impact of aging from other reasons why age and political interest might correlate. (Technically, the darkest lines are based on OLS estimation of Equation 6.1 without π^{BC}_i in the model and with $\alpha_i + \varepsilon_{it}$ as one combined error term.)

The lines with medium shading come from an estimator that attempts to determine panelists' long-term political interest averages (the α_i's discussed above, which are also called "unit effects") and adjust for them while estimating how much aging matters. This is a considerable improvement over the naïve estimates (shown by the dark lines) because it begins to take into account that some interest differences between people of different ages could be due to variation in stable individual characteristics, not aging. But just like the darkest lines, the lines with medium shading still ignore cohort effects. (These lines are based on random-effects estimates of Equation 6.1 without π^{BC}_i in the model. The Chapter Appendix explains how this violates a critical assumption underlying the random-effects estimator.)

Only the lightest lines fully remove spurious effects of birth cohort and any other constant between-subject differences. (These lines are based on fixed-effects estimates of model 6.1.)

The differences matter. In all three countries, moving from the darkest lines to the lightest lines reduces the steepness of the relationship between age and political interest. What looked like age differences to the naïve estimator are in fact stable differences between individuals that do not depend on age. The relationship between *aging* and interest is considerably less steep than the relationship between *age* and interest. In fact, aging largely ceases to raise political interest after early adulthood (for the average citizen). This conclusion is hidden from us in cross-sectional data or naïvely aggregated panel data in Figure 6.2.

---

[7] All measures of interestingness of the environment are held at zero, that is, no elections within a half year of the interview, no global or national news events, zero growth, and a flat stock market.

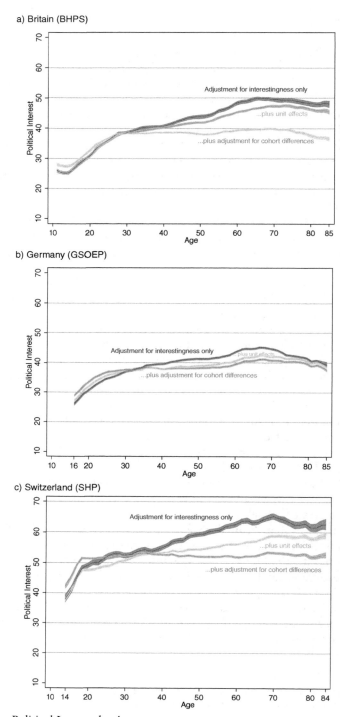

a) Britain (BHPS)

Adjustment for interestingness only

...plus unit effects

...plus adjustment for cohort differences

b) Germany (GSOEP)

Adjustment for interestingness only

plus unit effects

...plus adjustment for cohort differences

c) Switzerland (SHP)

Adjustment for interestingness only

...plus unit effects

...plus adjustment for cohort differences

FIGURE 6.3 Political Interest by Age

Comparing the medium- and lightly-shaded lines demonstrates that the impact of growing older is easily exaggerated when cohort differences are not accounted for. Without cohort adjustment, the relationship between age and political interest is steeper and positive until at least age 60. In Britain and Switzerland in particular, older people are more interested partly because they belong to more interested cohorts, not because they developed greater interest as adolescents or adults. When the goal is to explain why some people become more politically interested as they get older, unmodeled cohort differences induce bias. Not all panel estimators automatically remove the possible confounding of aging and birth cohort. (A fixed-effects estimator is the safest choice.)

Despite different political systems and histories, different survey procedures, and different questions to measure political interest, getting older has remarkably similar effects on political interest in all three countries examined here. For the average person, aging raises political interest by 10–15 points (on the 0–100 scale). This rise occurs almost entirely in adolescence and young adulthood.

Among young teenagers, political interest does not increase yet (at least on average). The youth sample of the BHPS is the only data source used here that covers panelists in their early teens. It indicates that average political interest starts to increase only around age 14 or 15. By the time the Swiss household panel starts interviewing at age 14, the rise of political interest has already started. These findings are roughly consistent with Russo and Stattin's (2016) study of young Swedish adolescents. They begin interviewing at age 12 but only find a noticeable rise after age 15. Hess and Torney's study ended with 8th grade – before children reach that age – and finds a slight decline of interest "in the government and current events" between the ages of 7 and 13. Dostie-Goulet (2009) reports increasing political interest after age 14 in Canada, and Quintelier and van Deth (2014) after age 16 in Belgium, but neither can determine the onset of growth because these are the youngest panelists included in their studies.

Cohort Differences in Political Interest

For the purpose of explaining why political interest changes as people get older, removing the influence of stable interest differences and isolating the impact of aging is essential. But for descriptive purposes, and to possibly understand why people born at different times exhibit different levels of interest, it is also useful to quantify cohort differences. Figure 6.4 does that. Panels on the left plot political interest scores before adjustments for birth cohort and other constant between-subject differences are made. (Only sample and interestingness effects are held constant. Graphs use the same predicted values as the dark lines in Figure 6.3.) Lines, distinguished by pattern and shading, plot smoothed interest trajectories for subsets of the sample who share the same birth decade. (The earliest cohort for each country comprises more than one birth decade to preserve sample size.)

In the German data, the 1940s cohort, shown by the solid black line at the center of the age range, stands out for their high level of political interest. Members

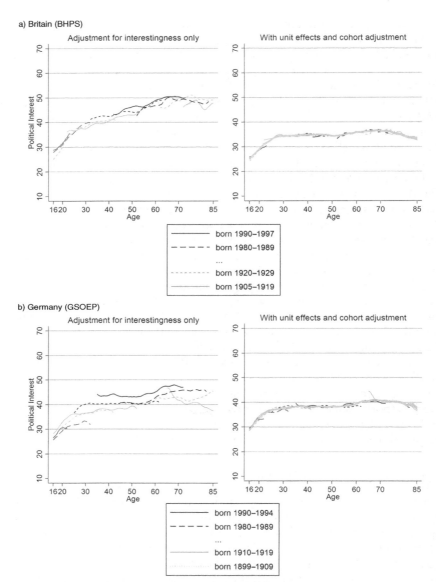

FIGURE 6.4 Aging Effects on Political Interest by Birth Decade

of this birth decade, who came of age in the 1960s, are fairly consistently about 5 points more interested than Germans of the same age who were born in the 1930s (long-dashed black line) or the 1950s (short-dashed black line). The long cohort born before 1910 is the least interested, about 10 points below interest levels of the youngest cohort observed over the same age range (those born in the

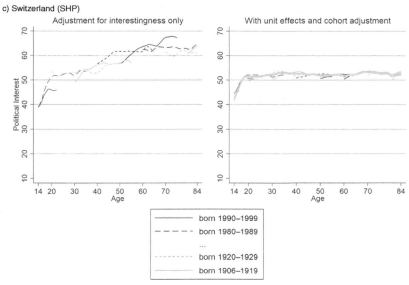

FIGURE 6.4 (*cont.*)

1930s). Another cohort difference occurs among panelists in their twenties: Germans born in the 1980s are about 5 points less interested than Germans born in the 1970s and 1960s, and almost 10 points less than those born in 1950s. (It is important to note that these differences cannot be explained by noteworthy events occurring at different ages for different cohorts because effects of interestingness, including the salient years around reunification, are held constant.)

Cohort differences in Britain are somewhat less prevalent. While in their thirties and forties, British people born in the 1930s and 1940s are about 5 points more interested than members of the two more recent birth decades (and perhaps older cohorts, too). As in Germany, political interest in the oldest cohort is lower at high age than the two following cohorts. But the four youngest cohorts in Britain are essentially indistinguishable. If anything, 16-year-olds born since 1980 are a bit more interested than those born in the 1970s. In Switzerland, finally, individuals born between 1940 and 1959 are a few points more politically interested than the preceding and succeeding cohorts. There is a suggestion that the youngest cohort, those born in the 1990s, developed political interest less quickly than the 1980s cohort.

The right panel for each country in Figure 6.4 shows political interest scores, again by cohort, but this time after the influence of constant predictors of political interest has been removed (using the same procedure as for the lightly-shaded lines in Figure 6.3). The thick light line in each graph repeats the 95-percent confidence interval of the mean-smoothed age-interest relationship across the full age range shown by the lightly-shaded line in Figure 6.3.

This line hides the individual cohort line segments almost completely, indicating that the fixed-effects transformation effectively removes most cohort differences. For all three countries, the shapes of the cohort trajectories closely resemble the full trajectory, so very few line segments "stick out" of the full-range confidence interval. As cohort lines also have sampling uncertainty that is not represented, Figure 6.4 provides strong evidence to conclude that constant cohort differences have been successfully removed and that different birth cohorts do not change much differently over time, so cohort-specific aging trajectories do not require separate modeling as long as cohort differences in levels are accounted for.

Sample and Panel Effects

The aging trajectories estimated so far are based on multiple samples administered as part of each household panel survey. The GSOEP and the SHP have added refreshment samples to their original panel. The BHPS boosted the number of households in Scotland and Wales halfway through the study, and USoc constitutes a massive refreshment sample. I tested for differences in intercept and trajectory between these different samples of the same population. Results generate no reason for concerns about systematic panel or sample effects (see Online Supplementary Materials).

It is remarkable that the age trajectories of newly empaneled respondents are mostly statistically indistinguishable from those of panelists who have completed interviews for as many as 15–20 years. The scarceness of evidence for panel effects in this chapter follows analyses in Chapter 5 that showed at best minor and directionally inconsistent panel effects. But it is not too surprising that BHPS, GSOEP, and SHP interviews do not make panelists more interested in politics or lead politically less interested panelists to refuse future participation. These surveys do not cover politics in great detail. The bulk of the questions each year is about respondents' jobs, financial situation, and changes in their household. Although the low number of questions about politics has a clear downside – many theoretically important political concepts cannot be measured – it quite possibly explains why panel effects with respect to political interest are so small.

THE IMPACT OF ELECTIONS, EVENTS, AND ECONOMIC CONDITIONS

Having isolated the impact of aging on political interest as well as the differences between birth cohorts, the remaining piece of the age-period-cohort triad is the effect of conditions at the time of the measurement that affect people across the board (that is, independent of age and birth cohort): Does an interesting political environment raise situational political interest? To answer this question, the environment's interestingness is measured independently of people's expressions of political interest, by relying on professionals in the business of discerning interesting events and by measuring uncommon economic conditions. Using measures introduced in Chapter 5, the analysis asks if a recent global news event – an event or topic that editors of *TIME*, *The Economist*, and *Der Spiegel* all deemed important enough to put on the cover at the same time – raises people's political interest. It also examines if political events in, or relating to, a country – newsworthy enough to warrant coverage in the *New York Times* front section – increase political interest in that country. The analysis includes measures of economic interestingness, related to both economic growth and stock market performance, that might spill over into the political realm and affect how interesting people find politics to be. Lastly, the analysis offers another way to gauge the impact of elections, either impending or in the recent past, on political interest.

Whereas Chapter 5 compared annual political interest averages in years with and without elections, this chapter compares political interest levels of the same panelists over time and examines if they report higher interest when they are interviewed close to an election, or just after a global or national news event, or at the beginning of a recession, or during a period of stock market turmoil. The analysis is thus less blunt than in Chapter 5 because it avoids the assumption that elections and other events have lasting effects. With the present approach, even short-term effects that influence only a subset of panelists interviewed in a given year can be detected.

Table 6.1 shows how much the interestingness of the environment affects political interest reports in the three panel studies. The first column for each country gives information on the frequency of these events in the sample. For indicator variables, it displays the share of interviews that occur within the noted proximity to an event. For continuous variables, it shows the mean across all observations. For example, the average number of global events, as identified by matching magazine covers, in the two weeks before an interview was between .14 and .22 in the three countries, so roughly one in five interviews occurred in proximity to a global event. The second column reports the regression coefficients, with standard errors in parentheses, based on the same model depicted in Figure 6.3 by the green line. When the coefficient is significant at $p < 0.05$, the third column displays the marginal effect on political interest. For indicator variables, the column simply repeats the regression coefficient. For continuous variables, it shows the effect of an above-average level of interestingness (one global event, a noticeable national event marked by 5 *New York Times* stories, a net stock market change of 3 percent or more over two weeks, and market volatility roughly twice the average).

Interestingness of the environment affects political interest. About half of the measures of interestingness have significant effects. The most important statistic in Table 6.1 appears in the penultimate row, however. It lists the within-person variance explained by variation in interestingness. In none of the countries do

TABLE 6.1 *The Impact of Interestingness*

	Britain (BHPS)			Germany (GSOEP)			Switzerland (SHP)		
	Freq.	Coef (se)	Effect	Freq.	Coef (se)	Effect	Freq.	Coef (se)	Effect
Election Campaign									
Days before election									
1–14 days	.4	4.5 (.6)***	4.5	.05	1.6 (1.3)		5.1	-1.1 (.2)***	-1.1
15–30 days	.6	4.1 (.6)***	3.1	.1	.7 (1.0)		6.1	-1.3 (.2)***	-1.3
31–90 days	2.1	.8 (.3)**	.8	1.0	-.002 (.3)		5.3	-1.3 (.2)***	-1.3
91–180 days	4.9	-.2 (.2)		6.1	-.8 (.1)***	-.8			
Election Aftermath									
Days after last election									
1–14 days	.6	2.5 (.5)***	2.5	.03	1.0 (1.5)		3.9	-1.1 (.2)***	-1.1
15–30 days	.5	3.1 (.6)***	3.1	.2	.5 (.7)		3.3	-.3 (.3)	
31–90 days	2.1	2.3 (.3)***	2.3	2.1	1.1 (.2)***	1.1	4.6	-1.0 (.3)***	-1.0
91–180 days	10.8	1.2 (.1)***	1.2	15.0	1.2 (.1)***	1.2	2.1	-1.5 (.4)***	-1.5
Global Events									
Matching covers									
1–14 days	.19	.06 (.09)		.14	.23 (.08)**	.2	.22	.32 (.10)***	.3
15–30 days	.21	-.15 (.08)		.12	.48 (.09)***	.5	.26	.16 (.09)	
31–90 days	.60	.09 (.04)*	.1	.50	.54 (.03)***	.5	.83	-.06 (.04)	
National Events									
NYT mentions (logged)									
1–14 days	2.0	.24 (.07)***	.4	3.0	.25 (.06)***	.5	.3	.19 (.16)	
15–30 days	2.1	.02 (.07)		3.3	.44 (.06)***	.8	.3	-.55 (.17)***	-1.0
31–90 days	8.8	.24 (.10)*	.4	12.4	.70 (.08)***	1.2	1.0	-1.01 (.10)***	-1.8
Change in GDP									
drop > 1%	.5	-.8 (.6)		1.4	-.4 (.3)		1.1	3.0 (.9)**	3.0
drop < 1%	6.2	-.1 (.2)		7.5	.2 (.1)		8.6	.1 (.2)	
rise < 1%	4.8	-.1 (.2)		7.8	-.2 (.1)*		9.5	.4 (.2)*	.4
rise > 1%	.6	.6 (.5)		1.8	-.2 (.3)				
Start of Recession	.2	1.8 (1.1)		2.4	-.9 (.3)**	-.9	1.1	-1.0 (1.0)	
Stock Market									
% increase	1.4	-.05 (.02)*	-.2	1.9	.02 (.01)		1.4	-.15 (.03)***	-.5
% decrease	1.3	.01 (.02)		1.3	.02 (.02)		1.2	-.02 (.02)	
market volatility	17	.005 (.001)**	.2	19	.007 (.002)***	.3	21	.005 (.001)***	.2
ΔR^2 (within)	.0017			.0175			.0048		
N (persons; obs.)	63,470; 315,024			39,005; 337,557			18,690; 110,373		

*** $p < .001$, ** $p < .01$, * $p < .05$

Note: The first column for each country shows the share of observations (as a percentage of the estimation sample) for indicator variables or, in italics, the mean for continuous variables. The second column reports the regression coefficients, with standard errors in parentheses, from fixed-effects (FE) estimation of model 6.1. For coefficients that are significant at $p < 0.05$, the third column displays the marginal effect on political interest (of 1 instance of

all interestingness measures combined account for even one percent of the within-person variance. High statistical power of the estimation (with hundreds of thousands of interviews in each country) generates many statistically significant individual measures. Yet substantively, political or economic events do not contribute much to movement in political interest. This is broadly consistent with the aggregate patterns in Chapter 5, which showed minimal year-to-year variation. Much of political interest is dispositional and not subject to short-term variation in the political stimuli people encounter.

The impact of elections in Britain is by far the largest effect in Table 6.1. Panelists were 4 points more interested when they were interviewed in the month before an election compared to a non-election period. In the 90 days after an election, British people remained 2–3 points more interested than usual. It turns out that these results are based on just one election, the election of 2010, which was the first election for members of the new, larger USoc sample. Unlike USoc, which is in the field throughout the year, the earlier BHPS began interviewing in September and typically conducted about 90 percent of interviews by the end of November. As elections in Great Britain occurred in April, May, or June, the original BHPS provides very few cases within three months of an election. Interview timing explains why such a small share of panelists in Britain are interviewed close to an election (although the small share of just over 2 percent within 30 days of an election still amounts to over 5,000 respondents, and the effects easily attain statistical significance).

The GSOEP provides even less data in the months before or after an election. Since 1990, Germans have elected the Bundestag in late September or early October, while the GSOEP field period begins in January, and by May about 90 percent of interviews have usually been conducted.[8] Results suggest a slight buildup of political interest in the month before an election, but the estimated 1.7 point increase in the last two weeks of the campaign is based on too few cases to be significant. Two to six months after Election Day, interest is still significantly higher, by about one point. Although interview timing makes it difficult to estimate the impact of elections in the GSOEP, the suggestion of small effects is entirely consistent with the conclusions based on election studies in Chapter 4 (especially Figure 4.3).

---

[8] The 1987 election was held on January 25, just about the same time when GSOEP interviewing for that year began. It produces only 30 interviews within 6 months before the election. Day of interview is not available for some GSOEP panelists who completed written questionnaires (about 1.8 percent of all observations). Political interest in these interviews is not significantly different from in-person interviews. As interview month is known, monthly means of interestingness are assigned to retain these cases. Election proximity is calculated based on the average interview date in the month for other interviews (plus a random draw from the uniform distribution [-5;10] to account for some delay relative to immediate face-to-face interviews). Models include dummy variables for interviews missing day they were conducted and for all interviews completed by mail-in questionnaire (about 12 percent of all observations).

Election effects in Switzerland, which holds national elections in October and where the SHP field period begins in September, can be well estimated with these data. They are uniformly and significantly negative: Swiss panelists report lower political interest in the months surrounding an election. Rather than a disconfirmation of the general expectation that elections raise interest, this result most likely reflects the unique Swiss political system. The composition of the national government follows a consensus formula that almost ensures representation of all major political parties. Most contentious political issues are decided through referenda or initiatives, of which there are dozens every term. Political interest appears to drop around national elections not because Swiss people are oblivious to political drama, but because Swiss national elections are not as consequential for policy outcomes as direct democracy or election in other countries.

Global or national political events raise political interest significantly in Germany, but the magnitude of these effects is small. Both global and national events appear to take a few weeks to develop their most pronounced effects. The largest effect, associated with the exceptional amount of coverage during the fall of the Berlin Wall and ensuing reunification (see Chapter 5), is still only about 3 points (the maximum joint effect of global and national news events). By comparison, political interest among East Germans was 13 points higher in 1990 before it quickly dropped to West German levels. Other events, many of them also quite exceptional by any other standard than the peaceful collapse of an entire political system, cause an increase of at most 1 point. Political events have some significant but even smaller effects in Britain. In two cases, *New York Times* mentions are even negatively related to political interest in Switzerland, a pattern that is difficult to explain.[9]

Changes in economic conditions are not particularly impactful, but appear to follow similar patterns across countries. In all three countries, stock market volatility has a significant positive effect on interest, but it is substantively negligible. In a few cases, positive economic news lowers interest, while economic contractions raise interest. Most effects, however, are not distinguishable from zero.

Event-Driven Socialization?

Although elections and other political events have generally very small effects on political interest, the Impressionable Years Hypothesis and previous research on political socialization recommends a closer look at their effects on

---

[9] The *New York Times* tends to cover German politics more heavily in the weeks around an election. The total effect of elections on political interest thus has to include the indirect impact through the NYT measure. Yet when the model is rerun without the media-based measures, estimates of election impact change only marginally. The same holds in Britain and Switzerland.

young people in particular. Sears and Valentino (1997) propose that socialization may be "event-driven" – it "may occur in bursts ... rather than through the gradual and incremental accretion of experience" (58). U.S. presidential campaigns, for example, promote the development of political attitudes among adolescents by encouraging news exposure (Valentino and Sears 1998). Pacheco (2008) shows that the closeness of local and state elections during individuals' adolescence (eighth grade) is positively related to self-reported turnout in follow-up surveys 6–12 years later, even among participants who had since moved. These findings support the Impressionable Years Hypothesis, according to which political attitudes are more malleable early in their development. With respect to political interest, it predicts more pronounced and lasting effects of events on young panelists.

Table 6.2 offers a partial test of the Impressionable Years Hypothesis that compares the effects of interestingness in different age segments. It drops respondents over 65 years of age from the previous model and adds dummy variables for respondents under 20 and for respondents aged 20–24. Table 6.2 shows all instances where these interactions are significant at $p < 0.10$ *and* the estimated effect of the interestingness measure is at least one percentage point in either age segment (so significant but substantively minuscule effects do not appear).

Evidence for event-driven socialization of political interest is limited and inconsistent. The approaching 2010 election in Britain (the first one fully captured by the BHPS data due to the change in field period) raises political interest by a substantial 11 points in the two young age groups, compared to 4 points among older respondents. Young people also stay somewhat more interested in the aftermath of the election. The two significant findings for Switzerland, while much smaller, also indicate greater interest caused by elections among the young. The German data, by contrast, reveal several age interactions in the opposite direction. Elections lowering interest particularly among young respondents is not obviously indicative of event-driven socialization.

As far as the effects of other political and economic events are concerned, they rarely vary by age. Young people are affected by events in much the same way as adults. A few exceptions appear in Table 6.2, but they show smaller effects among the young as often as they show larger ones.

The notion of event-driven socialization implies more than disproportionate contemporaneous effects on the young. If these effects indeed socialize individuals into finding politics interesting, they should remain detectable years after they occurred. There is no evidence for this proposition. Lags of the variables that make the largest difference in Table 6.2 are statistically insignificant or have the opposite sign of their contemporaneous effect. Even the few events that raised young people's interest in particular have no lasting effects. Events, it seems, can affect political interest, but their impact is not only minor, but also fleeting.

TABLE 6.2 *The Impact of Interestingness, by Age*

Age		Britain (BHPS)			Germany (GSOEP)			Switzerland (SHP)		
		16–19	20–24	25–65	16–19	20–24	25–65	14–19	20–24	25–65
Election Campaign	1–14 days	11.5	11.0	4.2						
	15–30 days					−5.6	2.0			
	31–90 days						.2			
	91–180 days	−2.1		−.4	−2.6					
Election Aftermath	1–14 days							2.7		−1.3
	15–30 days		8.3	2.5		−3.1	1.3			
	31–90 days	5.0	4.2	2.2	2.4	2.5	1.1		.5	−1.3
	91–180 days		2.6	1.2	2.5		1.1			
Global Events	1–14 days									
	15–30 days									
	31–90 days									
National Events	1–14 days		2.0	.5				−2.9		.4
	15–30 days									
	31–90 days				.1	1.8	1.5			
Change in GDP	drop > 1%							14.6		2.1
	drop < 1%									
	rise < 1%									
	rise > 1%		−3.7	.8						
Start of recession			−6.1	3.2						
Stock market	% increase									
	% decrease									
	market volatility									

Note: Cell entries are estimated effects of interestingness derived as in Table 6.1 but for separate age segments. Effects are shown if age interactions are significant at *p* < .10 and the estimated effect is at least one percentage point for age 16–19 or age 20–24.

CONCLUSION

Empirical analysis supports the Aging Hypothesis, but the positive effect of aging on political interest diminishes among adults. The average young Brit, German, and Swiss becomes modestly but significantly more politically interested in adolescence and early adulthood. Data from the BHPS youth interviews, which start at age 11, show little increase until age 14 or 15. The SHP, which starts interviewing at age 14, reveals growth among its youngest panelists. The beginning of political interest development is thus difficult to pinpoint consistently with these data. In all three countries, however, the period between the mid-teens and mid-twenties clearly marks the time of steepest growth. In order to understand why aging raises political interest, it is clearly necessary to break with common practice in political science that limits data to voting-age samples. By the time young people turn eighteen, large individual differences in political interest already exist. Including minors in this study makes it possible to observe important developmental changes as they happen.

The average impact of aging on political interest is about 10–15 points on the 0–100 scales I use to make different questions comparable. On the underlying 4-point scales used in the British and German surveys, this magnitude amounts to a rise of less than half a category over the life course for the average person. One reason why aging affects political interest less than we may have come to believe is that the raw data – and previous studies examining cross-sectional data – cannot eliminate the contribution of stable cohort differences to the positive relationship between age and political interest.

Distinguishing aging and cohort differences is important because of their different implications for understanding the development of political interest. Only to the extent that political interest changes as people get older should we be looking for the reasons for this change in adolescence, young adulthood, or even later in life. Cohort differences have their origins early in life, and the data used here are not as well suited to understanding them. The reasons for cohort differences are bound to lie before the start of data collection for the panel surveys and we therefore cannot observe the before and after for presumptive causes. The developmental archeology by Pacheco (2008) is a nice example of going back to measure conditions (in her case, electoral competitiveness) in which survey respondents grew up. But even she cannot go back and measure the change in political interest before and after those conditions changed. The best we can do is to see if accounting for conditions in place by the first interview with a young panelist can reduce estimates of cohort effects – and thus potentially narrow the search for explanations.

In all three countries, panelists who were born in the 1940s, and who thus came of age in the 1960s, are the most interested cohort. In light of the common view of the 1960s as a tumultuous period with wide-reaching youth and student movements and culminating struggles for political incorporation, this finding seems consistent with the Impressionable Years Hypothesis. Older cohorts may also fit this pattern, although with the twist that growing up in Germany during and between the two world wars turned people away from politics, at least by the time the GSOEP began speaking to them in the mid-1980s.

Lack of political interest among young people is a common concern with the workings of democratic governance. It is easily overblown. Young people eventually become more interested (for a similar conclusion in several other countries, see Howe 2010, 74–6). And evidence for lower interest in recent cohorts – differences young people won't make up as they get older – is mixed and modest. Cohort trajectories are very similar for people under 20 years of age in all three countries. Among Germans and Swiss in their twenties, cohorts born more recently are somewhat less interested. There is no sign of this in Britain, however.

Isolating and explaining the impact of aging on political interest also requires removing the effects of contemporaneous influences that briefly lift or lower everyone's political interest. To accomplish this goal and not fall into the collinearity trap that makes it statistically impossible to assess age, period, and cohort effects all at once, I included direct measures of events instead of a set of year dummies. These measures of interestingness, introduced in Chapter 5, do account for some temporary ups and downs in political interest. The magnitude of these effects is small, but that was to be expected given the remarkably constant aggregate levels of political interest seen in Chapters 4 and 5.

Proximity of the interview to an election is one of the measures of interestingness. Many people would probably expect approaching elections to increase political interest in the population, at least temporarily. Campaigns raise the salience of politics in the news and in many social interactions, remind people of the opportunity to affect policy, and create curiosity about alternatives to the current government. The analysis in this chapter produces the odd bit of supporting evidence for this expectation. In Britain, the 2010 election – which, because of the timing of fieldwork in the old BHPS, is the only election that can be examined with the household panel – raised interest by about 4 points. This is a temporary boost, but at about a third of the average life-course increase in interest, its magnitude is noticeable. Among young people, it was more than twice as large, but disappeared again within a year.

In Germany, however, elections have smaller effects on political interest, as seen both here and in previous chapters. While interview timing of the GSOEP produced few data points within weeks of an election, the magnitude of the effect for those cases, about a point or two at most, is reminiscent of the small changes in general political interest ahead of the German elections of 2009 and 2013 observed in Chapter 4. In Switzerland, finally, elections depress political interest by a point or two, although this result should probably be attributed to the idiosyncratic Swiss political system with its frequent referenda and initiatives in times without elections. The conclusion that elections have small and fleeting effects is consistent with the aggregate patterns shown in Chapter 5. In a number of different time series (not limited to the household panels used in this chapter), it was often impossible to infer from the yearly political interest averages which years featured elections. This is true even for the 2010 British election because the duration of the 4-point increase is so short. Even allowing for the somewhat larger but equally transitory effects of elections on campaign-specific interest, it is difficult to see elections as the motivational spark that produces strong and lasting civic involvement.

Much of this book has so far summarized political interest by describing population averages. Over time, average political interest does not vary much. Over the life course, it initially increases before leveling off among young adults. But would we expect everyone to follow this trajectory? Only if every-one experienced the same set of causal influences in adolescence, which is implausible even for the most common influences. Almost all adolescents complete compulsory schooling, but there are different tracks to do so and after about age 16, some young people leave school. Almost all adolescents live with their parents for a while, but some parents separate and not all parents are interested in politics. Our expectation should be that the average relationship between aging and political interest we saw in this chapter averages over a good amount of variation in individual political interest trajectories. The observed averages are consistent with any number of individual-level patterns. None of the evidence presented so far rules out that some individuals develop an intense interest in politics as they get older, that others lose interest, or that people swing widely between high and low political interest. Quantifying this variation and characterizing individual-level interest trajectories is the goal of the next chapter.

Appendix to Chapter 6

Model 6.1, in the main text, derives from an age-period-cohort formulation of political interest:

$$PI_{it} = \pi^{AGE}_{it} + \pi^{BC}_i + \pi^S_i + \mu_t + \alpha_i + \varepsilon_{it} \qquad (A6.1)$$

To break up the collinearity between age, period, and cohort, the period effects μ_t are replaced in (6.1) by x^N_t, which contains several different measures of interestingness: closeness to the next election, time since the last election, recent national and global news events, recent announcement of economic growth, and recent stock market variation. The measures of news events, growth announcements, and stock market variation were introduced in Chapter 5. National and global news events are measured by *New York Times* coverage of the country and matching covers of news magazines, respectively. For each metric, three measures are included: the number of stories in the 14 days, 15–30 days, and 31–90 days before the interview. The natural log of the *New York Times* counts is used to reduce the weight for events that receive very large amounts of coverage.

Economic and stock market indicators are measured in the 14 days before the interview. Change in quarterly GDP is coded as a series of indicator variables (drop by more than 1 percent, drop by less than one percent, rise by less than one percent, and rise by more than 1 percent) if the information was released within 14 days of the interview. If no new growth data were released in this period, or if the growth rate did not differ from last quarter's, the measure is coded as zero and treated as the omitted baseline. An indicator variable is coded 1 if the quarterly growth data signaled the beginning of a recession (two quarters of declining GDP) and were released within 14 days before the interview. Stock market performance is also assessed over the 14 days before the interview and measured by the percent increase in the market over this period (set to zero if the market declined), the percent decrease (set to zero if the market increased), market volatility (the sum of squared daily changes), and the largest daily change (coded separately for positive and negative values). Temporal proximity of the interview to the most recent and the next election enters as a set of dummy variables for the following intervals: within 14 days, 15–30 days, 31–90 days, and 91–180 days before and after an election.

It is reasonable to treat interestingness as exogenous because interview date or refusals are unlikely to depend on the political environment as interview schedules are usually determined well ahead of time and the survey is predominantly not about politics. Correlations between the different measures of interestingness (or the same measures over different time periods) never exceed .5 and are usually much lower. In the BHPS, the measures of interestingness do not fully capture the decline in interest between 1992 and 1996 discussed in the previous chapter. Year dummies for that period are included because otherwise the aging trajectory degenerates.[10] Dummies are also added for the first two waves of the new USoc sample. The GSOEP model includes a dummy for the first panel wave of the East German sample in 1990 because their political interest level was so considerably higher than in the West in just that year (see Figure 5.5).

Applying the demeaning transformation to (6.1) yields

$$\ddot{P}I_{it} = \pi_{it}^{\ddot{A}GE} + X_t^{\ddot{N}} + \ddot{\varepsilon}_{it} \tag{A6.2}$$

The two dots above the variable denote the demeaning operator such that $\ddot{P}I_{it} = PI_{it} - \bar{PI}_i$, where $\bar{PI}_i$ is the mean of PI across all panel waves for individual i. Unlike (6.1), Equation A6.2 uses only within-subject variation to infer the age-interest relationship.

Figure OL6.1 in the Online Supplementary Material plots estimates of the age dummies for four different combinations of models and estimators. "OLS wo/ cohort" is generated by OLS estimation of (6.1) without π^{BC}_i in the model and without the ability to estimate α_i and ε_{it} separately. "RE wo/ cohort" is based on random-effects estimation of the same model. It estimates α_i, the constant level of political interest for each panelist (also known as a "unit effect,") but it does so based on a tenuous assumption about α_i, that the unit effects are uncorrelated with aging. This random effects assumption is violated when panelists of the same age who were born in different years differ systematically in their political interest and this cohort difference is not modeled. This is the case for the "RE wo/ cohort" estimates, so the age coefficients do not consistently estimate the effect of aging on political interest. More precisely, if π_{BCi} is omitted from (6.1), $E(\pi_{AGEit}, \pi_{BCi}) \neq 0$ violates the random effects

---

[10] The coefficients for the five year dummies included in the BHPS model for 1991 to 1995 are 4.6, 5.2, 4.0, 3.3, and 2.4. (Together, they account for .2 percent of within-person variance.)

assumption that $E(\pi_{AGEit}, \alpha_i) = 0$ because $E(\pi_{BCi}, \alpha_i) \neq 0$. OLS also yields biased aging estimates because $v_{it} = \alpha_i + \varepsilon_{it}$ correlates with π_{AGEit}.

"RE w/ cohort" comes from random-effects estimation of (6.1), which explicitly controls for cohort membership π^{BC}_i. "FE" is based on the fixed-effects estimator of (6.1) shown in (A6.2), which eliminates both α_i and π_{BC} through fixed-effects transformation, so a correlation between the two cannot bias estimates of aging effects. (Estimating (6.1) using the fixed effects estimator is equivalent to OLS estimates of (A6.2) with adjustments to standard errors.)

In each of the three datasets, the two solutions produce highly similar results, so the "FE" estimates appear almost exactly on top of the "RE w/ cohort" estimates. The similarity is not automatic. The random-effects model still requires the assumption that α_i is independent of π^{AGE}_{it}, conditional on the other independent variables in the model. With cohort membership controlled for, there are fewer theoretically plausible reasons why the assumption may not hold, but a violation would invalidate the interpretation of the results as the effect of aging on political interest. As α_i is not observed, the assumption cannot be tested directly. The fixed-effects estimates do not rely on this assumption (because α_i is eliminated by transformation rather than modeled). Both estimates fully control for cohort differences and isolate the impact of aging on political interest.

The predicted values plotted in Figure 6.3 are based on the "OLS wo/ cohorts," "RE wo/cohorts," and "FE" estimates shown in Figure OL6.1. Because estimates of the observation-specific residuals ε_{it}, are not removed, the predicted values still reflect idiosyncratic deviations from panelists' aging trajectories.

7

Stability and Variation in Political Interest

For the average Brit, German, and Swiss, political interest increases by 10–15 points on a 0–100 scale in adolescence and early adulthood before it becomes pretty much constant. That was a key result in Chapter 6. Of course, nobody has ever met the average Brit or the average German. They are conceptual simplifications to describe a population. Population averages can be informative: If you randomly met an adult from one of these countries (another useful simplification, as you would never actually meet anyone in truly random fashion), your best guess should be that her political interest rose by 10–15 points when she was in her teens and twenties and has since stopped increasing.

Now imagine randomly meeting thirty British people. Your best guess for each one of them would still be an early 10–15 point increase followed by little systematic change. But if each of these thirty Brits could accurately recall for you their annual political interest since they were teenagers, how many different trajectory shapes would you hear about? Maybe political interest developed exactly the same way for all thirty Brits, rising 10–15 points early, then leveling off – and so the shape of the average trajectory equals the individual trajectories. But an average trajectory of the same shape would also emerge if most of the thirty Brits maintained a constant level of political interest throughout their entire lives, while a handful of them saw their political interest rise very steeply in their youth before it flattened out. It is even possible to obtain the average trajectories we saw in Chapter 6 if some people experienced declines in political interest as they grew older. As long as their decreases are outweighed by more or steeper increases among other people, the average of these trajectories could be mildly increasing at first before later stabilizing. In short, the last chapter characterized the average population trajectories in Britain, Germany, and Switzerland very precisely – but told us nothing about the extent to which people differ in their political interest.

This chapter is about the variation in political interest trajectories. The distinction between average and variation is not particularly complicated, but it is easy to confuse the precision with which the average age trajectory is estimated and the extent to which the average age trajectory characterizes an individual member of the population. The household panels provide so much data that the precision of the average age trajectory is very high. The first half of this chapter examines how much individuals' trajectories deviate from this average.

The second half looks at individual-level change in political interest from a different perspective. How stable is political interest at the individual level? Instead of seeking to describe political interest trajectories over decades of people's lives, it asks to what extent someone who is politically interested today will still be interested next year or next decade. Chapter 5 demonstrated that aggregate political interest – the average level of interest in the population – has been nearly constant over several decades. Again, different individual patterns could underlie this population summary: Maybe most people retain whatever interest they have in politics over long periods of time, and so the country as a whole looks stable, too. Or people's interest bounces up and down wildly from year to year, but about the same number of people bounce up as bounce down, and so the country as a whole looks stable. I test the **Stabilization Hypothesis** that is derived from the psychological model of interest and predicts increasing stability with age. High individual-level stability would provide the final piece of evidence necessary to diagnose dispositional political interest.

The question of individual-level stability in political interest has important implications for the civic foundation of a country, the pattern of citizenship behavior motivated by political interest. If political interest varied a lot at the individual level from one moment to the next, it would serve as an unreliable, fickle foundation – but one that could perhaps be mobilized quickly in important times. If political interest instead changed little over people's lives, whatever foundation exists would be solid – but possibly quite difficult to extend by raising interest further.

Put together, the two elements of this chapter, variation in political interest trajectories and individual-level stability of interest, move us from describing populations to understanding the diverse sets of people that make up these populations.

BETWEEN-PERSON VARIATION IN POLITICAL INTEREST

The previous chapter already gave a hint that there is considerable between-person variation in political interest and that some citizens deviate considerably from the average age trajectory. The plot of political interest reports by age in Figure 6.2 (before any corrections for cohort differences and effects of interestingness) did show that, on average, political interest

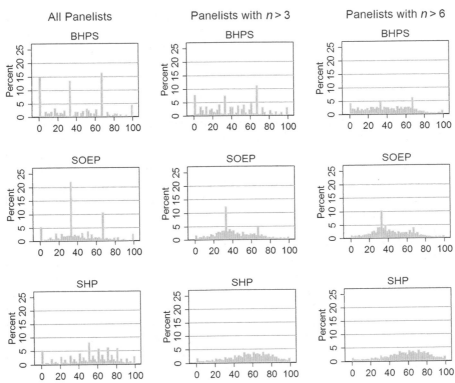

FIGURE 7.1 Political Interest Person Means
Note: Plots show distributions of political interest averaged by panelist (excluding the BHPS youth sample). *n* refers to the number of valid political interest reports per panelist.

increases as people become adults, but it also showed a good share of older respondents reporting no interest and some very young respondents already reporting the highest levels of political interest.

Another quick way to illustrate variation in political interest between different people is to plot panelists' mean interest over all reports they gave as panel members. As Figure 7.1 shows, some people never once indicated any political interest in their multiple interviews. Others consistently reported maximum interest. The figure presents person means for three sets: all eligible panelists (left column), panelists who reported their interest on at least four different occasions (center column), and panelists with at least seven interest reports (right column). Even among panelists who gave more than a half dozen interest reports, some have means of 0 or 100. Means in the left-hand plots naturally cluster around the values of the underlying response scales because panelists who contribute only one response have means at those values. Excluding panelists with few observations yields a smoother distribution of means, but hardly affects the spread of the means across the scale range. There is *a lot* of variation in political interest.[1]

INDIVIDUAL POLITICAL INTEREST TRAJECTORIES

Mean levels of political interest for an individual are useful to show the large between-person variation, but the mean glosses over too much within-person change to be an appropriate summary of many individuals' interest trajectories. Figure 7.2 illustrates this point by plotting the political interest reports given by 24 panelists (12 each from the SHP and the GSOEP) during their participation on the panel. The cases were randomly selected from all panelists who answered the political interest question at least four times.

Even just these few cases make clear that there are quite a number of different political interest trajectories. In order to say anything more about this variety, it is necessary to summarize each trajectory – more succinctly than by plotting every data point for tens of thousands of panelists, but not as succinctly as just calculating each panelist's mean political interest. A time (or age) polynomial is a convenient option. Figure 7.2 fits a quartic polynomial to each panelist's responses. For most panelists, the repeated political interest reports – up to 29 data points – are fairly well summarized as a function of age by a small

---

[1]   In the German SOEP, the mean of the person means – the average level of political interest among citizens in the sample, unweighted by the number of measurement occasions, n – is 42.9 across all panelists ($N = 39{,}019$), 43.1 across panelists with $n > 3$ ($N = 23{,}768$), and 43.8 across panelists with $n > 6$ ($N = 19{,}001$). In the BHPS adult sample, the respective means are 41.5 ($N = 62{,}546$), 43.3 ($N = 37{,}556$), and 42.4 ($N = 11{,}630$). Only in the Swiss data is the difference slightly greater with means of 53.1 ($N = 18{,}696$), 55.2 ($N = 9{,}311$), and 57.0 ($N = 6{,}710$). Especially in the GSOEP and the BHPS, the similarity in means across different subsets of panelists is remarkable and underlines that panel effects are a minor concern in these data. (The person mean is conceptually similar to estimates of α_i in (6.1), but does not remove variance explained by other variables in the model.)

One way to quantify the variation in political interest means plotted in Figure 7.1 is through the between-person standard deviation. It is 22 in the GSOEP, 27 in the BHPS, and 24 in the SHP. (These are values for panelists with $n > 3$.) This confirms what we see in the graphs: The person mean plus/minus twice the between-person standard deviation takes up pretty much the full range of the 0–100 political interest scale.

Figure 7.1 averages across a different type of variation: variation around each panelist's mean. This within-person variation is smaller than between-person variation in all three countries. Within-person standard deviations depend little on n and are 16 in the GSOEP, 17 in the BHPS, and 13 in the SHP. As a fraction of the overall variance in political interest, the within-person component is .34 in the GSOEP, .29 in the BHPS, and .22 in the SHP. While people's political interest means take up the full 0–100 range, the repeated political interest reports from the same individual typically do not, even with measurement error still part of the estimates.

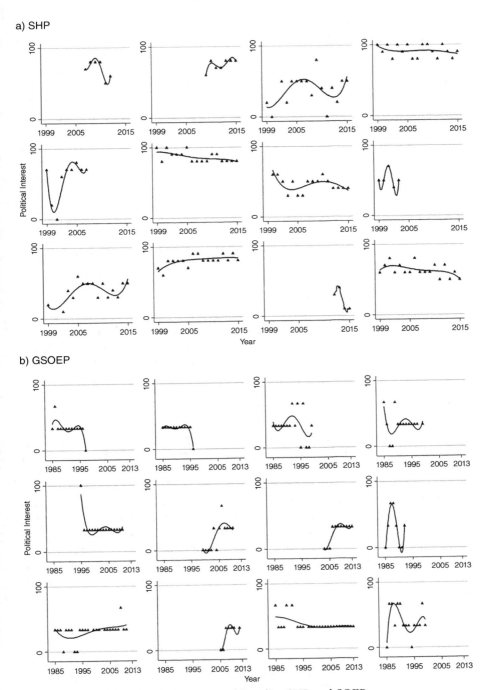

FIGURE 7.2 Political Interest by Year and Panelist, SHP and SOEP

Note: The triangles show political interest responses by 12 panelists randomly selected from all panelists in the SHP and GSOEP, respectively, who answered the political interest question at least four times. The lines show quartic time trends fit to each panelist's responses.

number of parameters – five for a quartic polynomial. The advantage of summarizing each panelist's political interest trajectory with a few parameters is parsimony. This permits the analysis to focus on explaining differences between these parameters rather than each interest observation. The trajectory parameters can essentially become dependent variables.

But why a quartic polynomial? A cubic trend would be even more parsimonious; a quintic polynomial would summarize trajectories more accurately.[2] It is tempting to make this decision based on the average age trajectories shown in Chapter 5, which suggested perhaps a cubic relationship between age and interest. But the functional form of the population trajectory does not tell us about the functional form of individual trajectories. Instead, to gauge what order of a time polynomial provides a suitable summary of most panelists' political interest trajectories, I regressed each panelists' interest reports on six different polynomials, ranging from zero-order (constant only) to fifth-order (quintic). Panelists with at least two observations are included. Figure 7.3 summarizes the fit of these OLS regressions by plotting their R^2 averaged across panelists. (Panelists who report the same interest level in every wave are assigned an R^2 of 1.) The results are very similar across the three datasets.

Not surprisingly, linear trends explain a lot more of the variance in political interest than only a constant, but quadratic trends do considerably better yet. A cubic polynomial adds another 10 percentage points to the average explained variance, but the additional explanatory power declines with every order of the polynomial. A cubic or quartic polynomial suggests a reasonable compromise between accuracy and parsimony, explaining around three quarters of the variance in the average panelist's political interest responses with four or five parameters.

The parameters – the coefficients on the age terms for each individual panelist, one regression at a time – could become dependent variables in a new model to explain who has, say, already high political interest at a young age (a large intercept) and whose trajectory is particularly steep early on (a large coefficient on the linear age term). The following analysis performs essentially this task, but to run separate regressions is not an efficient way to do so. The OLS estimates of the growth parameters from individual regressions are very noisy and ignore the fact that some OLS estimates are more precise than others (because estimates are based on different numbers of observations, because observations are differently spaced, and because a given age polynomial fits

---

[2] It is possible that trajectories would in fact be more accurately characterized by another functional form. This limitation is less critical than it might sound because deviations from a parameterized age trajectory can be modeled by adding explanatory variables. The parameters of the age trajectory only need to capture the trajectory conditional on other components of the model.

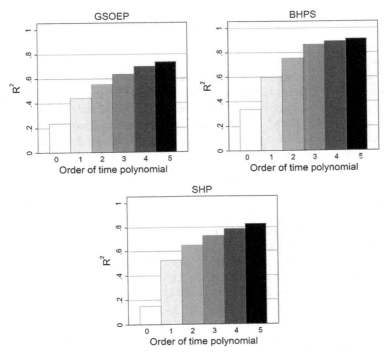

FIGURE 7.3 Mean R^2 across Panelists Accounted for by Time Polynomials

some panelists better than others.) A multilevel model offers a more efficient approach that can also easily account for cohort, period, and panel effects.

GROWTH CURVE MODELS OF POLITICAL INTEREST

Instead of estimating a trajectory for each panelist separately and then averaging across these estimates, growth curve analysis estimates the average trajectories across all panelists and then models the variance around this average (see, e.g., Bollen and Curran 2006; Preacher et al. 2008; Singer and Willett 2003; Weiss 2005; for an early political science application, see Plutzer 2002). Growth curve analysis treats panel studies as multilevel data with measurement occasions nested within panel respondents. It takes into account the dependence of observations from the same respondent by modeling the covariance structure. This section describes the logic of the growth curve model. A more detailed explanation appears in the appendix to this chapter.

Starting with the formal representation of the growth curve model is instructive because it highlights the close similarity to the model in Chapter 6. Replacing the age dummies in (6.1) with a quartic age trajectory and renaming α_i as b_{0i} yields

$$PI_{it} = b_{0i} + b_{1i}AGE_{it} + b_{2i}AGE_{it}^2 + b_{3i}AGE_{it}^3 + b_{4i}AGE_{it}^4 + x_t^N + \pi_i^{BC} + \pi_i^S + \varepsilon_{it}$$

$$(7.1)$$

The main difference between this model and (6.1) is that the age coefficients have *i* subscripts to indicate that they vary across individuals. Model 6.1 did this only for the intercept (allowing each panelist to have his or her own one, α_i). In (7.1), each component of the quartic age trajectory may be different across individuals. Each measurement of political interest is modeled as a combination of structural parameters estimating average age trajectories and person-specific deviations from these averages. The parameters of the age trajectory $b_{\cdot i}$ are the sum of two components, the average of each growth component across panelists and individual deviation from this average. The purpose of the average growth parameters (referred to as $\gamma_{\cdot 0}$ in the appendix) is to do the same thing as the coefficients for the age dummies in Chapter 6: characterize how aging relates to political interest averaged across the entire population. The individual deviation from this average (labeled $\zeta_{\cdot i}$) is new. It aims to summarize how people differ from each other. For example, the linear component of the age trajectory is $b_{1i} = \gamma_{10} + \zeta_{1i}$. It gauges the slope of the age trajectory at age 16 (because I center age on that value), which is steeper for some people than others.

Because they capture variation in the population (between panelists), $\zeta_{\cdot i}$. are variance parameters. These variances could easily be correlated: Individuals with high starting levels of political interest in adolescence (positive deviations from the mean starting level in the population) might increase less steeply later (negative deviations from the mean linear or higher-order growth components). In this case, the covariance between the intercept estimates and the estimates of (some) higher-order growth components would be negative. The model accommodates this possibility by freely estimating these covariances.

Table 7.1 presents the estimates of the quartic growth curve model in Equation A7.1 for each of the three datasets. Age is centered on 16, the first age covered by all three studies. The coefficients for the trajectory components are all highly statistically significant and very similar across countries. It is easier to understand the shape of the estimated trajectory by examining the predicted values plotted in Figure 7.4. The graphs show the quartic age trajectory predicted by the model and a non-parametric summary of the data (repeating the lightest lines in Figure 6.3). Both lines are drawn with 95-percent confidence bounds around them. The close overlap of raw data and model prediction indicates that the five growth parameters used to model the average age trajectory capture the underlying data quite well.[3] In the Swiss data, the

---

[3] For comparison, Figure OL7.1 in the Online Supplementary Materials shows predicted values from a cubic growth curve model. The cubic model understates the steepness of the initial growth in interest, especially in the Swiss data, so the one additional parameter required for a quartic

TABLE 7.1 *Quartic Age Trajectories of Political Interest*

		Britain (BHPS)	Germany (GSOEP)	Switzerland (SHP)
Intercept	γ_{00}	31.4 (1.0)	30.5 (.9)	49.3 (1.4)
(Age − 16)	γ_{10}	1.28 (.06)	1.36 (.04)	1.19 (.06)
(Age − 16)^2	γ_{20}	−.062 (.003)	−.069 (.003)	−.061 (.004)
(Age − 16)^3	γ_{30}	.0012 (.0001)	.0014 (.0001)	.0012 (.0001)
(Age − 16)^4	γ_{30}	−.000008 (.000001)	−.000010 (.000001)	−.000008 (.000001)
Birth year				
(1960 omitted)	π^{BC}_i	included	included	included
Sample	π^{S}_i	included	included	included
Interestingness	x^{N}_t	included	included	included
Variance Components (as standard deviations				
and correlations)				
intercept	ψ_{00}	28.7 (.2)	24.5 (.2)	28.1 (.3)
linear term	ψ_{11}	.58 (.01)	.59 (.01)	.66 (.01)
r(intercept, linear)	ψ_{01}	−.54 (.01)	−.60 (.01)	−.62 (.01)
within-person	σ	17.6 (.03)	15.7 (.02)	13.1 (.03)
Log Likelihood		−1423517	−1461541	−467433
No. of observations		315,025	337,557	110,373
No. of panelists		63,470	39,005	18,690

Note: Models estimated by full maximum likelihood. Cell entries for fixed effects are coefficients with standard errors in parentheses. BHPS uses adult sample only. GSOEP also includes indicator variables for whether interview day is available and whether a written questionnaire was used.

quartic trajectory understates the steepness of the rise before age 18 and the sudden leveling off that follows. The largest difference occurs at age 18, when the non-parametric estimates show a year-to-year increase of 3.5 points, compared to 2.2 points in the two years prior and 1.0 implied by the quartic trajectory. It may not be coincidence that this jump occurs just before Swiss citizens become eligible to vote at age eighteen and begin to receive frequent government information about referenda and initiatives.

The similarity of the variance components across datasets is also remarkable. (The Chapter Appendix explains why some variance components are not estimated.) In all countries, the standard deviation of the intercept is about a quarter of the full range of the interest scale, indicating that starting levels of political interest anywhere between 0 and 100 are not uncommon. The standard deviation of the linear component is consistently around .6 with coefficients of 1.2–1.4, so very few people are estimated to have negative linear growth

model seems justified. Dee (2004) and Milligan et al. (2004) use quartic polynomials to control for age. The Online Supplementary Materials also provide results for the joint youth-adult sample of BHPS.

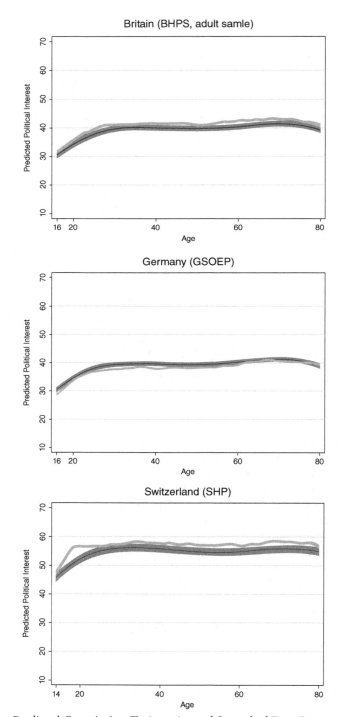

FIGURE 7.4 Predicted Quartic Age Trajectories and Smoothed Raw Data
Note: Graphs show predicted values based on Table 7.1 with 95-percent confidence intervals. Grey band shows adjusted locally mean-smoothed political interest scores (the lightest lines in Figure 6.3).

components. Importantly, these two components of the growth trajectory are not independent of each other. In all three panel studies, respondents with high starting levels of political interest tend to have lower linear growth components, as indicated by the negative correlations of around .6 between the two random effects.

To illustrate the substantive implication of the variance estimates, Figure 7.5 plots thirty political interest trajectories as they are predicted based on the model in Table 7.1. This is the statistical equivalent of randomly meeting thirty Brits, Germans, and Swiss. They are generated by drawing values from the joint distribution of intercepts and linear components and then calculating predicted values using these deviations as well as the population average trajectory. The thick black line is the population average (the same line that already appeared in Figure 7.4.)

There is considerable variation in age trajectories of political interest. Political interest at age 16 varies widely. Most trajectories have a gentle upward slope, but there are also some steep increases and a good number of trajectories that drop with age. The negative covariance of intercept and linear term is evident here in the tendency of trajectories with lower starting levels of interest to increase at a higher rate.

The point of Figure 7.5 is to provide an intuition for the variety of trajectory shapes that can appear in the population, not to characterize any individual's political interest. The example trajectories are based on data and model. Without using the model, it would not be possible to draw trajectories covering the entire age range: No panelist provided data over 60 years, so the model is used to extrapolate the trajectories. Even with a correct model, the statistical uncertainty around the individual trajectories, which is not shown in the graph, would be substantial. But Figure 7.5 is helpful in visualizing the difference between the average trajectory and variation in this trajectory in the population. Individuals clearly do not all develop political interest at the same age or to the same extent. But some types of political interest trajectories are more common than others: More of them exhibit change early in life than late. Gentle growth is more common than either steep growth or gentle decline. (As a different way to visualize variation in growth trajectories, Appendix Figure A7.1 plots confidence bands around the average trajectories derived from the estimated variance components.)

INDIVIDUAL-STABILITY OF POLITICAL INTEREST

Whether "politics" is interesting is difficult to know without a good idea of what "politics" is. Experience with politics is bound to increase with age, but an evolving understanding and new encounters with politics may still change assessments of politics more frequently at young ages. As they get older, the store of political experiences grows for many people and situational interest in

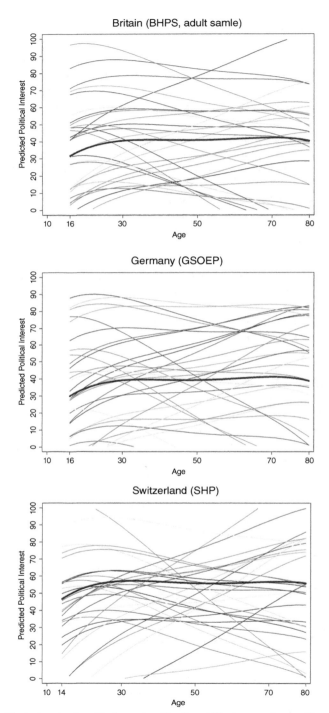

FIGURE 7.5 Variation in Age Trajectories (Predicted Trajectory for 30 Randomly Chosen Individuals)

Note: Graphs show predicted age trajectories for thirty randomly chosen panelists based on Table 7.1 as well as the predicted population trajectory (thick black line).

politics may develop into more enduring dispositional interest, so additional experiences may carry less weight.

The first half of this chapter demonstrated that "the average" person develops interest in politics during adolescence and then maintains a fairly unchanging level for much of life. This pattern, so consistent across the three countries, suggests lower stability of interest – and perhaps less certainty about "politics" – early in life. Conceptually, growth of political interest is distinct from stability, however. Essentially horizontal interest trajectories among adults only show the absence of an average long-term trend, not the absence of temporary ups and downs around the flat trajectory.

Research on the stability of political attitudes has focused mostly on attitudes toward politically contested objects, such as parties, policies, and candidates.[4] These studies do not provide much guidance for understanding stability of political interest. Low stability of political evaluations does not preclude a stable habit of political involvement, as Merelman and King (1986, 479, 476) point out. Instead, "early learning [may produce] a lasting proclivity toward activism, coupled with strong motives to search the environment flexibly and imaginatively for a satisfying political stance." In this "sensitization model," young people become involved and experienced in politics early "while keeping the direction of their political allegiances and the content of their political belief systems open." It is a useful way to think about changing political stances among politically interested individuals, but it does not offer much help in understanding whether and why political interest might wax and wane.

Research on stability of political evaluations does supply useful typologies with respect to timing of change. Scholars distinguish a persistence model according to which only early experiences influence attitudes from a "lifelong openness" model which emphasizes change throughout people's lives as they continue to update their attitudes (e.g., Sears 1983; Alwin 1994; Sears and Funk 1999; see also Merelman and King 1986). Other model trajectories are mixtures of these two types, specifying the varying probability of attitude change over the course of a lifetime (Sears 1983; Alwin 1994, 142–5). According to one of them, the "impressionable years" model, early experiences matter disproportionately and attitudes stabilize in early adulthood.

---

[4] The vast majority of empirical studies, at least in the United States, has focused on stability of party identification, concluding that many people identify with the same party for years and even decades (e.g., Jennings and Markus 1984; Sears and Funk 1999; Green et al. 2002). Many other political attitudes, including issue positions, group evaluations, and ideology are also very stable, at least in adulthood (Alwin and Krosnick 1991; Alwin 1994; Ansolabehere et al. 2008). Issue positions appear to be quite stable over shorter campaign periods with strong information flow as well. Candidate evaluations, on the other hand, can change considerably during a campaign (Feldman 1989).

Sears (1983, 94–102) explains different levels of stability as a function of the attitude object. High stability would emerge when the attitude object is salient, receives frequent public attention, and has constant meaning over time. Among adults, the attitude object "politics" probably has the first two attributes. (Politics can be a salient concept even to people who rarely think about, or participate in, politics.) Sears (1983, 102) suggests that the meaning of politics is too complex, contested, and subjective to induce persistent evaluations. But high stability might still emerge if individuals tend to maintain their definitions of politics, even if these definitions vary widely between individuals. Like the psychological model of interest, the "impressionable years" pattern also predicts support for the Stabilization Hypothesis because politics is not salient from birth or its meaning self-evident to children. Gradually, stability in political interest should increase and become very high in adulthood unless the political system undergoes extraordinary change. When the impressionable years end is an empirical question.

The straight-up persistence model without much early malleability is another theoretical possibility. Personality traits and some elements of people's identity exhibit high stability starting in childhood (e.g, Roberts and DelVecchio 2000; Caspi et al. 2005, 466–7). Although the increase in average interest levels during adolescence is inconsistent with a strict persistence view, it is worth remembering that the magnitude of this increase, 10–15 points on a 0–100 scale, was modest.

Finally, if Sears (1983, 102) is right that politics is so complex and contested as to thwart persistent evaluations and that new information about, and changing interpretations of, politics modify people's evaluations of its appeal, political interest may not stabilize even after the impressionable years. As Sapiro (1994, 203) notes, people may be "impressionable" at other points in their lives. The empirically demonstrated absence of aggregate change among adults does not imply absence of individual change, so the alternative of "lifelong openness" remains in the running.

To test the Stabilization Hypothesis and adjudicate between the lifelong openness, impressionable years, and persistence models, this section gauges the stability of political interest by examining its correlation over time. Using correlations implies a relative definition of stability. To what extent is the ordering of less to more interested individuals preserved over time? A high correlation and a constant ordering (relative stability) could emerge even if everyone became more interested by a similar amount (absolute change). Yet, in the case of political interest, we already know that aggregate interest in the population is almost constant, so high relative stability would also indicate high absolute stability. (An alternative operationalization takes stability to be the pace with which interest returns to its long-run equilibrium after it unexpectedly changed. In Prior (2010), I provide a detailed exposition of this approach. It also emerges naturally in Part III of this book. Both analyses confirm that perturbations of political interest among adults dissipate very quickly.)

In Prior (2010), I reported stability estimates for a large number of datasets, including then available waves of the three household panels. Analyses corrected for measurement error and allowed the error to have unequal variance and be correlated over time. The models generated relative stability estimates of .978 on a year-to-year basis, very high (but not complete) stability. This result is strong evidence against the widespread operation of "lifelong openness" when it comes to political interest. In the same analysis, I found almost the same level of stability among the youngest panel members, but the split into two age groups was somewhat clunky. The oldest "young people" were already 29 at the beginning of the panel, and I reported average stability over a half dozen or more annual waves. This approach may have missed lower stability limited to the very youngest panelists. (The analysis did not include the BHPS youth interviews.)

For a more precise description of how political interest varies with age, Figure 7.6 plots stability over two years as a function of age. For a given age, both graphs show the correlation between interest reports by panelists at that age and reports by the same respondents two years later. The top graph plots Pearson correlations. The bottom graph applies Wiley and Wiley's (1970) correction for random measurement error to account for attenuation in the observed correlations. For each dataset, a line through the individual estimates provides a mildly smoothed summary of the age trend in stability. The BHPS data include the youth interviews, so the first three correlations are between two 3-point scales. Starting at age 16, the correlations are entirely between the 4-point interest reports recorded in adult interviews. Including the youth interviews in Figure 7.6 is important enough to tolerate this measurement transition because stability turns out to increase rapidly in people's teens.

Juxtaposing the corrected and uncorrected sets of correlations nicely illustrates the general value of adjusting for measurement error. According to the uncorrected correlations in the top graph, political interest is more stable in Switzerland than in Germany and Britain. This is an artifact of the difference in response scales: The 4-point scales used by the GSOEP and the BHPS generate more measurement error than the more nuanced 11-point scale in the SHP. With corrections for random error, the country differences disappear. Among adults, stability is about .95 in all three datasets, very similar to the average I obtained in Prior (2010) when transformed to the one-year interval. With or without correction for measurement error, political interest becomes more stable with age in all three countries. In the Swiss panel, error-corrected two-year stability rises from .6 at age 14 to around .9 in people's twenties. The British data reveal an even steeper increase because stability at age 11 is only about .5. Regardless of the change in response scale, the rapid firming of political interest is supported by the British data because it is evident for the first three estimates that rely only on youth interviews and for estimates starting at age 16 that use only adult

a) Pearson Correlation

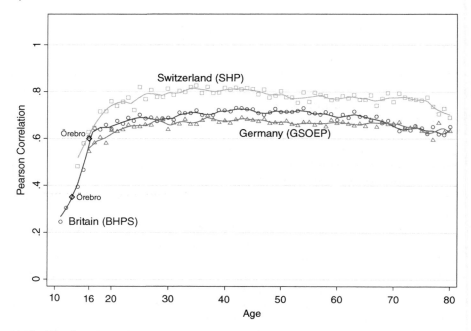

b) Stability Correlation Corrected for Random Measurement Error

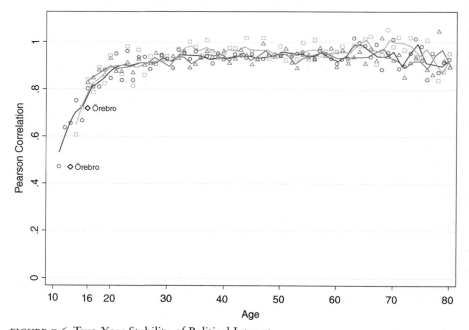

FIGURE 7.6 Two-Year Stability of Political Interest

Note: Markers are correlations between political interest at current age and political interest two years later. The top graph plots Pearson correlations; the bottom graph applies Wiley and Wiley's (1970) correction for random measurement error. Lines apply mean smoothing. "Örebro" indicates estimates by Russo and Stattin (2016) for a local Swedish population.

interviews. The German SOEP misses most of the rise in stability because it begins interviewing only at age 16. For available age ranges, the three household panels yield very similar estimates of stability by age. As further confirmation, the graph includes identically calculated stability estimates from a recent study of Swedish youths (Russo and Stattin 2016). Corrected two-year stability rises from .47 at age 13 to .72 at age 16 – matching the magnitude of the increase observed in Britain and Switzerland almost exactly.

The Youth-Parent Socialization Panel Study (Jennings et al. 2004) provides a somewhat less precise comparison with the United States. The study started with a sample of students who were in high school in 1965, so it is not representative of the entire U.S. population and covers a period that precedes the earliest household panel by two decades. It did reinterview the original sample three times (last in 1997) and included the ANES *Follow Public Affairs* question (see Chapter 3) in every wave, making it possible to assess stability over long time spans. The Pearson correlation between political interest in Wave 1 (at age 18) and Wave 2 (at age 26) is .32 (Jennings and Niemi 1981; Shani 2009b, 73). It increases to .42 for the next pair of waves (between ages 26 and 35) and finally to .51 (between ages 35 and 50). Transformed to the two-year interval (for comparison with Figure 7.6), these correlations are .75, .82, and .91. Using the correction for measurement error provided by Shani (2009b, 73), the equivalent two-year estimates are .966, .974, and .993. According to all of these calculations, stability of political interest increases with age even though the eligibility age of 18 misses the period of greatest instability. The extent of stability is even slightly greater than for comparable ages in Figure 7.6, perhaps because the Jennings sample excludes high-school dropouts or because coming of age in 1960s' America was especially formative.

All told, five different panel studies support the Stabilization Hypothesis: Stability of political interest increases with age. Disattenuated stability correlations of .5 and lower for panelists in their early teens indicate a considerable amount of updating and change. Yet, the window for change closes quickly (if not completely). Stability of political interest over two years approaches .9 by age 20 and about .95 in people's early thirties.

Although stabilization of political interest typically has already occurred among teenagers, extraordinary events have the potential to delay it. Further analysis shows that in the years after reunification (1990–4), individual-level stability was lower for the GSOEP sample of East German residents recruited in 1990. This East-West difference has a strong age gradient. Among panelists under 20 years of age, East Germans have disattenuated stability correlations of .60, much lower than the .89 among other panelists of the same age in the same period. The East-West difference is already much lower among 20- to 24-year-olds (.10) and not evident at all among people over 55.

CONCLUSION

Variation in political interest is immense as far as differences between people are concerned, but much lower when it comes to differences within the same people over time. This chapter has examined variation from two perspectives: How similar are different people's political interest trajectories? (Not very similar.) And how strongly is a person's political interest today related to her political interest next year? (Very strongly.)

One main qualification to this summary is of considerable importance for the rest of this book: There is a time early in life – from the first appraisals of politics in childhood through adolescence and into early adulthood – when political interest is still malleable. Especially among teenagers, political interest is not yet stable. Stability rises rapidly as people approach their twenties, and in their early thirties, most of them have conclusively decided how interesting they find politics. This pattern is a textbook example of the "impressionable years" model of socialization that expects significant change but concentrated early in life. It advises against thinking of political interest as akin to a personality trait because personality stabilizes sooner, typically in childhood (e.g, Roberts and DelVecchio 2000; Caspi et al. 2005, 466–7). The "impressionable years" character of political interest development provides a very helpful clue for the search for causes of political interest in Part III of this book: focus on young people and the most common ways for them to encounter politics.

But as crucial as adolescence looks to be for the development of political interest, it would be premature to drop older adults entirely from the analysis. This is where averaging over all political interest trajectories in the population particularly hurts intuition. It is true that the average age trajectory flattens out after about age 30 and political interest becomes very stable. For the large majority of adults, political interest is essentially constant. That does not mean, however, that *all* adults retain their level of interest. The growth curve model shows that positively or negatively sloped trajectories occasionally occur even in adulthood. And the estimated annual stability of .978 for adults (Prior 2010) implies stability of .8 over ten years and .57 over twenty-five years – even small yearly deviations from perfect stability compound to produce some change over longer periods. Although the results in this chapter clearly indicate that widespread change of political interest among adults is exceedingly unlikely, they are consistent with isolated change in small subpopulations. Hence, it still bears asking what happens to the political interest of those few adults who join a political organization or have a spouse who, against the odds, does become more interested. Both of these are rare events, and the results in this chapter leave room for rare events to affect political interest, even among adults.

It is a mark of politically interested people to be interested even when the environment is relatively uneventful. Commenting on the high stability of many other political predispositions among adults, Sears (1983, 94) cautioned that "whether this obtained persistence is due to the intrinsic psychological strength of early-learned attitudes or to a waning level of discrepant communication in one's proximal environments as one ages is more arguable." In the case of political interest, the strength of an existing, oft-confirmed predisposition appears to be the more important factor in explaining stability. Close elections, financial crises, and other political and economic events probably produce "discrepant communication" salient enough to remind even less interested people that politics is out there. Yet, as earlier chapters have shown, September 11, 2001, the election of Tony Blair, the end of the Kohl era, and the adoption of the Euro are only some examples of salient events that caused hardly any change in political interest. Political interest is stable for most adults not because they are never prompted to reconsider their appraisal, but because they stick with their existing judgment in the face of salient events.

This chapter has demonstrated considerable variation in political interest trajectories. Averaged over the entire population, political interest rises only in adolescence and young adulthood. But there are plenty of individuals who do not develop political interest at that age or lose it. Other people exhibit much steeper interest growth than the population average. And yet others are already quite interested at a young age and often retain this interest as adults. The next chapter examines if this variation is associated with known characteristics of individuals. Who are the people with steeper-than-average growth of political interest in adolescence? Who starts out strongly interested in childhood already? Answering these questions is still mostly descriptive, but identifying types of people with distinct political interest trajectories promises help in focusing the search for causes of interest in Part III of the book.

Appendix to Chapter 7

SPECIFICATION AND ESTIMATION DETAILS FOR MODEL 7.1

The full growth curve model with variance components in square brackets is

$$PI_{it} = \gamma_{00} + \gamma_{10}AGE_{it} + \gamma_{20}AGE_{it}^2 + \gamma_{30}AGE_{it}^3 + \gamma_{40}AGE_{it}^4 + x^N_t$$
$$+ \pi^{BC}_i + \pi^S_i + \left[\zeta_{oi} + \zeta_{1i}AGE_{it} + \zeta_{2i}AGE_{it}^2 + \zeta_{3i}AGE_{it}^3 + \zeta_{4i}AGE_{it}^4 + \varepsilon_{it} \right]$$

$$(A7.1)$$

The $b_{\cdot i}$ terms in (7.1) are assumed to be normal variables whose mean $\gamma_{\cdot o}$ and variance $\zeta_{\cdot i}$ can be estimated. The ζ_{1i}'s are assumed to be independent across subjects and distributed multivariate normal with means of zero and covariance matrix ψ. The diagonal elements of ψ are the variances of the random effects (e.g., ζ_{oi} has a mean of zero and variance ψ_{oo}). The off-diagonal elements of ψ indicate the covariances between different random effects. For example, ψ_{o1} represents the relationship between the random intercept ζ_{oi} and the linear component of the growth trajectory ζ_{1i}. ε_{ij} is the error component at the observation level, i.e., the variance not explained by average trajectories, person-specific trajectory deviations, and other variables in the model. The simplest assumption is to treat it as following a normal distribution with mean zero and variance σ^2, but this assumption can be relaxed to accommodate serial error correlation. ψ and ε are assumed to be independent of each other.

In (A7.1), the control variables affect the intercept ($b_{oi} = \gamma_{00} + x^N_t + \pi^{BC}_i + \pi^S_i + \zeta_{oi}$), but not higher-order growth parameters. It is straightforward to allow sample or cohort differences in higher-order growth parameters as well and assess the improvement in model fit to detect significant panel and cohort effects.

Equation A7.1 bears close resemblance to the random effects estimator of model 6.1. Whereas (6.1) includes a series of age dummies, (A7.1) uses a quartic polynomial in age. While only the intercept is allowed to vary across panelists in (6.1), (A7.1) allows all trajectory components to vary. Switching to a quartic age function in (6.1) and dropping the variance components ζ_{1i} AGE$_{it}$, ζ_{2i} AGE$_{it}^2$, ζ_{3i} AGE$_{it}^3$ and ζ_{4i} AGE$_{it}^4$ in (A7.1) makes the two models identical, with $\zeta_{0i} = \alpha_i$ (see Halaby 2003).

The terms in square brackets in (A7.1) are the different stochastic components of the model, sometimes also referred to as the composite residual. The terms ζ_{1i} AGE$_{it}$, ζ_{2i} AGE$_{it}^2$, ζ_{3i} AGE$_{it}^3$, and ζ_{4i} AGE$_{it}^4$ allow the composite residual to vary across measurement occasions by making it a function of age and across individuals by treating $\zeta_{.i}$ as a distribution. This way, the composite residual accommodates autocorrelation and heteroscedasticity even when the error term ε_{ij} is assumed to be independent across time. Each element of the marginal covariance matrix of the repeated measures of PI$_{it}$ is the sum of the covariance implied by the random effects ψ and the covariance implied by the error term ε_{ij}:

$$V = \text{Cov}(Z_i\zeta_i) + \text{Cov}(\varepsilon_i) = Z_i\psi Z_i' + \sigma^2\Omega_i \qquad (A7.2)$$

Equation A7.2 shows the induced covariance structure of the model in A7.1. The first component captures deviations from the population trajectory that can be different for each panelist. The second component allows for error dependence at the level of the observation that is the same for all panelists. The covariance structure thus explicitly separates between-subject and within-subject variation in PI$_{it}$. Z_i is the design matrix for the random effects, in this case composed of five columns for intercept, AGE$_{it}$, AGE$_{it}^2$, AGE$_{it}^3$, and AGE$_{it}^4$. Ω is the autocorrelation matrix for the observation-level errors. When ε is assumed to be uncorrelated over time, Ω simplifies to the identity matrix. The assumption that the individual errors ε_{ij} are conditionally independent implies that the random effects for the growth components are sufficient to model the autocorrelation in the data. This could be unrealistic if the political interest questions induce the same kind of measurement error in consecutive panel waves, so it is prudent to verify the conditional independence assumption.

Growth curve models are estimated in two (iterated) steps using maximum likelihood estimation. First, the structural (or fixed) part of the model is estimated for the entire sample (not panelist-by-panelist, as in the individual regression approach.) Second, the residuals are used to estimate the stochastic (or random) part of the model. Hedeker and Gibbons (2006, 129) note that different combinations of between- and within-person variance components often fit the data about equally well and "typically" do not "greatly" affect the fixed (population average) estimates. They and others recommend first including all covariates, then testing variance specifications. One of the advantages of growth curve models is that panelists with missing data for some waves can still be included in the analysis. As in Chapter 6, responses from the oldest 1 percent of respondents are excluded because coverage is very thin.

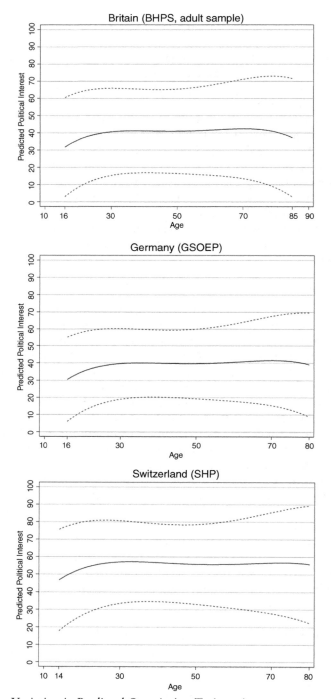

FIGURE A7.1 Variation in Predicted Quartic Age Trajectories
Note: The solid line in each graph shows the predicted quartic population age trajectory. Dashed lines mark the area that is expected to contain about 68 percent of the quartic age trajectories (one standard deviation above and below the mean trajectory).

Estimates of the variance components appear in the bottom half of Table 7.1 (expressed, for convenience, as standard deviations and correlations). Only three of them, for the intercept, the linear term, and the covariance between them, are included because most variances of the higher-order terms are not statistically significant or are so small that standard errors cannot be estimated. Even the few statistically significant variances are tiny. The variance for the quadratic term of 2.0×10^{-16} in the BHPS and 1.8×10^{-19} in the GSOEP are distinguishable from zero, but two standard deviations equal only .00000002 and .00000001, respectively, around coefficient estimates of −.062 and −.069. For all practical purposes, the higher-order variances can be treated as zero.

GRAPHING RANDOM EFFECTS

Like Figure 7.5 in the text, Figure A7.1 graphically illustrates the variation in age trajectories. It marks the area that is expected to contain 68 percent of the age trajectories (see Rabe-Hesketh and Skrondal 2008, 219–20). The between-subject variation around the mean age trajectory is derived from the estimated variance of the random effects:

$$\mathrm{var}\left[\zeta_{0i} + \zeta_{1i}\mathrm{AGE} + \zeta_{2i}\mathrm{AGE}^2 + \zeta_{3i}\mathrm{AGE}^3 + \zeta_{4i}\mathrm{AGE}^4\right] =$$
$$\mathrm{var}[\zeta_{0i}] + 2\,\mathrm{cov}[\zeta_{0i}, \zeta_{1i}\mathrm{AGE}] + \mathrm{var}\left[\zeta_{1i}\mathrm{AGE}\right] + \mathrm{var}[\zeta_{2i}\mathrm{AGE}^2] + \mathrm{var}\left[\zeta_{3i}\mathrm{AGE}^3\right]$$
$$+\mathrm{var}\left[\zeta_{4i}\mathrm{AGE}^4\right] =$$
$$\psi_{00} + 2\,\mathrm{AGE}\,\psi_{01} + \mathrm{AGE}^2\psi_{11} + \mathrm{AGE}^4\psi_{22} + \mathrm{AGE}^6\psi_{33} + \mathrm{AGE}^8\psi_{44} \qquad (A7.3)$$

The bands in Figure A7.1 are calculated by adding and subtracting the square root of the expression in Equation A7.3 from the predicted interest level for a given age.[5] The bands contain an estimated 68 percent of the predicted political interest scores at a given age. The area marked by the bands does *not* indicate the precision with which the average trajectory is estimated. (The graph does not show the confidence interval around the trajectory estimate. The bands themselves are estimated with some imprecision due to sampling error, which is not represented in the graph either.) The figure shows 68-percent bands instead of more common 95-percent bands because even the narrower bands contain a lot of different individual political interest trajectories. The 95-percent bands cover almost the entire area of the charts (except for the upper left corner).

---

[5] Equation A7.3 illustrates the first of the two variance components in (A7.2). The quartic growth curve model implies a particular covariance matrix, $\mathrm{Cov}(Z_i\zeta_i) = Z_i\psi Z_i'$. This matrix implies heteroscedastic and autocorrelated errors within subjects. The second variance component in (A7.2), $\mathrm{Cov}(\varepsilon_i) = \sigma^2\Omega_i$, allows further autocorrelation in the error structure. It has been constrained to $\sigma^2\Omega_i = \sigma_2 I$, which assumes that the first variance component is sufficient to model any autocorrelation in the data. Completely unconstrained estimation of Ω_i requires many additional parameters, especially when the number of observations per subject is high. But more parsimonious alternative parameterizations are possible (see, e.g., Singer and Willett 2003, 246–65; Weiss 2005, 243–94). Alternative parameterizations leave the fixed effects estimates unbiased, but can change their precision.

8

Differences in Age Trajectories

If you think back to the thirty random Brits we met in the previous chapter, you now know that their political interest follows different trajectories as they get older. Not only do some find politics more interesting than others, but such differences between people can wax and wane over their lives. So, who exactly are the people with greater interest or steeper growth trajectories? If we had met the 30 Brits when they were still young, could we have predicted how their political interest would develop?

This chapter examines if stable characteristics that differ between people can account for variation in trajectories. A large literature in political socialization proposes factors already present in childhood as particularly formative in people's subsequent development of political orientations. Potentially relevant variables include both the conditions in which a child grows up and the enduring predispositions that form early in life, before children even begin to discover politics as a domain of potential interest. To represent the former category, this chapter analyzes the association of political interest with family origin and parental education. With respect to early non-political characteristics, I consider personality, cognitive skills, and gender.

The **Curiosity Hypothesis** suggests that specific personality traits, most prominently curiosity and openness to new experiences, contribute to interest development. Curious individuals may not necessarily end up enjoying politics, but their curiosity leads them to experience situational interest in a greater variety of domains – situational interest that may evolve into a sustained dispositional interest. According to the **Cognitive Ability Hypothesis**, political interest is higher among people with high cognitive ability because objective ability engenders a subjective sense of efficacy (not part of the analysis in this chapter) which in turn makes formation of political interest more likely.

This chapter reaps the benefits of explicitly considering aging and growth trajectories over people's lives. Instead of just comparing overall means of different groups – political interest levels of more and less curious people, say – this chapter will investigate the development of such differences over time, as people get older. For example, past research summarized later in this chapter has repeatedly found men to be more interested in politics than women, but we know much less about gender differences at different stages of life. I examine if the gender gap in political interest is already present early in life when boys and girls are just starting to encounter politics or only develops as men and women accumulate more political experiences. The advantage of this approach is that we can not only detect interest gaps between different groups of people, but sometimes even see these gaps emerge.

This chapter is the last in Part II of the book, and by answering questions about between-person differences, it largely concludes the descriptive analysis. It also takes a step toward explaining political interest, albeit a halfhearted one. Analyses in Part III will rely centrally on the argument that causality involves a change in one variable followed by a change in another variable. For the kind of variables examined in this chapter, which are fixed, almost fixed, or determined early, change is either not theoretically defined or very rare. This feature creates both conceptual and statistical challenges to interpretations of cause and effect.

STABLE PERSONAL CHARACTERISTICS AND POLITICAL INTEREST TRAJECTORIES

Conceptually, explaining a time-varying characteristic such as political interest with a time-invariant variable, such as gender at birth, is incomplete: If men and women have different political interest trajectories, what exactly is it that gender does to change interest? Men and women may have different experiences or develop different attitudes that in turn affect their political interest. But in that case, experiences or attitudes are the more proximate cause – and vary over time. Time-varying variables permit the more intuitive change-on-change analysis. But if we do not know what the more proximate causal factors might even be, the incomplete analysis using the more removed stable characteristics can at least narrow the search.

Statistically, time-invariant variables as causal factors are subject to strong challenges. Precisely because time-invariant characteristics never change for any individual, their within-person effect cannot be observed. As a result, the threat from omitted variable bias severely limits causal interpretation. If individuals with an open personality are more interested in politics, but personality hardly changes at all (as many psychologists believe), we cannot see if people who become more open to experience also develop greater political interest, and any other stable variable that correlates with an open personality could be the true cause.

The personal characteristics examined in this chapter fall into two categories. Characteristics in the first category are so stable over people's lives that there is no or hardly any change to exploit in change-on-change analyses. Personality is considered to be highly stable, and so are cognitive skills. Gender changes very infrequently (and gender at birth, the variable measured in the household panel studies, is constant by design).

The second category of personal characteristics comprises variables that could plausibly change but that are deemed particularly important ("formative") at an early point in life. Parental education and socioeconomic status fall in this category. Some people still attend educational institutions when they become parents, but according to theories of socialization and youth development, parents' education is most relevant when their children are still young. The following analysis relies mostly on parents' characteristics measured when their child is between 6 and 10 years of age, a time when children are just starting to become politically conscious. As the earliest measurement of political interest occurs at age 11 (in the BHPS youth interviews), this definition has the added advantage that the independent variable is measured before the dependent variable which makes causal inference somewhat easier.

For both categories of predictors, the quartic growth curve model introduced in the previous chapter now allows the five trajectory parameters to vary as a function of time-invariant independent variables.

Parental Education

Parental education is frequently used to measure family resources and socioeconomic background during a person's early political development (e.g., Verba et al. 1995; Plutzer 2002). It is positively related to the offspring's political participation (Condon and Holleque 2013) and political interest (Verba et al. 2005, 103). To the extent that this is a causal effect on political interest, it could arise through different mechanisms, including easing of resource constraints, family communication patterns, and prestige. All of those things can change year-to-year, and some of them will be examined in detail in Part III. Here, I use parental education (which is already constant for most panelists when they first report their political interest) as a general proxy for socioeconomic background.

Individuals develop greater political interest if their parents are well educated. Figure 8.1 shows predicted political interest trajectories in Britain, Germany, and Switzerland separately for three groups of panelists: those whose parents both obtained an upper secondary schooling degree, those who had only one parent with such a high level of education, and those whose parents both did not complete this level of education.[1] The graphs are based on quartic growth curve models introduced in the previous chapter, now with added time-

---

[1] Parental education was reported by the child. Upper secondary degree is defined as Abitur in Germany, Matura in Switzerland, and post-school qualifications or certificates in Britain.

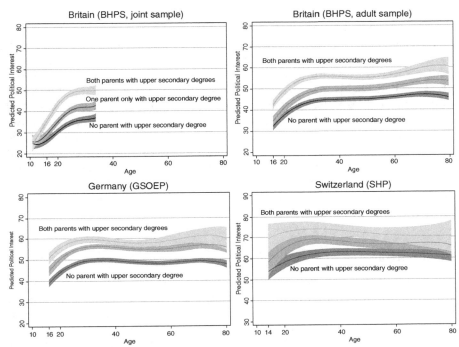

FIGURE 8.1 Predicted Quartic Age Trajectories by Parental Education

Note: Graphs show predicted values with 95-percent confidence intervals around average trajectory estimates for a quartic growth curve model.

invariant predictors for gender, personality, parental education, and country-specific measures of family origin. (Cognitive ability will only be added later because it significantly reduces the sample size.) The purpose of this analysis is to test if the components of the growth trajectory differ depending on those predictors. The appendix to this chapter explains the details of this approach. (For the BHPS, I present two sets of results, one that uses only the adult sample and one that combines youth and adults but focuses on a limited age range to parsimoniously capture the early trajectory shape.)

For all three countries, intercept differences are statistically different, indicating that parental education is associated with political interest at age 16 (the value on which age is centered). Joint tests of the interactions with the four other trajectory parameters (linear through quartic) assess if the trajectories also differ based on the time-invariant predictor. Here, trajectories for higher parental education are indeed statistically different from the trajectory for individuals whose parents both had little education. The patterns are remarkably similar for all three countries (even if results are noisier for Switzerland because the SHP sample is smaller).

Parental education becomes more strongly associated with political interest as people grow older. In fact, the joint BHPS sample that integrates the youth interviews shows no association at all among 11-year-olds. In Switzerland, too, the difference associated with one educated parent only develops in adolescence. Trajectories diverge in all three countries as age increases. Whatever causal mechanism is operating to raise political interest among children of more educated parents, it appears to be (still) operating throughout their teenage years. The mechanism does not necessarily involve education, however. Adding a measure of parents' occupational status, which is only available for the SHP and a subset of GSOEP cases, reduces the differences associated with parental education and shows occupational status to be significantly related to political interest as well.[2] It is probably best to think of the associations in Figure 8.1 as relating to socioeconomic status broadly rather than one particular component of it.

Family Origins

To the extent that political interest depends on being integrated into a society and its domestic political system, nationality and time spent in a country might be related to interest development. This is an area where differences between Britain, Germany, and Switzerland are pronounced. For all three countries, this book examines citizens, largely because the samples do not contain many non-citizens.[3] In addition, I also excluded the few German citizens who were born outside the country and British citizens who moved to Britain after 1950.

In the Swiss SHP, however, 20 percent of panelists who are citizens were not born in Switzerland, a much higher share than in Britain or Germany. Excluding them would diminish the sample size for Switzerland, already the smallest study. More importantly, the higher share of foreign-born citizens in the SHP is not a sampling problem, but a feature of the Swiss immigration system after World War II. Does political interest develop differently for Swiss citizens depending on whether they were born in Switzerland or not? It does not, according to the quartic growth curve model. Neither the intercept nor the growth trajectory can be statistically distinguished for the two groups.

Even for citizens who were born in their country of residence or have lived there for a long time, family origins vary. Models for all three countries include

---

[2] In both the SHP and GSOEP, trajectory differences are no longer significantly associated with parental education and the intercept differences are reduced by about a third. Occupational status of parents is associated with trajectory differences in the SHP, but not in the GSOEP. Predicted trajectories by parents' occupational status are graphed in Figure OL8.1 in the Online Supplementary Material.

[3] This is not true in the GSOEP, which has interviewed substantial oversamples of guestworkers and recent immigrants and contains enough panelists to model interest among non-citizens. The British and Swiss data, however, would not permit this type of analysis.

an indicator variable for panelists whose parents were both citizens of the study country at birth. The percentage of these panelists is 91 in the BHPS, 94 in the GSOEP, and 83 in the SHP. The relationship between this variable and political interest varies by country, as shown in Figure 8.2.

The most intriguing result occurs in Switzerland. When they are young, children of parents who themselves were not Swiss citizens at birth are considerably less interested in politics than offspring of Swiss citizens. Their interest deficit at age 14 of about 20 points is large. And yet, by mid-adulthood they have caught up and their political interest is indistinguishable from that of children whose parents were Swiss at birth. Neither the initial deficit nor the catching-up is evident in Britain or Germany. Panelists whose parents were not German at birth are significantly less interested in politics, but the magnitude of this difference is substantively small through the life course. In Britain, the difference is also small, but its direction is reversed. It is difficult to come up with a plausible explanation for the contrast between Germany and Britain in this respect. In Switzerland, the country with the highest share of first-generation citizens, the initial interest deficit of these individuals is stark, but they catch up with the rest of the citizenry very effectively as adolescents and young adults.

One last variation in family origin is unique to Germany. Although the German SOEP did not operate in East Germany before the fall of the Wall, it started interviewing there in 1990, even before reunification, and thus includes many panelists who grew up in the German Democratic Republic. The growth curve model uses an indicator variable for place of residence in 1989 (East or West Germany) to understand the impact of this difference. Both intercept and growth trajectory differ significantly depending on this variable. As the plot of predicted values at the bottom of Figure 8.2 shows, the magnitude of the difference is fairly modest. Germans who grew up in the East are about 4 points less interested in politics than their Western counterparts. The difference increases late in life as older East Germans, asked in the two decades after reunification, report declining political interest.

In sum, family origin has detectable, but mostly small and sometimes inconsistent associations with political interest. Caution is warranted in interpreting even these small differences: They might arise due to other factors that happen to correlate with family origin, such as income. (Parental education is controlled for here, however.)

Personality

Personality traits are thought to be very stable over the lifecycle (e.g, Roberts and DelVecchio 2000; Caspi et al. 2005, 466–8; Anusic et al. 2012), quite likely because they have a firm biological basis characterized by high heritability (see Mondak et al. 2010 for a summary of evidence and application to political behavior). Personality measured at an early age is related to behaviors that only manifest themselves in adulthood. Childhood agreeableness (being

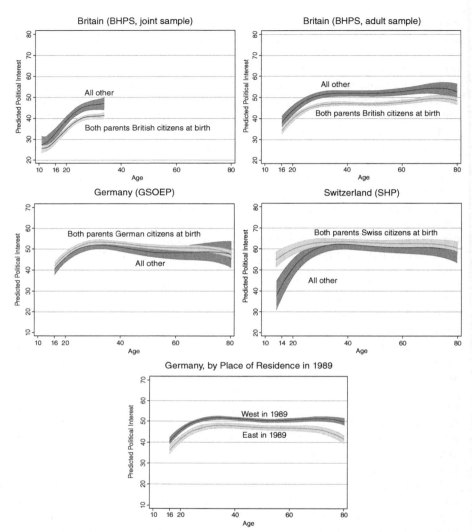

FIGURE 8.2 Predicted Quartic Age Trajectories by Parental Citizenship and Residence in 1989

Note: Graphs show predicted values with 95-percent confidence intervals around average trajectory estimate for a quartic growth curve model.

"cooperative with limits set by adults, generous, kind, and considerate"), for example, has a (small) positive effect on work competence at age 30 (Shiner et al. 2003). These findings have led some to argue that personality causally precedes to political development.[4]

---

[4] This assumption may be overly strong. Personality is quite stable, but not self-evidently more stable than party identification or political interest. According to Caspi et al. (2005, 466–8),

According to the psychological accounts of interest formation reviewed in Chapter 2, initial situational interest typically involves a positive affective reaction to an environmental stimulus that may later develop into dispositional interest. Curious people with a personality open to new experiences might find themselves in such stimulating situations more often or have a greater proclivity to react positively to a given environmental stimulus – including politics. Among the Big Five personality traits, a standard classification of personality along five dimensions (McCrae and Costa 1987; Goldberg 1990; John and Srivastava 1999), a link between "openness to experience" and political interest is arguably the most compelling theoretical prediction.

In all three datasets, adults with an open personality report greater political interest.[5] This association, graphed in Figure 8.3 by comparing predicted values by age for the 10th and the 90th percentile of openness, is very strong. Figure 8.3 also shows that it develops in adolescence: Among the youngest British and Swiss youths, personality differences are not yet statistically detectable. The gap widens with age, generating statistically different age trajectories. This result is consistent with the notion that an open personality leads to greater sampling of interest domains early on, and thus a gradually increasing chance of recognizing politics as interesting.

It is conceivable that other personality factors also predispose people to develop more or deeper interests, including perhaps interest in politics. The negative correlation of political interest and conflict avoidance (Blais and St-Vincent 2011) and the link between adults' political interest and their teachers' ratings of them as aggressive when they were 16 years old (Denny and Doyle 2008) may be picking up the same personality influence. The theories reviewed for this book do not provide a ready explanation for why aggressive individuals would develop greater political interest, however. For the closest Big Five factor, agreeableness, results provide only partial confirmation. In Britain, individuals high on agreeableness are about 10 points less interested in politics, a difference that is constant through the life course. In Germany and Switzerland, this personality factor is not related to political interest in any way, however. Furthermore, Blais and St-Vincent's (2011) finding that political interest and altruism are positively correlated throws a wrench into any general conclusion because altruism is thought to be a subcomponent of agreeableness,

---

"test-retest correlations over time (a) are moderate in magnitude, even from childhood to early adulthood. Furthermore, rank-order stability (b) increases with age ... [and] peaks some time after age 50... [T]he majority of personality change occurs in young adulthood, not in adolescence." Analyzing Big Five scale means by age shows some increase in conscientiousness and agreeableness. Openness, the strongest correlate of political interest in the following analysis, is mean-stable, including in the SHP starting at age 14 (Srivastava et al. 2003; Anusic et al. 2012).

[5] Big Five dimensions of personality are measured with shortened versions of the 44-item Big Five Inventory (John and Srivastava 1999) using 15 items on 7-point scales in BHPS and GSOEP and 10 items on 11-point scales in the SHP. Further details appear in the Online Supplementary Materials.

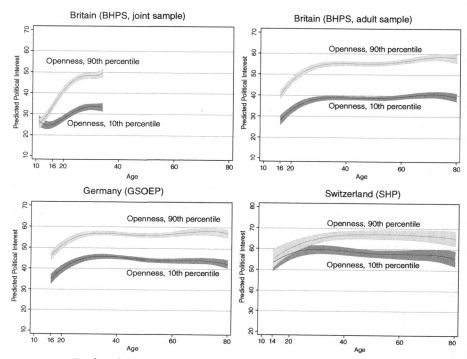

FIGURE 8.3 Predicted Quartic Age Trajectories by Openness
Note: Graphs show predicted values with 95-percent confidence intervals around average trajectory estimate for a quartic growth curve model.

so the correlation should be negative if agreeable individuals are less politically interested than aggressive/antagonistic people.[6]

In the household surveys, a significant but smaller association exists between conscientiousness and political interest in Britain and Germany. More conscientious individuals have somewhat lower interest in politics. The predicted values in Figure 8.4 locate this effect among adolescents and young adults in Germany, but later in life in Britain. Given this inconsistency and the small magnitudes, this personality factor might not contribute much to a general explanation of political interest development.[7]

---

[6] In Gerber et al.'s (2011) analysis, agreeableness is not significantly related to political interest either in several different tests. In all three household panel studies, agreeableness is the Big Five trait with the lowest measurement reliability. In the SHP, which used only two items per factor, reliability is below .2.

[7] Several studies (Condra 1992; David 2009; Sohlberg 2015) have shown an empirical association between political interest and need for cognition, a measure of general appreciation of thinking and cognitive effort (Cacioppo and Petty 1982; Cacioppo et al. 1996). Need for cognition is also

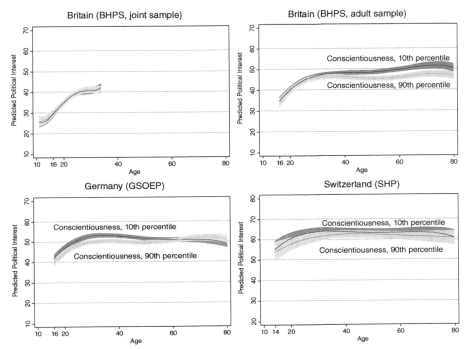

FIGURE 8.4 Predicted Quartic Age Trajectories by Conscientiousness
Note: Graphs show predicted values with 95-percent confidence intervals around average trajectory estimate for a quartic growth curve model.

Extraversion has no consistent relationship with political interest across the three studies. This result is only seemingly at odds with the documentation of a link between extraversion and political participation in other research: Extraverted individuals are indeed more likely to participate, but only if the participatory behavior involves social interactions, such as attendance at meetings or discussion (Mondak et al. 2010). Politics can be interesting with or without a social component, so extraversion is neither conducive nor inhibiting to the development of political interest.[8]

---

related to the exploration dimension of Kashdan et al.'s (2004) curiosity measure. David finds a correlation between political interest and need to evaluate (Jarvis and Petty 1996). Neither of these scales is available in the household panel studies.

[8] Gerber et al. (2011, 279) find a correlation between political interest and extraversion using a short Big Five instrument, but not using the longer inventory. Blais and St-Vincent (2011) do find that shyness is negatively related to political interest. They do not use the Big Five scales, however. Finally, the interaction of neuroticism with the age trajectory is also inconsistent in its direction across studies and substantively minor.

Gender

Gender may be the most researched demographic in political behavior research. Women typically express less interest in politics than men (Lazarsfeld et al. 1948 [1944], 45; Berelson et al. 1954, 25; Glenn and Grimes 1968; Bennett 1986; Verba et al. 1995; Kroh 2006; Neundorf et al. 2013). Scholars have suggested that there is "a genuine [gender] difference in the taste for politics" (Verba et al. 1997, 1064, 1070) and that "politics is still very much a man's world" (Gidengil et al. 2006, 246).

Figure 8.5 shows predicted political interest trajectories in Britain, Germany, and Switzerland separately for men and women. Among adults, a gender gap in political interest is clearly evident and of about the same magnitude in all three countries: Men are 10–15 points more interested than women. (This is controlling for the variables already discussed in this chapter, but the gender trajectories are very similar with and without them in the model.) The gender gap increases in adolescence. In all three countries, it is smaller among the youngest respondents. The emergence of the gender gap is more evident in Britain. In fact, when the BHPS youth sample is used along with the adult interviews, we can just observe panelists at a young age when gender differences in political interest do not exist yet. The model does not affect this conclusion: In the raw BHPS data, mean interest of boys and girls is within 1 point until age 13 and within 2 points until age 15. By contrast, mean differences are already 8 and 11 points, respectively, at age 14 and 15 in Switzerland, and 7 points at age 16 in Germany. These results are consistent with other research that shows a gender gap in political interest emerging in the mid-teens. Boys and girls have similar interest levels among the youngest American elementary-school children in Hess and Torney's (1967) study and among German 12-to-13-year-olds in research by Westle (2006), but Ingrisch (1997, 152–4) finds significant gender differences in political interest among German students between the ages of 13 and 16.[9]

Cognitive Skills

Psychological models of interest formation point to coping potential or efficacy as a factor that can trigger and sustain interest in a domain leading to the Cognitive Ability Hypothesis. General cognitive skills may both contribute to a subjective sense of political efficacy and make it objectively easier to participate in politics. In cross-sectional models, cognitive skills are indeed positively associated with political involvement (Luskin 1990; Verba et al. 1995; Nie

---

[9] Because of the clear differences between men and women in Figure 8.5, statistical models in Part III will allow quartic age trajectories to vary by gender. (Unlike other stable predictors, gender is available throughout so the age-by-gender interactions can be included without reducing the number of observations.)

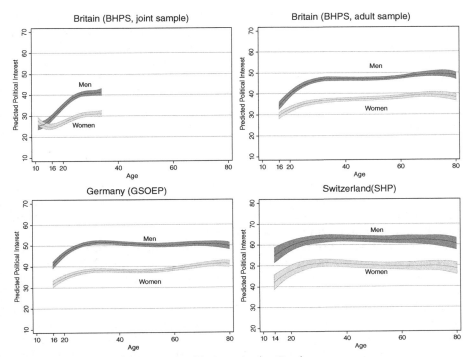

FIGURE 8.5 Predicted Quartic Age Trajectories by Gender
Note: Graphs show predicted values with 95-percent confidence intervals around average trajectory estimate for a quartic growth curve model.

et al. 1996; Highton 2009). Measured in childhood, cognitive skills have been shown to correlate with political interest (Hess and Torney 1967, 153) and predict turnout and political interest among adults (Deary et al. 2008; Denny and Doyle 2008).

Only two of the three household studies, the BHPS and GSOEP, include measures of cognitive ability (see, e.g., Anger and Heineck 2010). Only a subset of panelists took the tests and most took them only once. Cognitive ability is thus measured at different ages for different panelists. As I explicitly control for age (and use age-adjusted ability scores) and as cognitive ability is very stable (Caspi et al. 2005, 466–7), these measurement conditions are suitable for an analysis of cognitive skills as a time-invariant predictor. Cognitive skills measures are available for over 85 percent of the BHPS sample examined in this chapter, but only for about a fifth of the GSOEP sample, thus producing much noisier results for Germany.

Cognitive ability is positively related to political interest, but there is clear indication that this association only develops, or at least becomes considerably stronger, in adulthood, a finding that is broadly consistent with Hess and

Torney's (1967, 153) data for American children which also shows the gradual emergence of cognitive ability as a predictor of political interest (starting in high school). Figure 8.6 shows the pattern of results based on a test of verbal fluency, which was included in both BHPS and GSOEP and asks respondents to name as many animals as they can in 60 seconds. (For measurement details, see Online Supplementary Materials.) In both studies, the growing divergence of the political interest trajectories of more and less skilled individuals is clearly statistically significant. At age 16, however, interest in Germany is not yet stratified by cognitive ability. In the British study, the difference at age 16 is already significant, but the joint sample confirms the lack of relationship among younger children.

Other tests included in the two studies permit additional differentiation of the kinds of skills most clearly related to political interest. The GSOEP also uses a non-verbal symbol correspondence test that asks respondents to match numbers and symbols using a computer interface (provided by the interviewer). When both tests of cognitive ability are included in the model, performance on the symbol correspondence test is not statistically related to political interest and the results for the verbal fluency test remain much the same.

The BHPS includes two other tests of cognitive ability, a word recall test and a test of numerical skills that covers arithmetic and probabilities. When these two tests are added to the model, the verbal fluency test becomes insignificant, whereas the other two tests are significantly related to political interest. (Performance on the different tests in the BHPS is correlated at about .4.) Performance on the recall test is positively associated with political interest regardless of age, but the magnitude is fairly small. Differences are larger for numerical skills and follow a pattern very similar to the verbal fluency test in Figure 8.6 when no other tests are included in the model. Together, these results do not permit clean generalization about what kind of ability is most relevant for political interest development. In the German study, a verbal test is more predictive than a non-verbal symbols test. In the British study, a numerical test outperforms both verbal (recall and fluency) tests.

The addition of cognitive skills to the quartic growth curve model has little effect on the relationships of political interest with the other variables examined in this chapter. The trajectory differences by gender, parental education, openness to experience, and conscientiousness remain about the same (albeit with more noise, especially in the German data). The reason is simple: Cognitive ability is not strongly related to any of these other variables. The strongest correlation, between gender and numerical skills in Britain, is only -.14. None of the skills measures correlate with parental education more strongly than .11.

It is important to note that openness retains its association with political interest after controlling for cognitive ability. Openness has two notable subcomponents, imagination/creativity and intellect (Caspi et al. 2005, 459-60). Examining these subscales, Gerber et al. (2011, 278-9) find intellect, but not

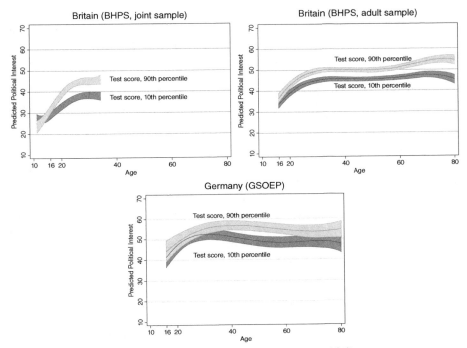

FIGURE 8.6 Predicted Quartic Age Trajectories by Cognitive Ability
Note: Graphs show predicted values with 95-percent confidence intervals around average trajectory estimate for a quartic growth curve model. Cognitive skills are measured using a verbal fluency test.

imagination/creativity, related to political interest. Their analysis controls only for education, not cognitive ability. At a minimum, the empirical findings here show that objective ability and the personality trait of openness/intellect have independent associations with political interest.

FROM PART II TO PART III

This chapter concludes the description of when political interest develops and stabilizes. Population averages have revealed a significant but substantively moderate increase of political interest in adolescence and early adulthood. The individual-level stability of political interest rises very quickly during this period, so by people's mid-twenties or early thirties, interest levels are typically where they will remain for the rest of people's lives. The conditional growth curves in this chapter – age trajectories that take different shapes depending on stable, or nearly stable, individual characteristics – show some substantial differences in political interest development in different subgroups of the population, but even for these subgroups, trajectories become horizontal early in adulthood. This does not preclude the occasional update among adults, but the analysis leaves little doubt that development of political interest follows an "impressionable years" pattern, according to which early malleability evolves into high stability by early adulthood. Cross-sectional data easily mislead on this point because they cannot distinguish aging from cohort differences. Older people happen to be even more politically interested than young adults in the data analyzed here, but that is *not* an effect of aging. Instead, people who came of age in the 1960s, the most interested cohort in all three countries, were more interested in politics even before they did their aging.

Growth curve analysis supports both the Curiosity Hypothesis and the Cognitive Ability Hypothesis. People with an open personality and intellectual curiosity are more interested in politics, as are people with stronger cognitive skills. Both of these between-person differences are consistent with the psychological model of interest. Both increase from small, sometimes insignificant associations among teenagers to large differences among adults. That, too, is consistent with curiosity and ability (or its subjective correlate, efficacy) as factors operating during the development of political interest in adolescence.

Two other stable characteristics, neither directly predicted by the psychological model, also distinguish more and less politically interested individuals: Parental socioeconomic status (measured by parental education or, when available, occupational status) and gender. Men and the children of parents with higher socioeconomic status find politics more interesting. These differences also grow in adolescence and early adulthood.

As causal explanations, the results are not quite satisfying. That openness to experience would be related to political interest is clearly consistent with psychological models of interest formation. But the causal mechanism from this personality trait to political interest must involve intervening steps that actually produce the change in interest, perhaps experiences with the domain of politics that generate curiosity or positive affect. As neither experiences nor the accompanying affective states are measured in the data used here, a direct test of the causal process remains elusive.

Why, for example, do the gender gap and interest differences by parental education persist and even grow as young people become older and leave their parents' household? According to one possibility, early-life conditions have long-lasting effects. But it is also possible that parental socioeconomic status is a marker for experiences that continue to happen from early on (at least from before the start of data collection) and happen more often as young people grow up. In this scenario, a relationship between a stable characteristic and an outcome that changes as people get older is explained by a mediating variable that is also time-varying. Children of more educated parents tend to complete more years of schooling and attend more advanced educational institutions. Their income also tends to be higher when they are young and increase faster as they get older. Could changes in attendance of educational institutions or changes in income be the causal factors that explain their rise in political interest, not anything specifically about their parents? This is one of the questions I take up in Part III.

Even if the empirical analyses in this chapter do not clearly identify causes of political interest, they help by telling us where to look and which subpopulations to look at particularly carefully. Women, closed-minded individuals, older people, and children of parents with lower socioeconomic status do not lack political interest, but they do develop it at lower rates. Whatever influences generate political interest, they happen more, or more effectively, to men, individuals open to new experiences, the young, and children of better educated parents.

Appendix to Chapter 8

SPECIFICATION AND ESTIMATION DETAILS FOR GROWTH CURVE MODELS

In the quartic growth model, five person-specific parameters characterize an individual's trajectory. These parameters are expressed as functions of time-invariant explanatory variables. For example, the equation for the linear component becomes $b_{1i} = \gamma_{10} + \gamma_{11}$ GENDER$_i$ + γ_{12} PARENTAL EDU$_i$ + γ_{13} FAMILY ORIGIN$_i$ + γ_{1k} PERSONALITY^k_i + ζ_{1i}, where k indexes dimensions of personality. These independent variables only have i subscripts, because they are constant across age t. To allow the complete age trajectory to vary by these predictors, the same independent variables are also included in the equations for the intercept, quadratic, cubic, and quartic trajectory components. The resulting composite model, using only gender for presentation convenience, is

$$
\begin{aligned}
PI_{it} = {} & \gamma_{00} + \gamma_{01}\text{GENDER}_i + \gamma_{10}\text{AGE}_{it} + \gamma_{20}\text{AGE}_{it}{}^2 + \gamma_{30}\text{AGE}_{it}{}^3 \\
& + \gamma_{40}\text{AGE}_{it}{}^4 + \gamma_{11}\text{GENDER}_i \times \text{AGE}_{it} + \gamma_{21}\text{GENDER}_i \times \text{AGE}_{it}{}^2 \\
& + \gamma_{31}\text{GENDER}_i \times \text{AGE}_{it}{}^3 + \gamma_{41}\text{GENDER}_i \times \text{AGE}_{it}{}^4 + \pi^{BC}{}_i + \pi^S{}_i \\
& + \mathbf{x}^N{}_t + \left[\zeta_{0i} + \zeta_{1i}\text{AGE}_{it} + \zeta_{2i}\text{AGE}_{it}{}^2 + \zeta_{3i}\text{AGE}_{it}{}^3 + \zeta_{4i}\text{AGE}_{it}{}^4 + \varepsilon_{it} \right]
\end{aligned}
$$

$$(A8.1)$$

Covariates are assumed to be uncorrelated with the variance components ζ_{0i}, ζ_{1i}, ζ_{2i}, ζ_{3i}, ζ_{4i}, ε_{it}. (A random effect for gender, or any other time-invariant predictor, does not make sense because it would attempt to quantify the variability in the effect of gender, even though the effect of gender for individual panelists cannot be estimated. It is possible to include a random intercept with different variances for men and women.)

Graphs of predicted values hold other covariates at their means (personality, news events), actual values (parental education, year of birth), or modal categories (other measures of interestingness). Gender is set to male, residence in 1989 (Germany) to West, and birth place (Switzerland) to Switzerland. Parental citizenship is held constant at both parents being citizens for BHPS and SHP, the modal value. In the GSOEP, the variable is held at actual values, including missing, because it was only asked starting in 2000 and is unavailable for 48 percent of the sample. Full results appear in Table OL8.1 in the Online Supplementary Materials. The Online Supplementary Materials also present more information on the difference between using the adult BHPS sample and the joint youth-adult sample.

EXPLAINING CHANGE IN POLITICAL INTEREST

9

The Big Benefits of Panel Data Analysis

Political interest develops predominantly in adolescence and early adulthood. As Part II of this book showed, new members of the self-governing class often join in this period. Political interest rises rapidly early in life and takes on a stability that makes it more difficult to change later. But *why* does political interest build at this stage in life? What is it that makes people grow interested? Those are more difficult questions than depicting different interest trajectories because they involve statements of cause and effect. Addressing them requires some additional conceptual legwork and more sophisticated analytical tools. The early formation of political interest suggests that influences operating in adolescence hold some answers, so Part III begins with careful consideration of education and parents. The principal challenge is to distinguish causal impact from mere association.

This chapter explains what more we can learn about causal impact when we measure the purported cause and effect not just once, but repeatedly over time. The analytical approach in Part III rests on the notion that causality necessarily involves a change in one variable followed by a change in another variable. Panel data make it possible to gauge individual change. When potential explanatory variables vary over time for an individual, it is possible to assess if changes in those variables are followed by changes in the individual's political interest. In and of itself, that is not enough to establish causality, but it can often get us closer. Importantly, changes in political interest caused by those other variables may be slow to occur. Even with panel data, we may miss them if political interest is only measured a few times or analysts do not look for changes in effect size. Elaborating this logic, the chapter clarifies why it is conceptually confusing to talk about "the effect" of a causal factor: Effects may vary in their duration, so a complete characterization of causal impact includes information about their delay and decay.

Panel data provide considerably more leverage for causal inference than cross-sectional observational data, but their analysis involves a few extra steps. The goal of this chapter is to lay out these extra steps clearly and intuitively, so empirical inferences remain transparent and their advantages over cross-sectional comparisons become evident. Things are relatively straightforward when changes in the hypothesized cause of political interest cannot have been influenced, directly or indirectly, by past changes in political interest, the anticipation of future changes, or other variables that change with political interest. Completing compulsory schooling probably fits those conditions: Young people are highly unlikely to stay in school because of their political interest or because they seek and expect secondary schooling to raise it. When those conditions are not met, inferences from panel data must build on additional assumptions, and panel estimators become more complicated. Appreciating the intuition behind the Big Benefits of panel data does not require detailed statistical knowledge, however. Graphical analysis of the rich household panel data makes it possible to "see" the Big Benefits and use them to understand the causes of political interest.

This chapter provides the toolkit for the third part of the book. Subsequent chapters will use these tools to evaluate the hypotheses derived from psychological theories of political interest in Chapter 2. The main task of this chapter is to explain the logic of causal inference from panel data to readers regardless of their statistical training. It is possible to learn much about causes of political interest from the graphical analyses of change that I introduce here. A model-based approach in the later parts of each section permits greater statistical precision and adds capacity to analyze many potential causes at once. In covering panel estimators, I focus on conceptual explanation of the particular inferential challenges. To be transparent about the statistical procedures and assumptions underlying these estimators, I provide some technical notation, but move much of it to the Chapter Appendix.

There are three principal advantages panel data offer over observational cross-sectional data: The ability to focus on changes, not levels; the ability to detect temporal variation in causal impact; and greater leverage in distinguishing cause and effect by exploiting the timing of their respective changes. The first two of these Big Benefits are straightforward and unambiguous. The third one often depends on critical assumptions that cannot be directly verified. They are weaker than the assumptions necessary to identify causal effects using cross-sectional observational data, but stronger than the assumptions experimental designs require. Especially for potential causes of political interest that defy random assignment, the Third Big Benefit is thus of great practical value, but the intricacy of its assumptions imposes more methodological, and occasionally technical, exposition. The organization of this chapter follows the three benefits and provides empirical illustrations for each of them using potential predictors of political interest.

COMPARING CHANGE, NOT LEVELS

The First Big Benefit of panel data is the ability to rule out observed or unobserved constant variables as alternative explanations for a causal effect. It solves one critical challenge to causal inference inherent in non-experimental cross-sectional data analysis. The relationship between education and political interest illustrates this benefit. Among British, German, and Swiss adults between the ages of 25 and 40, political interest is between 14 and 19 points higher if they hold an upper secondary schooling degree. At almost a fifth of the full scale, this is a large difference equivalent to the average lifetime effect of aging. But does this difference mean that upper-secondary schooling increases political interest?

A causal effect of education is the change in political interest that arises because someone receives additional schooling. A difference in the level of political interest between people who received different amounts of education is not sufficient. At a minimum, we need to see political interest change at some point *after* the additional "dose" of education began. The change need not occur immediately, but if there is no change or it occurs *before* education began, there is probably no causal effect.

Figure 9.1 sows considerable doubt about the causal impact of education. The figure summarizes the association between political interest and education by graphing interest as a function of age in groups with different educational attainment. Educational attainment is the highest level of education panelists obtain while part of the study – regardless of whether they already finished this level at a given age. Panel data are thus necessary to create this graph because it requires information about political interest in years before individuals complete their education. For example, the dark solid lines at the top for postsecondary education plot the political interest of people who eventually finished a university degree during their time on the panel. In the years until these individuals reached their early-to-mid-twenties, we could observe their political interest before they completed their university education.

Among adults, Figure 9.1 indicates a strong and largely monotonic relationship between education and political interest in all three countries. By their mid-to-late twenties, university graduates are 20–30 points more interested than people with no more than compulsory (lower secondary) education and about 10 points more interested than people with only an upper secondary schooling degree. The ordering of educational attainment and political interest among adults is very similar in all three countries. For the most part, more education goes together with greater political interest.

Yet this strong cross-sectional association between education and political interest among adults, which is familiar from many previous one-shot studies, does not necessarily imply that the two variables are causally related. It is also possible that the association reflects a preexisting difference in political interest

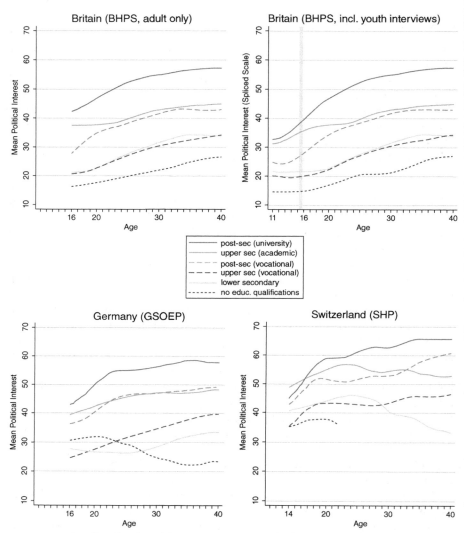

FIGURE 9.1 Predicted Political Interest Trajectories, by Highest Level of Education
Note: Minimum of three panel waves required to be included. Within each educational tier, academic qualifications are considered higher than vocational qualifications (so a panelist with the highest general educational qualification and a secondary vocational degree is coded as "upper secondary (academic)." Graphs use data from panelists who completed at least three panel waves. In order to put BHPS youth and adult interviews on the same scale, calculations apply the splicing introduced in Chapter 6 separately for each education category. The gray vertical bar shows the transition from youth to adult interviews.

between more and less educated panelists, a difference that is caused by other variables that happen to be related to both education and political interest. In fact, Figure 9.1 provides several hints that a considerable portion of the cross-sectional association between education and interest does not arise because education has a causal effect on political interest. In a number of instances, political interest in segments with higher eventual education exceeds interest in less educated segments *even before they could have obtained a particular degree.*

In all three countries, half or more of the adult difference in political interest between panelists with the highest level of secondary schooling and panelists who only complete lower secondary schooling is already evident at age 16, some two or three years *before* students typically finish the upper secondary track. In Switzerland, much of this difference is evident at age 14, and in Britain, it exists among 11-year-olds and does not change much as they get older. Swiss students who eventually earn post-secondary degrees (academic or vocational) develop greater political interest than their counterparts who never earn those degrees in their mid-to-late teens – but most post-secondary programs have not yet started at that age. Political interest differences between panelists who will complete a university degree (typically in their early to mid-twenties) and panelists who do not get a university degree are already in place *before* they enter university.[1]

Something other than the experience of upper secondary schooling or a university education must explain their graduates' higher interest levels as teenagers. Figure 9.1 does not take into account a measure of that other explanatory factor, however, so the association between education and political interest as an estimate of causal impact suffers from omitted variable bias: One or more variables related to both the dependent variable and the independent variable of interest are not included in the analysis.

The First Big Benefit of panel data is the ability to rule out other constant differences between people as alternative explanations for a causal effect – to reduce omitted variable bias. Examining differences between two or more political interest measurements for the same person transforms the analysis

---

[1] In the United States, too, college students participate more in politics than young people who do not go to college, but also already outperform them on standardized civics tests they took as high-school sophomores (Dee 2004, 1704). Niemi and Junn (1998) and Syvertsen et al. (2011) find large differences in civics knowledge and self-reported political participation, respectively, among high-school seniors depending on whether they plan to attend a 4-year college, a 2-year college, or not to go college. And the Jennings-Niemi panel study of a cohort of young Americans who were in high school in 1965 shows that much of the difference in political knowledge between those who had completed college by 1973, the next wave of the study, and those who never attended college was already present in 1965 (Highton 2009; Jennings and Niemi 1981; Smith 1989, 215–19). To the extent that differences in political interest, knowledge and participation are in place before students enter college, college education loses plausibility as a cause of these differences.

from a comparison of levels into a comparison of changes. Where cross-sectional data permit only between-person comparisons, panel data can take advantage of within-person comparisons. A variable that is constant for an individual – that takes the same value for this individual every time it is measured – cannot be related to a change in political interest. Hence, it cannot generate omitted variable bias. This benefit elevates panel analysis of observational data over cross-sectional analysis of observational data in many circumstances.

Chapter 8 revealed several variables that are correlated with political interest as early as age 11 and continuing throughout the lifecycle, including the personality trait of openness and cognitive ability. In a cross-sectional analysis, the effect of a supposed cause of political interest that is correlated with an open personality or cognitive ability would be measured with bias unless these two variables are controlled for. More importantly, there may be many other time-invariant correlates of political interest that we are unaware of or failed to measure. In a within-person analysis, it is sometimes possible to prevent these variables from biasing the estimates – even if we do not know what they are.

Graphical Analysis of Change

Figure 9.1 does well to show that something is wrong with naïve associations between education and political interest as estimates of causal effect. But by using only a panelist's eventual highest level of education, it does not exploit within-person variation. For many young panelists, education changes while they are panel members, making it possible to examine if completing an upper secondary schooling degree corresponds to a rise in political interest that is not observed among panelists who did not receive the degree. Answering this question is more informative than inferences based on a non-experimental cross-sectional correlation between political interest and highest level of education or years of schooling because the analysis holds constant unobserved differences between individuals. Even though educational attainment has changed, we know that a host of other attributes – including people's gender, personality, and cognitive ability – have not.

Figure 9.2 offers a way to see change. It compares panelists' political interest before and after they earned an upper secondary degree. Their interest development is compared to that of panelists who start out without a degree and are of roughly the same age, but never end up completing upper secondary school. The dark line plots political interest among the first group of panelists who earn an upper secondary schooling degree at some point while they are part of the study. The dark line is aligned so that $t = 0$ is the first year panelists report the degree. The first filled circle marks this time point. To the right of $t = 0$, the dark line graphs political interest among these panelists in the years after obtaining

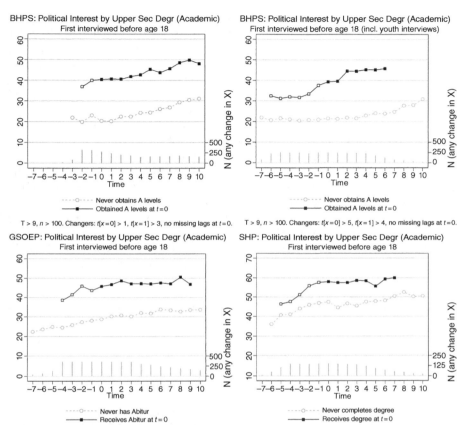

FIGURE 9.2 Within-Subject Change in Political Interest, by Upper Secondary Schooling Degree

the degree. The empty circles to the left of $t = 0$ show their interest levels before this transition. (The bars at the bottom of each graph show on how many observations the dark line is based.)

In the British data in the top row of Figure 9.2, the dark line reveals change in political interest in the years after panelists received their upper-secondary degree at $t = 0$. While education is not randomly assigned, we can loosely think of these panelists as the "treatment group" and the degree as the "treatment." To gain greater certainty that the degree caused this change, it is important to compare it to a "control group." The second, lighter, line in the graph therefore follows a group of panelists who were also first interviewed at a young age, but did not complete an upper secondary schooling degree (hence, empty circles represent their political interest averages throughout).[2] Because the research design involves no random assignment, I will avoid the term "control group" and usually refer to these panelists as the "reference group." If the degree has causal impact, the darker line should reveal greater change after $t = 0$ than the lighter line. Parallel lines, even if both display an upward trend, do not constitute evidence for causal impact because they indicate that the degree affected treatment and reference groups to a similar extent.

Figure 9.2 suggests causal impact of upper-secondary education in Britain, picking up two or three years before students finished their degree, during their time in school. The graphs in the first row compare panelists who earn *A levels* to those who do not. The graph on the left uses only the adult interviews; the graph on the right includes youth interviews. With youth interviews providing an earlier baseline, the graph indicates an increase in political interest associated with an upper secondary degree. Three to six years before some complete this degree – when they were still in lower secondary schools – future graduates are about 10 points more interested than those who will not complete *A levels*. In the two years before graduation, the difference between these two groups rises to about 20 points. There is no indication that the impact attenuates; if anything, it appears to increase after degree conferral.

Other graphs in Figure 9.2 display essentially parallel lines. Political interest develops about the same among degree recipients as in the reference group, albeit at a higher level. If the same interest difference existed years before degree conferral, the degree can hardly be its cause.

---

[2] Using the same minimum number of interviews and the same age limits at the first interview keeps the age distribution of the two groups similar. Panelists who do not earn an upper secondary degree are aligned with the "treatment group" by computing the distribution of age of degree recipients and assigning panelists who never make this transition a $t = 0$ point based on a random draw from this distribution. Simply plotting interest by age in the "no transition" group so that $t = 0$ aligns with the average age of entering upper secondary school in the "transition" group would skew the comparison because panelists who made this transition did not all make it at the same age, and age is non-linearly related to political interest.

Graphs aim to balance the requirement to include a sufficient number of observations at each time point with the need to minimize selection effects related to panel tenure. Following the exact same two groups of panelists (one at some point experiencing a transition, the other not) would provide the cleanest comparison of their respective political interest levels. But it would also discard a lot of data from panelists who provided fewer observations – and risk bias if panelists with many observations are atypical in their political interest development (a possibility for which there is little evidence here or elsewhere in the data). Notes below the graphs state how panelists were selected for inclusion.

Because political interest was not asked in BHPS adult interviews between 1997 and 2000, graphs include some data from panelists who do not provide observations immediately before and after obtaining a degree (or other transitions, in other graphs). For example, political interest for a panelist who obtained *A levels* in 1998 may only be observed in 1995 and 1996, and again after 2000. As long as the gap in political interest is unrelated to other variables in the analysis, this limitation should not bias patterns in the graphs.

Data for Germany suggest parallel trends most clearly. In Switzerland, the graph provides a hint that a degree might raise political interest. In the two years before and after earning an upper secondary degree, panelists' interest increases slightly more than among their counterparts who do not earn the degree. This difference is no more than a few points, however, and does not last. Three to four years after earning their degree, panelists differ by about the same amount from their counterparts without degrees as they did three to four years before earning the degree.

To sum up, graphical examination of within-person change can assess the plausibility of causal impact. For Germany and Switzerland, it indicates at best very small causal effects of education on political interest. The double-digit cross-sectional differences between adults with and without an upper secondary schooling degree reported at the beginning of this section look like poor estimates of causal impact. Analysis of within-person change suggests that strong associations between political interest and education among adults that are so evident in Figure 9.1 and in many previous studies are largely the consequence of omitted variables that happen to be correlated with education.

As the results for Britain show, graphical analysis can detect bigger effects. The joint BHPS sample provides initial evidence for a causal effect of education in Britain by showing that political interest increases more among recipients of an upper secondary degree than among panelists of similar age who did not complete the degree. I will return to this evidence later in the chapter and assess several challenges to this preliminary conclusion.

Graphical analysis of within-person change is an intuitive tool to "see" what happens to political interest before and after a hypothesized cause occurred. It is transparent because it displays summaries of the raw data. Yet this style of analysis also has downsides. It does not take into account statistical uncertainty. Partly as a result, graphs can turn out to be inconclusive regarding the presence of effects. As a complement to graphical analysis, I now introduce model-based panel estimators that provide a roughly equivalent analysis.

Model-Based Analysis of Change

The formal way to switch from analyzing levels of a variable to analyzing change comes in two basic flavors: Either, subtract a panelist's response in one wave from her response in the previous wave. Or, calculate the mean for a panelist across all of her responses, then subtract this mean from each response. Change as the difference between adjacent panel waves is known as the first-difference (FD) transformation. Δ is the first difference operator, so $\Delta PI_{it} = PI_{it} - PI_{it-1}$. Defining change as the deviation from the person mean is referred to as the within or fixed-effects (FE) transformation. Two dots above a variable denote this demeaning operator such that $\ddot{PI}_{it} = PI_{it} - \bar{PI}_i$, where $\bar{PI}_i$ is the mean of PI across all panel waves for individual i. Instead of the level of political interest PI_{it}, ΔPI_{it} or $\ddot{P}I_{it}$ becomes the dependent variable in the transformed statistical model.

A panel estimator applies these transformations not only to the dependent variable, but also to all independent variables on the right-hand side of the model. This is how it achieves the First Big Benefit of panel data. The best way to see it is to look at the model before and after the transformation. Here is the model of political interest from Chapter 6, which distinguishes the contribution of four different variables on political interest: age (π^{AGE}_{it}), birth cohort (π^{BC}_{i}), sample (π^{S}_{i}), and the interestingness of the environment (x^{N}_{t}):

$$PI_{it} = \beta_1 D_{it} + \pi^{AGE}_{it} + \pi^{BC}_{i} + \pi^{S}_{i} + x^{N}_{t} + \alpha_i + \varepsilon_{it} \tag{9.1}$$

The model includes two unobserved components: α_i, a separate intercept for each panelist that captures stable differences between panelists, and ε_{it}, the remaining difference between the level of political interest predicted by the model for a given time and panelist, and the political interest response the panelist actually gave. In order to test if an educational degree raises political interest, I added a dummy variable for degree holders: D_{it} is 1 for years when i is observed with a degree, 0 otherwise. (This simple specification assumes that the full effect of the degree occurs right away. The Second Big Benefit will allow us to relax this restrictive assumption.) In estimating the causal impact of the degree, an acute threat is correlation between D_{it} and the two error components, α_i and ε_{it}. For example, stable cognitive skills might be related to political interest. Because the model does not account for cognitive skills, α_i will be greater for panelists with high cognitive skills. Cognitive skills also affect whether people obtain an upper-secondary degree, so the error term and D_{it} will be correlated – and violate a key assumption of OLS regression. Ignoring this would incorrectly attribute causal impact to the degree which in fact belongs to cognitive skills. With cross-sectional data, there is no way to measure α_i and remove its biasing effect because with only one observation per person, it is not possible to separate someone's long-term stable level from a short-term deviation.

With panel data, on the other hand, there are options to get rid of α_i. Here is what model 9.1 looks like after the first-difference transformation:

$$\Delta PI_{it} = \beta_1^{FD} \Delta D_{it} + \Delta \pi^{AGE}_{it} + \Delta x^{N}_{t} + \Delta \varepsilon_{it} \tag{9.2}$$

The troublemaker α_i is gone! It no longer appears in Equation 9.2 because α_i at t and α_i at $t-1$ equal each other, so subtracting one from the other yields zero. The same is true for cohort and sample differences, which are also constant over time and thus drop out. (The variables that change over time, education, age, and interestingness, remain in the model. For example, Δx^{N}_{t} captures differences in interestingness of the political and economic environment between $t-1$ and t.)

Alternatively, after the within or fixed-effects transformation, model 9.1 becomes:

$$\ddot{P}I_{it} = \beta_1^{FE}\ddot{D}_{it} + \ddot{\pi}_{it}^{AGE} + \ddot{x}_t^N + \ddot{\epsilon}_{it} \tag{9.3}$$

Again, α_i is eliminated, this time because it equals its subject mean and is thus subtracted from itself. Cohort and sample differences drop out for the same reason.

Both transformations make causal inference easier if we are willing to assume that α_i has an additive and separable effect on political interest. Because they remove α_i from the estimation, it can be arbitrarily correlated with the error term without introducing bias. A correlation between the educational degree and stable cognitive skills is no longer a threat to causal inference. More generally, unobserved constant variables do not lead to omitted variable bias after the FE or FD transformation. (This First Big Benefit of panel data does not guard against omitted variable bias through unobserved variables that change over time.)

In slightly different ways, the FD and FE transformations are a model-based representation of plotting change over time. In graphs, we can visually examine if the trend in political interest is broken by a presumed cause that happens at $t = 0$ and compare it to the trend among people who did not experience the cause. In a model, we use a transformation to convert variables into within-person changes and then use a regression approach to see if changes in political interest are related to changes in other variables. Models 9.2 and 9.3 yield, respectively, estimates of β_1^{FD} and β_1^{FE}. Significant estimates indicate that within-person change in political interest is statistically related to within-person change in the independent variable, in this case holding an educational degree.

THE CHANGING EFFECTS BENEFIT

When we talk about "the effect" on an outcome, our language is imprecise. We are describing an effect that occurred over a specific period between the time the cause unfolded and the time we measured the outcome – but we do not typically mention those details of timing, or do so elsewhere in our report, often in the fine print. In the household panels used here, multiple measurements of political interest in the years after a purported effect occurred make it possible to estimate different effects of a potential causal factor at different times. The effect of a college degree on political interest, for example, can be assessed in the first reinterview after the panelist obtained the degree and again once every year until the study's most recent wave. It no longer works to talk about "the effect" of a variable, because the answer can differ depending on when we look. Effects can occur all at once or gradually; they can decay or grow in strength. Being able to detect changing effects is the Second Big Benefit of panel data – if the panel includes enough waves.

The Second Big Benefit of panel data strengthens both observational and experimental research. Studies that measure outcomes only once at the same interval for all participants – whether they use random assignment or not –

estimate causal impact over one, often arbitrary, time period. We can think of these research designs as "minimally dynamic" – they examine change either by measuring a variable twice or by using random assignment (to argue that control and treatment group used to be indistinguishable.) Many social scientists train their intuitions and methodological facilities on such minimally dynamic research designs. In most laboratory or survey experiments, for example, the outcome is measured minutes after the treatment. Random assignment yields strong identification of a causal effect, but it is only one of many conceivable effects, specific to the duration between treatment and measurement, and to whatever the subjects ended up doing in this interim. Adding repeated outcome measurements, especially in the period after the treatment has occurred, can strengthen the research design by characterizing how the effect evolves over time. An effect might unfold gradually, for example over several years of schooling before graduation, as in Figure 9.2 for British youths. Long panels with many waves thus increase leverage for causal inference considerably.

Model 9.1 proposes a dynamically unrealistic effect of an upper secondary schooling degree. It implies that the effect on political interest occurs entirely in the year when the degree was received and remains constant afterwards. Figure 9.2 suggests that this is not always true. Political interest levels of British panelists with and without a degree diverge in the years after the degree was awarded. In Germany, they converge very slightly. The graphs also show that political interest of future degree recipients already rises in the years before graduation. Theoretically, this makes sense: The degree per se is not a particularly relevant causal variable. The supposed treatment is not the reception of the degree, but the educational experience that culminates in its reception, so any rise in political interest is likely to be gradual over the period of schooling. Model 9.1 is thus dynamically misspecified. In that situation, FD and FE estimators are bound to generate different results. (The Chapter Appendix explains why.)

To estimate treatment effects more flexibly, model 9.1 can be modified to allow the treatment to have different effects over different intervals. Laporte and Windmeijer (2005) recommend a series of "pulse variables," used here instead of the step variable D_{it}:

$$PI_{it} = \sum \beta^j_1 PD^j_{it} + \pi^{AGE}_{it} + \pi^{BC}_i + \pi^S_i + \mathbf{x}^N_t + \alpha_i + \varepsilon_{it} \qquad (9.4)$$

Pulse variables PD^j_{it} are dummies that are 1 if the number of years between t and receiving the degree is j, 0 otherwise. For example, PD^0_{it} is 1 in the year in which i is first observed with the degree. PD^1_{it} is 1 in the second year in which i is observed with the degree. Negative values for j indicate dummies for years before i received the degree. For example, PD^{-3}_{it} is 1 three years before receiving the degree. We could include one dummy for every possible temporal distance between degree receipt and year of interview. With pulse variables, the model can pick up gradual, temporary, and delayed effects. β^j_i quantifies the impact of a degree j years after (or, for negative j, before) i received the degree.

To illustrate this approach, Figure 9.3 plots estimates of the full set of pulse variables for upper secondary schooling degrees.[3] The pulse variable for one year must be omitted from the model and serves as the baseline for the effects over different intervals. I set the baseline to capture the typical length of upper-secondary education. It is two years in Britain and three years in both Germany and Switzerland (Schneider 2008; Seitz et al. 2005), so the omitted pulse variables are $t = -2$ in BHPS and $t = -3$ in the GSOEP and the SHP. The coefficients for the other pulse variables, plotted in the graphs with standard errors, show difference to these baselines.[4]

Figure 9.3 demonstrates the need to specify panel models in a way that allows for non-constant effects. The effect of the German *Abitur* on political interest, for example, occurs while students are still attending upper secondary school (at $t = -2, -1$), is at best marginally statistically significant at $t = 0$, the year panelists receive their degree (marked by the vertical line), and drops to zero thereafter. Upper-secondary education in Germany has only a temporary (and rather small) effect on political interest.

The effects of *A levels* in Britain and the *Matura* in Switzerland are larger and more sustained. Formal tests described in the Chapter Appendix indicate that they are constant after degree conferral in both countries. In both countries, significant effects on political interest already appear at $t = -1$ (and $t = -2$, in Switzerland), before panelists receive their degree. They are somewhat smaller than the post-degree effect, demonstrating a gradual build-up.

For Britain, the graph based on the joint BHPS sample shows another manifestation of non-constant effects: Most estimates are statistically significant and negative for t between -7 and -3. Panelists who eventually complete

---

[3] Following the empirical results in Chapter 8, I allow age trajectories to vary by gender and use a quartic age polynomial instead of age dummies (starting here and continuing through the rest of the book).

[4] The most common ages to first observe an upper secondary degree are 17 and 18 in the British BHPS (71 percent), 19 and 20 in the German GSOEP (67 percent), and 19 and 20 in the Swiss SHP (63 percent). (Extending the range by 1 year on each end captures 86 percent of degree-earning panelists in the GSOEP, 87 percent in the SHP, and 87 percent in the BHPS.) This leaves at least two waves before the typical start of upper-secondary education in the SHP (eligibility age 14) and four waves in the combined BHPS sample (eligibility age 11 for youth interviews). In the GSOEP, with eligibility age of 16, only three observations before degree are available for panelists who first report their *Abitur* at age 19, so some panelists are not observed before the start of upper-secondary education. In the adult component of the BHPS, the eligibility age 16 leaves little time before degree. At least two observations before degrees are available only for the older half of degree-earners (see Chapter Appendix for details).

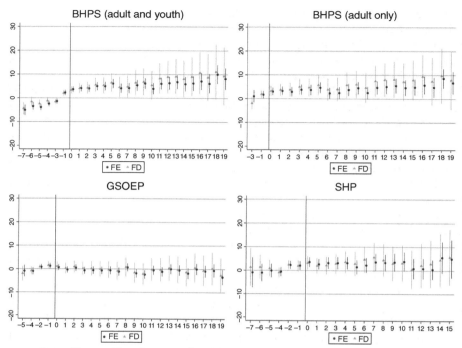

FIGURE 9.3 Year-to-Year Impact of Upper Secondary Degrees on Political Interest
Note: Graphs plot coefficients and 90% confidence intervals for pulse variables based on Equation 9.4 for upper secondary schooling degrees. Vertical lines indicate reception of degree. Minimum of three panel waves and age below 40 required to be included. Omits the GSOEP East German sample before 1996.

A levels were less politically interested already between 3 and 7 years before graduation than those who would not finish upper-secondary education. It is likely that this result is partly explained by a causal effect of upper-secondary education on panelists who were already attending this level before $t = -2$ (as the two-year interval between interviews is unlikely to coincide precisely with two-year attendance of an upper-secondary institution), so the post-degree effect in Figure 9.3 is probably an underestimate. This argument is not plausible for the earliest significant and still lower estimates, however, so the results also suggest that something happens in lower-secondary education that affects ultimate *A level* recipients differently (such as advanced classes to prepare for Sixth Form College).

Results for the three countries thus reveal subtly different types of effect: A small, fleeting effect in Germany, a larger effect in Switzerland that appears to dissipate eventually (but estimates become increasingly noisy because few panelists earned a degree while on the panel and then remained on it for more than decade), and a robust effect in Britain that is still statistically detectable almost two decades after the degree was awarded. A model that allows only a constant effect following graduation is misspecified for all three countries and would yield biased estimates (with FE and FD estimators differently biased, as explained in the Chapter Appendix).

Displaying the results for each independent variable graphically as in Figure 9.3 takes up a lot of space. It is easy to summarize the key dynamic effect estimates numerically instead. For example, the average impact of a degree (relative to the pre-program baseline) in the first three years after conferral is 4 points in Britain, 3 points in Switzerland, and indistinguishable from zero in Germany. These effects are calculated by jointly estimating coefficients for PD^{0}_{it}, PD^{1}_{it}, PD^{2}_{it}, and PD^{3}_{it} while they are constrained to be equal. Tests of the equality constraints indicate that these yearly effects are statistically indistinguishable, so the effects of education in Britain and Switzerland were constant for three years after degree conferral. Effects in Britain would be underestimated by a point or two if $t = -3$ is a more appropriate baseline. (These summaries consider both FE and FD estimates. The Chapter Appendix presents details.) I return to the topic of education in Chapter 10, providing some background about the education systems of Britain, Germany, and Switzerland and presenting causal inferences not only for upper secondary schooling, but other programs and qualifications as well.

The FE and FD estimates presented here rarely differ by more than a point and their confidence intervals in Figure 9.3 always overlap with nearly identical point estimates – so why take additional space to present both sets of results? When the full set of pulse variables is included and the model otherwise correctly specified, FD and FE estimates converge (for balanced panels) even when effects are not constant over time (Laporte and Windmeijer 2005). But this conclusion does not apply when the model fails to account for delayed or attenuating effects. Indeed, results for naïve models that do not take account of the gradual build-up and later decline of education effects prove bafflingly divergent in many cases. Because correct model specification cannot be empirically ascertained, the convergence of FD and FE estimates is not a foolproof diagnostic. Nonetheless, comparison of both estimators can serve as a useful heuristic.

The Changing Effects Benefit also applies for continuous variables. Model 9.1 estimates the impact of a discrete one-time event, the reception of a specific educational degree, and allows year-by-year variation in effect size starting long before the event and continuing for decades. This highly flexible approach is feasible for other unique discrete events. With some modifications, it could also be used for events (such as job loss) that can occur repeatedly over a person's time on the panel. But continuous time-varying measures can also have gradual or decaying effects. They require another modeling strategy.

To put it succinctly and technically for one paragraph, I include contemporaneous values and a number of lags of continuous time-varying variables w_{it} to accommodate their dynamic effects. With lags, the specification becomes a distributed lag model (Wooldridge 2009, 342–5):

$$PI_{it} = \gamma_0 w_{it} + \gamma_1 w_{it-1} + \ldots + \gamma_k w_{it-k} + \beta x_{it} + \alpha_i + \varepsilon_{it} \qquad (9.5)$$

where $x_{it} = \pi^{AGE}_{it} + \pi^{BC}_i + \pi^S_i + \beta_N x^N_t$ collects the terms covered previously. While all available lags (and leads)[5] can be included, it would constrain the sample to panelists who completed every wave or require some imputation of missing values. Limiting the number of lags to k avoids this problem and still accommodates the most plausible dynamic effects. (Effects that operate with a delay[6] of many years are theoretically unlikely.) The effect of w can vary over time for k periods. After k periods, the *long-run effect* is assumed to become constant. The long-run effect (also referred to as the long-run multiplier) is calculated as the sum of the coefficients γ_0, $\gamma_1, \ldots, \gamma_k$. It makes no functional form assumptions regarding the dynamics of effects for up to k periods after the change in the independent variable. Applications of this approach later in Part III use graphs to show both the yearly effects and how they accumulate to create a long-run effect.

THE THIRD BENEFIT OF PANEL DATA: UNTANGLING CAUSE AND EFFECT

The first two Big Benefits of panel data improve analysis of cause and effect by comparing changes in variables, not their levels, and by picking up changes that occur with delay or decay. Yet a relationship between changes is still only an association. Taking it as evidence for causal impact requires additional evidence. Sometimes, the direction of causality between two variables is easy to determine. Random assignment as part of an experiment is the easiest case because the researcher controls variation in one of the variables. By definition, random variation cannot be the consequence of changes in another variable, so any robust association between them is caused by the randomized treatment.

The data I analyze in Part III of this book are observational, so randomization is not available to support causal claims, and stronger assumptions are necessary to draw causal inferences. The Third Big Benefit of panel data is to provide analytic options that make these assumptions more plausible than they would be for cross-sectional observational data. For example, panel data can sometimes establish that one change clearly preceded another change. While

---

[5] A distributed lag model can also include leads (Blanden et al. 2012; Gallego et al. 2016) much like the pulse variable specification (Laporte and Windmeijer 2005). In fact, for a binary variable, the distributed lag model with all leads and lags is equivalent to a pulse variable specification with different parameterization.

[6] With annual panel data, a "delayed" effect describes a change of w observed at t that affects PI at $t + 1$ or later. "Without delay" means that a change in w observed at time t has already affected PI at t.

not as dispositive as random assignment, temporal order can back up claims about causal order.

Additional analytic options to support identifying assumptions are a benefit of panel data, but the necessity to rely on modeling assumptions in the first place makes this benefit less unequivocal than the first two Big Benefits. An experiment is designed to be sure that a predictor is causal because it was assigned randomly. Even with the benefit of panel data, causal inferences in the absence of randomization are based on non-trivial assumptions, making them second best, at least in principle. Panel data help disentangle some questions of causality, but they cannot offer the same peace of mind regarding identification that we would get from randomly assigning people to, say, stay in school for another year, or join a civic organization, and then observing their political interest after these treatments. For some independent variables, future experimental studies may thus overturn current findings on the basis of fewer, more self-evident assumptions. For other potential causes of political interest, it would require years and perhaps decades to demonstrate experimentally the dynamic effects that some of the predictors of political interest appear to have. And for yet other predictors, experiments may never be feasible, so panel estimators represent our best chance for understanding their impact.

Because the causal claims that follow cannot rest on the simple truth of random assignment, they take more time to make and more conceptual exposition to justify. In order to be transparent about the assumptions underlying advanced panel estimators, the remainder of this chapter offers a mostly non-technical explanation for readers who want to gauge the plausibility of the inferential foundation. For greater precision, statistical details of these panel estimators appear in the Chapter Appendix.

There are several logical reasons why a correlation between change in an independent variable and change in political interest might not in fact result from a causal effect of the independent variable on political interest. Each reason constitutes a form of endogeneity that could invalidate causal claims. One common form of endogeneity is omitted variable bias. Although constant omitted variables do not bias causal inferences thanks to the First Big Benefit of panel data, this protection does not extend to variables that change over time. If another time-varying predictor exists that is correlated with the presumed cause of political interest, and this predictor is also related to a change in political interest during the same period, and this other predictor does not appear in the model – then estimates will be biased. The presumed causal factor is in effect stealing from this other variable, which is the real cause but remains unaccounted for.

For example, we will see later in the book that as individuals become more interested in politics, they also become more likely to be members of civic organizations. It is conceivable that involvement in a civic organization could raise political interest. A politically uninterested participant might realize that she finds it exciting and rewarding to plan and carry out the group's initiatives and influence its decisions, develop an understanding of the political issues involved, or be inspired by other group members eager to discuss policy and politics in the group's area of engagement and beyond – and become more politically interested as a result. According to an alternative explanation, however, the individual developed greater trust in the political system, which both led her to join the civic organization and raised her political interest. When trust is not accounted for, the relationship between joining civic organizations and increasing political interest might not indicate a causal effect of membership, but instead an effect of trust in the political system (the omitted variable).

Another form of endogeneity is reverse causation. It seems just as plausible that a rise in political interest causes someone to join a civic organization as the other way around. A statistical relationship between changes in interest and changes in organizational membership might indicate causation in either direction – and to simply assume that the causal arrow goes only one way amounts to risking faulty estimates due to endogeneity bias.

Reverse causation is subtly different from selection effects, another common source of endogeneity. It is not a secret that civic organizations dedicate time and effort to discussion and initiatives involving political topics. Precisely as a result of this expectation, more politically interested individuals are prone to join civic organizations in the first place. With cross-sectional data, when we cannot calculate if people's political interest changed, this selection effect could explain some or all of the relationship between the levels of the two variables. With panel data, the First Big Benefit addresses this problem: If people's political interest has been constantly high, but they just joined an organization, examining change in the two variables does not in fact turn up a statistical association that we might mistake for a causal effect (because we would see change in membership, but no change in political interest). In short, examining changes, not levels already takes care of some forms of endogeneity, but reverse causation is not among them.

Sometimes, strong theoretical grounds minimize some (or even all) of the concerns about endogeneity. We may be fairly certain that selection or reciprocal causation do not operate when influences occur regardless of a person's existing political interest. A young person cannot choose her parents. Compulsory schooling laws make it very hard to avoid several years of schooling. But the degree of selectivity or reciprocal causation can be difficult to determine and may differ in idiosyncratic ways. While a young person cannot choose her parents, she can choose to avoid political discussions with them. Several years of schooling are required for everyone, but civics classes are sometimes optional.

Statistically, different forms endogeneity amount to the same problem: They invalidate the assumption that the presumed causal factor is exogenous even after adjusting for all the other relationships specified by the statistical model. As a general way to define exogeneity, it requires covariates to be independent to the model's error term – but omitted variable bias and reciprocal causation induce correlation between covariate and error. The key to understanding how the household panel data can help with this challenge is thus the statistical concept of the error term.

What Is an Error Term?

The error term absorbs whatever components of political interest the model did not capture. If, according to the model, someone is predicted to have a political interest score of 50, but the actually observed response is 60, the error is 10. Something happened that raised the person's political interest report over and above what the model anticipated. It is useful to think of this as a "shock" to political interest that has nowhere to go but in the error term. Some shocks are literally errors, as when the interviewer marks the wrong box. Other shocks reflect genuinely higher (or lower) political interest. When shocks occur randomly – when they are not systematically related to anything else in the model, that is – they do not generate endogeneity. Unfortunately, there are many ways for shocks to be related to other variables and thus to violate the assumption of exogeneity.

In cross-sectional models, there is only one period and thus one error term and one value for each covariate per person. Exogeneity requires independence of the error and the covariates. In panel models, the definition of exogeneity becomes more complex because there are more periods per person and a covariate is observed repeatedly. For a covariate to be exogenous in a panel model, its past, current, and future values must be independent of the error term. Understanding the implications of this definition is critically important and requires consideration of some details of the model.

The relevant error term is the error term of the equation we wish to estimate. For panel models, this is the equation after the transformation to eliminate the unit effect α_i (the First Big Benefit). With FD and FE, we get two different transformed equations – with two different error terms. Hence, the assumption of exogeneity means something different for the two estimators.

After the FE transformation, the error term in 9.3 is $\ddot{\varepsilon}it$, the difference between error ε at time t and the mean of ε over all waves for which the panelist provides data. In other words, the error term is the average of all the shocks to her political interest over the years subtracted from this year's shock. (So if this year's shock is unusually big and positive, the error term will probably also be positive.) After the FD transformation, the error term in 9.2 is $\Delta\varepsilon_{it}$, the difference between ε at time t and ε at time $t-1$. The error term is last year's shock to political interest subtracted from this year's shock. (So if this year's shock is bigger, the error term will be positive.)

This does not sound like much, but the difference between FE and FD is very consequential. Because the error term in the transformed equations differs, the exogeneity assumption differs, too. In the fixed-effects (FE) estimator, *shocks from all periods appear in the error term* because it includes the mean shock over all panel waves. For a covariate to be independent of the error term, it thus needs to be independent at each and every panel wave. This is known as strict exogeneity. The error term of the first-difference (FD) estimator is $\varepsilon_{it} - \varepsilon_{it-1}$, so it involves *shocks at only two panel waves*. For this error to be independent of the covariate Δx_{it} ($= x_{it} - x_{it-1}$), none of the terms can be correlated, so correlations between x and ε at $t-1$, t, and $t+1$ must all be zero. This is sometimes called weak exogeneity.

What seems like an arcane detail has big implications for accommodating violations of exogeneity because the FD estimator imposes no restrictions on how values of the independent variable at $t-2$ and earlier may be related to the error term.[7] In contrast, the FE estimator requires a stricter definition of exogeneity that applies to the independent variable at all time periods. Before explaining suitable methods when exogeneity is not met that exploit this feature of the FD estimator, it may help to describe more precisely how the three forms of endogeneity generate correlations between the presumed causal factor and the error term that violate the exogeneity assumption.[8]

In the example of omitted variable bias, an increase in political trust between time $t-1$ and time t causes a rise in political interest by time t. When trust does not appear as a covariate in the model, its effect is absorbed by the error term, so both $\Delta \varepsilon_{it}$ (in the FD estimator 9.2) and $\ddot{e}it$, (in the FE estimator 9.3) are higher for panelists with greater political trust. This violates the assumption of exogeneity if people who joined the civic organization had different changes in trust than those who did not join (and the timing of changes in group membership and political trust is the same).

The fix for the violation of exogeneity is obvious in this case: include political trust as a covariate. Yet omitted variable bias is often serious precisely because we do not know what other omitted time-varying predictor might be related to both political interest and our presumed causal predictor, or because we do not have appropriate measures available. The trust example does emphasize that the correlation with an omitted covariate must be between differences, not levels, and occur (predominantly) between differences in the same period to threaten exogeneity. That is often less likely than conditions for omitted variable bias in cross-sectional data.

In the example of reciprocal causation, a shock between $t-1$ and t leads an individual to experience unexpectedly high political interest for unknown

---

[7] This is only true if the errors at different times t are not correlated. This serial error assumption is important, but I find little evidence that it is a problem for models of political interest using the household panel data and thus discuss it only briefly.

[8] For some variables, logical arguments and auxiliary evidence can strengthen assumptions. I have assumed in previous chapters that interestingness of the environment is exogenous. It is highly unlikely that frequency of *New York Times* coverage, the state of the economy, or the timing of the next election are affected by European panelists' political interest or a variable correlated with it.

reasons. Because the model cannot account for it otherwise, the shock ends up in the error term. If, as a result of this shock, the individual joins a civic education organization, the $\Delta\varepsilon_{it}$ and the first difference of the membership variable at t will both be positive and correlated, violating the assumption of exogeneity. The estimate would falsely credit the civic organization with creating the rise in political interest because it does not "know" that joining was a consequence of earlier political interest.

For many non-political variables, reciprocal causation (or selection effects) seem implausible on theoretical grounds. Unexpectedly higher political interest is not going to lead someone to get married, buy a house, or have children. It probably won't lead people to lose their jobs or their parents to get divorced. But there are other covariates for which selection of this kind is still theoretically remote, but not beyond imagination. Perhaps unexpectedly high political interest causes someone to quit her job at an insurance company and work as a high-school teacher instead. If teachers make less money than insurance agents, the political interest shock ultimately affects income, thus invalidating the assumption that income is an exogenous covariate.

These are the problems caused by different forms of endogeneity. If present, they lead to a violation of the exogeneity assumption.[9] To get consistent estimates for variables that are not exogenous, it is necessary to either adjust the model or relax the assumptions. The price to pay in both cases is more complicated estimation procedures and other assumptions that, although weaker than exogeneity, still need to be justified.

Controlling for Last Year's Political Interest

Although exogenous effects are a lot easier to estimate, panel data do offer some leverage for understanding if highly selective behaviors like joining civic organizations change political interest or only reflect existing political interest. The idea is to isolate the effect of selective activities by holding constant the effect of past political interest in motivating the activity in the first place. This requires including the lagged dependent variable – the political interest report in the previous interview, about a year earlier – as a predictor. Adding it to model 9.5 yields

$$PI_{it} = \lambda PI_{i,t-1} + \gamma_0 w_{it} + \gamma_1 w_{it-1} + \ldots + \gamma_k w_{it-k} + \beta x_{it} + \alpha_i + \varepsilon_{it} \qquad (9.6)$$

Model 9.6 removes some forms of endogeneity because the error term ε_{it} no longer absorbs the leftover portion of shocks to past political interest as those are now modeled directly. More technically, the independence requirement of

---

[9] Formal tests exist to detect violations empirically. In FD models, significant coefficients for the undifferenced predictor would indicate violations of exogeneity. In FE models, exogeneity can be tested by including x_{it+1} as an additional regressor (Wooldridge 2002, 302).

the exogeneity assumption is now conditional on PI_{it-1}. The lagged dependent variable reduces endogeneity bias through slow omitted time-varying predictors because their effects on PI_{it} are controlled for to the extent that they happen before $t - 1$. Selection effects and reciprocal causation can be mitigated for the same reason.[10] As I discuss in the next section, (9.6) continues to suffer from endogeneity bias when these processes operate in the period between $t - 1$ and t (so controlling for PI_{it-1} does not capture them).

In the case of political interest, a lagged dependent variable is also theoretically more appropriate. According to the psychological model, interest is an enduring predisposition, not a sentiment that is created anew at every interview, as model 9.5 suggests. Adding lagged political interest to the model specification makes this dynamic element of political interest more explicit. In model 9.5, current political interest is a function of a person's constant political interest "base level" α_i, various covariates w_{it} and their lags, age, and current interestingness of the political and economic environment. Lagged political interest in (9.6) allows for the possibility that last year's unanticipatedly high (or low) political interest still affects current political interest. The parameter λ captures the extent to which the previous interest report is related to the current interest report after the other elements of the model have been accounted for. If last year's shock was caused by a clerical error, the possibility that λ would be different from zero seems very remote; the panelist would not even be aware of it. But if a panelist was genuinely more interested at $t - 1$ than the model implied, some (or all) of this shock could still be present at t. This is referred to as persistence, so λ measures the extent of persistence in political interest. It is important to understand that the estimate of persistence is not a characteristic of political interest as such, but is conditional on the model. If a different model leads to more accurate accounting for interest at $t - 1$, the shock is smaller and the estimate of λ could change. (Moreover, α_i is the ultimate vehicle for persistence, at least in the colloquial sense, because it captures the portion of political interest that is entirely stable over the period of the panel.)[11]

---

[10] Including a lagged dependent variable can also reduce serial error correlation because remnants of a shock to political interest at $t - 1$ no longer end up in the error term at t but are instead modeling explicitly.

[11] A model with a lagged dependent variable is sometimes referred to as a "dynamic panel model." This terminology is confusing because even model 9.5 permits dynamics in the form of effects of independent variables that change over time, like the ones plotted earlier. Even a model that includes no lagged terms at all is still dynamic when the unit effect for panelists α_i is included because it implies an equilibrium level of political interest that can be adjusted through changes in other independent variables. Hence, even a simple panel model is consistent with the theoretical notion that political interest is a lasting predisposition. Model 9.5 allows for more complex dynamic patterns, and model 9.6 is explicit about persistence in political interest and permits slow-moving equilibration.

After adding lagged political interest, the model can be rewritten to emphasize the focus on explaining *change* in political interest. Subtracting $PI_{i,t-1}$ from (9.6) yields:

$$\Delta PI_{it} = (\lambda - 1)PI_{i,t-1} + \gamma_0 w_{it} + \gamma_1 w_{it-1} + \ldots + \gamma_k w_{it-k} + \beta x_{it} + \alpha_i + \varepsilon_{it} \quad (9.7)$$

Equation 9.7 expresses the change in political interest between this year and last year as a function of last year's political interest, the long-run person average, and the other covariates. In this formulation, the implications of shocks to political interest at $t - 1$ for change between $t - 1$ and t are apparent. If there is no persistence, perhaps because the shocks are all clerical errors, $\lambda = 0$ simplifies the first term in (9.7) to negative $PI_{i,t-1}$. Hence, if the shock at $t - 1$ was positive, political interest is expected to decline by the amount of the shock between $t - 1$ and t. (And vice versa for a negative shock. This is assuming that none of the independent variables change, so based on the rest of the model, political interest is expected to remain the same.) This is why a model like (9.7) is often referred to as an "error correction model" (e.g., De Boef and Keele 2008). If there is some persistence in political interest ($0 < \lambda < 1$), a shock at $t - 1$ will not be fully corrected, but the adjustment still happens in the same direction.

Dynamic panel models such as (9.6) are more difficult to estimate than models without a lagged dependent variable. The lagged dependent variable violates exogeneity by design. The solution to this problem takes advantage of the fact, discussed earlier, that the FD estimator requires only weak exogeneity, so early lags of political interest may be arbitrarily correlated with the error term $\Delta \varepsilon_{it}$. They can serve as "instruments" for $PI_{i,t-1}$, which appears in the differenced lagged dependent variable and would violate weak exogeneity through correlation with the ε_{it-1} term in the differenced error. The basic idea of an instrument here is to use early lags of a variable that can be considered exogenous. Instead of including the invalid $PI_{i,t-1}$ itself, instruments build up a kind of "scaffolding" from earlier, exogenous lags of political interest that can predict the invalid $t - 1$ term. Technical details appear in the Chapter Appendix.

The scaffolding to identify a dynamic panel model is not automatically durable. The appropriate estimator for this model requires careful verification of two assumptions. First, serial error correlation invalidates certain lags as instruments. Second, valid but weak instruments reduce the efficiency of the estimator and can exacerbate finite sample bias. The estimator also requires attention to the number of instruments as too many instruments can dramatically increase finite sample bias. Specification tests are available to evaluate these requirements. I apply this method first in Chapter 11. Instruments for $PI_{i,t-1}$ turn out to be sufficiently strong and the models pass the requirements for serial correlation.

Estimating the Effect of Predetermined and Endogenous Predictors

Including a lagged dependent variable in no way guarantees that independent variables meet the exogeneity assumption. "Feedback" is another way to think of the correlation between a predictor and the error term that amounts to a violation of exogeneity. The dynamic connotation of the word "feedback" is helpful in a panel context because we are worried about a sequence of influences unfolding in a direction opposite to the presumed causal path. A shock to political interest ends up in the error terms because the model did not account for it. This shock may "feed back" into an independent variable causing the correlation that violates exogeneity. Model 9.6 can only control for feedback that has already occurred by the panel wave at $t - 1$. To obtain consistent estimates for independent variables that still violate exogeneity, an approach similar to the treatment of lagged political interest is required. If some observations of a covariate could be affected by (shocks to) political interest, then estimation must use only observations that occurred early enough they cannot have been subject to this influence. (Those observations could have been subject to shocks at earlier waves, but those shocks do not appear in the error term of the estimation equation, so they do not bias the model. This is only true in the FD estimator, whose error term only includes shocks going back to $t - 1$.)

There are two types of feedback, distinguished by their speed. For example, deciding on an occupation and deciding what civic organizations to join involves different considerations. Many people commit to a profession early (as young adults) and revisit their choice infrequently. Organizational involvement, on the other hand, is often more temporary and involves less of a commitment. The speed of feedback – an unexpected rise in political interest leading someone to take a politically impinged job or join a civic organization, or an unexpected drop in interest leading someone to quit that job or leave that organization – is likely slower for occupational choice than for organizational membership.

The general logic of the fix is to use lags of variables unaffected by feedback from the model's error as instruments for following observations. The speed of feedback governs whether a predictor that violates strict exogeneity is *predetermined* or *endogenous*. If feedback is slow, so it affects future values of a covariate w^P_{it}, but not current or past values, w^P_{it} is said to be *predetermined* because it was determined prior to t, so a shock at t cannot change it. This assumption is also known as dynamic sequential exogeneity.

Fast feedback exacerbates the estimation problem. There is an econometrically sound fix, but it is more taxing to implement even with large panel datasets because it is built on weaker scaffolding. When w^P_{it} is predetermined, its current value is uncorrelated with ε_{is}, so the shock to political interest does not yet affect w^P_{it} at time t. If this is not true and even current values of the covariate could be subject to feedback, we can only justify a weaker assumption. Whereas predetermined covariates w^P_{it} may only be correlated with future values of the error term, endogenous variables w^E_{it} may also be correlated with the contemporaneous error. To accommodate this weaker assumption, instruments must be measured earlier which threatens to make them weaker (because they are further removed in time from the variable they are instrumenting).

The speed of feedback is relative to the interval at which panel waves occur. The shorter the intervals between waves, the easier to justify that a variable is predetermined. As far as political interest development is concerned, if waves at $t-1$ and t occurred within a few days of each other, a typical shock at t would be unlikely to be big (because a shock is defined over and above $PI_{i,t-1}$, so the shock has only a few days to occur) and feedback would be unlikely to occur by t (because the time between the shock and t is too short for many substantive processes to play out that affect the covariate). If decades passed between waves, on the other hand, shocks would potentially be bigger (because they comprise unexpected deviations over many years) and feedback more likely (because years may lie between the shock sometime after $t-1$ and the next measurement at t, giving feedback time to play out by t). Similarly, if an omitted time-varying third variable causes the violation of exogeneity through its effect on both w_i and ε_{it}, longer panel intervals make it more likely that both of these effects will occur in between $t-1$ and t, rendering w_{it} endogenous, not just predetermined.

To continue the example, assuming organizational membership to be predetermined is plausible only if feedback from political interest affects group membership with some delay. Individuals who experience an unexpected rise in political interest after $t-1$ may need time to identify and join the group that is right for them and therefore not yet be a member at t. If any effect of political interest on joining the group and any effect of a third variable on both interest and group membership operate with this kind of delay, then past *and current* group membership is uncorrelated with the error term. Group membership at $t-1$ can serve as a valid instrument for the difference in group membership between $t-1$ and t.

However, since the time between panel waves is at least a year in the data used here, treating group membership as predetermined may be unrealistic. It is certainly easy to leave a group quickly in response to a drop in political interest. Fast feedback invalidates $w_{i,t-1}$ as an instrument. Similarly, if an omitted third variable causes people to change their political interest and their group membership between $t-1$ and t, estimates using $w_{i,t-1}$ as an instrument will be biased. To address this problem, group membership has to be treated as endogenous, allowing $w_{i,t-1}$ and ε_{it} to be correlated. In this case, group membership has to be lagged at least twice to be a valid instrument for the difference in group membership between $t-1$ and t.

The recipe for addressing violations of exogeneity is theoretically sound, but it rests on two key empirical premises: that tests can detect when it is invalid to treat a covariate as predetermined (as opposed to endogenous) and that lags of a covariate provide an instrument of sufficient strength. Both of these premises can be individually difficult to satisfy, but they also work against each other because a more conservative approach to the first makes the second harder to achieve. The Chapter Appendix describes this tradeoff and the tests available to adjudicate it.

Even though the solution of instrumenting endogenous terms with their lagged values is appropriate as an econometric principle, practice can make it impossible to implement this solution for a given data set when the scaffolding is just too weak. In those cases, I will be unable to estimate some effects of interest. More often, the method meets specification tests and produces informative results but is credible only with thorough documentation of estimation details. The presentation of results in the following chapters reports the necessary auxiliary statistics, either in the tables or as footnotes.

CONCLUSION

Part III of this book focuses on dynamics. At its core is the categorical difference between cross-sectional and longitudinal data. Regardless of the details of the panel design, observing the same individual-level characteristic more than once provides a fundamental advantage: the ability to correlate changes rather than levels of a variable. As simple as that sounds, this analytical shift is eye-opening when it comes to considering what factors might plausibly be central to the outcomes we study. In many instances, the following analysis will reveal robust cross-sectional associations between political interest and other variables. Almost as often, however, these associations turn out to be widely off the mark as estimates of causal impact. When a variable changes that is cross-sectionally associated with political interest, changes in political interest rarely follow, and when they do, the magnitude is much smaller than the cross-sectional association.

Panel estimators provide some opportunities to disentangle cause and effect even when there is feedback between the two, a serious problem in analyses of observational data. The design of a panel, especially the number and spacing of reinterviews, has important consequences for how much more analytical force a panel provides. Although panels with two or three waves provide more leverage than cross-sectional studies, they do not permit implementation of the methods described in the second half of this chapter. Fortunately, the European household panels each have over a dozen waves and offer a chance to understand causal effects on political interest using sophisticated panel estimators.

The remainder of Part III examines possible causes of political interest in an order roughly corresponding to their location in the life cycle and their potential speed of feedback. In the next chapter, I analyze the influence of education on political interest. Attendance of educational institutions is a possible cause of political interest that operates in adolescence and raises relatively few concerns about feedback (because young people are unlikely to leave school, or advance to higher education, as a consequence of their political interest). Parental influence, the other most usual suspect in political socialization research, is the topic of Chapter 11. It also operates early in life, but might involve much more complicated feedback processes (parents affecting their children, children affecting their parents, possibly in fast iteration). The analysis of parental impact thus has to draw on the more advanced panel estimators introduced in this chapter.

Chapter 12 examines the effects of resources, well-being, and several other demographic and social factors that are not directly political. Feedback poses little threat theoretically and, as best as we can tell, empirically. This makes it possible to let the Second Big Benefit of panel data speak to the durability of causal effects with considerable nuance. In Chapters 13 and 14, in contrast, estimating variation in effects over time must take a backseat because addressing the severe challenge from rapid feedback alone can stretch the data to their limit (sometimes to the point where an unambiguous effect estimate remains elusive). Chapters 13 and 14 cover the impact of (more or less expected) encounters with politics and attitudes about politics and political parties. The plausibility of rapid feedback varies even for predictors in these two chapters, but the possibilities of fast feedback cycles for political attitudes in particular reveal the limits of causal inference with observational data.

Thanks to the First Big Benefit of panel data, the following analyses can rule out important alternative explanations for observed effects. Personality and parental education are theoretically or practically constant starting at a young age, so they cannot be causes in any straightforward way. (They could still predispose people to be more receptive to other causal influences, something I will check along the way.) Education and parental influence are constant for most adults and thus accounted for through the First Big Benefit or, when they still change, controlled in the empirical models.

Appendix to Chapter 9

DIVERGENCE OF FIXED-EFFECTS AND FIRST-DIFFERENCE ESTIMATES IN THE PRESENCE OF DYNAMIC MISSPECIFICATION

FD and FE estimators are bound to generate different results when the dynamics of the causal effect are not captured adequately by the model. (The following discussion uses the example of an educational degree and assumes that degree conferral can be treated as exogenous.)

β_1^{FD} in (9.2) compares ΔPI_t between the last year before obtaining the degree and the following year to ΔPI_t over the same period among panelists who did not obtain a degree or have a degree in both years. If the true effect of obtaining the degree emerges gradually over more than one period (or starts before the degree is earned), this comparison will not accurately capture the causal effect of the degree. For example, if the full positive impact emerges gradually over two periods and then stabilizes, the comparison would understate the causal impact because interest among panelists in their second period after graduating would still rise, but the comparison would treat this period as a "control" observation because their degree status did not change (again) at this point.

When panelists are observed for more than two waves, those who obtain a degree are also observed for pairs of waves in which their degree status does not change. If the model is specified correctly, this will not bias results, but it requires the correct specification of the control variables. In Equations 9.1 and 9.2, the age dummies and interestingness measures are used to adjust ΔPI_t for changes in political interest that occur due to aging or a changing environment regardless of (change in) degree status. For example, if the interest of a panelist who just obtained a degree rises a lot at a time when the sample as a whole becomes more interested due to unusually salient political events, the portion of the rise that is common across the sample is not due to the degree. *Only* when treatment dynamics and control variables are both correctly specified in a model with more than two waves, is the comparison still between observations for which $\Delta D_{it} = 1$ and observations with $\Delta D_{it} = 0$ still informative, either from other panelists of the same age and in the same environment or from the same panelist adjusted for age and environment. When, contrary to model specification, true effects are not constant over time, the treatment effects beyond the first period after degree conferral bias this comparison.

The FE estimator is based on a different comparison. Rather than isolate change in political interest at just the point when the panelist obtains the degree, β_1^{FE} compares average political interest across all years in which *i* holds a degree to average interest across all years in which she does not. If the true degree impact begins to decline after several periods, this would therefore lower estimates of β_1^{FE}, but not of β_1^{FD} (assuming an otherwise correctly specified model). Roughly speaking and in the absence of anticipatory effects, the FD estimator in Equation 9.2 characterizes the immediate effect of earning a degree, whereas the FE estimator in Equation 9.3 gives the average effect over the entire period for which a panelist is observed with the degree. In unbalanced panels, where different panelists complete different numbers of interviews, this complicates comparisons across subgroups or datasets.

SUMMARIZING CAUSAL IMPACT IN FIGURE 9.3

This section presents the precise estimates of an upper-secondary degree in the first three years after graduation relative to the baseline before the (typical) start of a program ($t - 2$ in Britain, $t - 3$ in Germany and Switzerland). Results are the same as those shown graphically in Figure 9.3. With robust standard errors and *p* values in parentheses, estimates for Switzerland are 3.3 (1.2, $p = .006$) using FE and 3.2 (1.7, $p = .064$) using FD. In Britain, estimates based on the joint sample are 4.0 (.7, $p < .001$) with FE and 3.3 (1.0, $p = .001$) with FD. Using the adult sample only yields smaller but still clearly significant estimates: 3.1 (1.0, $p = .001$) for FE and 3.1 (1.3, $p = .015$) for FD. For all of these estimates, *p* values for the equality constraint are .20 or greater, indicating that the variation in the yearly effects of the degree program is statistically indistinguishable. The equivalent procedure for the German data produces non-significant estimates for both estimators: .3 (.7, $p = .65$) for FE and 1.3 (1.2, $p = .29$) for FD. (Equality of coefficients is rejected for the FE model. Figure 9.3 indicates declining impact in this period.) When separate effects are estimated for each year, the coefficients are bound to be noisy even when they are based on many thousand panelists. Treating estimates for longer periods as equal (and verifying that they are) can increase the efficiency of the statistical inferences.

Repeating this procedure for pulse variables for years 4–6 gives the average education effect in the following three-year stretch. In Britain, estimates grow slightly to about 5 points (but so do their standard errors). In the Swiss data, the impact of the *Matura* degree remains at about 3 points about a half-decade later, but is more difficult to detect statistically. (Britain: 5.1 (1.0, $p < .001$) for FE-joint; 5.5 (2.1, $p = .008$) for FD-joint; 3.6 (1.2, $p = .004$, rejects equality) for FE-adult; and 4.8 (2.3, $p = .037$) for FD-adult. Switzerland: 2.8 (1.6, $p = .07$) for FE and 3.7 (2.8, $p = .19$) for FD.) Estimates for Germany are even smaller and non-significant.

Another way to summarize the post-degree impact is to calculate the average education effect across the longest period for which year-by-year effects cannot be distinguished. The length of this period is determined by testing if $PD°_{it}$ and PD^1_{it} are statistically different and then adding one additional constraint at a time. The first joint test with a p value below .10 indicates that the post-degree effect is no longer constant. Because the FE estimator is more efficient than the FD estimator, it can detect smaller deviations from constancy. Across all specifications for the British and Swiss data, the equality constraint on the yearly post-degree effects is never rejected, confirming the impression in Figure 9.3 that the impact of an upper-secondary degree is roughly constant. The estimates are always within a few decimal points of the estimates for the first three years (testifying to the much greater number of observations in the years close to degree conferral). In this instance, one indicator variable for any period after degree conferral instead of 20 different variables would have given a very similar but slightly more efficient estimate (Britain: 4.2 (.7) for FE-joint, 3.3 (.9) for FD-joint, 2.8 (1.0) for FE-adult, and 3.0 (1.2) for FD-adult; Switzerland 3.1 (1.3, $p = .015$) for FE, and 3.2 (1.7, $p = .069$) for FD.) Of course, the more detailed model is necessary to establish if the simpler one is biased by non-constant effects. For Germany, the simple model assuming constant effects yields biased results because it misses the short-term effect of education.

An even simpler model that also drops pre-degree indicator variables exacerbates bias because it incorrectly considers observations before degree conferral as not involving treatment. This naïve model would understate the impact of education. Larger differences between FE and FD estimates illustrate the different types of distortions caused by misspecification for the two estimators (Britain: 4.7 (.6) for FE-joint, 1.3 (.6) for FD-joint, 2.2 (.7) for FE-adult, and 1.2 (.7) for FD-adult; Germany –.6 (.5) for FE, and –.5 (.6) for FD; Switzerland 2.2 (.9, $p = .017$) for FE, and 1.7 (.8, $p = .048$) for FD.)

IDENTIFICATION AND ESTIMATION OF DYNAMIC PANEL MODELS

Estimating (9.6) by OLS violates the assumption that right-hand side variables and error term be independent because α_i and $PI_{i,t-1}$ are correlated by design. This is most easily seen by lagging (9.6) by one period:

$$PI_{it-1} = \lambda PI_{i,t-2} + \gamma_0 w_{it-1} + \gamma_1 w_{it-2} + \ldots + \gamma_k w_{it-k-1} + \beta x_{it-1} + \alpha_i + \varepsilon_{it-1}$$

$$(9.8)$$

The first-difference transformation – subtracting (9.8) from (9.6) – solves this problem by removing α_i:

$$\Delta PI_{it} = \lambda \Delta PI_{i,t-1} + \gamma_0 \Delta w_{it} + \gamma_1 \Delta w_{it-1} + \ldots + \gamma_k \Delta w_{it-k} + \beta \Delta x_{it} + \Delta \varepsilon_{it} \quad (9.9)$$

Yet in (9.9), $\Delta PI_{i,t-1}$ and $\Delta \varepsilon_{it}$ are now correlated because, as seen in (9.8), $PI_{i,t-1}$ and ε_{it-1} are correlated, so OLS estimates of (9.9) are still biased. The correlation is negative because $PI_{i,t-1}$ on the right-hand side of (9.9) has a positive sign and ε_{it-1} a negative sign, leading to downward bias in λ. The FD estimator I have used to this point would not yield consistent estimates of (9.9).

Lags of $\Delta PI_{i,t-1}$ can be used as instruments that break up the correlation with the error term. Anderson and Hsiao (1981) showed that, in the absence of serial error correlation, $PI_{i,t-2}$ can serve as an instrument for $\Delta PI_{i,t-1}$ because it is correlated with $\Delta PI_{i,t-1} (= PI_{i,t-1} - PI_{i,t-2})$, but not with the error term in (9.9), $\Delta \varepsilon_{it} (= \varepsilon_{it} - \varepsilon_{it-1})$. By the same logic, $\Delta PI_{i,t-2} (= PI_{i,t-2} - PI_{i,t-3})$ is a valid instrument for $\Delta PI_{i,t-1}$ because neither $PI_{i,t-2}$ nor $PI_{i,t-3}$ is correlated with $\Delta \varepsilon_{it}$. In order for $\Delta PI_{i,t-2}$ or $PI_{i,t-2}$ to be valid instruments, ε_{it} must thus not be autocorrelated because otherwise $E(\varepsilon_{it-1}, \varepsilon_{it-2}) \neq 0$, so $E(\varepsilon_{it} - \Delta \varepsilon_{it}, \varepsilon_{it-2}) \neq 0$, $E(\Delta \varepsilon_{it}, PI_{it-2}) \neq 0$ and $E(\Delta \varepsilon_{it}, \Delta PI_{it-2}) \neq 0$. Using either of these instruments, estimation of (9.9) by two-stage least squares (2SLS) provides consistent estimates.

Holtz-Eakin et al. (1988) and Arellano and Bond (1991) extended the Anderson/Hsiao approach by using all available lags as possible instruments in a generalized method-of-moments (GMM) framework. For example, with three panel waves ($T = 3$) and no autocorrelation in ε_{it}, the Arellano and Bond difference estimator is just identified, with $PI_{i,1}$ as the instrument for $\Delta PI_{i,2}$ based on the moment condition $E(PI_{i,1} \Delta \varepsilon_3) = 0$. For $T = 5$, six moment conditions $(E(PI_{i,1} \Delta \varepsilon_{it}) = 0$ for $t = 3,4,5$; $E(PI_{i,2} \Delta \varepsilon_{it}) = 0$ for $t = 4,5$; and $E(PI_{i,3} \Delta \varepsilon_{i5}) = 0)$ provide the following instruments: $PI_{i,1}$, $PI_{i,2}$, and $PI_{i,3}$ for $\Delta PI_{i,5}$; $PI_{i,1}$ and $PI_{i,2}$ for $\Delta PI_{i,4}$; and $PI_{i,1}$ for $\Delta PI_{i,3}$. As the number of waves increases, the number of available instruments grows quadratically in T.

The initial Arellano-Bond estimator used levels of lagged variables as instruments in the differenced Equation 9.9. Arellano and Bover (1995) and Blundell and Bond (1998) show that, at the expense of an additional assumption, differences can be used as instruments for levels in the levels Equation 9.6. One of the motivations for this extension was the finding that the Arellano-Bond estimator is downward biased for highly persistent data, i.e., high autoregression in the dependent variable with $\lambda > .8$. This bias occurs because lagged levels become very weak instruments as λ approaches unity. Differences as instruments for levels, on the other hand, are stronger in this case, so the extensions by Arellano/Bover and Blundell/Bond eliminate the bias in λ even for persistent processes. The class of estimators that instrument both the level and the difference equation are known as system GMM. For the current application, the weakness of the Arellano-Bond estimator for highly persistent dependent variables is not a concern because persistence in political interest turns out to be very low, justifying the Arellano-Bond difference GMM (see, e.g., Bond 2002; Green et al. 2002, 59–63; Wawro 2002).

A dynamic panel model changes the calculation of the long-term effects of w. Adding and subtracting $\gamma_0 w_{it-1}$ in 9.7 explicates the notion that the model estimates the effect of change (in the independent variables) on change (in the dependent variable):

$$\Delta PI_{it} = (\lambda - 1)PI_{i,t-1} + \gamma_0 \Delta w_{it} + (\gamma_0 + \gamma_1)w_{it-1} + \ldots + \gamma_k w_{it-k} + \beta x_{it} + \alpha_i + \varepsilon_{it}$$

(9.10)

For three lags of w ($k = 3$), the following transformation expresses change in political interest between last year and this year as a function of the level of w three years ago and the yearly changes in w since then:

$$\Delta PI_{it} = (\lambda - 1)PI_{i,t-1} + \gamma_0 \Delta w_{it} + \tau^{(1)}\Delta w_{it-1} + \tau^{(2)}\Delta w_{it-2} + \tau^{(3)}w_{it-3} + \beta x_{it} + \alpha_i + \varepsilon_{it}$$

(9.11)

where $\tau^{(k)} = \gamma_0 + \ldots + \gamma_k$. When current and lagged political interest are equal, the dynamic process is in equilibrium at

$$PI_{it} = \alpha_i/(1 - \lambda) + \gamma_0/(1 - \lambda)w_{it} + \ldots + \tau^{(k)}/(1 - \lambda)w_{it-k} + \beta/(1 - \lambda)x_{it}$$

(9.12)

The equilibrium level of political interest for an individual can change permanently due to changes in explanatory variables w_{it-k} (and age). Time-specific shocks through x_{it} and ε_{it} can generate temporary departures from equilibrium. λ indicates how quickly people return to their equilibrium after a shock or transition to a new equilibrium. As a result, the immediate effect of a change in w_{it}, γ_0, differs from its full effect $\tau^{(k)}/(1 - \lambda) = (\gamma_0 + \gamma_1 + \ldots + \gamma_k)/(1 - \lambda)$.

ESTIMATING THE EFFECT OF PREDETERMINED AND
ENDOGENOUS PREDICTORS

Dynamic sequential exogeneity is defined as follows. For w^P_{it} to be predetermind in model 9.6, ε_{it} must be independent of current and past values of w^P_{it} and of past values of the lagged dependent variable (conditional on the other variables): $E(\varepsilon_{it}|w^P_{it}, w^P_{it-1}, \ldots, w^P_{i1}, y_{i,t-1}, y_{i,t-2}, \ldots, y_{i,1}, x_{it}, \alpha_i) = 0$.

To generate consistent estimates of predetermined independent variables, we can use the same method as for the lagged dependent variable (which is technically also predetermined). Instrumenting Δw^P_{it} works analogously to instrumenting ΔPI_{it-1}. If the dynamic sequential exogeneity assumption holds and w^P_{it} is predetermined, $w^P_{i,t-1}$ can serve as an instrument for $\Delta w^P_{it}(= w^P_{it} - w^P_{i,t-1})$ in (9.9) because it is not correlated with $\Delta \varepsilon_{it}$, ε_{it} or $\varepsilon_{i,t-1}$.

A variable w^E_{it} is endogenous if $E(\varepsilon_{it}|w^E_{it-1}, \ldots, w^E_{i1}, y_{i,t-1}, y_{i,t-2}, \ldots, y_{i,1}, x_{it}, \alpha_i) = 0$. (Hence the difference between a predetermined and an endogenous variable is that the latter permits $E\left(\varepsilon_{it} | w^E_{it}\right) \neq 0$.) When w^E_{it} is endogenous, $w^E_{i,t-1}$ *cannot* serve as an instrument for $\Delta w^E_{it}\left(= w^E_{it} - w^E_{i,t-1}\right)$ in (9.9) because it is correlated with $\Delta\varepsilon_{it}$ through $\varepsilon_{i,t-1}$. In this case, w^E_{it} has to be lagged at least twice, so $w^E_{i,t-2}$, $\Delta w^E_{i,t-2}$, and earlier lags are valid instruments for Δw^E_{it}.

To determine if it is justified to treat a covariate as predetermined rather than endogenous, the difference-in-Sargan/Hansen test is available. It assesses if $w^E_{i,t-1}$ (or $\Delta w^E_{i,t-1}$) is correlated with estimates of the error term. A significant test statistic calls for treating the covariate as endogenous. One weakness of the test is that it must use estimates of the error term (because we cannot observe the true error), which could be poor if the model is not correctly specified. Interpretation of this test can be ambiguous when p values are greater than conventional levels of significance (e.g., $p < .05$) but still relatively small. In those cases, it is prudent to treat a covariate as endogenous rather than predetermined, but this results in considerably stronger demands on the data because earlier lags typically make for weaker instruments: w_{it-2} or Δw_{it-2} as instruments tend to be much less strongly related to Δw_{it} than $w_{i,t-1}$ or $\Delta w_{i,t-1}$. Weaker instruments lead to larger standard errors for the estimate effect, sometimes so much so that they become entirely uninformative. In practice, this can lead to the choice between accepting a marginal statistic on the specification test and inability to estimate an effect at all. In those instances, I report both sets of estimates.

The second premise – availability of sufficiently strong instruments – is also an empirical matter. With a large number of panel waves, many lagged variables are indeed available as potential instruments, but lags, especially long lags, can be very weak instruments. This risks bias in the coefficient estimates through overfitting of the endogenous variables with many weakly related instruments (Wawro 2002, 38; Roodman 2009b). Several statistics provide guidance for instrument design and will be reported when relevant.

When Δw_{it} has to be instrumented, lags of w_{it} in a distributed lag model can exacerbate instrument weakness because the relevant consideration is the instrument strength of the excluded instruments. With lags 0, 1, 2, and 3 of w_{it} in the structural model, as in 9.5 or 9.6, the differenced model includes Δw_{it}, $\Delta w_{i,t-1}$, $\Delta w_{i,t-2}$ and $\Delta w_{i,t-3}$. With w_{it} assumed endogenous, the first two of these differences must be instrumented. $\Delta w_{i,t-2}$ and $\Delta w_{i,t-3}$ are valid instruments, but they are also included in the second stage, so their contribution as instruments for Δw_{it} and Δw_{it-1} is lost. Keeping three lagged differences in the second stage thus weakens identification. Using some of those lags as excluded instruments instead improves the strength of the instrument. This ultimately amounts to a trade-off between addressing the endogeneity problem at $t = 0$ and accurately capturing delayed effects at $t < 0$. Leaving at least $w_{i,t-1}$ in the second stage is desirable given how frequently exogenous variables have non-constant effects (in the education example in this chapter and in the rest of the book), but there may be situations in which even this minimally dynamic specification would make the standard errors for the coefficient on w_{it} so large as to be uninformative.

Another trade-off occurs when applying this method to data for the youngest panelists. Each lag included in the structural model or as an additional instrument moves up the minimum age at which causal impact can be assessed. The problem is most severe for the German study which has an eligibility age of 16. A model without lagged predictors and no violations of exogeneity that might require lags as instruments can help us understand the difference in political interest between age 16 and 17. Adding a lagged dependent variable makes that political interest between 17 and 18 because the earlier difference is now on the right-hand side of the model. Political interest at 16 can serve as an instrument, but if additional lags are needed to strengthen the instrument, the dependent variable becomes the political interest difference between 18 and 19. That model can barely estimate the impact of secondary education anymore and misses other potential influences in adolescence.

10

Education

To some, it might seem a foregone conclusion that education raises political interest. Education is, after all, the "universal solvent" (Converse 1972, 324) that is related to all kinds of components of political involvement. And there are theoretical reasons to expect more education to generate greater political interest. But, it turns out, there are also some pretty compelling reasons why a strong association between education and political interest might not reflect causal impact of education. This chapter ultimately reveals much smaller education effects than many readers might intuitively expect. It takes panel data and the estimation techniques described in the previous chapter to see that correlation does not equal causation as far as education is concerned.

Education appears in the psychology of interest in an indirect role. Many models of interest agree that a sense of efficacy facilitates the formation of interest because it is often more rewarding to be interested in content that one can hope to understand and cope with intellectually (Bandura 1997; Eccles and Wigfield 2002; Silvia 2006). Evidence discussed in Chapter 2 supports the role of efficacy. Education enhances one's sense of efficacy by teaching reasoning skills and increasing one's store of knowledge (e.g., Pasek et al. 2008). Especially when efficacy is not included in the estimation, as is the case in this chapter, education should thus increase political interest. This **Education Hypothesis** can also be derived from psychological models that emphasize the direct role of competence in the development of interest (Masten et al. 2005; Obradović and Masten 2007).

A similar argument appears in the literature on political participation. General education may teach skills and verbal proficiency that make participation easier (Nie et al. 1996; Verba et al. 1995). Skills include the capacity to follow voting instructions, locate polling places, distinguish choices, and "circumvent the various bureaucratic and technological impediments to civic participation" (Dee 2004, 1699). Although the participation literature typically emphasizes the instrumental value of skills and ability in turnout and activism, the psychological model would predict heightened political interest as well.

Political interest is indeed higher among the better educated (e.g., Bennett 1986, 74–8; Berelson et al. 1954, 25; Blais and St-Vincent 2011; Denny and Doyle 2008; Glenn and Grimes 1968; Lazarsfeld et al. 1948 [1944], 43; Milligan et al. 2004; Neundorf et al. 2013; Siedler 2010; Verba et al. 1995, ch.12). Chapter 9 confirmed this association for the household panel data used in this book.

Yet, there is considerable debate in the literature, mostly with respect to political participation as an outcome, whether education is in fact a causal factor. Some scholars have argued that education is linked with political participation only because it serves as a marker for social status. In this account, increasing education thus does little to change participation levels because its effect is to confer relative status, which will remain unchanged if all or most people receive more education (Campbell 2009; Nie et al. 1996). The implications of this explanation for the education-interest link are ambiguous. If education expands social networks, and status manifests itself through more links with politically active or influential individuals, education might indirectly inspire political interest.

Methodologically, the problem of omitted variable bias looms large in cross-sectional studies of educational effects. Berinsky and Lenz (2011, 358) explain why the cross-sectional relationship between education and political involvement may not be causal: "Perhaps education is ... an index of status in society, cognitive skills, and personality traits that leads to civic engagement. Education, in this view, is a proxy for the types of characteristics that lead to a taste for politics." To the extent that cognitive ability and personality are stable at the individual level (see Chapter 8), the methods applied here will rule out these kinds of selection effects that lead people with a greater "taste for politics" to opt for more education.[1]

---

[1] Several past studies have tried to correct for omitted variable bias through an instrumental variables approach. Most of them do not examine political interest specifically, however, and results across types of political involvement do not yield a consensus. Changes in laws guiding the length of compulsory schooling are related to how many years young people spend in school and appear to be unrelated to political involvement. They can therefore serve as exogenous instruments for respondents' education. Using this approach, Milligan et al. (2004) find that differences in political interest between U.S. high school graduates and drop-outs become more pronounced when education is instrumented, thus supporting a causal effect of education on interest. For the United Kingdom, they find support for causal effects of education on some measures of political involvement, but not others. (Whether or not a respondent "consider[s] oneself politically active" is the measure closest to political interest and is positively affected by education using the IV approach.) Using the same IV approach to examine the effect of education in Germany, Siedler (2010) shows strong endogeneity bias, however. A positive cross-sectional relationship between years of schooling and political interest disappears (and may even become negative) when years of schooling is instrumented by an extension of compulsory schooling.

Selection effects and reciprocal causation are a particularly serious challenge to another potential explanation for a link between education and political interest. It argues that coursework and activities related to politics, not general education per se, raise political interest. A variety of components of education could contribute to increasing interest, including courses related to politics, civics, social life, and history, particular instructional methods, involvement in student government or other extracurricular activities, and community service facilitated or required by schools. A strong endogeneity challenge can be mounted against these expectations: Unless such components are required, they will be sought out by students who are more politically interested in the first place.

After a brief overview of the educational systems in Britain, Germany, and Switzerland, I use the methods explained in the previous chapter to estimate the impact of educational attainment on political interest. Using upper-secondary schooling as an example, Chapter 9 demonstrated that the education does not always have constant and lasting effects. This chapter examines other educational qualifications as predictors and adds time-varying covariates to the model to reduce omitted variable bias. In the second half of this chapter, I review past studies and conduct some limited original empirical tests to determine if the civics content of education specifically contributes to development of political interest.

A third study using an IV approach, Dee (2004), finds that the positive effect of education on self-reported newspaper reading does not suffer from endogeneity bias. All three studies also examine the effect on self-reported and/or validated turnout: Dee (2004) and Milligan et al. (2004) find positive causal effects in the United States; Milligan et al. find endogeneity bias and null effects in the United Kingdom; Siedler (2010) finds endogeneity bias and null effects in Germany. Another instrumental variables study in the Unites States (Berinsky and Lenz 2011), which uses exogenous variation over time in the Vietnam draft and policies for educational deferment, finds evidence for endogeneity bias in the relationship between education and turnout, but lacks statistical power to tell if any positive causal impact remains after accounting for it. Sondheimer and Green (2010) use randomized assignments to education programs as instruments and find large causal effects on turnout. For one of their studies, they also report a positive causal effect on political interest (p. 186).

A complication for comparisons of these results is that studies examine different independent variables: Siedler, Dee, and Milligan et al. (in the U.K.) estimate the effect of years of schooling; Milligan et al. (in the U.S.) and Sondheimer and Green, the effect of high school graduation; and Dee (in a second study) and Berinsky and Lenz the effect of college attendance. The period between exposure to education (treatment) and turnout self-reports (outcome) also varies across these studies (which, with the exception of Sondheimer and Green, aggregate large ranges of treatment-outcome durations).

A limitation of the IV approach is that it is only informative for people who were affected by the instruments, i.e., students who only stayed in school because of compulsory schooling laws or the Vietnam draft (Berinsky and Lenz 2011, 371; Siedler 2010, 323; Sondheimer and Green 2010, 178). The effect of education on individuals who would have stayed (or not have stayed) in school with or without these interventions could be different.

EDUCATION IN BRITAIN, GERMANY, AND SWITZERLAND

In all three countries, primary school typically starts at age six or seven, and children have to attend school for a minimum compulsory education of nine years. Few, mostly older, panelists left school without completing compulsory education.[2] Much more common is to hold at least a lower-secondary degree typically obtained after nine years of schooling. This is the highest level of schooling for about 60 percent of twenty-year-olds in Germany and Switzerland, and about 40 percent in Britain.[3] Schooling through upper-secondary education typically takes 12–13 years and entitles graduates to attend institutions of post-secondary education. The share of panelists in their twenties with an upper-secondary degree is 34 percent in Germany, 47 percent in Britain, and 28 percent in Switzerland.[4]

Germany and Switzerland offer highly structured vocational education starting after nine years of compulsory schooling. Firm-centered vocational education as part of an apprenticeship of 3–4 years is the most common form, but full-time vocational schools provide an alternative. The share of panelists in

---

[2] In a few German states, 10 years of schooling are compulsory. Among panelists in their twenties, 10 percent in Britain, 6 percent in Germany, and 8 percent in Switzerland did not complete compulsory schooling or a standard lower-secondary degree. Percentages refer to panelists who do not report completed schooling in any of the panel interviews they completed in their twenties. Non-citizens are excluded, as they are throughout this chapter. Because of the way SHP and USoc measure education, there is some ambiguity in these estimates. In the SHP, first-time panelists were not asked about specific degrees, but given a chance to report their qualifications in a series of open-ended questions. They may have reported vocational degrees without reporting early school-leaving degrees. In USoc, first-time panelists were asked to report their highest schooling or post-secondary academic degree in one question, so for panelists with higher degrees, it remains unmeasured whether they also hold lower schooling degrees. I assume that they completed upper-secondary education because that is typically the entry requirement for higher degrees. Importantly, none of these measurement limitations concern panelists' highest level of education (used in Figure 9.1) or qualifications obtained while on the panel. Changes in educational attainment, the critical independent variables in causal inference estimates, are thus measured without ambiguities (other than standard measurement error).

[3] In Germany, the two types of lower-secondary schools are *Hauptschule* and *Realschule*. For 62 percent of GSOEP panelists in their twenties, a degree from one of these two school types is the highest level of schooling. In Britain, lower-secondary education degrees include O-levels, Certificates of Secondary Education (CSEs), and General Certificates of Secondary Education (GSCEs). GSCEs replaced O-levels and CSEs in 1986. CSEs and GSCEs are awarded in specific subjects. For 42 percent of BHPS panelists in their twenties, one of these lower-secondary school degrees is the highest level of schooling. In Switzerland, several lower-secondary school tracks offer different requirements. For 62 percent of SHP panelists in their twenties, the highest completed level of schooling is lower secondary. This category includes 4 percent of panelists whose highest schooling degree is from an *allgemeinbildende Schule*.

[4] The most common upper-secondary schools, leading to the highest general educational qualification, are *Gymnasium* in Germany (leading to the *Abitur* degree), Sixth Form College in Britain (leading to *A levels*), and *Gymnasium* in Switzerland (leading to the *Matura* degree). Percentage for Germany includes 7 percent with *Fachhochschulreife*, which qualifies students to enter vocational post-secondary tracks, but not university.

their twenties with these qualifications is about 70 percent in Germany and 50 percent in Switzerland. (Most of them also hold a schooling degree, typically a lower-secondary degree.)[5]

Britain does not have a dual system of vocational training, but high schools and further education colleges offer a variety of vocational qualifications. About 50 percent of BHPS panelists in their twenties have a vocational qualification.[6] Post-secondary vocational degrees are uncommon in Britain, so the following analysis examines the pooled effect of all vocational degrees and qualifications. In Britain, 24 percent of panelists in their twenties hold a university degree (either only a "first" or also a "higher" university degree, comparable to undergraduate and graduate degrees in the United States).

Post-secondary education in Germany and Switzerland can be divided into vocational and academic programs. In Germany, 9 percent of panelists in their twenties have university degrees and 10 percent have a vocational post-secondary degree. In Switzerland, an "academic" university degree is the highest degree for 11 percent in the same age group, while another 3 percent hold more applied university degrees. Another 10 percent have completed post-secondary programs that offer professional preparation rather than university education.[7]

---

[5] In Switzerland, *Berufslehre* is a dual system of apprenticeship and general learning that many students enter after completing compulsory schooling. Students are placed within firms, and apprenticeships typically last 3–4 years, depending on the profession, and result in a federal vocational certificate (*Fähigkeitsausweis*). At the conclusion of a *Berufslehre*, graduates may receive a vocational matura degree (which is different from a general *Matura* obtained in *Gymnasium*). In the SHP, 47 percent of panelists in their twenties completed a *Berufslehre* (with or without vocational matura degree). Individuals can also pursue vocational training organized through schools rather than firms, attending full-time vocational schools (*Vollzeitberufsschule*), which last 2–3 years. Four percent of SHP panelists in their twenties completed full-time vocational school and another 3 percent hold other secondary vocational qualifications (typically from shorter programs). Germany also has a dual system of vocational training. A *Lehre* or *Berufsausbildung* is a formalized professional qualification similar to the Swiss *Berufslehre*. As in Switzerland, full-time vocational schools (*Berufsfachschule*, *Berufskolleg*) provide an alternative to more firm-centered vocational education. Among panelists in their twenties, 64 percent completed a *Lehre* or *Berufsausbildung* and another 8 percent a vocational school degree. In Switzerland and Germany, it is possible to enter post-secondary institutions with degrees obtained in the vocational track of secondary education.

[6] Vocational qualifications include National Vocational Qualifications, which were developed in the 1980s and offer different levels of vocational training. Vocational qualifications also include clerical or commercial qualifications and trade apprenticeships as well as Higher National Certificates or Diplomas (HNC, HND). Two percent hold teaching or nursing qualifications. Five percent of panelists report a university diploma (some of them ultimately earn a first or higher university degree). University certificate programs are usually much shorter than a typical Bachelor program, and are therefore not considered in the following analysis.

[7] For 7 percent of panelists in their twenties, a higher vocational degree is the highest post-secondary qualification; another 4 percent hold an advanced professional diploma or license (e.g., *Berufsprüfung mit Meisterdiplom*).

THE RELATIONSHIP BETWEEN GAINING EDUCATION
AND CHANGE IN POLITICAL INTEREST

Analysis in this section uses the graphical tool introduced in Chapter 9 to compare panelists of similar age who do or do not obtain a particular educational qualification. The graphical analysis has the advantage of not imposing a model on the data, but cannot provide very precise estimates. The eligibility age for the three household panel studies dictates which educational stages can be examined. In the German study, for instance, individuals become eligible to be interviewed at an age when many have either finished lower-secondary schooling or are months away from it, making a comprehensive before/after comparison impossible.[8]

Figure 10.1 suggests that a lower-secondary degree raises political interest, according to the British and Swiss studies, which begin interviewing early enough to examine this educational qualification. Figure 10.1 excludes panelists who eventually complete upper-secondary school, so most individuals represented in the graphs go on to vocational training or jobs soon after $t = 0$. In Britain, panelists who earn lower-secondary degrees start out slightly more interested than those who do not, but this divergence grows to become more pronounced starting in the years before graduation. In Switzerland, the two

---

[8] In the German GSOEP, adolescents become eligible for interviews when they turn 16. At that age, about a third of them have already left school and typically started some form of vocational education. We do observe other adolescents make this transition a year or two later, which makes it possible to track their political interest during their last year or two in lower-secondary education and throughout vocational training. Both groups can be compared to individuals who stay in school for another 3–4 years through the end of secondary schooling. Other key educational transitions that occur during panel tenure are completion of upper-secondary degrees, completion of vocational qualifications, moving from upper-secondary school to post-secondary education, and completion of post-secondary degrees.

Eligibility in the Swiss SHP starts at age 14, and almost all panelists are still in school at that age. Many of them are interviewed twice before they leave school or transition to upper-secondary schools, making it somewhat easier to observe transitions out of compulsory schooling than in the German data. The most common education after compulsory schooling is a dual-system vocational education that combines apprenticeship at a company with additional schooling (*Berufslehre*). The path from lower-secondary schooling to upper-secondary schooling (*Gymnasium*) and degree (*Matura*) is the next most frequent. All transitions into post-secondary education occur while people are panel members.

The British BHPS begins interviewing children at age 11, but uses a youth questionnaire until age 15 that differs from the questionnaire for adult panel members age 16 and older. As previously shown, the data from these youth interviews provide important information about political interest during several years when children are still in compulsory schooling. This allows for a systematic analysis of the transitions from lower-secondary education to upper-secondary education, vocational training (less common in Britain), and employment. The price for using the youth interviews is slight uncertainty about the break in the data that occurs at age 16 because the BHPS did not use the same response options for lower levels of political interest in youth and adult interviews. Other common educational paths involve completion of upper-secondary education (A-levels) and post-secondary education.

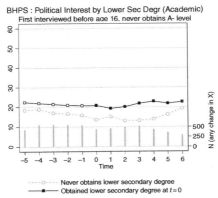

BHPS : Political Interest by Lower Sec Degr (Academic)
First interviewed before age 16. never obtains A- level

- - - -○- - - - Never obtains lower secondary degree
—■— Obtained lower secondary degree at *t* = 0

T > 5, *n* > 75. Changers: *t*[*x* = 0] > 3, *t*[*x* = 1] > 3, no missing lags at *t* = 0.

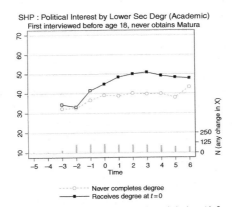

SHP : Political Interest by Lower Sec Degr (Academic)
First interviewed before age 18, never obtains Matura

- - - -○- - - - Never completes degree
—■— Receives degree at *t* = 0

T > 5, *n* > 30. Changers: *t*[*x* = 0] > 1, *t*[*x* = 1] > 3, no missing lags at *t* = 0.

FIGURE 10.1 Within-Subject Change in Political Interest, by Lower-Secondary Degree

groups of individuals have very similar interest levels until about a year before degree conferral. Political interest among those with a lower-secondary degree then increases almost ten points more.

Eventually, the effect of lower-secondary schooling appears to attenuate. In both Britain and Switzerland, the difference between the two groups declines again about 4 or 5 years after degree conferral. Comparing Figure 10.1 to the equivalent analysis of upper-secondary degrees in Chapter 9 indicates effects of similar size in Switzerland and somewhat smaller effects of lower-secondary degrees in Britain.

Secondary vocational training is a common educational path in both Germany and Switzerland. It typically occurs after lower-secondary (compulsory) school, but my analysis also includes panelists who first completed some upper-secondary education. In order to keep comparison focused on secondary education, I exclude panelists who attend university at any time on the panel. Graphs appear in Appendix Figure A10.1. There is little evidence that a vocational degree has any effect on the political interest of German youths. In Switzerland, political interest does noticeably increase in the two years prior to completing the vocational degree (which usually takes about three years), but the effect declines again after individuals complete the program. Results for vocational education in Britain show panelists with vocational qualifications to be slightly more interested in politics, but this difference may be in place before training starts – and thus likely not reflect a causal effect.

Effects of university education are examined in Figure 10.2. These graphs include panelists who end up with an upper-secondary school degree that entitles them to attend university. Among them, those who go on to complete a university degree are more politically interested by about 10 points, as we have already seen. But this difference exists years before degree conferral, so it cannot be the consequence of university attendance. During the years leading up to the degree, when panelists shown by the darker line studied for their degree, the two lines are close to parallel in Germany. In Switzerland, some divergence after $t = -4$ suggests a small effect. In Britain, the lines diverge after $t = -3$, also suggesting some, likely temporary, educational impact.

Summing up, graphical examination suggests effects of secondary education in both Britain and Switzerland. Political interest increases more among recipients of a secondary schooling degree than among panelists of similar age who did not complete the degree. Analyses of vocational and post-secondary education, as well as secondary schooling in Germany (in Chapter 9) reveal small or nonexistent causal effects of education on political interest, however. The cross-sectional differences in political interest associated with different levels of education among adults that were so evident in Figure 9.1 and many previous studies look to a large extent like the consequence of omitted variables that happen to be correlated with education.

Estimating the Effect of Educational Degrees on Political Interest

Graphical analysis offers an intuitive way to "see" education effects (or their absence). They focus on one type of degree at a time even though individuals likely go on to different types of education after earning the degree. To examine the effects of all educational paths simultaneously, this section provides a model-based analysis of the same question as the graphical analysis. It is evident from the graphical displays that the model needs to accommodate effects that are temporary and change over time. The method introduced in Chapter 9 meets this demand by estimating dynamically flexible effects with a series of pulse variables (see model 9.1).

Models reported in this and subsequent chapters control for a series of time-varying demographic variables, including income, social class, employment status of the panelist and, if known, the panelist's parents, parental

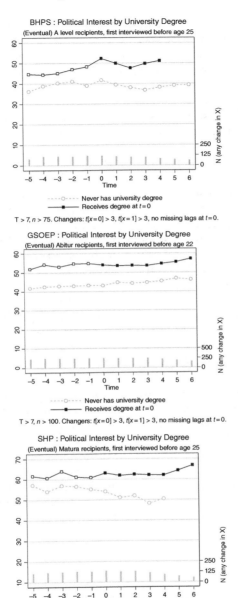

FIGURE 10.2 Within-Subject Change in Political Interest, by University Degree

divorce, marital status, residential mobility, and number of siblings and children. When available, the specification controls not only for the temporary effects of these variables, but also for effects delayed by up to two years. This is a solid way of accounting for the impact of economic resources, conditions in the parental household, and life transitions such as moving out or starting a family. I describe results for these control variables in Chapter 12. Only observations from panelists under 40 years of age are included here because most people complete their education in their twenties or early thirties.

As in the analysis of upper-secondary education using pulse variables in Chapter 9, the models here must again specify a baseline year to which political interest in subsequent years will be compared. For upper-secondary education, I use the same baseline as in Chapter 9 ($t-2$ for Britain, $t-3$ in Germany and Switzerland). The same baselines are appropriate for secondary vocational degrees because the typical programs in Germany and Switzerland last three years whereas the British system offers a greater variety of usually shorter options.[9] Duration of post-secondary education is often longer and generally varies a lot in all countries, so $t-4$ is used as the baseline in order to capture possible early effects. Lastly, the baseline for lower-secondary degree is dictated largely by the eligibility ages of the panel studies (see footnote 8). The BHPS youth sample permits $t-4$ as a baseline, while $t-2$ is the earliest baseline with good data coverage in the SHP. (The GSOEP does not provide enough data to estimate the effect of lower-secondary degrees.)

The results in Table 10.1 confirm the impact of upper-secondary schooling on political interest in Britain when other educational paths are accounted for.[10] A *levels* raise political interest by about 4–5 points according to both FE and FD. The pulse variable for $t = -1$ shows that this effect starts to build significantly in the year leading up to the degree. The results for Switzerland are more marginal. Only the FE estimator shows a significant impact. The FD estimates suggest that there may be a small temporary effect, but no hint left of this effect even a few years after graduation. An upper-secondary degree does not increase political interest in Germany.

---

[9] Whereas post-secondary education is common in Switzerland and Germany and consists of either quasi-university education or master craftsman's certificate programs, Britain has few vocational degree programs that are clearly post-secondary so all vocational degrees are pooled. For consistency between countries, British nursing and teaching degrees are grouped with post-secondary university degrees.

[10] The number of observations after transformation is lower for the FD estimator because there are logically fewer differences than demeaned levels and because observations for which the immediate lag is missing drop out of FD but not FE. This does not affect the estimators' ability to detect changes that happen between the first and second observation for a panelist: FD uses the first observation as a baseline in $\Delta PI_{i2} = PI_{i2} - PI_{i1}$; FE uses the demeaned first observation.

TABLE 10.1 *The Impact of Obtaining Educational Qualifications on Political Interest*

	BHPS FD	BHPS FE	BHPS (incl youth) FD	BHPS (incl youth) FE	GSOEP FD	GSOEP FE	SHP FD	SHP FE
Lower-Secondary School								
Year -3	-2.9 (2.3)	.7 (2.0)	-.04 (.5)	.1 (.5)			-4.7 (3.3)	-.7 (3.4)
-2	*baseline*	*baseline*	-.1 (.7)	.05 (.6)			*baseline*	*baseline*
-1	2.1 (1.4)	2.1 (1.2)	-.4 (1.0)	.05 (.7)			3.0 (1.8)	4.9 (1.7)
0-3	3.5 (1.7)	3.0 (1.2)	-.1 (1.3)	.4 (1.0)			2.5 (2.5)	4.1 (1.8)
4-6	5.9 (2.9)	3.4 (1.5)	.5 (2.5)	.04 (1.3)			3.0 (3.8)	4.4 (2.2)
Upper-Secondary School								
Year -3			-1.9 (.8)	-1.0 (.7)	*baseline*	*baseline*	*baseline*	*baseline*
-2			*baseline*	*baseline*	.5 (.8)	.5 (.7)	1.9 (1.3)	2.4 (1.2)
-1			2.4 (.9)	2.6 (.9)	1.1 (1.1)	1.2 (.8)	-.2 (1.7)	1.0 (1.3)
0-3			3.7 (1.3)	4.4 (.9)	1.1 (1.3)	.5 (.8)†	2.2 (2.1)	3.6 (1.4)
4-6			6.7 (2.7)	5.5 (1.2)†	-.7 (2.1)	-1.0 (1.1)	-.2 (3.5)	3.4 (1.9)
Secondary Vocational Degree								
Year -3	.8 (1.1)	1.4 (1.1)	.8 (.8)	.9 (.7)	*baseline*	*baseline*	*baseline*	*baseline*
-2	*baseline*	*baseline*	*baseline*	*baseline*	1.4 (.8)	.7 (.8)	-.6 (1.2)	.8 (1.1)
-1	1.6 (1.0)	2.2 (.9)	1.2 (.8)	1.5 (.7)	1.2 (1.1)	.7 (.8)	-2.4 (1.7)	.3 (1.2)
0-3	1.4 (1.2)	1.2 (.9)	.9 (1.1)	.9 (.7)	.3 (1.3)	-.3 (.8)	-3.3 (2.0)†	.4 (1.3)
4-6	.5 (2.1)	-.1 (1.1)	.1 (2.0)	-.4 (1.0)	.6 (2.0)	-.04 (1.0)	-5.8 (3.6)	2.2 (1.8)
Post-Sec Vocational Degree								
Year -3					2.3 (1.3)	2.7 (1.3)	.2 (1.3)	-.3 (1.3)
-2					.4 (1.7)	.5 (1.3)	-2.0 (1.8)	-1.4 (1.5)
-1					-.2 (2.1)	.8 (1.3)	-2.7 (2.2)	-2.4 (1.5)

(continued)

TABLE 10.1 (*continued*)

	BHPS		BHPS (incl youth)		GSOEP		SHP	
	FD	FE	FD	FE	FD	FE	FD	FE
0–3					.2 (2.3)	–.4 (1.3)[†]	–1.8 (2.5)	–1.5 (1.3)
4–6					–2.3 (3.5)	–2.1 (1.5)	–.9 (3.9)	–1.2 (1.7)
University Degree								
Year –3	1.7 (1.2)	1.9 (1.1)	1.8 (1.2)	2.0 (1.1)	.5 (1.1)	.8 (1.1)	1.3 (1.0)	1.2 (1.0)
–2	**3.2 (1.7)**	**3.9 (1.3)**	**3.2 (1.7)**	**3.9 (1.3)**	1.7 (1.5)	1.9 (1.1)	–.3 (1.4)	–.04 (1.0)
–1	2.3 (2.0)	2.7 (1.3)	2.4 (1.9)	2.8 (1.3)	1.4 (1.9)	1.9 (1.1)	–.04 (1.7)	.3 (1.1)
0–3	**4.3 (2.2)**	**4.3 (1.3)**	**4.4 (2.1)**	**4.3 (1.3)**	1.0 (2.1)	1.0 (1.1)	1.4 (2.0)	.9 (1.2)
4–6	1.4 (3.3)	2.7 (1.6)	1.4 (3.3)	2.7 (1.6)	–1.5 (3.1)	–.2 (1.4)	–2.9 (3.1)	–.1 (1.4)
N obs	71,598	95,255	83,291	109,392	82,286	95,429	23,288	30,049
N panelists	16,852	18,419	18,596	19,650	12,012	12,485	4,553	4,866

[†] equality of coefficients rejected ($p < .10$)

Note: Coefficients are based on first-difference or fixed effects models as noted. Models control for up to two lags of time-varying demographic variables reported in Chapter 12. Bolded coefficients are significant at $p < .10$. Unless indicated otherwise, the omitted baseline for the pulse variables is $t - 4$. Minimum of three panel waves and age below 40 required to be included. The East German sample before 1996 is omitted.

Lower-secondary schooling can only be assessed in Britain and Switzerland, and in Switzerland the estimation is somewhat handicapped by the necessary baseline of $t = -2$. Relative to two years before earning the degree, students' interest rises by 2–4 points before graduation and remains at this level for several years. The effect is statistically significant only in the more efficient FE estimator. A lower-secondary degree in Britain, which looked in Figure 10.1 like it might have a small positive effect, does not appear to affect political interest.

If vocational education affects political interest, it does so only a little, only as long as people are in the program, and only in Britain and Germany. There is no evidence for vocational education effects in Switzerland at all.

A university degree in Britain raises political interest about as much as an upper-secondary schooling degree – about 4 points – but, unlike the latter, does so only temporarily. Effects 4–6 years after graduation are smaller and statistically significant only for one of the estimators. More than three years after graduation, the effect is no longer statistically detectable. In Germany, the effect of a university degree is half as large and present only while people attend the institution. University degrees in Switzerland have no effect on political interest.

Estimating the Effect of Educational Attendance on Political Interest

Educational degrees neatly delimit years before and after education or transitions to higher educational levels, and a lot of previous scholarship has drawn on them to measure education. Theoretically, the supposed treatment is not the reception of the degree, however, but the educational activities that lead to the degree. In fact, whether or not a student receives a degree may be largely irrelevant after accounting for the years she studies for it. The graphical examinations of education effects and models estimating degree effects show no signs of sharp changes immediately following a degree and, in several cases, gradual change in the years preceding the degree. Another relevant causal variable is thus time spent in education, possibly distinguishing between different types or stages of education.

To estimate the impact of educational attendance, the model specification needs to be modified. It estimates a substantively different effect than the Degrees Model in Table 10.1. Not everyone who attends an educational institution also earns a degree. For example, about a quarter of observations in Sixth Form College in Britain stem from panelists who did not complete an upper-secondary schooling degree. The equivalent share among university attendees is slightly higher still. If attendance of these institutions is sufficient to raise political interest, the model using degree completion might underestimate their impact.

This section examines the effect of attending different types of educational institutions in one model (see Chapter Appendix for specification). Results from this model are in Table 10.2. For each type of education, the first table entry shows the estimate of the per-year effect on political interest of attending a particular educational institution (β_3 in Equation A10.3).[11] The next two estimates give the parameters of a quadratic decay function after leaving education (β_4 in Equation A10.3).

Results confirm the effect of secondary schooling in Britain. Attendance of Sixth Form College increases political interest at a rate of around 3 points per year. As in the Degrees Model, these effects last after leaving school as indicated by consistently non-significant decay parameters. Lower-secondary schooling in Britain also has significant and lasting effects.[12]

The average length of equivalent educational experiences varies between countries. German panelists who attend upper-secondary schooling are observed for an average 2.5 years in *Gymnasium*, whereas British attendees spend only 1.4 years in Sixth Form College. (The equivalent mean in the Swiss data is 1.8 years.) University attendees also spend about a year more at university in Germany than in the other two countries (2.6 years compared to 1.5 and 1.3), whereas spells in German lower-secondary schooling are somewhat shorter.[13] For a comparison that removes the impact of difference in spell length, the bottom part of each set of estimates assumes two years in a program and translates these coefficients into the predicted political interest effect immediately after completion, three years after completing it, and six years after completing to provide standardized estimates.

Schooling in Britain stands out as the largest educational political interest booster – and in fact the only sizable one. Two years of Sixth Form College raise political interest by 4–8 points. There is no indication of decay. Attending British lower-secondary schools also raises interest. The effect is about two points smaller than for the upper-secondary variety, but appears reliably in

[11] These per-year effects are calibrated by the age eligibility of panel studies: Estimates for Switzerland average over per-year effects of education starting at age 14, whereas the German study provides no information about schooling effects before age 16. Different per-year estimates for the two countries could thus arise if the impact of schooling on political interest depends on the age of the student. Students also attend equivalent types of schooling at different rates and ages in the three countries. The share of eighteen-year-olds in school is more than twice as large in Switzerland and Germany than it is in Britain. At age 19, almost one in five panelists are still in school in the former two countries, but hardly anyone is in Britain.

[12] With a few exceptions, FE and FD estimates in Table 10.2 are similar. Unlike the pulse variable approach in (9.4), the model in (A10.3) risks some misspecification in return for greater efficiency. The linear increase in years spent in school and the quadratic decline afterwards are both approximations. Deviations bias the two estimators differently. The fairly close fit between FE and FD again suggests that the model is not too far from the correct specification.

[13] The BHPS youth interview checks only if respondents are still in school, not which school. Assuming that all attendees are still in lower-secondary schooling, the mean number of observed years of lower-secondary schooling among those who ever attend is 4.6 in the combined sample, compared to .9 in the adult-only sample. The equivalent means for GSOEP and SHP are 1.3 and 1.8, respectively.

TABLE 10.2 The Impact of Educational Attendance on Political Interest

	BHPS		BHPS (incl youth)		GSOEP		SHP	
	FD	FE	FD	FE	FD	FE	FD	FE
Lower-Secondary School								
Years of ...	1.5 (1.0)	1.9 (.9)	2.1 (.6)	2.6 (.4)	1.3 (1.1)	.9 (.8)	.5 (1.1)	1.3 (.8)
Years since ...	.10 (.48)	-.10 (.20)	.28 (.48)	.08 (.21)	-.08 (.40)	-.09 (.16)	-1.2 (.7)	-1.0 (.4)
(Years since ...)^2	-.004 (.027)	-.002 (.010)	-.008 (.023)	.004 (.010)	-.004 (.021)	.001 (.009)	.076 (.047)	.038 (.025)
end of 2 yrs	3.1 (1.9)	3.8 (1.7)	4.1 (1.3)	5.2 (.8)	2.6 (2.1)	1.9 (1.5)	1.0 (2.3)	2.5 (1.6)
2 yrs, 3 yrs after	3.4 (2.4)	3.5 (1.7)	4.9 (2.3)	5.5 (1.1)	2.45 (2.4)	1.6 (1.5)	-2.0 (3.4)	-.3 (2.0)
2 yrs, 6 yrs after	3.6 (3.1)	3.2 (1.8)	5.3 (3.1)	5.9 (1.5)	2.3 (2.9)	1.4 (1.6)	-3.6 (4.4)	-2.4 (2.4)
Upper-Secondary School								
Years of ...	3.1 (.8)	2.2 (.7)	3.3 (.7)	3.9 (.5)	1.1 (.5)	.8 (.3)	-.5 (.8)	1.4 (.5)
Years since ...	-.02 (.54)	-.09 (.22)	.23 (.53)	-.02 (.22)	-.52 (.38)	-.41 (.17)	.09 (.66)	-.13 (.36)
(Years since ...)^2	-.019 (.031)	.017 (.013)	.006 (.031)	.010 (.013)	.020 (.020)	.021 (.009)	-.015 (.050)	.014 (.027)
end of 2 yrs	6.2 (1.7)	4.4 (1.4)	6.6 (1.5)	7.9 (1.1)	2.1 (1.1)	1.7 (.7)	-1.0 (1.5)	2.7 (1.1)
2 yrs, 3 yrs after	6.4 (2.3)	4.3 (1.4)	7.3 (2.1)	7.9 (1.1)	.8 (1.6)	.6 (.7)	-.9 (2.5)	2.5 (1.4)
2 yrs, 6 yrs after	6.8 (3.1)	4.5 (1.5)	8.2 (2.9)	8.1 (1.2)	-.3 (2.2)	-.02 (.9)	-1.0 (3.5)	2.5 (1.8)
Secondary Vocational Training								
Years of ...	1.0 (.6)	1.4 (.4)	1.0 (.6)	.8 (.4)	-.4 (.3)	-.02 (.20)	-.1 (.6)	.8 (.4)
Years since ...	-.15 (.42)	-.18 (.18)	.005 (.41)	-.09 (.18)	.07 (.28)	-.032 (.12)	-1.1 (.5)	-.30 (.29)
(Years since ...)^2	.015 (.026)	.015 (.011)	.009 (.026)	.009 (.011)	-.001 (.015)	.001 (.006)	.066 (.047)	.040 (.024)
end of 2 yrs	2.0 (1.3)	2.8 (.8)	2.0 (1.1)	1.7 (.7)	-.8 (.7)	-.05 (.4)	-.3 (1.1)	1.5 (.8)
2 yrs, 3 yrs after	1.7 (1.8)	2.4 (.9)	2.1 (1.6)	1.5 (.8)	-1.0 (1.2)	.1 (.5)	-3.0 (2.1)	1.0 (1.1)
2 yrs, 6 yrs after	1.7 (2.4)	2.3 (1.0)	2.4 (2.3)	1.5 (.9)	-1.2 (1.7)	.2 (.7)	-4.5 (2.9)	1.2 (1.4)

(continued)

225

TABLE 10.2 (continued)

	BHPS		BHPS (incl youth)		GSOEP		SHP	
	FD	FE	FD	FE	FD	FE	FD	FE
Post-Secondary Vocational Training								
Years of ...					.8 (.5)	.8 (.3)	-.2 (.5)	-.09 (.4)
Years since ...					.07 (.48)	-.33 (.18)	.03 (.54)	-.06 (.28)
(Years since ...)²					-.007 (.034)	.008 (.012)	-.021 (.057)	.030 (.027)
end of 2 yrs					1.6 (1.0)	1.7 (.6)	-.5 (1.0)	-.2 (.7)
2 yrs, 3 yrs after					1.8 (1.6)	.8 (.6)	-.6 (1.7)	-.6 (.9)
2 yrs, 6 yrs after					1.8 (2.3)	-.01 (.8)	-1.0 (2.5)	-1.6 (1.1)
University								
Years of ...	.5 (.5)	.9 (.3)	.7 (.5)	1.7 (.3)	.1 (.3)	.3 (.2)	.1 (.4)	.6 (.2)
Years since ...	-.19 (.49)	-.30 (.22)	-.29 (.49)	-.39 (.22)	-.64 (.45)	-.55 (.20)	-.70 (.55)	-.43 (.29)
(Years since ...)²	.019 (.031)	.034 (.013)	.026 (.030)	.037 (.013)	.030 (.035)	.017 (.014)	.041 (.048)	.027 (.025)
end of 2 yrs	1.0 (.9)	1.7 (.6)	1.4 (.9)	3.4 (.6)	.3 (.7)	.5 (.3)	.1 (.9)	1.3 (.5)
2 yrs, 3 yrs after	.6 (1.6)	1.2 (.7)	.7 (1.6)	2.6 (.7)	-1.4 (1.4)	-1.0 (.5)	-1.6 (1.7)	.2 (.8)
2 yrs, 6 yrs after	.5 (2.5)	1.2 (1.0)	.6 (2.4)	2.4 (.9)	-2.5 (2.1)	-2.2 (.8)	-2.6 (2.7)	-.3 (1.2)
N obs	77,230	102,218	89,282	116,917	95,135	109,981	23,285	30,436
N panelists	18,162	19,191	19,384	20,445	13,507	14,001	4,799	5,156

Note: Coefficients are based on first-difference or fixed effects models as noted. Models control for up to two lags of time-varying demographic variables reported in Chapter 12. Bottom three rows for each type of education calculate predicted political interest effect of two years in the program zero, three and six years, respectively, after completing it. Bolded coefficients are significant at $p < .1$. Minimum of three panel waves required to be included. The East German sample before 1996 is omitted.

three out of the four models and the imprecise FD estimate is of comparable magnitude to the more efficient FE estimate.

Whether attendance or degree completion is concerned, schooling in Germany barely registers as a cause of political interest. Attending *Gymnasium* for two years raises political interest by a significant 2 points, but this effect decays very quickly, a pattern that was also apparent in the Degrees Model and in Figure 9.3. The impact of lower-secondary education can now be estimated in Germany as well (because more panelists attend this type of school than earn a degree), but not with sufficient precision to determine if the 2-point increase is more than statistical noise. Evidence for an effect of school attendance in Switzerland is slightly weaker than in the Degrees model. There is some suggestion of marginal endogeneity bias in the FD estimate (discussed further in the last section of this chapter), however, so the estimates converge on a small but positive effect of secondary schooling in Switzerland.

The impact of vocational education is very similar when attendance rather than degree conferral is considered. In several instances, vocational programs raise political interest by around 2 points, but these effects appear to decay. These results illustrate once again the need to allow for non-constant effects and the usefulness of estimating decay rates.

Effects of university education, lastly, are smaller when attendance is considered. Attending university does not consistently increase political interest even in Britain, where the Degrees Model showed a robust if temporary impact. It is possible that the differences between the two models are genuine and occur for substantive reasons: Attending university may indeed raise political interest, predominantly among students who end up earning a degree.

In sum, the results for school attendance largely match the conclusions from the Degrees Model (with university education in Britain as the main exception). Both modeling approaches find that schooling has lasting effects on political interest in Britain and possibly Switzerland, that vocational education raises interest marginally and temporarily, and that education effects in Germany are small and fleeting across the board.

The Effect of Civics Coursework or General Education?

What, exactly, is it about schooling in Britain and possibly Switzerland that inspires students' political interest? Civics courses are the most intuitive explanation, but it is also possible that instruction in other subjects or the overall experience of attending school generates interest, perhaps by teaching skills, giving students a sense of efficacy, or raising their curiosity. It is almost impossible to differentiate between these mechanisms with the household panel surveys used here because the data do not include information about attendance of courses on civics or other topics related to politics. Curriculum changes in England mandated by the government following the Crick Report (Advisory Group on Citizenship 1998) present one opportunity.[14]

Since 1989, the United Kingdom had used a national curriculum that includes compulsory classes in history and geography, but not civics. Starting in 2002, civics education was made mandatory in English schools at the lower-secondary level (Key Stages 3 and 4, typically attended by kids between 11 and 16). Although some variation remained from school to school, the reforms strengthened citizenship education by requiring a place in the curriculum, specifying learning goals, and evaluating achievement (Keating et al. 2009). Panelists born in 1991 or later were 11 or younger in 2002 and thus likely experienced the reformed civics curriculum. Those born before 1987 were already 16 or older when the reforms began, so they could not have been affected. Wales and Scotland were not covered by the reform (Kisby and Sloam 2012). Across Great Britain and the full time period, a lower-secondary schooling degree did not affect political interest (Table 10.1). If the reforms raised political interest, the effects of lower-secondary education in England should have increased among the youngest panelists relative to panelists who were 16 or older before 2002 – and this increase should have been greater than in Wales or Scotland.

Figure 10.3 shows the results of running the degrees model on lower-secondary degrees in England before and after curriculum reform for a comparable age range. Most panelists leave lower-secondary school before they turn 18. Panelists who went to this type of school under the post-reform curriculum are therefore no older than 22 at the latest panel wave included in the analysis. Limiting observations for panelists who attended lower-secondary school before the reforms to interviews before they turned 23 thus provides a balanced comparison. Estimates for the ten years around degree conferral are not statistically significant either before or after reform except for $t = 0$ before reform. If anything, the pattern of year-by-year effects suggests a more positive effect before the reforms were implemented.

The analysis of attending educational institutions in Table 10.2 revealed a more precisely estimated, statistically significant effect of lower-secondary school attendance. These estimates also pooled over pre- and post-reform periods and included parts of Great Britain that did not see reform (Wales and Scotland). To estimate the impact of reform on the impact of school attendance, I add interaction terms to compare the coefficients on lower-secondary school attendance before and after reform, and this pre-post change in England to that in Wales and Scotland (essentially a difference-in-differences design). Because the post-attendance period is short, I only include a linear trend after leaving lower-secondary school. The interactive model is estimated using the more efficient fixed-effects estimator.

---

[14] Switzerland has no national curriculum for civics education. In secondary schools, civics is often covered as part of other subjects, such as history. According to the International Civic and Citizenship Education Study, only 5 cantons offered civics courses at the lower-secondary level (as of 2009), but it was impossible for me to identify those cantons.

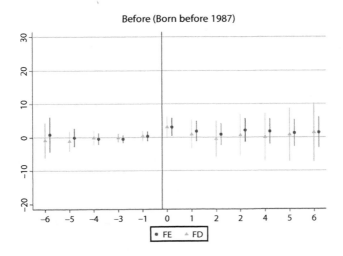

Before (Born before 1987)

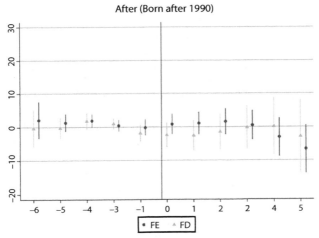

After (Born after 1990)

FIGURE 10.3 The Impact of a Lower-Secondary Degree before and after Reform Curriculum in Britain

Note: Graphs plot coefficients and 90% confidence intervals for pulse variables. Vertical lines indicate reception of degree. Minimum of three panel waves required to be included. Residents of England only.

The immediate impact of attending lower-secondary school did not change significantly after reform. In England, two years in school raised political interest by 5 points before reform and by 6.1 points after reform. In Wales and Scotland combined, these effects were slightly but not significantly smaller at 4.4 before and 4.7 after reform. The difference in these differences is a non-significant reform effect of .8 points.

Before reform, the impact of two years in lower-secondary school in England increased slightly (and non-significantly) in the years after leaving school, to 6.1 points three years later. In Wales and Scotland, the impact remained essentially unchanged, at 4.0 points. After reform in England, attendance effects decay noticeably, from 6.1 points immediately to 3.6 points three years later. But decay is also steeper in Wales and Scotland in the post-reform period, from an immediate 4.7 point effect to 2.7 points three years later. Post-reform decay is greater in England, but the difference in differences is not significant ($p = .20$). Using two measures of education, there is no evidence that adding and mandating civics courses to the curriculum raises students' political interest.

Previous research on civics coursework and political involvement more generally does not provide clear evidence for a causal link either. It has demonstrated an association between civics education and students' political knowledge and engagement. Niemi and Junn (1998, 68) show that high-school seniors who report having completed "American government or civics course work" perform better on a thorough test of civics knowledge. The difference is small (a probability difference of about .1 in answering a question correctly) and only 8 percent of students reported no civics coursework. The reported *amount* of civics coursework is *not* related to civics knowledge (see also Highton 2009, 1574). In Canada, Howe (2010, 129) finds a significant association between self-reported coursework "on government and politics" and both political interest and political knowledge. As a measure of causal effects, these cross-sectional associations between coursework and involvement suffer from all the same biases as the relationship between education and interest in Figure 9.1.

Using panel data, Shani (2009b, ch.7) shows that the number of civics courses a student reports predicts political interest measured contemporaneously as well as 8 and 17 years later. Reducing concerns about self-report error, the relationship remains when the average of civics courses reported by other panelists in the same high school is used. Each additional class is associated with 1.3 points of political interest (on a 0–100 scale).[15]

Yet, analyzing data for 22 EU members countries collected by the 2009 International Civic and Citizenship Education Study, Garcia-Albacete (2013) finds no differences in political interest between schools with and without civics education. To measure the curricular role of civics education, head teachers at each school were asked if civics was part of the curriculum at all and if it was taught as a separate subject. Across all schools and countries, political interest does not depend on whether civics is part of the curriculum and is lower in schools in which it is taught as a separate subject. And using panel data, McFarland and Thomas (2006) find no effect of civics courses reported when individuals are in high school on their political participation as adults.

A number of studies have compared civics courses using different curricula to understand their impact on learning and attitudinal change among students

---

[15] Enjoying social studies as an adolescent has a positive effect on adults' political interest, although, as Shani notes, liking of social studies may be a marker, not a cause.

(Feldman et al. 2007; McDevitt and Chaffee 2000; McDevitt and Kiousis 2004; Pasek et al. 2008; Patrick 1970) or measured political involvement before and after taking a civics course (Hartry and Porter 2004; Meirick and Wackman 2004). Because these studies either lack a control group or evaluate different civics curricula, they cannot tell us how taking a civics course compares to not taking one. (Levy et al.'s 2016 study is an exception that compares political interest among students before, during, and after they took either a course covering politics or a course without political relevance such as English or Psychology. Politics classes attracted more politically interested students but did not lead to greater interest gains than the non-political classes.)

Some of the other examined programs include substantial extra-curricular components or unusual classroom activities. The Student Voices program in Philadelphia (Feldman et al. 2007; Pasek et al. 2008) featured "class room visits from elected officials, candidates, policy makers, and journalists" (Pasek et al. 2008, 28). In the Kids Voting program (McDevitt and Chaffee 2000; McDevitt and Kiousis 2004; Meirick and Wackman 2004), in addition to classroom components, "students participated in their own convention . . . and cast ballots in a mock voting exercise" (McDevitt and Chaffee 2000, 269). The studies are thus not designed to assess the effects on political involvement of typical government or civics courses.

Even as evaluations of different ways of teaching civics courses, these studies do not provide unambiguous answers. None of the studies used random assignment of the civics treatment, so alternative explanations cannot be ruled out. For example, the seemingly more effective curricula may instead have been adopted by effective or motivated teachers or in classrooms that were prone to benefit the most.[16] Manning and Edwards (2014) located thousands of studies examining the relationship between civic education and political participation, but could not find a single experiment with random assignment to a civics treatment or a control condition that did not involve civics instruction. They conclude that "it seems a missed opportunity not to have followed the classical experimental design used to investigate causal links" (38).[17]

---

[16] Several studies use student-reported recall of curriculum components instead of independent observed participation in the course as their independent variable. This adds a further confound as students with stronger civics outcomes may have been more likely to remember curriculum components. Campbell (2008) uses hierarchical models on cross-sectional data to study the effect of classroom climate on 14-year-olds. Open classroom climate is positively associated with civic knowledge and intention to participate in politics. The alternative hypothesis that open climate is more feasible (or more apparent) when students are civically engaged cannot be tested.

[17] Berti and Andriolo (2001) test the impact of a curriculum designed to teach knowledge of politics by comparing two classrooms in pre- and post-tests. The treated classroom received about two weekly hours of instruction over three months. Whether this was on top or instead of other civics-related instruction in the comparison classroom is not clear. With a total of 43 third-graders, the study is underpowered, but the results suggest clear evidence for political learning, both in absolute terms and relative to the comparison group.

After finding a surprisingly low relationship between coursework in college and political involvement (in observational data), Delli Carpini and Keeter (1996, 193) infer that other aspects of education (in the United States) are at least as important:

[A]mong respondents who attended college, political knowledge (and political interest) varied very little according to undergraduate major. Those who studied subjects far afield of politics or social sciences had average scores on indexes of political knowledge, political interest, and media use that were only slightly lower than those who majored in these disciplines. Of course, this does not indicate that courses in politics, history, or social sciences make no contribution to the college effect – general education require- ments still exist in most colleges, guaranteeing that students have some exposure to this material. But the fact that concentration in these areas does not leave a distinctive mark on most citizens is consistent with the notion that higher education promotes the acquisition of political knowledge through the stimulation of political interest and the development of cognitive skills.

There is one question related to the content of study in the three household panels that permits a test of their conclusion. The GSOEP asks its respondents in which subject they completed their post-secondary degree. Of 596 panelists who are observed receiving a university degree and give information about their field of study, 13 percent earned the degree in law, social science, humanities, or history. In the year when they first reported this degree, their political interest was 11 points higher than the interest of other university degree recipients. (The most common degrees are economics or business, natural sciences, and engin- eering. About 20 percent of reported fields are classified as "other" by the GSOEP.)

For a test of whether these differences arise while panelists attend univer- sity, Figure 10.4 reports year-by-year estimates from the Degrees Model separately for politics-related fields of study (left panel) and all others (right panel). Due to the small number of cases earning a politics-related degree (about 80 at $t = 0$, and considerably fewer several years earlier or later), the estimates are very noisy. None of them are positive after the omitted baseline of $t = -4$, however, and there is a hint of negative post-degree effects. There are only two positive estimates that even approach significance. They occur at $t = -6$ and $t = -5$. At that point, most of the individuals who eventually receive a politics-related degree are not yet in university education (only 9 and 16 percent are, respectively). Although statistically imprecise, these results are most consistent with reciprocal causation: Because they become more politically interested for other reasons, individuals decide to study politics or related fields at university. Their studies do not further increase their political interest and, if anything, it declines again in the decade after they completed their degree.

A degree in a field unrelated to politics does not raise political interest either. While at university, it leaves interest unchanged. In the decade after conferral, it may eventually lead to a small decline. (Recall from Table 10.2 that university

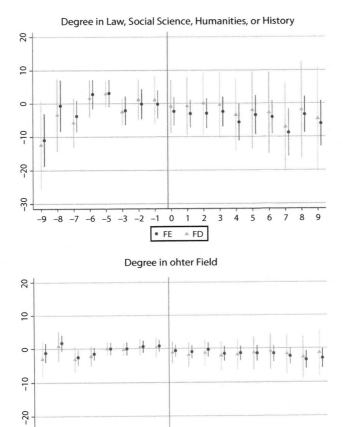

FIGURE 10.4 The Conditioning Effect of Field of Study on University Degree Impact
Note: Graphs plot coefficients and 90% confidence intervals for pulse variables. Vertical lines indicate reception of degree. Minimum of three panel waves required to be included. Includes panelists who never attended university and panelists who received a university degree and reported their field of study.

attendance in Germany may possibly have a small, delayed negative effect.) But the pattern at $t = -6$ and $t = -5$ is the reverse of that for students of politics-relevant subjects: Marginally significant negative estimates indicate that business, engineering, and natural sciences disproportionately attract students who experienced a drop in political interest before they decided what to study. At least at the post-secondary level, where individuals have a clear choice of specialization, politics-related studies are not a cause of political interest but a consequence.

Is Education Endogenous?

Reciprocal causation of the kind suggested for university education in the German data demand consideration of endogeneity bias. The claim of education effects on political interest is based on the notion that something about the educational experience operates as a treatment causing political interest to change. Endogeneity threatens this claim insofar as political interest affects selection into the treatment. For example, if the treatment is instruction on topics related to politics and if politically interested individuals are more likely to select fields of study that feature this treatment, then estimates of the impact of field of study on political interest are bound to be biased if field of study is assumed to be exogenous.

Evidence for reciprocal causation at the university level in Germany does not necessarily call into question the other education effects examined in this chapter, however. First, while university students have great leeway over what they want to study, pupils in secondary schools are often required to take classes in a wide array of subjects, including civics education or subjects that include politics-related instruction. The school curricula in Britain, Germany, and Switzerland all contain some required civics instruction. (As referenced by Delli Carpini and Keeter, many colleges in the United States also have some general education requirements that expose all students to coursework related to politics.) In order to avoid all required civics education, students would have to completely change educational tracks or even drop out of school – a selection that seems a lot less probable.

Second, the treatment that potentially causes political interest to change may be broader than civics coursework and include instruction in other areas, instructional styles, length of school day and year, and interactions with peers, among other things. It is more difficult to select out of this broader treatment and less clear why politically less interested individuals would be disproportionately more inclined to do so.

As a theoretical matter, selection into the treatment based on political interest and reverse causation are thus less likely in the case of general education examined here. It is probably rare for students to leave school early or fail the required tests for a degree just because they are not interested in politics. This is not to say that endogeneity disappears as a concern for analyses in this chapter. Better research designs may in the future show civics coursework per se to be a more relevant treatment than the general educational experience. If that were the case, endogeneity would be a particular threat at the advanced secondary and post-secondary levels where selectivity is greatest. My description may also understate the extent to which children in Britain, Germany, and Switzerland can opt out of subjects they do not like or the extent to which decisions to stay in school, attend a particular type of educational institution, or complete a degree are affected by a person's political interest. The more customizable the curriculum, the greater the threat from endogeneity.

Formal tests of the exogeneity assumption show a few signs of violations, but only for some estimators. As the Chapter Appendix details, discounting results with violations of exogeneity and using more advanced (although often noisy) estimators that reduce endogeneity bias leaves the general thrust of the analysis in place. In particular, the positive effect of secondary schooling in Britain is sustained although probably closer to the lower range of magnitude.

CONCLUSION

This chapter has produced some qualified support for the Education Hypothesis. Like past work on political participation, I examined the impact of attending educational institutions and earning degrees. Many influential analyses of the link between education and political participation use measures of formal schooling and overall educational attainment (Nie et al. 1996; much of Verba et al. 1995), as do instrumental variables designs of education and political involvement (Dee 2004; Milligan et al. 2004; Siedler 2010; Berinsky and Lenz 2011). Overall, graphical analyses and the two statistical models reveal largely consistent results. Education has some detectable effects on political interest, but the magnitude of many of these effects is not large and they often do not last long. The strongest claim of unambiguous and durable effects of education on political interest arises for secondary schooling. Vocational and university education have no or very short-lived impact on political interest.[18]

The pattern of findings also speaks to two other hypotheses. The largest causal effects occur in secondary schooling, which not only involves more civics coursework than vocational school and many university majors, but also makes it hard to avoid civics. This might look like support for the Inadvertent Political Encounters Hypothesis, according to which political experiences that cannot be avoided have the largest potential to raise political interest. There is a caveat to this conclusion, however. A limitation of my analysis is the inability to isolate the impact of civics education from other components of general education. The one test, taking advantage of a curriculum change in Britain that made civics mandatory in lower-secondary schools, did not produce evidence that civics coursework specifically is responsible for raising political interest. Some past studies reach the same conclusion. If civics is not behind the interest-boosting effect of secondary schooling, then results are more supportive of the Education Hypothesis which centers on general ability than on the Inadvertent Political Encounters Hypothesis which postulates an effect of exposure to political content.

---

[18] Denny and Doyle (2008, 307) find a non-linear relationship between education and political interest: Adults who stayed in education past the age of 16 are more politically interested regardless of how many years of education they completed.

Some university programs, degrees in political science foremost among them, are dominated by politically relevant content – but individuals who lack political interest will feel no obligation to pursue them. Consistent with the Selectivity Hypothesis, the more selective the exposure to political content, the less likely it is to raise political interest. The most effective way for education to generate political interest may be to require politically relevant coursework or other activities.

In a dramatic way, this chapter again illustrates how misleading cross-sectional estimates of education effects can be. Figure 9.1 showed university graduates to be decidedly more politically interested than individuals whose education ends with an upper-secondary degree, who, in turn, are clearly more interested than those with only lower-secondary degrees or, even more so, no degrees at all. But this chapter demonstrated fairly unambiguously that university education has no lasting causal impact on political interest. Instead, more interested individuals are more likely to attend university or develop disproportionate interest for some other reason. (The finding that education does cause some of the cross-sectional interest differences between the least educated and those with secondary education simply means that cross-sectional differences are not related to causal effects in a systematic fashion.)

While analysis of panel data can convincingly debunk cross-sectional differences by educational attainment as even remotely plausible estimates of causal effects, determining the true effects of education precisely is more difficult. For one, many effects are no larger than a few points on the 0–100 political interest scale. Whether or not these effects are statistically significant is almost beside the point – because their magnitude often amounts to less than one tenth of the distance between two categories on the underlying response scale (in BHPS and GSOEP). Second, the possibility that political interest causes education, not the way around, is theoretically unlikely, but empirical confirmation is not always conclusive because it asks more of the data and yields fairly noisy estimates.

The ideal research design to study the impact of general education or civics coursework would be to randomly assign education and measure political interest repeatedly over several decades afterwards. To randomize some aspects of the educational experience that might cause political interest raises ethical and practical concerns. Moreover, such a study would take a long time to complete. In the meantime, analysis of panel data without random assignment of education and field experiments that evaluate short-term impact (such as Sondheimer and Green 2010) are strong second-best designs. Results in this chapter demonstrate that education, while not entirely inconsequential, has much more limited effects on political interest than past research (usually examining other elements of political involvement, however) might lead us to expect.

Appendix to Chapter 10

The hypothesis that a year in school corresponds to a greater rise in political interest than a year not in school can be stated as

$$\Delta PI_t | (\text{in school between } t\text{-1 and } t) > \Delta PI_t | (\text{not in school between } t\text{-1 and } t)$$
(A10.1)

The dependent variable, political interest, is expressed in its differenced form, $\Delta PI_t = PI_t - PI_{t-1}$. The independent variable, spending the year between interviews (or at least some portion of it) in school, is also a difference: the difference between the number of years an individual has spent in school at t ($YSCL_{it}$) minus the number of years in school at $t - 1$. Before taking differences, the terms in (A10.1) are thus an equation expressed in levels of political interest:

$$PI_{it} = \beta_3 YSCL_{it} + \mu_t + \alpha_i + \varepsilon_{it}$$
(A10.2)

Equation A10.2 implies permanent effects of each additional school year. Judging by the estimated effects of educational degrees, this assumption is not always met. Equation A10.3 therefore also includes YafSCL, a measure of time since leaving school that allows the impact of schooling to decay (or grow). (Years after school are zero for panelists who are not ever observed in school.) The equation also substitutes in the measures of aging, cohorts, samples, and environmental effects:

$$PI_{it} = \beta_3 YSCL_{it} + \beta_4 f(YafSCL_{it}) + \pi^{AGE}_{it} + \pi^{BC}_i + \pi^S_i + x^N_t + \alpha_i + \varepsilon_{it}$$
(A10.3)

The model specifies β_3 to be the increase in political interest due to a year of schooling and β_4 the change over time in this increase after leaving school.

The first-difference estimate of β_3 compares the change in political interest during years in school to the change among panelists of the same age who are not in school (while also holding constant year-to-year variations in ΔPI and changes caused by long-run effects of earlier education). Likewise β_4^{FD} compares interest changes in years after leaving school to changes among panelists of the same age who never attended that type of school. If β_4 (an individual coefficient for a linear time trend or a coefficient vector for higher-order trends or sets of indicators), is indistinguishable from zero, the post-attendance effect of schooling is constant over the duration of the panel. In the absence of anticipatory effects, fixed-effects (FE) estimates of Equation A10.3 have a similar interpretation as first-difference estimates. β_3^{FE} assesses the extent to which deviations from the panelist's mean level of political interest correlate with years in school, and β_4^{FE} quantifies the correlation between mean deviations and time since leaving school.

TESTING FOR ENDOGENEITY BIAS IN RESULTS IN TABLES 10.1 AND 10.2

Formal tests of the exogeneity assumption (Wooldridge 2002, 302) are available. In FD models, significant coefficients for the undifferenced education variables would indicate violations of exogeneity. The test (adding $YSCL_{it}$ to the differenced model) rejects endogeneity at $p < .10$ for all models in Table 10.2.

In FE models, exogeneity can be tested by including x_{it+1} as an additional regressor. Adding $YSCL_{it+1}$ to the models in Table 10.2 yields significant coefficients (at $p < .05$) for years in university education in the BHPS and for both types of post-secondary education in the GSOEP. In the British data, lower and upper-secondary schooling both meet the specification test in the adult-only sample, but not in the joint sample ($p < .001$). FD tests are marginal ($p = .14$–.15) for upper-secondary schooling in Britain using either sample.

For the Degrees Model in Table 10.1, coefficients for a subset of pulse variables before the baseline can be used to test for endogeneity. This also identifies upper-secondary schooling estimates (both FE and FD) in the joint BHPS sample as affected by selection effects (even when $t = -5, -6, -7$ is used, years so long before panelists completed *A levels* that they could not have been attending Sixth Form College already). Estimates for the adult-only sample do not cause these violations, however. Both BHPS samples indicate violations for vocational education for FE ($p = .05$–.08). In the SHP, FE estimates of secondary vocational degrees are flagged ($p = .02$).

Put together, these violations raise the clearest concerns about the positive upper-secondary schooling estimates for Britain. But even for this type of education, the BHPS adult-only sample generates only one marginal violation, yet effect estimates almost as large as in the joint sample. To investigate possible violations of exogeneity further, I estimated dynamic panel models that control for lagged political interest and instrument education with its lags (see Chapter 9). These models require several lags of political interest as instruments, so the age rises at which effects can be detected. In the joint BHPS sample, instrumenting $\Delta PI_{i,t-1}$ requires two lags of the difference to meet the specification tests of the dynamic panel model, so the earliest detectable effects occur among 15-year-olds. They are similar in size to estimates in Tables 10.1 and 10.2, but relatively weak instruments increase their standard errors too much to draw firm conclusions. Difference-in-Hansen tests, which are used in dynamic panel models to check for violations of exogeneity, show no evidence of endogeneity with only a lagged dependent variable in the model but no instrumenting of education – and estimates for upper-secondary schooling increase. Overall, these analyses suggest that upper-secondary schooling in Britain does

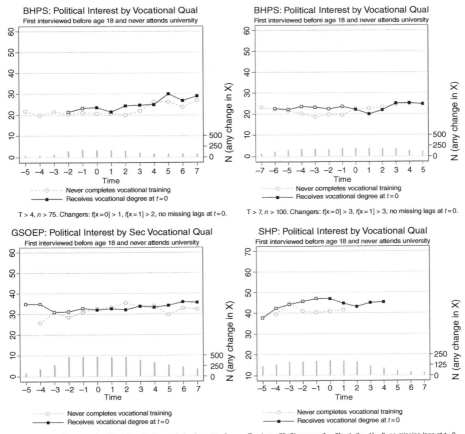

FIGURE A10.1 Within-Subject Change in Political Interest, by Vocational Qualification
Note: Right-hand graph for BHPS includes youth interviews.

increase political interest, but that endogeneity bias inflates the effect size in the joint sample, so the magnitude is closer to about 5 points than the upper range of the estimates in Tables 10.1 and 10.2.

Endogeneity bias does not necessarily reduce estimates. For upper-secondary schooling in Switzerland, the FD test suggests a violation of exogeneity ($p = .14$), and a dynamic panel model that instruments schooling generates larger, albeit very noisy, estimates that are similar to the significant FE estimates reported in Table 10.2 which meet tests for exogeneity. (Due to the eligibility age of 14, a dynamic panel model estimates effects on political interest in the Swiss data for individuals as early as age 17. Upper-secondary school enrollment is still at its peak at this age, so the SHP data can provide an informative estimate.) Appropriate modeling of reciprocal effects thus strengthens the case for upper-secondary schooling in Switzerland as a causal factor in the development of political interest.

Violations of exogeneity in Britain for university attendance (Table 10.2), but not for the clearly positive (if temporary) effects of university degrees (Table 10.1) are hard to interpret. Discounting the positive FE estimates in Table 10.2 would reinforce the conclusion that attendance has little effect unless students also complete a degree.

11

Parents

Family members, and especially parents, exert the first socializing influences on children. Most of the literature on parental influence on children's political socialization covers political orientations, such as candidate preference and, most prominently, party identification. The empirical finding of positive, moderately strong correlations between party identification of child and parent (e.g., Achen 2002; Jennings and Niemi 1968; Niemi and Jennings 1991) was initially taken as evidence for "transmission" (e.g., Jennings et al. 2009) from parent to child, a theoretical perspective deriving from social learning theory (Bandura 1969) that sees the child as modeling parents and passively adopting their attitudes and values. The moderate magnitude of child-parent correspondence appeared to indicate that lack of communication could limit parental influence. Child-parent correspondence indeed is significantly lower when children do not correctly perceive their parents' party identification (Ojeda and Hatemi 2015b) and when parents are not politically involved (Dinas 2014; Jennings et al. 2009). But more recent findings question the causal direction assumed in the transmission model by demonstrating that children can also influence their parents (McDevitt and Chaffee 2002; Saphir and Chaffee 2002; Stattin et al. 2017).

This chapter analyzes child-parent correspondence with respect to political interest, but asks a similar question as the literature on party identification: Do parents pass on their political interest to their children, as the **Parental Influence Hypothesis** predicts? The analysis begins with a description of the correspondence between parents' and child's political interest. But this correspondence could arise even if parents do not influence their children's political interest. Perhaps all members of a household are subject to influences that make their interest more alike. Or children affect their parents' interest. Examining parent-child correspondence as a function of family characteristics, including residence in the same household and the consistency of parents' interest, provides more clues about the sort of influence that makes parents and children resemble each other.

Directly estimating the causal impact of parental political interest on children's political interest would provide the clearest answer to the question of who influences whom. The second half of this chapter offers such an analysis. But because the causal arrow may point in the other direction and because influence between people sharing so much of their lives could happen very quickly, establishing causal order is a very challenging task.

PARENT–CHILD CORRESPONDENCE OF POLITICAL INTEREST

Past research on the link between political involvement of parents and their children presents a puzzling combination of findings. For some indicators, empirical results document a good degree of child-parent correspondence. Parents' self-reported news exposure predicts how often children say they watch the news (Conway et al. 1981; Niemi and Chapman 1998), and children of poorly informed parents have below-average political knowledge themselves (Jennings and Niemi 1981; Jennings 1996; McIntosh et al. 2007). Parents' political participation correlates with that of their children (Plutzer 2002). Cesarini et al. (2014) show a relationship between turnout of parents and adopted children, so post-birth/socialization factors are likely at play. (The relationship is stronger for biological children.)

It is only natural in light of these findings to expect a strong association between the political interest of parents and their offspring, as Luskin (1990, 337), for example, does: "Through both observational learning and direct reinforcement, children should tend to absorb the political enthusiasm or apathy of their parents." Yet the workhorse of socialization studies, the long-running Youth-Parent Socialization Panel Study (Jennings et al. 2004), shows a very weak link. Jennings et al. (2009) describe this low correlation as "inexplicable" because "we might expect higher consonance [between parents and their children] on the basis of family socioeconomic status alone" (785–6). In Zuckerman et al.'s (2007) analysis of German and British data (early waves of the GSOEP and BHPS), the bivariate relationship between political interest of children and their parents is also low and pales against the strong child-parent correspondence of partisan preferences, religion, and the frequency of religious attendance (as it does in Jennings et al. 2009). Other analyses of the same data at least establish a statistically significant contemporaneous relationship between political interest of children and their parents (Neundorf et al. 2013 for the BHPS; Kroh 2006 for the GSOEP). Nonetheless, the weakness of these associations does not appear compatible with unconditional "transmission" of political interest from parent to child. Is political interest an exception to the otherwise common modeling of parents by their children?

Not quite. But parent–child correspondence of political interest does not happen automatically or regardless of the child's stage of development. Parents may influence their children, but not as deterministically as social learning implies, so children's own judgment could weaken the relationship. Past research has largely ignored the dynamics and age-specificity of parent–child relationships. Social learning theory does not imply a strong relationship throughout the lives of parents and their children. It suggests age variation in parent–child correspondence: Children begin to model their parents' political interest as they start to perceive politics and form their first assessments of it, in their early teens. Over the following years, while children still live in the parental household, opportunities for social learning should be plentiful, so correspondence might peak before offspring, in their later teens and twenties, experience politics in new and more varied ways outside the home. This more nuanced prediction of social learning has not been empirically tested, partly for lack of appropriate data. The main U.S. dataset, the Youth-Parent Socialization Panel Study, interviewed high school seniors – and then reinterviewed them eight years later. That is not enough data to analyze variation in parent–child correspondence during the theoretically important age range.

Figure 11.1 offers a detailed look at parent–child correspondence of political interest.[1] The horizontal axis indicates the age of the child, so the graphs track the parent–child correlations as children get older. Connected lines show the smoothed age trend in the correlations. The figure plots two types of correlations between children's political interest and that of their parents. Circles and the darker lines show the contemporaneous correlations between child and parents. The second type of correlation, shown by triangles and the lighter line, summarizes the relationship between a child's current political interest and her parents' political interest when she was between 8 and 10 years of age.[2] When their children are this young, parents can hardly be affected by their political interest because children in this age range are barely starting to develop political consciousness (see Chapter 6). Because children's interest is too undeveloped to exert influence on their parents, a relationship between parents' interest

---

[1] The household panels are designed to follow panelists over time, even when they leave their original households. As a result, children remain in the dataset even after they move out of their parents' household. (If a child does not live in the same household as her parents for at least one panel wave, the child's household would not automatically be part of the sample.) Because children under the eligibility age are not interviewed, but their parents are, the studies usually provide more interview data for parents than children. In all three studies, we observe hundreds and even thousands of children and their parents repeatedly as children grow up, sometimes from the time the children were very young and often after the time they leave the parental household.

[2] Both contemporaneous and early parental interest average one interest report by each parent, if available, so measurement error affects both types of correlations the same way. For early interest, this is the latest report available for the mother and father when the child is between 8 and 10 years old. Both sets of correlations are calculated only for panelists for whom early parental interest is available, so they compare the same samples.

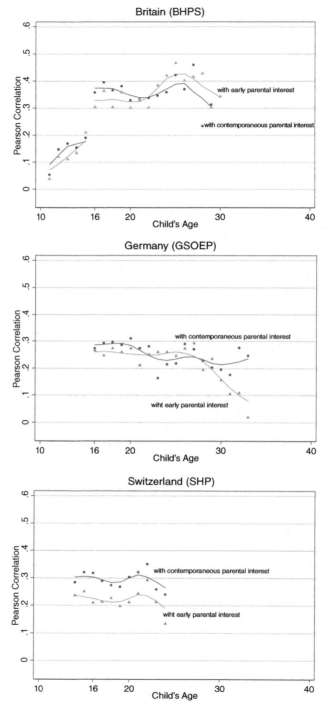

FIGURE 11.1 Correspondence of Child's Political Interest with Early and Contemporaneous Parental Interest

measured so early and their children's interest a few years later is thus bound to represent a directional influence from parent to child. As children get older, the possibility that their political interest affects that of their parents becomes an increasing threat to causal interpretation.

Figure 11.1 reveals a remarkable result: Political interest of the youngest teenagers is not yet related to interest of their parents. The British dataset is the only one to show this finding because only the BHPS started interviewing as early as age 11. Correlations strengthen over the course of the BHPS youth interviews, between ages 11 and 15. The jump in magnitude between ages 15 and 16 is partly explained by the switch from a three-point to a four-point scale in the adult questionnaire (which increases correlations by reducing measurement error), but the rise continues for at least another year after age 16.

Comparing the two types of correlations in Figure 11.1 strongly suggests that British teenagers change their political interest and increasingly come to share their parents' political interest. Influence is, at least initially, one-directional from parent to child. Evidence for this conclusion is indirect: Regardless of whether the analysis uses contemporaneous parental interest or parental interest before the child turned 11, the correlations are very similar (compare the dark and light lines). This pattern implies that the rising correlations in the British data are caused by a change in children's interest because if parents had changed, the contemporaneous correlations would exceed the correlations with early parental interest.

By the time the German study begins to interview children, the parent–child association is already close to its maximum. But in the GSOEP, too, the correlations are very similar regardless of whether contemporaneous parental interest is used or parental interest measured years earlier when the child was between 8 and 10 years old. If, like young British teenagers, young German teenagers do not yet share their parents' political interest, but the GSOEP missed it because of its higher eligibility age, then the similarity between the two sets of correlations implies that children must have changed to resemble their parents. (The Swiss data in Figure 11.1 are inconclusive with respect to parental influence. The youngest panelists, aged 14, already show peak levels of parent–child correspondence. And contemporaneous correlations are consistently higher than correlations with early parental interest. It is possible that Swiss parents' interest changed and their children continued to model them, but the pattern of correlations in Figure 11.1 is consistent with many alternative explanations as well.)

FIGURE 11.1 (*cont.*) *Note:* Correlations based on a minimum of 100 observations at each age. Parents' early political interest is the average of one interest report each by mother and father, if available, when the child is between 8 and 10 years old. Lines apply lowess smoothing to age trend. The BHPS line is not connected between the ages of 15 and 16 to highlight the transition from youth to adult questionnaire that happens at that point for most panelists.

Though indicative of some parental influence, the maximum correlations in Figure 11.1 are not very high. At around .3, the parent–child correlations are not as low as the correlations reported by Jennings et al. (2009) and Zuckerman et al. (2007), but neither do they provide particularly strong support for widespread "transmission." Judged against correlations between different indicators of political interest for the same person – which often exceeded .6 even without corrections for measurement error (see Chapter 3) – maximum correlations of .3 point to limited parental influence.

Measurement error understates the correlations in Figure 11.1, but not all that much. A quick way to see this is to first average over each individual's interest reports and then calculate the parent–child correlation between these averages. Because averaging interest reports reduces measurement error, these correlations provide a sense of how much error attenuates correlations calculated separately for each wave. During the peak period of parent–child correspondence, when the child is between 16 and 30 years old, the average uncorrected correlations in Figure 11.1 are .30 (BHPS), .30 (GSOEP), and .27 (SHP). Averaging interest reports first to reduce measurement error changes these estimates to .40, .41, and .33, respectively.[3] Hence, attenuation turns out to be present but moderate in magnitude. Even after accounting for measurement error, the data point to "transmission problems" in the influence of parents on their children's political interest.

Inconsistent parental interest is one reason for "transmission problems." When mother and father differ from one another in their political interest or waver between more and less interest, children may find it harder to model their parents or model them for a while without following all of their parents' reassessments. Variation in conditions for social learning may lower overall correspondence. Jennings et al. (2009) find significantly stronger parent–child similarity of political interest when parents are consistent in their political interest levels, either over time or (in two-parent families) between each other.[4] Figure 11.2 tests this idea by separating parents with consistent and inconsistent levels of political interest. Consistency is measured by the standard

---

[3] The calculations are for panelists with at least five interest reports by themselves and their parents while the panelist is between 16 and 30 years old.

[4] This finding recalls the argument in the literature on party identification that influence is easier or more reliable when the "signal" is strong and obvious. But measures of "signal strength" used there, such as politicization or the frequency of political discussion in the family, are not suitable as conditioning variables for social learning of political interest because they are correlates, possibly consequences, of parental political interest and thus lead to a circular argument. For example, children of parents who encourage discussion and do not shy away from conflict and controversy in their family communications tend to be more interested in public affairs (Chaffee and Yang 1990; McLeod 2000; Verba et al. 1995).

Non-political factors could still affect the conspicuousness of parental political interest or the likelihood that children will adopt it. With respect to party identification, Ojeda and Hatemi (2015a; 2015b) demonstrate that perceived parental support and emotional closeness of parent

deviation of parental interest reports over the three years leading up to and including the current interview year (provided that parents contribute a combined three or more interest reports in this period). Consistency is thus a household-level property that combines parental variation over time and differences between the two parents. (For single-parent households, it captures only the former.) Figure 11.2 shows the role of parental consistency separately for mother-child and father-child dyads.

When parents are consistent in the extent to which they find politics interesting, children are more likely to adopt parental interest. The British data reveal most clearly how child-parent correspondence rises during the teenage years. At elementary school age, children do not yet share their parents' political interest, but they appear to pick it up quite rapidly as teenagers – if their parents are consistent. This conclusion does not rest on the BHPS youth interviews alone; it is also clearly visible in the Swiss data. In fact, in Switzerland, parental consistency does not yet distinguish the parent–child correlations at age 14, the eligibility age of the SHP. Yet in the ensuing years, children of consistent parents begin to resemble their parents, whereas children of inconsistent parents do not. The German study appears to start interviewing children too late to observe the growing correspondence of parents and their children. The maximum difference depending on parental consistency is already in place at the eligibility age of 16.

The results in Figure 11.2 are strongly suggestive of parental influence. When children are just starting to notice politics, their budding political interest is not yet related to their parents' interest (and may not yet be particularly reliable or still highly situational). Child-parent correspondence grows quickly among teenagers, but it is mostly confined to children whose parents offer suitable conditions for social learning by providing a consistent signal of how interesting politics is to them.[5]

Correspondence of political interest between parents and child depends on frequent exposure. Figure 11.3 demonstrates this point by plotting correlations

---

and child affect correspondence by influencing the probability that children who accurately recognize the partisan leanings of their parents also adopt them. To the extent that these family characteristics facilitate social learning, they might also affect whether children share their parents' interest in politics.

[5] Figure 11.2 also shows that political interest levels of the mother tend to be more strongly related to children's interest. Match between child's and parent's gender has inconsistent implications across the three studies. The correlation of five-year averages is always highest for mother-daughter pairs, but the magnitude of this difference is meaningfully large only in the BHPS (.43 compared to .31–.34 for other gender combinations) and the SHP (.36 compared to .20 and .21 for father-daughter and father-son, respectively, and .31 for mother-son).

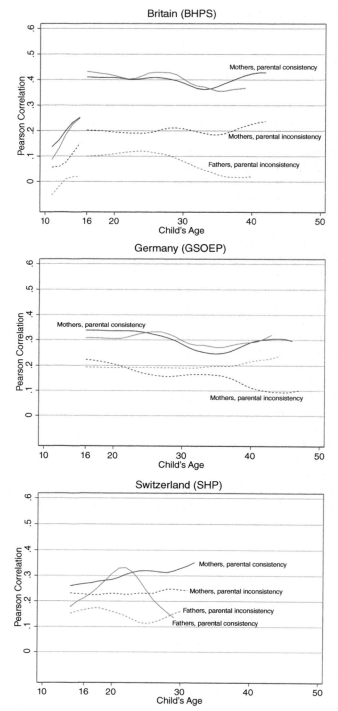

FIGURE 11.2 Contemporaneous Relationship by Consistency of Parental Political Interest

between contemporaneous interest of parents and their children depending on when children moved out of their parents' home. (The shading of the lines in Figure 11.3 corresponds to the age at which children moved out, with darker shading indicating earlier move-out ages.) Parent–child correspondence tends to peak just around the time children move out. In all three countries, children who move out after they turned 25 retain the strongest links with the parents, often well into their thirties. In contrast, parent–child correspondence in the opposite group, young people who leave their parents' home very early, drops rapidly in their twenties in Germany and Switzerland (and more gradually in Britain). Many of the other lines display peaks and drops in between those two extremes, roughly in order of move-out age.

All told, the evidence so far is consistent with *catch-up* parental influence: Starting in their early teenage years, children begin to adopt the political interest of their parents if their parents present a clearly discernable model. Then, as children get older, and especially after they leave the parental household, parents cease to be the only or primary influence, so parent–child correspondence declines.

In this version of parental influence, children slowly catch up to their largely unchanging parents. Catch-up parental influence is theoretically appealing because it proposes parental effects even in the absence of change among adults – which is rare when it comes to political interest, as shown in Part II. Children observe, assess, and sometimes adopt their parents' political interest – a process that can operate even, and perhaps more easily, when parents' interest remains unchanged. Catch-up parental influence is difficult to demonstrate unambiguously, however, because the underlying causal factor, parental political interest, does not have to vary over time for the effect to occur. What does change is the child's awareness of her parents' political interest or her readiness to adopt it, but this change is not measured in the data used here.

Conceptually, catch-up parental influence alone cannot provide a complete account of parental influence. It does not address what happens when parental interest changes. Although such change occurs infrequently, its effect when it does occur constitutes critical evidence for the fate of the Parental Influence Hypothesis. Does a change in parents' political interest trigger, possibly with

---

FIGURE 11.2 (*cont.*) *Note*: Lines are smoothed contemporaneous correlations between parent's and child's political interest by age and parental consistency. Consistency of parental political interest is based on median split of the standard deviation of mother's and father's political interest at t, $t-1$, and $t-2$ (minimum of three non-missing values to be included). Minimum of 100 observations at each age. The BHPS line is not connected between the ages of 15 and 16 to highlight the transition from youth to adult questionnaire that happens at that point for most panelists.

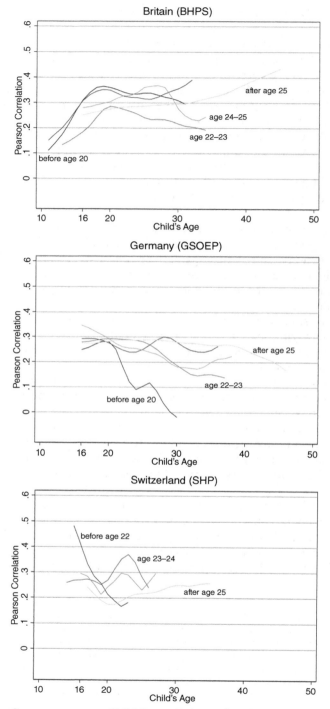

FIGURE 11.3 Contemporaneous Child-Parent Relationship, by Child's Move-Out Age

some delay and possibly only temporarily, a corresponding change in their children's political interest? This process describes *ongoing* parental influence. Its presence would considerably strengthen the hypothesis. Failure to find empirical support would raise doubts about the extent to which children's political interest really follows that of their parents. The next section looks for ongoing parental influence by identifying parents whose political interest changes and measuring their children's interest change in the years that follow.

DOES PARENTAL POLITICAL INTEREST CAUSE CHILDREN'S POLITICAL INTEREST?

Ongoing parental influence is a causal process that involves a change in one variable – a parent's political interest – leading to a change in another variable – her child's political interest. To see if this process occurs, this section again takes advantage of the First Big Benefit of panel data, the ability to analyze the effect of change on change. It begins by applying the same graphical template introduced in Chapter 9 to parental influence on children's political interest. Graphs show trends in children's political interest before and after their parents' interest changes. By following children for many years, this tool can detect delayed and gradual impact.

To accommodate these complexities, the graphs for parental interest in Figure 11.4 have four lines, two for children of a parent whose political interest changes, and two for children whose parent has largely stable levels of political interest. Lines for changes track what happens when a parent's political interest rises or falls. Lines for stable levels distinguish parents who are consistently interested in politics from those with consistently low political interest. Children of the former are expected to be more interested themselves, but not to develop even greater interest as their parent's interest remained unchanged in the period covered by the graph.

The dark line with square markers in Figure 11.4 shows political interest among panelists whose parent experienced an increase in political interest at some point while both were part of the study. The graph centers the line so that this increase occurs at $t = 0$. To the right of $t = 0$, the line thus graphs political interest among panelists in the years after their parent's interest increased. The

---

FIGURE 11.3 (*cont.*) *Note*: Lines are smoothed contemporaneous correlations between parent's and child's political interest by age. Correlations must be based on at least 100 observations to be included. Different lines distinguish children by the age at which they no longer share the same household with either of their parents. Darker shading indicates earlier move-out ages. The share of children living in their parents' household drops below two thirds at age 23 in Britain and Germany, and at 25 in Switzerland. It drops below one half at age 26, 25, and 27, respectively.

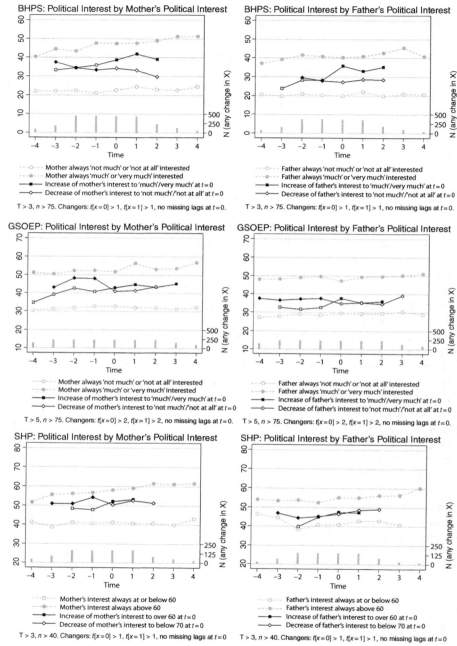

FIGURE 11.4 Political Interest after Large Change in Parental Political Interest
Note: Definition of change explained in the text. For details on graphs, see Book Appendix B.

empty squares to the left of $t = 0$ show their interest levels before this increase occurred. The dark line using diamond-shaped markers shows the reverse of the other dark line, following panelists whose parent lost political interest. The first open diamond marks the time of this decrease and is also aligned at $t = 0$. (This line is new in this graph because the equivalent of this group does not exist for education, which does not decline.) Figure 11.4 also includes two lines that represent political interest among children whose parent has largely stable political interest. The dashed line with all open circles plots political interest for panelists whose parent is not particularly interested in politics and never changes much. The dashed line with all filled circles is for children of parents with stronger and largely stable political interest.

Distinguishing parents who change from those who do not for Figure 11.4 is more challenging than it was for educational degrees in Chapter 10. Unlike binary degree variables, parental political interest is based on multi-category measurement of political interest. That is why the language in the previous paragraph is vaguer, referring to parents represented by the solid lines as "largely stable." Change is defined in the most straightforward way for Britain and Germany, taking the top two categories as "high" parental political interest, the other two categories as "low" interest, and movement between "high" and "low" as "change." For Switzerland, the cutpoint between "high" and "low" is between 60 and 70 on the 0-to-100 scale. This simple dichotomization has the advantage of pinpointing the timing of change as precisely as possible. The disadvantage is that some differences may represent measurement error, not genuine change, and that changes that happen entirely below or above the cutpoint are treated as stability. An alternative method, less susceptible to measurement error, more flexible in picking up change of different magnitude and anywhere on the scale, but less precise with respect to timing, yields similar results.[6]

As before, the panelists in the stable reference groups are selected to be of similar age at $t = 0$ as the changers.[7] All panelists represented in a graph must

---

[6] The alternative method defines "change" based on change of the moving average, the difference in the two-year average before t and the two-year average in years t and $t + 1$. At least some of the change must occur between $t - 1$ and t. Using the moving window to identify change makes it possible to rule out preceding and subsequent change in the opposite direction. Although a two-year window limits the ability to pinpoint the order of change among parent and child, it is necessary to ascertain that parental change is more than temporary oscillation or measurement error. In Figure OL11.1 (in the Online Supplementary Materials), I examine only the largest changes in parental interest, based on the expectations that they should generate the largest impact among children if ongoing parental influence occurs. For the four-point scales in the BHPS and GSOEP, a before/after difference of at least one-and-a-half categories yields just enough instances of change. An example of a change of this magnitude that meets this condition is a parent in the German data increasing from at least two years of being "not so strongly interested" to "strongly interested" at t and "very strongly interested" at $t + 1$. The largest change on the 11-point SHP scale that yields enough cases is three categories. Figure OL11.2 lowers the cutoff for what constitutes "change," defining changes as a one-category change instead of a 1.5-

also have completed a minimum number of waves (stated at the bottom of each graph). The bars in the graph show the combined number of observations on which the two solid lines are based, that is, the number of panelists who changed while on the panel and meet the minimum observation requirements. Book Appendix B provides more detail on change graphs such as Figure 11.4.

When parental interest changes, children's interest tends to change, too. This pattern is evident repeatedly in Figure 11.4, most clearly in the British and German data. An increase in political interest of mother or father is associated with an increase in children's interest of close to 10 points in the BHPS (dark line with square markers). A similar but somewhat smaller effect occurs for both parents in Germany (with children's interest dropping, more so than in Britain, when their parents lose interest). Swiss parents seem to affect their children's political interest a lot less if at all.

For Britain and Germany, the graphical analysis leaves no doubt that changes in parental interest are associated with changes in their children's interest. These results establish the plausibility of ongoing parental influence. Who learns from whom can be difficult to discern, however. The cleanest evidence for parents as the cause comes from change in children's interest after $t = 0$ as that change most likely postdates the parental change. There is only one instance of such a pattern, however (for mothers in Britain in Figure 11.1). The largest changes among children typically occur between $t - 1$ and t. In one or two instances, the child's interest starts to move in the direction of the parent between $t - 2$ and $t - 1$. While it has the benefit of avoiding any modeling assumptions, the graphical analysis thus has a hard time disentangling causal direction.

A model-based approach offers more nuanced assessment of magnitude, timing, and possibly even causal direction. A regression model examines the effect of any movement on the multi-category variable of parental interest while continuing to pinpoint the timing of this movement to within one year. Furthermore, a regression approach can explicitly hold constant children's interest at $t - 1$, ruling out at least some forms of reverse causation (with earlier changes among children in fact causing the parental change). It also directly estimates the role that living in the same household plays for ongoing parental influence. The price for more nuance is a more complex estimation procedure.

category change for the BHPS and GSOEP, and a 2.5-category change instead of a three-category change in the SHP. As expected, if effects are proportional to the trigger, the magnitude of change among children is somewhat smaller than in Figure OL11.1.

[7] To avoid relying on adult children, Figure 11.4 excludes panelists who never lived with their parent and either joined the panel after turning 25 or had an average age greater than 25 across their completed panel waves. Children who left their parent's household before they turned 18 are excluded from the figure.

Model-Based Analysis of Ongoing Parental Influence of Political Interest

To estimate the impact of parental interest, its contemporaneous value and up to two of its lags are added to the model used in the previous chapter. A distributed lag model (see Equation 9.5) is necessary because the graphical analysis indicates that parental influence is not necessarily stable over time. The model includes controls for education, employment status, income, and household composition (whose effects are covered in Chapter 12). Up to two lags of these controls account for the possibility of temporary or delayed effects.[8] Models also take into account whether child and parent live in the same household.

Isolating changes in children's interest that can be attributed to causal influence of their parents presents the biggest challenge in estimating the parental effects consistently. Violations of exogeneity could occur if children (also) influence their parents or if factors operating on the household change the interest of all household members in the same direction. Indeed, the fixed-effects (FE) estimator, which is more susceptible to exogeneity violations, fails the relevant specification test in many cases, so I do not rely on it here. Table 11.1 reports results based on the first-difference (FD) estimator, which only requires independence of the error term at $t-1$, t, and $t+1$ (see Chapter 9). With a few exceptions, noted in the table, the FD models meet the specification tests. To address these exceptions and take into account the compelling theoretical case for violations of exogeneity, Table 11.1 also presents results from a model that includes a lagged dependent variable. As Chapter 9 explained, this dynamic panel model (see Equation 9.6) guards more actively against selection effects and reverse causation.[9]

---

[8] As long as they reported their political interest, panelists are retained in the FD model even when these lags of control variables are missing due to non-response. First and last values are used for extrapolations. An indicator variable is included in the model that marks all values imputed in this way. Missing data on parental interest is handled equivalently (for both FD and Arellano-Bond models). In most cases, parental interest is available for several years before a child becomes eligible for interviewing, limiting the need to backfill values. Carrying forward the last measured parental interest when a parent drops out of the sample does not affect substantive estimates – because parental interest at this point becomes a constant by design – but ensures that the child remains in the estimation sample. When one parent is missing altogether for a panelist, the parent's political interest is set to zero (and the imputation indicator to one), in order for the panelist to remain in the estimation sample. A parent with constant interest (whether imputed or observed) does not contribute to the identification of the effect estimate. Kroh (2006) uses "no information about parents" as the baseline to include panelists for whom parental data is unavailable. In a FD estimator, this leads to jumps between "no info" and measured parental interest.

TABLE 11.1 *Effect of Parental Political Interest on Child's Political Interest*

	Britain			Germany			Switzerland		
	FD Age < 21	FD Age < 40	AB Age < 40	FD Age < 21	FD Age < 40	AB Age < 40	FD Age < 21	FD Age < 40	AB Age < 40
Mother's Pol. Int.	[.08*** (.03)‡]			.09*** (.03)+			.04 (.06)		
in same HH		[.08*** (.02)‡‡]	.09*** (.03)‡‡		.10*** (.02)‡‡	.10*** (.02)‡‡		.05 (.04)+	.06 (.04)+
in separate HH		.03 (.03)	.02 (.03)		.03 (.02)+	.04** (.02)+		.06 (.05)+	.05 (.05)+
Father's Pol. Int.	[.004 (.03)]			.01 (.03)+			-.08 (.07)		
in same HH		.06*** (.02)+	.05* (.03)+		.04* (.02)+	.03 (.02)+		-.02 (.04)	.05 (.05)
in separate HH		.02 (.03)	.03 (.03)		.05 (.02)+	.05** (.02)+		.02 (.05)	.06 (.05)
Lives with									
Mother	-1.1 (3.4)	-1.9 (2.1)-	-2.6 (2.4)-	-5.2 (3.7)	-5.8*** (1.9)	-5.0*** (1.7)-	-6.7 (7.1)	.4 (3.7)	1.2 (3.7)
Lives with Father	.7 (2.8)	-1.5 (2.3)	.1 (2.6)	1.6 (3.5)	1.5 (2.1)	1.5 (1.8)	-1.5 (6.8)	2.4 (3.7)	-.1 (3.8)
Political Interest$_{t-1}$			.12*** (.03)			.03*** (.01)			.08** (.03)
Political Interest$_{t-2}$			.03* (.02)						
AB test for AR(1)			-17.6, $p<.001$			-34.5, $p<.001$			-12.9, $p<.001$
AB test for AR(2)			-1.6, $p=.10$			1.2, $p=.24$			-.7, $p=.47$
Sargan test			$\chi^2(4)=1.8$, $p=.77$			$\chi^2(2)=1.3$, $p=.52$			$\chi^2(2)=.4$, $p=.81$
Hansen test			$\chi^2(4)=1.5$, $p=.83$			$\chi^2(2)=1.1$, $p=.57$			$\chi^2(2)=.3$, $p=.85$
R^2 (within)	.021	.013		.034	.021		.045	.030	
No. of panelists	4,242	6,737	5,135	4,091	5,750	4,976	1,500	2,107	1,703
No. of observations	11,050	26,240	19,325	11,961	42,964	34,913	4,655	10,263	7,305

*** $p<.01$, ** $p<.05$, * $p<.10$. Cell entries are long-run effects for t, $t-1$, and $t-2$, with standard errors in parentheses. Coefficients in brackets indicate violations of exogeneity at $p<.10$. Columns labelled "AB" show results from Arellano-Bond difference estimator. $\Delta PI_{i,t-2}$ is a required instrument. Optional instruments are $\Delta PI_{i,t-m}$ with $m = 3, \ldots, 7$ in BHPS, $m = 3,4$ in GSOEP and SHP. The model includes controls for education and demographic variables with up to two lags (see Chapter 12 for results).

+ Coefficients of contemporaneous short-run effect is positive at $p<.05$

- Coefficients of contemporaneous short-run effect is negative at $p<.05$

‡ Same-household interaction significant at $p<.05$

Columns labelled "AB" report the results of the dynamic panel model. The table shows coefficient estimates for the lagged dependent variable. They are substantively very small, but statistically distinguishable from zero. If political interest deviates from a person's underlying political trajectory one year, this deviation barely carries forward at all and is almost entirely gone a year later.[10] Neither the overall fit statistics (shown in the bottom section of the table and discussed in detail in the Chapter Appendix) nor difference-in-Hansen tests for the specific variables indicate any violations of the exogeneity assumption for parental interest or joint household residence.

The political interest of mothers affects their children's interest. When their mother develops greater interest in politics, children follow and become more interested themselves. When their mother loses interest, so do they. This effect is significantly stronger when mother and child live in the same household, suggesting that observing the parent is indeed important to parental influence on political interest. Fathers have less influence on their children's interest, and shared residence does not affect it.

The results in Table 11.1 strongly support these conclusions for Britain and Germany. In the BHPS, the FD estimator produces several results that violate exogeneity (shaded in the table), but the dynamic panel model meets all specification tests. Results are more ambiguous for Switzerland. Only the contemporaneous impact of maternal political interest is statistically significant, joint residence does not affect the impact, and a difference between mothers and fathers is not clearly evident.

When the sample is limited to the youngest panelists, individuals no older than twenty years, their mother's influence is already present, at about the same magnitude as in the larger (older) sample. Fathers' political interest, on the

---

[9] A dynamic panel model pushes up the minimal age at which effects can be detected. In theory, the model eats up only two lags (because the level at $t-2$ can serve as a valid instrument for the difference at $t-1$, see Chapter 9). In practice, instrumenting $\Delta PI_{i,t-1}$ works only with the difference at $t-2$, and thus requires the third lag of political interest. In the German data, this makes the change in education between ages 18 and 19 the earliest change whose contemporaneous effect on political interest can be detected using a dynamic panel model. Due to the lower eligibility age of 14, a dynamic panel model estimates effects on political interest in the Swiss data for individuals as early as age 17. For the British data, the youth sample with its eligibility age of 11 permits estimates among 15-year-olds. (For the BHPS, the model includes $PI_{i,t-2}$ because it noticeably improves the specification tests.) In short, there is a trade-off between the dynamic panel model and the FD estimator without a lagged dependent variable: The former misses the earliest parental influences, but offers greater protection against reciprocal causation.

[10] Coefficients for the lagged dependent variable in the dynamic panel model speak to long-term stability in political interest. They have little to say about stability from one year to the next. Even if λ (in Equation 9.6) is zero, frequent and large disturbances may generate low year-to-year stability in interest. Whereas the Wiley-Wiley measurement model used in Chapter 6 expresses (relative) stability directly as correspondence between interest reports in consecutive time periods, the dynamic panel model provides information about stability by showing that political interest returns to a person's equilibrium very quickly after a disturbance (see also Prior 2010).

other hand, has no impact yet. It emerges only when the sample is extended to panelists in their twenties and thirties. (These conclusions are similar for sons and daughters. Interacting mother's and father's political interest with the gender of the child reveals no statistically significant differences.)

Most panelists under twenty years of age still live with their parents, so the impact of moving out is imprecisely estimated in the young sample, and parental influence inside and outside the household cannot yet be distinguished. But when young people move out of their mother's house, a transition better captured in the larger sample, their political interest tends to go up. This effect is large in Germany, smaller and temporary in Britain, and not evident in Switzerland. In the first two countries, it adds a noteworthy wrinkle to maternal influence on political interest. The rise in children's interest after moving out occurs regardless of whether their mother was herself politically interested. At the same time, moving out considerably weakens the ongoing impact that mothers have. For children of less politically interested mothers, both of these effects serve to raise interest: They gain interest from starting their own households, and moving out removes them from the dampening effect of their mother's low interest.

CONCLUSION

Children are affected by their parents' political interest. They become more interested when their parents do, and lose interest when their parents lose interest. It is helpful to distinguish two versions of parental influence, *catch-up* and *ongoing*. Thanks to catch-up parental influence, children whose political interest at a young age differs from that of their parents become more similar to their parents' interest levels over time. This form of parental influence entails a change in children's political interest even when their parents' interest remains stable. The more proximate causal factor in this process is presumably the child's growing awareness (and acceptance) of their parents' political interest, but awareness was not measured in the data used here.

Ongoing parental influence results in children changing their political interest when (and because) their parents' interest has changed. As Part II of the book revealed, political interest among adults rarely changes. Yet, it is important to demonstrate that children respond when it does change because ongoing parental influence is subject to fewer alternative explanations than the catch-up version. Put together, empirical evidence for both processes offers considerable support for the Parental Influence Hypothesis.

Because it was not possible to randomly vary the political interest of parents, the analytical strategy in this chapter built on a variety of more circumstantial evidence to make the case for a causal effect of parents on their children. The British dataset, the only one to measure interest in panelists' early teenage years, shows that children's political interest is not yet related to that of their parents. It is apparently not the case that inherited predispositions, early parenting, or shared household influences produce parent–child correspondence right when children develop their political consciousness and make their first assessments of politics as something that does, or does not, interest them.

As children become adolescents, their political interest starts to increasingly resemble that of their parents. Because they also increasingly resemble their parents' interest levels of years earlier, the most logical explanation for this growing similarity is one-directional influence from parent to child. Differences in parent–child correspondence depending on consistency of parental interest and residence in the same household provide evidence that awareness and accurate perception of parents underlie parental influence. Adopting parental political interest should *not* work very well when parents do not agree on their political interest or change it a lot. It should work less well when parent and child do not interact frequently because they do not live together. Both of these expectations are consistently supported by the data, demonstrating that parental influence operates more powerfully in suitable conditions. Additional evidence cements the case that living together is critical for both catch-up and ongoing parental influence. Parent–child correspondence tends to peak just around the time children move out. And the regression models examining ongoing parental influence show the more forceful impact of mother's political interest to be significantly stronger when mother and child live in the same household.

The final piece of the empirical analysis illustrates the payoff from appropriate modeling of parental influence. While graphical analyses show that parental change in political interest often coincides with change among their children, a model-based approach pinpoints the timing with which the respective changes occur more precisely and holds constant the child's interest when the parent begins to change. Although still based on critical (but empirically supported) assumptions, the dynamic panel model strongly suggests that parents, especially mothers, contribute to their children's political interest.

The most obvious benefit of the household panel data used here is the annual measurement of political interest which makes it possible to examine change over time and implement the demanding dynamic panel models. Yet, possibly just as important is the independent measurement of political interest among parents and children. Past research has often had to rely on respondents' memories and ability to report them accurately. McIntosh et al. (2007), for example, use the child's report of political discussion between child and parents in their demonstration that youth-parent discussion is positively related to young people's political knowledge and attention to news. Verba et al. (1995; 2005) ask their adult survey respondents to report their parents' political activity and political discussion when they were teenagers. Decades later, it is difficult to remember parents' behavior, and politically interested respondents may remember it more easily or exaggerate the frequency of political elements. Asking parents themselves, and asking them to report on their present state, ensures much greater validity.

Despite plenty of consistent evidence showing parental influence, some questions remain, perhaps none more curious than the role of parents in Switzerland. In several different analyses in this chapter, results from the SHP differ from the other two countries. After accounting for the fact that the SHP measures interest with less error (because its response scale offers more options), parent–child correspondence in Switzerland is about 20 percent lower than in Britain or Germany. Only in Switzerland, correlations with early parental interest are already lower than contemporaneous correlations at age 14. Graphical and model-based analyses of ongoing parental influence showed smaller, mostly statistically insignificant effects of parental interest and living in the parental household on Swiss children's political interest. Some of these differences might be due to the smaller size of the SHP, but this analysis cannot rule out that parental influence works differently in Switzerland.

Appendix to Chapter 11

ESTIMATION OF DYNAMIC PANEL MODELS

In all three datasets, the difference $\Delta PI_{i,t-2}$ turns out to be a stronger instrument for $\Delta PI_{i,t-1}$ than the level $PI_{i,t-2}$. Regressing differenced political interest on the lag of this difference generates an R^2 of .21 (BHPS), .21 (GSOEP), and .20 (SHP). The respective R^2 statistics for the regression of ΔPI_{it} on $PI_{i,t-1}$ are .14, .15, and .10, by comparison. Using additional lags increases instrument strength further. Three lags of the difference yield an R^2 of .30, .31, and .29. To retain as many cases as possible, I use additional lags of differences if they are available, up to the lag length indicated in Table 11.1.

By other standard benchmarks, too, lagged differences are strong instruments. Consideration of the first-stage equation in a 2SLS model provides further confirmation. Kleibergen and Paap (2006) developed a modified F test robust to heteroscedasticity. For the three datasets, these test statistics are 3701, 15809, and 1636, respectively, more than two orders of magnitude larger than the critical values recommended to reject weak instruments (see, e.g., Baum et al. 2007).[11]

A valid specification using levels or differences of political interest at $t - 2$ as instruments must not have serial error correlation beyond order one. If errors ε_{it} are serially uncorrelated, the errors in the differenced model should exhibit negative first-order autocorrelation (which they do in the FD model without lagged political interest, as seen in Table 12.1), but no higher-order autocorrelation (Arellano and Bond 1991). The test developed by Arellano

---

[11] Exogenous covariates also help to instrument $\Delta PI_{i,t-1}$. The partial R^2 for the excluded instruments is particularly relevant for instrument strength (see, e.g., Baum et al. 2007).

and Bond (1991) evaluates this key assumption and is shown in Table 11.1.[12]

When a model has more instruments than instrumented variables (that is, some instruments are excluded from the second-stage equation), the model is overidentified and the assumption of no correlation between the instrument(s) and the second-stage error term can be tested using a Sargan/Hansen test. A significant χ^2 value on the Sargan/Hansen test indicates that the restrictions are not valid, i.e., the moment conditions assumed to hold are not in fact zero judging by the estimated sample moments. Unlike the related Sargan test, the Hansen test is robust to heteroscedasticity in ε_{it} (Roodman 2009a). As Table 11.1 shows, Sargan/Hansen tests are met in all datasets. Lagged levels always violate the Sargan/Hansen tests.[13]

The test of covariate endogeneity assumes that the overidentifying restrictions imposed by using lags of political interest as excluded instruments are valid, so they can be used to test the exogeneity assumptions made regarding covariates.[14] These tests generate no violations of exogeneity at $p < .10$ for parental interest or household residence in Table 11.1.

---

[12] When AR(2) in the transformed errors indicates first-order correlation in the untransformed level equation and there is no higher-order error correlation, $PI_{i,t-2}$ is not a valid instrument, but $PI_{i,t-3}$ and earlier lags can be used as instruments for $\Delta PI_{i,t-1}$.

[13] These models are unusual in requiring differences as instruments. While Anderson and Hsiao (1981) showed the validity of either lagged levels or differences as instruments, the approach made popular by Holtz-Eakin et al. (1988) and Arellano and Bond (1991) proposed the use of levels to instrument differenced endogenous regressors. All models presented here meet the specification tests proposed by Arellano and Bond (1991).

[14] In this case, the Sargan/Hansen test is used to check if the correlation between the differenced contemporaneous term of an independent variable and the estimated difference of the second-stage error term is distinguishable from zero. Rejection of this hypothesis indicates that the contemporaneous term can be treated as exogenous (assuming that the model is correctly specified and all other identifying assumptions are met).

12

Money, Health, and Happiness

Economic inequality is on the rise and has political implications as elected officials appear to be more responsive to the preferences of wealthy citizens (e.g., Bartels 2008; Gilens 2012). On its face, this type of economic and political inequality is different from inequality in the distribution of political interest because the latter appears to reflect a voluntary decision not to engage with politics. But there is a solid empirical association between economic resources and political interest.

Wealthy, economically comfortable people with high-status jobs are more interested in politics. The political interest difference between the lowest and highest income decile of household income (after governmental transfers) is 16 points in Britain, 15 points in Germany, and 14 points in Switzerland. In each of the three countries, individuals between 30 and 60 in higher-level professional, administrative or managerial occupations, the top category in prominent class coding schemes (Erikson and Goldthorpe 2002; Ganzeboom and Treiman 1996), are 20 points more politically interested than unskilled manual workers. Using a slightly different class coding scheme in Britain (Rose and Pevalin 2003), the difference between top and bottom is close to 25 points.

If these differences exist because economic resources produce political interest, the implications for inequality, and specifically the link between economic and political inequality, would be momentous. They would demonstrate that economic and social hardship hits twice, not only by lowering people's standard of living and well-being, but also by draining their motivation for political involvement. Socioeconomic inequality would exacerbate inequality in the distribution of political interest – and consequently, the distribution of political involvement. Attempts to remedy political inequality would have to begin with efforts to reduce socioeconomic inequality. The main goal of this chapter is to understand if socioeconomic inequality, in addition to its other detrimental effects, also exacerbates inequality in political interest.

In *Voice and Equality*, a widely cited study of political participation, Verba, Schlozman, and Brady (1995) make a strong claim that economic inequality indeed contributes to inequality in political interest. They see three broad groups of reasons why people do not participate, "because they can't; because they don't want to; or because nobody asked" (15), and include political interest in the second set of reasons, motivation. But political interest, according to Verba et al., is itself affected by the first group, resources, as "the roots of political interest are, at least in part, in socioeconomic factors ... The process that produces greater participation for the advantaged also produces greater political interest. Hence, although an index of *wanting* to take part, political interest is also related to *being able* to take part. Therefore, political interest also works to reduce the representation of the needy" (494, emphasis in the original), so "if the less advantaged are less interested in politics, or are otherwise less politically engaged, these predispositions reflect resources as well as choice" (527).[1]

Verba et al. advance this claim on the basis of a cross-sectional survey, however – just the kind of data that have shown strong associations between education and political interest, even though the causal impact, according to Chapter 10, is much smaller. This chapter puts their claim to a more rigorous test, one that examines if changes in political interest follow changes in resources.

There is a second reason to be cautious about a causal role of economic inequality. Unlike the case for a causal link between resources and some forms of political participation, the theoretical argument for a causal impact of resources on political interest is not so clear. Economic resources buy a car that gets you to the polling place, pay for the nanny who watches your children while you attend a volunteer event, and allow you to give money to political causes. But these obstacles are monetary opportunity costs to participating in politics. It doesn't cost to be interested in politics.

Economic resources do not appear in the psychological model of interest. One central component of the resource argument, the importance of skills learned in school in explaining political participation, is consistent with the psychological model if the effect works through efficacy. In fact, Chapter 10 offered some qualified support for general education as a cause of political interest. But money, material resources, and occupational status do not directly figure into psychological explanations of interest formation. After accounting for education, there is no obvious theoretical reason why material resources should affect political interest. According to the psychology of interest, economic inequality should have little effect on political interest.

Some political scientists have speculated that economic resources may affect interest through a subjective sense of insecurity or worry. Financial hardship

---

[1] Elsewhere, Verba, Schlozman, and Burns (2005, 102) argue that political interest "would seem to be a clear measure of motivation not dependent on resources."

may occupy people to an extent that crowds out politics because "when a person experiences economic adversity his scare resources are spent on holding body and soul together – surviving – not on remote concerns like politics" (Rosenstone 1982, 26). Analyzing the "sorts of problems [people] have to deal with in their daily lives," Brody and Sniderman (1977, 340, 346) voice a similar expectation that centers even more directly on people's cognitive involvement with politics: "Citizens whose chief worry is making ends meet ... may well find any interest they might have in the broad affairs of politics deflected to coping with finding a way to deal now, or as soon as possible, with the most immediate and pressing of 'bread-and-butter' problems." Neither Brody and Sniderman nor Rosenstone examine effects on political interest empirically, yet this chapter follows their reasoning and includes not only objective resources, but also subjective assessments of finances and well-being more generally.

Dynamic effects – temporary, delayed, or building gradually – are a main analytic theme in this chapter because changes in resources, employment (or loss of it), living arrangements, and well-being are not as directly connected to political life as, say, parents whose own interest makes them discuss politics frequently. Their effects might thus not be instantaneous. Of course, if the connection is too remote for most people, there may be no effect at all.

To start, this chapter shows the results for covariates already included in the models analyzing education and parental interest in the previous two chapters. They fall into two broad categories, socioeconomic resources and major life transitions, and were selected somewhat opportunistically: They are available in all panel waves and show no clear signs of endogeneity, thus keeping the modeling approach simple. Unlike education and parents, economic resources and life transitions might have their impact at any point in the lifecycle. In addition to the sample of people under 40, the chapter will therefore also examine their impact in the full sample. In the second half of the chapter, I add variables to the baseline specification to take a more in-depth look at specific areas of economic circumstances, subjective concerns, and general well-being. Some of them exhibit patterns of endogeneity – the causal arrow does not point unambiguously from them to political interest – so the more advanced panel estimators will be needed again.

THE IMPACT OF RESOURCES AND SOCIOECONOMIC STATUS ON POLITICAL INTEREST

Socioeconomic status includes material resources, such as income and ownership of one's home. The type of employment and, saliently, the loss of employment are both manifestations of, and further contributing factors to, socioeconomic status. Some life transitions, such as divorce or single parenthood, can aggravate social and economic hardship. These variables, as well as measures of major life transitions discussed subsequently and educational attendance[2], enter the baseline specification with up to two lags, so for the first two years after a change in an independent variable, the model allows full dynamic flexibility as estimates pick up immediate, delayed, and gradual changes. The baseline model answers two questions: Two years after a change in material resources, a change in employment, or a major life transition, is there any change in political interest? Which variables have only short-term effects that have dissipated by that time?[3]

Table 12.1 shows results for the sample examined in Chapters 9–11 using only observations from panelists under the age of 40. (Estimates for the full age range differ little and appear in Table OL12.1 in the Online Supplementary Materials.) Table 12.1 shows estimates of the two-year long-run effect for each variable (following the specification in Equation 9.5). Long-run effects do not measure temporary impact: If an independent variable moves political interest one year, but its delayed effect is in the opposite direction and occurs within the two-year window, political interest is not affected in the long run. The underlying year-by-year estimates (γ_k in Equation 9.5) are not shown, but the table notes two tests for non-constant effects. Estimates with + or − superscripts indicate that the variable has a contemporaneous effect (γ_o) at $p < .05$ (in the direction implied by the respective symbol). A dagger also provides evidence of non-constant effects. It indicates rejection of the hypothesis that the coefficients for lags of a variable are equal to zero. It is possible for some or all lagged coefficients to be different from zero even in the absence of a long-run effect. When these tests indicate short-run effects, I will often use graphical tools to depict the dynamics of the effect.[4]

Most variables examined here are theoretically unlikely to be themselves influenced by political interest. It is difficult to come up with a compelling reason

---

[2] Different levels of schooling are pooled here because Table 10.2 shows very similar effects of lower- and upper-secondary schooling. The model for the full age range in Table OL12.1 uses two lags instead of estimating post-attendance quadratic decay.

[3] Gaps of up to two waves are interpolated with averages of adjacent non-missing responses, and missing observations for lags before a panelist joined the study are backfilled using the earliest response for the panelist. The model adds indicator variables for imputed values so that the backfilled values do not add information to the estimation of the substantive effects. In the absence of panel effects, these estimates should be very similar to the estimates from the model that drops panelists with missing data, but have tighter confidence intervals. Backfilled values are the same as the first valid response, so difference scores are zero for all backfilled waves. The indicator for imputed waves removes their influence from the FE estimation. The only effect of backfilling is that panelists with fewer waves are retained and the information contained in their valid responses goes into the estimation.

[4] The model with long-run multipliers of order 2 assumes that all dynamic variation in effects occurs within three years of the initial change in the independent variable. If this is not true and some effects take even longer to disappear or stabilize, the model is misspecified and estimates will be biased. For a heuristic check of this violation, Table 12.1 again presents results from both the within (FE) estimator and the first-difference (FD) estimator. Although there could be many reasons why different estimators of these complex models with dozens of independent variables yield different results, Chapter 10 illustrated how rough similarity of long-run impact can provide some measure of reassurance. (The FE estimator is more efficient, so standard errors should be systematically larger for the FD results.)

TABLE 12.1 *Long-Run Multiplier Effects of Socioeconomic Status (Age under 40)*

	BHPS		GSOEP		SHP	
	FE	FD	FE	FD	FE	FD
Resources						
Household Income (Pre-Transfer)	.017 (.017)+	.010 (.023)	.004 (.008)	.002 (.01)	.005 (.006)	.005 (.007)
Owns home	-.1 (.5)	.6 (.8)	-.5 (.3)⁻	-.9 (.6)⁻	1.8** (.8)	.6 (1.1)
Mobility	-.5*** (.2)+	-.6 (.4)+	-.5*** (.2)	-.3 (.4)	-.2 (.4)	-.1 (.7)
Employment						
Employed (full time)	-2.0*** (.6)+⁻	-2.0** (.9)⁻	-.03 (.4)⁻	-.4 (.6)⁻	-1.7** (.8)	-.8 (1.1)
Employed (part time)	-.4 (.6)	-.9 (.9)⁻	-.6 (.4)⁻	-.1 (.7)	.3 (.8)⁻	1.0 (1.2)
Occupational Status (Omitted: routine nonmanual employees)						
Higher service professionals	-.1 (.8)	.1 (1.3)	-.8 (.6)	-.3 (.9)	-.6 (.9)	-2.8** (1.2)+
Lower service professionals	.02 (.6)	-.5 (.9)	-.8** (.4)	-.5 (.6)	-.2 (.7)	-1.3 (.9)
Self-employed	-.5 (1.0)	-.6 (1.5)	-.6 (.7)	1.5 (1.3)	-1.2 (2.0)	-1.8 (3.9)
Lower supervisory	-1.1 (.9)	-1.0 (1.4)	-.6 (.7)		-2.3* (1.3)	-4.6** (2.1)⁻
Skilled manual/semi-routine	-.6 (.5)+	-.5 (.9)	-.8 (.5)	-2.0** (.8)⁻	-2.1** (1.1)	-1.6 (1.7)
Semi-/unskilled manual/routine	-2.4*** (.7)⁻	-1.1 (1.0)	-.5* (.5)+	-.4 (.7)	-3.8*** (1.0)+	-2.9* (1.5)
Unemployed	-1.7* (.7)+	-.0002 (1.1)	.6* (.4)+	.2 (.6)	-2.5 (1.9)	-5.0* (2.7)
Parents						
Lives in mother's HH	-1.6** (.8)	1.1 (1.2)	-.5 (.8)⁻	-2.1 (1.4)+	-1.4 (1.3)	.2 (1.9)
Lives in father's HH	.1 (.8)	.1 (1.2)	-.8 (.8)	.8 (1.4)+	-1.1 (1.4)	-2.8 (1.0)
Mother works full time	.1 (.6)	.7 (.9)	-1.2** (.6)	.5 (1.0)	.2 (1.6)	-1.7 (2.6)
Mother works part time	.3 (.6)	-.01 (.8)	-.5 (.5)	1.2 (.9)	.9 (.9)	.6 (1.6)
Father works	-.1 (.6)	-.3 (1.0)	-.3 (.4)	-.4 (.8)	-.9 (1.1)	.2 (1.9)
At least one parent unemployed	-.1 (.7)	-.04 (1.0)	.5 (.5)	1.3 (.8)	.5 (2.2)	.1 (3.3)
Parental divorce/separation	-.8 (1.9)	-2.0 (3.4)	.6 (1.2)	.6 (2.2)	.1 (2.0)	1.3 (3.3)

(continued)

267

TABLE 12.1 (continued)

	BHPS		GSOEP		SHP	
	FE	FD	FE	FD	FE	FD
Spouse, Children						
Married	-.4 (.6)	.2 (1.0)	-.1 (.5)	-.5 (.8)†	-1.1 (.9)	-2.7* (1.4)⁻
Divorced, separated	-2.5** (1.0)	2.3 (1.8)	-.7 (.8)	-2.2 (1.6)†	-2.5* (2.4)	-1.0 (3.9)
Spouse in HH	1.1* (.6)†	2.0** (.9)†⁺	.5 (.5)	-.5 (.8)	.7 (.8)	1.3 (1.3)
Single parent	-.2 (1.0)	-1.4 (1.6)†	-.6 (.9)	-1.0 (1.6)⁻	-5.6** (2.6)⁻	-.4 (4.1)
Children in HH, age 0–1	-.3 (.6)	-.9 (.7)	.8 (.8)	.8 (.9)	-2.8 (3.5)	-6.2* (3.2)⁻
Children in HH, age 2–4	.02 (.4)⁺	.6 (.6)	1.4** (.6)	-.1 (.9)	-4.6* (2.7)	-5.7 (4.2)
Children in HH, age 5–10	.5 (.5)	1.1 (.8)	2.2*** (.5)⁺	1.4 (.8)	.1 (1.3)	2.1 (1.9)
Children in HH, age 11–15	-.5 (.5)	.8 (.9)	2.0*** (.5)	.4 (.9)	.5 (1.1)	2.1 (1.6)
Children in HH, age 16+	-.8 (.7)	-.3 (1.1)	2.4*** (.6)⁺	.7 (1.0)	-.4 (1.6)	-.1 (2.7)
Own children in HH, age 0–1	-.3 (.4)⁻	.4 (.5)	.03 (.4)	.1 (.5)	3.1 (3.5)	6.8** (3.2)⁺
Own children in HH, age 2–4	-.1 (.4)	-.1 (.5)	-.6 (.6)	.6 (.8)	4.6 (2.7)	5.8 (4.1)
Own children in HH, age 5–10	.4 (.4)	-.3 (.5)	-1.2** (.5)	-.9 (.7)	.05 (1.2)	-2.0 (1.7)
Own children in HH, age 11–15	-.1 (.3)	-.04 (.4)	-.7 (.3)⁻	-.3 (.5)	.4 (.7)	-1.0 (.9)
Own children in HH, age 16+			-.2 (.2)	-.4 (.4)	.9 (.5)	-.1 (.6)
R^2 (within)	.025	.008	.024	.011	.035	.016
AR(1) correlation of residuals	.02	-.44	.06	-.45	.07	-.40
AR(2) correlation of residuals	-.07	.002	-.02	-.01	-.04	-.02
No. of panelists	20,445	19,384	14,001	13,507	5,156	4,799
No. of observations	116,917	89,282	109,981	95,135	30,436	23,285

*** $p < .01$, ** $p < .05$, * $p < .10$. Cell entries are 2-year long-run multipliers with robust standard errors in parentheses (1-year LRM for children in household). Models also include dummy variables for age, measures of interestingness defined in Chapter 6, educational attendance with quadratic post-attendance decay (see Chapter 10), and indicator variables for any values that were interpolated.
† Lagged coefficients all equal to zero is rejected at $p < .10$
⁺ Coefficients of contemporaneous short-run effect is positive at $p < .05$
⁻ Coefficients of contemporaneous short-run effect is negative at $p < .05$

why a change in political interest should cause, say, divorce, income change, or job loss. Politically interested individuals might opt for different types of jobs, but this chapter will ignore those distinctions. (Chapter 13 will focus specifically on jobs with connections to politics or public administration.) The resources and life course events examined in this chapter are expected to operate as exogenous variables that causally precede political interest. Empirically, tests for endogeneity introduced in Chapter 10 largely confirm these expectations. In only one, theoretically implausible, case (own children between 16 and 18 in the SHP) do the tests indicate violations of exogeneity at $p < .05$ for both estimators. Hence, Table 12.1 shows only effects of variables that are likely exogenous.

The combined impact of economic resources, employment conditions, and life transitions is very small. The within-subject R^2 noted in Table 12.1 shows that the fraction of the individual-level change in political interest explained by changes in socioeconomic variables, life transitions, aging, and interestingness of the environment never exceeds .035. And decidedly more than half of that small fraction – almost all of it in the GSOEP – is accounted for by just aging and interestingness. A cross-sectional model of political interest with the same measures of socioeconomic status and life transitions, by comparison, yields a higher R^2. (The R^2 for yearly regressions without age or interestingness is up to .17 in BHPS, .21 in GSOEP, and .18 in SHP.) This comparison demonstrates that it is a lot easier to find variables that are associated with levels of political interest than it is to identify potential causes of it – variables that changed in advance of (or contemporaneous to) a change in political interest.

The estimated effect of income on political interest illustrates this point well. Income is measured in great detail in all three household panel surveys. The base specification uses real gross household income, which includes labor earnings, investment income, and private transfers, including private retirement income. It measures income before government transfers and taxes. The variable is adjusted for inflation and divided by the square-root of the number of people living in the household. As noted at the beginning of the chapter, the richest individuals in all three countries are about 15 points more politically interested than the poorest. Other studies have also found a positive association between political interest and income (Bennett 1986, 74–7; Verba et al. 1995, ch.12; although Blais and St-Vincent 2011 find no relationship).

Yet, despite a clear positive association, a change in income is *not* followed by any change in political interest, according to either Table 12.1 or the full-sample results in Table OL12.1. There are only two significant temporary effects (out of 12 estimates) and no long-term effects at all.[5] Home ownership, which may pick up other aspects of wealth, is equally anemic as a cause of interest.

---

[5] As far as household income is concerned, the biggest change for most young people occurs when they leave the parental household. To distinguish the effect of this transition from the effect of income, models control for living in the parental household.

A Closer Look at Income

Before concluding that income has no effect on political interest, it is worthwhile to assess three additional expectations about possibly more intricate income effects. First, it may not be gross income that affects interest, but the extent by which redistribution modifies someone's income. The difference between net and gross household income captures these public transfers (including government-run retirement benefits, unemployment aid, child benefits, and many others) and tax payments (including contributions to public retirement systems). Second, it may not be absolute income that affects interest, but the level of income relative to others in the country. Rescaling income in terms of (yearly) deciles picks up this relative income effect. Third, with respect to turnout, studies have found marginally declining effects suggesting that the same increase in income makes a bigger difference at low income levels (e.g., Rosenstone 1982). Entering pre-transfer income as a series of decile dummies instead of one continuous measure allows for such non-linear effects.

Empirical analyses generate no systematic evidence that relative income matters, that income has non-linear effects on political interest, or that government transfers affect interest. The FE model for Germany indicates a positive effect of government transfers, but the FD estimator does not confirm this finding, and one estimator shows a marginally negative effect in Switzerland. None of the variables make any kind of difference for political interest in Britain. Income really does not affect political interest, no matter how we look at it.

- - -

Employment status does appear to affect political interest, but the dynamics of this effect are not straightforward. Even if income does not influence their political interest, it is conceivable that other aspects of people's work life do. Looking for a job might stress the role of the state in the labor market, through provision of unemployment benefits, job training, and the common attribution of unemployment as a government responsibility. How much people work partly determines how much time they have for other things, including politics. Past research is inconsistent. Kroh and Könnecke (2014) find a clear negative cross-sectional relationship between unemployment and political interest, but the annual change in political interest that follows job loss is statistically insignificant. In Kroh's (2006) earlier analysis of GSOEP data, he finds political interest to be higher among unemployed people relative to (manual) workers. Also using the GSOEP, Emmenegger et al. (2017) demonstrate a negative effect of unemployment on political interest among young people. Rosenstone (1982), among many others, shows turnout to be lower for unemployed Americans, and more so the more closely before the election the job loss occurred.

The baseline model includes measures of full-time employment, part-time employment, and unemployment. The omitted reference category comprises people in education, in retirement, or not working for other reasons. For Britain, Table 12.1 shows that taking a full-time job leads to a significant two-point drop in political interest. The effect is one point in Switzerland, but only significant for the more efficient FE estimator and only using the full age range (see Table OL12.1). The estimates quantify the impact two years after people became employed. The dagger symbol next to the BHPS and SHP estimates indicates that a portion of the effect operates with a delay (the coefficients for the first and second lag of full-time employment are not both zero). And FD results for Germany in Table OL12.1 indicate a significant negative short-term effect of employment. These results demonstrate that employment status has an effect that is not immediate and constant, but does not fully characterize how it unfolds. The result summary tells us that a portion of the effect was immediate, but not what portion. It also suggests delayed effects, but not their direction and precise timing.

By providing more detail about effects that change over time, the Second Big Benefit of panel data really gets its chance to shine in this chapter. Figure 12.1 characterizes the dynamic relationship between full-time employment and political interest more fully. Separately for each country and estimator, it shows both cumulative long-run impact and year-to-year effects of employment. The purpose of the figure is to display immediate and delayed effects as estimated by the baseline specification, do so again allowing for much longer delays, and summarize the long-run effect over a decade. (Graphs are based on the full age range because the extended time frame makes information beyond age 40 relevant and increases the statistical efficiency of the analysis.)

Summary graphs in Figure 12.1 present three sets of year-by-year estimates and the cumulative effect as a function of the lag (with 95-percent confidence intervals). The horizontal axis charts the length of the lag k, that is, how many years have passed since the change in the independent variable. Moving rightward through a graph depicts the development of the long-run effect of a variable over increasing periods of time. The lighter square symbols show yearly effects up to lag two based on the baseline specification.[6] The triangles come from reestimating the model with a full decade of lags. Their confidence intervals are larger because they are based only on panelists who provide a response for 11 consecutive years. Requiring non-missing data on so many lags drops not only panelists who were panel members for just a few years, but also long-time participants who missed one or more yearly interviews. A third model therefore interpolates and backfills missing responses in order to include most panelists who were part of the baseline analysis. The circle graphs these estimates. The last statistic, shown in the graph by black squares and thicker

---

[6] There is one difference: The baseline specification interpolates short gaps and backfills data, as previously explained; the estimates shown by lighter squares in the graphs do not.

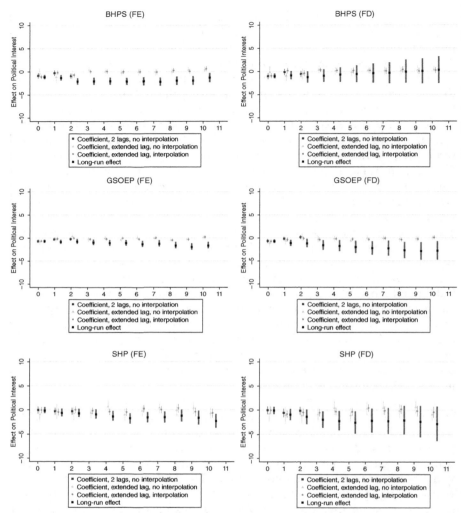

FIGURE 12.1 The Effect of Full-Time Employment on Political Interest

Note: Graphs plot estimates of γ_k (lighter squares, triangles, and circles symbols) and long-run multipliers (larger black squares) as a function of lag length k (the horizontal axis). 95-percent confidence intervals shown. Political interest is 0–100. Full-time employment is a dummy variable. Estimates are based on full age range (excluding the BHPS youth interviews).

lines for confidence intervals, is the long-run multiplier up to k from the interpolation model. Estimates in dark green and the long-run multiplier are thus identical for $k = 0$ (the value 0 on the horizontal axis).

The effect of full-time employment in all three countries is negative and builds up over several years, as seen by the dark squares in Figure 12.1, which track the long-term impact of taking a job. The effect is only about 2 points at its largest, and this maximum occurs at different times in different countries. In Britain, the negative effect is immediately significant, grows for another year or two, and begins to revert toward zero after about five years. In Germany and Switzerland, in contrast, it only develops to statistically detectable magnitudes after several years, but then shows no signs of reversion. Taking a job does appear to reduce political interest with some delay, but this effect is small enough that even the very large household panel studies can barely distinguish it from zero.

Even though unemployment is not the opposite of full-time employment, its effect appears to be. The results for unemployment again become clearer when their evolution over several years is considered, in Figure 12.2. In all three countries, unemployment raises political interest at some point. The effect is immediate and brief in Britain, but gradual in Germany and, probably, Switzerland.[7]

There is one additional wrinkle when it comes to unemployment, but even many tens of thousands of data points are not quite enough to be statistically sure: Results for Switzerland and Britain both suggest that the effect of unemployment might initially be negative when it happens early in life. Two of four estimates in Table 12.1 are statistically significant, a third is marginal, and plots of yearly effects (not shown) confirm negative effects within a year or two of becoming unemployed.

What type of job people have may also affect their political interest. Occupations vary in autonomy, task complexity, and the extent to which they teach politically relevant skills (Verba et al. 1995), which in turn build up the coping potential that facilitates interest.[8] Past research showed political interest in Britain to be higher among self-employed individuals (Denny and Doyle 2008) and individuals employed in professional or managerial/technical jobs (Deary et al. 2008). Turnout among these groups in the United States fits the same pattern and clearly exceeds turnout among manual workers (Hout et al. 1995).

Results presented so far have drawn conclusions about the "average" job or, more precisely, a job of middling prestige and task complexity. The baseline model includes additional variables to assess the impact of employment in occupations that are higher or lower on those dimensions, features that sociologists often describe as indicative of social class. For instance, in order

---

[7] Estimates for Switzerland have uninformatively large standard errors for several reasons: Unemployment is usually somewhat lower in Switzerland than in the other two countries. The SHP is the smallest of the three studies. Unlike the GSOEP, which combines two questions, about unemployment at the time of the interview and during the preceding year, the SHP (like the BHPS) only asks about unemployment at the time of the interview, thus missing people who are unemployed for shorter stretches.

[8] Following Almond and Verba (1963) and Pateman (1970), research has examined whether certain workplace experiences provide people with a greater sense of self-esteem or (general or political) efficacy (see, e.g., Adman 2008; Lafferty 1989). This argument links occupational status with coping potential, one of the theoretical underpinnings of interest. It implies that its estimated effect should shrink to zero when efficacy is included in the model.

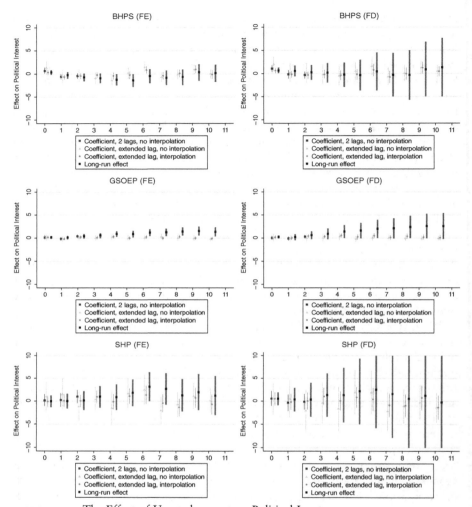

FIGURE 12.2 The Effect of Unemployment on Political Interest

Note: Graphs plot estimates of γ_k (lighter squares, triangles, and circles symbols) and long-run multipliers (larger black squares) as a function of lag length k (the horizontal axis). 95-percent confidence intervals shown. Political interest is 0–100. Unemployment is a dummy variable. Estimates are based on full age range (excluding the BHPS youth interviews).

to "capture qualitative differences in employment relations," Erikson and Goldthorpe (2002, 32–3) distinguish, principally, "employers, self-employed workers, and employees."

A slightly more nuanced version of the Erikson-Goldberg typology of occupations includes a higher and a lower category of professionals and managers, "routine nonmanual employees," skilled manual workers, non-skilled manual workers (including farm workers), and a group of nonprofessional self-employed workers, small employers, and farmers. A key distinction in employment relations is between a service relationship for professionals and managers, and labor contracts for workers and routine employees. Commitment is based more on contracts and regulations for the latter, more on employee trust for the former in that "service-class employees are controlled by the 'carrot' of long-term benefits, and workers by the 'stick' of close regulation and the labor contract" (Evans 1992, 214). Other typologies exist, but they produce similar classifications.[9]

Lower-status occupations appear to reduce political interest more than service professions, self-employment, or occupations with middling status. The omitted baseline in Table 12.1 includes panelists who are not working and those classified as "intermediate" or "routine nonmanual." Full-time employment thus captures political interest in the intermediate/routine nonmanual category. Coefficients for the other occupational types indicate whether the effect on interest differs among working people depending on their occupational status. All coefficients for the "lower supervisory" and manual occupations are negative, more than half are greater than a full point, and 7 out of 16 are statistically significant. Magnitudes are lower for the full age range in Table OL12.1, so to the extent that occupational status makes a difference for political interest, it does so at the outset of an individual's work life.

In sum, employment status and the type of employment shape political interest in small but fairly consistent ways. Working tends to lower political interest, and job loss increases it. These effects can be temporary (in Britain) or slow to emerge (in Germany and Switzerland), a conclusion that clearly illustrates the need to allow for changing effects over time. As best as we can tell, some effects are different for young people: For them, both unemployment and employment in lower status occupations appear to depress political interest.[10] (Results also show that employment status of parents does not affect the political interest of their children.[11])

---

[9] Ganzeboom and Treiman (1996, 216, 217) compare the Erikson and Goldthorpe typology to two other measures of "occupational status." They conclude that all measure "the role of occupation in the status attainment process" and correlate at .8 to .9. Analysis of the British data uses the National Statistics Socioeconomic Class (NS-SEC, see Rose and Pevalin 2003) measure because the Erikson and Goldthorpe typology is not consistently available. The two measures are similar, but NS-SEC prioritizes employment relations over task requirements and therefore classifies jobs as "routine" and "semi-routine" instead of coding simply whether they are skilled or unskilled and involve manual labor or not. Occupational status can be assessed either for individuals who work or for households based on the status of the highest-earning household member or the head of household (Goldthorpe 1999, 61, fn 3; Kohler 2005). My analysis uses person-specific classification.

[10] Even for the German data, which yield null results in Table 12.1, Emmeneger et al. (2017) show a negative effect of unemployment on political interest for panelists under 35 using a matching estimator that includes baseline political interest among the matched covariates.

[11] The baseline model includes employment status of mother and father when available. If fathers are employed, they almost always work full time. Mothers in the labor force tend to work part time,

THE IMPACT OF LIFE TRANSITIONS ON POLITICAL INTEREST

A second set of factors emphasized in the political socialization literature includes important life transitions, such as moving out of the parents' house, getting married, or having children, and these may change people's political interest, temporarily or in a lasting way. Past research has shown private life events to affect the propensity to vote. Focusing on the low turnout of young adults, Highton and Wolfinger (2001, 203) propose that in the transition from adolescence to early adulthood, "participating in politics, rarely a top priority for anyone, competes against and usually loses to ... other, more pressing personal concerns for young people." They argue that only the completion of these transitions allows young adults to focus on politics (again or for the first time). Distinguishing the effects on turnout of residential status, moving out of the parents' house, finishing school, and entering the labor force, they find some positive associations with turnout. Other transitions and early life events, such as teen parenthood, dropping out of high school, or parental divorce are associated with lower (future) participation (Plutzer 2002; Sandell and Plutzer 2005; Pacheco and Plutzer 2007). Consequential transitions are not limited to adolescence (Sigel 1989; Sapiro 1994).[12] Both marriage and divorce or separation, for example, appear to lower political participation of adults, at least initially (Stoker and Jennings 1995).

The mechanisms that link these transitions with political participation are not well understood, so the implications of these findings for political interest remain ambiguous. For example, residential mobility might be negatively related to political participation (as shown by, among others, Pacheco and Plutzer 2008), because people need to learn how to vote again after each move. Yet, whether mobility lowers political interest is less clear. Life transitions might cause changes in participation mostly by changing material resources and time constraints. Hener et al. (2016, 2) examine if parental divorce and being raised by an unmarried mother reduce political involvement "since they undermine, and in some cases prevent, the process and activities through which parents shape their children's political orientations." For political interest as an outcome, they do not find significant cross-sectional differences for either variable, however (in the GSOEP data).[13] Highton and Wolfinger (2001; see also Sapiro 1994, 214–16) argue that transitions affect political interest by

but there are enough cases of full-time employed mothers to distinguish both. Parental unemployment is rare in the data, so both parents are considered jointly to create an indicator for at least one parent being unemployed. The panel designs follow parents even when they no longer live in the same household as their children (as long as parent and child lived in the same household for at least one wave). Panel attrition among parents should be mostly a function of old age or parents leaving the country. Models include an indicator variable for availability of parental data.

[12] Sapiro (1994) points out that the timing and sequence of life events might condition their effect.
[13] A model with sibling fixed effects shows no effect of parental divorce, but a significant negative relationship with birth outside marriage (Hener et al. 2016).

refocusing attention and changing the salience and relevance of government and public policy. Parents of a young child, for example, may recognize more fully the role of the state in education policy.[14]

As Table 12.1 shows, most life transitions have little systematic impact on political interest. Residential mobility, measured by a count of residential moves since joining the panel, has statistically detectable negative effects for half the estimates, but they are small. Leaving the parental household may raise political interest a bit, but, as Chapter 11 has shown, this effect also depends on parental interest (not included in this chapter's models). To the extent that lack of mobility is in fact causally related to political participation, as some previous research suggests, familiarity with local voting arrangements and ways to participate seems like a better explanation than an increase in political interest. As far as interest is concerned, people appear to take it with them when they move.

The effect of parental divorce is difficult to establish because relatively few parents experience it, and the (non-significant) estimates are in the opposite direction in Britain as in the other two countries.[15] Having children or sharing the household with children (typically siblings) is mostly unrelated to political interest. The only credible exception occurs in Switzerland where young siblings appear to lower political interest levels of older children.[16] This is a rare scenario in the first place, however, as it entails an age gap between siblings exceeding ten years. Raising children alone significantly lowers political interest in Switzerland. (Teen parenthood, defined as a female panelist under the age of 20 reporting a child, is too rare in the data to provide an estimate: There are only 6 cases in the SHP, 38 in the GSOEP, and 70 in the BHPS.)

Overall, the association between adverse circumstances such as parental divorce or single parenthood and lower political involvement by young people that appeared in past research does not work through political interest, does not generalize in Western Europe, is not negative, or is possibly not causal.

Living with a spouse or partner might raise political interest by a point or two. Again, the effect is substantively small, but suggestive in across all three countries. (Graphs are available in the Online Supplementary Materials, Figure OL12.1.)

---

[14] In the absence of direct measures, demographics may indicate population segments with good reasons to care about policy, e.g., parents with children in school (Verba et al. 1995, ch.14).

[15] Parental divorce or separation is defined to occur either when one parent moves out of a dual-parent household or if the marital status of parents changes to separated/divorced while they are still in the same household as the child. The indicator variable remains at 1 for all waves after parental divorce.

[16] The baseline model includes two sets of counts, one for the panelists' own children, the other for children living in the household. (For parents, these two sets of measures will have mostly the same values. For other household members, especially young people, only the second set is relevant, for example by providing information about siblings in the household.) Each set comprises of counts of children within different age ranges living in the household: Infants under the age of 2, young children between 2 and 4, children of primary school age (age 5–10), young adolescents (11–15), and older adolescents (age 16 and older). An indicator for raising children as a single-parent is also included.

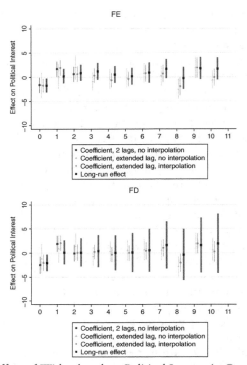

FIGURE 12.3 The Effect of Widowhood on Political Interest in Germany

Note: Graphs plot estimates of γ_k (lighter squares, triangles, and circles symbols) and long-run multipliers (larger black squares) as a function of lag length k (the horizontal axis). 95-percent confidence intervals shown. Political interest is 0–100. Estimates are based on full age range.

The effect builds up over several years of moving in with someone. The model controls for marital status which distinguishes unmarried individuals from married individuals, separated or divorced individuals, and widowed individuals. These two variables pick up different things: Married couples need not live in the same household, and people can cohabitate without being married.[17] It is cohabitation, not the formal status that produces the effects. (Marital status has no systematic effects even when spousal cohabitation is dropped.)

Insofar as the end of a marriage co-occurs with the end of cohabitation, it lowers political interest by a similar amount as moving in increases it. Beyond that, divorce or separation leave political interest unchanged. The death of a spouse may cause an additional short-term drop in interest. This effect is clearly present only in Germany (Figure 12.3), but at least for that country it cogently

---

[17] Because of the sampling design that recruits all members of randomly selected households, both partners in a couple (whether married or not) will initially only be part of the sample if they live in the same household.

illustrates effects that vary over time. Losing a spouse depresses political interest in the year in which a panelist first reports being widowed. A year later, interest rebounds by a similar amount, and the long-run effect is indistinguishable from zero.[18]

For the most part, however, life transitions do not have the impact past research attributed to them, at least when it comes to political interest and when the analysis looks for changes in the political outcome variable following changes in life circumstances.

THE IMPACT OF SUBJECTIVE ECONOMIC ASSESSMENTS

Although socioeconomic insecurity is typically defined in terms of objective conditions, worries about finances and the economy might make it a more subjective factor. In addition to income, resources, and type of work, a subjective sense of economic hardship, mounting financial constraints, and reduced standard of living constitutes another potential source of political interest. Economic anxiety has been related to lower turnout (Rosenstone 1982), and both Rosenstone and Brody and Sniderman (1977) argue that it should lower political interest by reducing people's capacity or inclination to focus on concerns beyond their immediate circumstances. A positive effect on political interest is also conceivable, however: Worry about the economy and one's personal finances may stimulate an interest in understanding the reasons for economic problems, including politics and economic policy.

Unlike the objective economic circumstances and life transitions examined in the first half of this chapter, subjective economic assessments could as easily be influenced by political interest as influence it. Taking an interest in politics for other reasons might lead people to pay more attention to economic policy and conditions – which, in turn, might cause them to worry about the state of the economy or their own finances. Hence, the analytical approach in the second half of the chapter must take greater precautions against reciprocal causation. As before, the first line of defense is the inclusion of lagged political interest as a predictor because it accounts for potentially higher preexisting interest among people feeling, or worried about, economic hardship. If this analytic move does not take care of the problem, using earlier lags of subjective economic assessments offers a stronger remedy for reciprocal causation. That approach, however, also puts greater demands on the data, as early lags are now needed to build the kind of scaffolding that permits the work-around in the presence of reciprocal causation (see Chapter 9). As a result, the following analysis will no

---

[18] The effects of widowhood on political interest are much lower than effects on turnout in Hobbs et al.'s (2014) recent study of California voter files. They find an immediate drop in turnout of over 20 percentage points and only partial recovery over the next year-and-a-half that still leaves turnout rates among widows 9 points lower.

longer go back as far as a whole decade in tracing potentially long-delayed and cumulative effects of changes in independent variables. For most variables, going back three years will be possible and should capture the bulk of effects that subjective sentiments might have.

All three household panel studies ask panelists every year how well they are "managing financially these days" (BHPS) or how satisfied they are with their financial situation (GSOEP, SHP; for exact wording of all questions used, see Online Supplementary Materials). When added to the FE/FD models from Table OL12.1, these variables raise only minor concerns (one test violation for the SHP) about reciprocal causation. With lagged political interest controlled for, all of them can be treated as exogenous. A second measure, available only in the German data, assesses panelists' worry about the economy. It shows clearer signs of violating the exogeneity assumption that are not remedied in a lagged dependent variable model. Economic Worry, therefore, needs to be treated as predetermined (see Chapter 9) in the following analysis.

Table 12.2 shows the results for the full age range. It also includes measures of health and well-being discussed shortly.[19] Models meet the specification requirements: Lagged differences of political interest are strong instruments for the current differenced political interest; the instruments are valid; and the model has no serial error correlation beyond first order. The bottom section of Table 12.2 shows the most important specification tests.[20]

Financial satisfaction has a positive effect on political interest in all three countries, but this effect unfolds differently over time and is only marginally significant in Britain. The coefficients in Table 12.2 are the 3-year long-run multipliers: how much greater satisfaction with personal finances affects political interest over the course of three years. The superscript "+" next to the GSOEP estimate indicates that the immediate effect at $t=0$ is positive and statistically significant at $p < .05$. The dagger symbol next to the estimate for Switzerland adds that the coefficients for lagged financial satisfaction are not all indistinguishable from zero – in other words, a change in financial satisfaction today leads to an additional change in political interest in the future, over and above the immediate effect. Figure 12.4 depicts the impact of financial

---

[19] Some variables are unavailable in a few panel waves. Table entries for them (in italics) are based on reestimation of the model for the subset of available waves. In the BHPS, life satisfaction was only asked in 1996–2000 and 2002–13, and objective health conditions are not available after 2008. Satisfaction with free time in the GSOEP was not asked in 1990 and 1995. Unlike Tables 12.1 and OL12.1, the models in Table 12.2 do not interpolate or backfill missing values. Because the lagged dependent variable and the lags required to instrument it preclude estimates for the youngest panelists anyway, there is less need to backfill.

[20] Instrument strength for Economic Worry in the GSOEP is sufficiently high: The F statistic for the excluded instruments (its difference at $t-2$ and $t-3$ and its level at $t-4$) is over 4500, easily exceeding the value of 20 that is considered acceptable according to a common rule of thumb. Treating the variable as endogenous instead of predetermined is not required according to a difference-in-Hansen test ($p < .89$).

TABLE 12.2 *Long-Run Multiplier Effects of Socioeconomic Status, Health and Well-Being*

	BHPS	GSOEP	SHP
Financial satisfaction	1.2 (.8)	.9 (.6)$^+$	1.3** (.8)†
Economic worry		2.0*** (.7)$^+$	
Physical health	−2.7** (1.0)$^{†−}$		−1.7** (.8)$^{†+}$
Mental health	−.1 (.8)$^+$		−.5 (.9)
Satisfaction with health		−.04 (.6)	
General life satisfaction $^{a)}$	1.4 (1.0)$^+$	2.3*** (.6)$^+$	2.2*** (.7)$^{†+}$
Satisfaction with free time		1.6** (.7)$^+$	.6 (.8)
Education			
Years in school $^{a)}$	−2.6 (8.7)†	1.0 (2.8)	.7 (1.1)
Years in secondary vocational $^{a)}$	1.0 (1.9)	.7 (.6)†	.5 (.6)
Years in post-sec. vocational $^{a)}$		.1 (.5)	−.2 (.4)
Years in post-sec. academic $^{a)}$	−.1 (.9)†	−.003 (.3)	.3 (.4)
Resources			
Household Income (Pre-Transfer)	.050* (.027)$^+$	−.007 (.010)	.003 (.003)
Owns home	−.8 (1.0)	−.0003 (.5)	.8 (.8)
Mobility	−.7 (.4)†	.2 (.3)	.2 (.5)
Employment			
Employed (full time)	−1.6 (1.0)$^−$	−1.4** (.6)$^−$	−2.9*** (.9)†
Employed (part time)	−1.5 (1.0)$^−$	.1 (.6)	−1.1 (.8)$^−$
Occupational Status (Omitted: routine nonmanual employees)			
Higher service professionals	.9 (1.2)	−.6 (.8)	.1 (.9)
Lower service professionals	−.1 (.8)	−1.1* (.6)†	−.5 (.7)
Self-employed	1.4 (1.4)	−.1 (1.0)	−.7 (2.3)
Lower supervisory	.9 (1.5)		−4.7*** (1.4)$^{†−}$
Skilled manual/ semi-routine	1.3 (1.0)	1.1 (.8)	−.8 (1.6)$^−$
Semi-/unskilled manual/ routine	2.8** (1.2)†	−.3 (.7)	−.2 (1.2)
Unemployed	1.4 (1.7)	−.1 (.5)	3.6 (2.3)
Parents			
Lives in mother's HH	.1 (2.0)	−1.5 (1.4)$^−$	−2.2 (2.3)
Lives in father's HH	−1.8 (2.2)	.3 (1.5)	−2.4 (2.4)
Mother works full time	−.3 (1.9)	.1 (1.2)	−1.0 (3.2)
Mother works part time	2.0 (1.9)†	−.6 (1.1)	.4 (1.7)
Father works	−2.6 (1.7)	.2 (.9)	.8 (2.2)

(*continued*)

TABLE 12.2 *(continued)*

	BHPS	GSOEP	SHP
At least one parent unemployed	1.5 (3.2)	.5 (1.0)	11.5** (5.1)†
Parental divorce/separation	14.3 (13.3)	3.0 (2.9)	−1.3 (3.7)
Spouse, Children			
Married	−1.1 (1.2)	−.1 (.9)	−.8 (1.3)
Divorced, separated	−.2 (1.5)	−.6 (1.2)	1.1 (1.9)
Widowed	.4 (2.3)	−.6 (1.5)$^-$	3.4 (2.8)
Spouse in HH	.8 (1.3)	.4 (.8)	1.2 (1.1)
Single parent	.1 (1.6)	−.3 (1.0)	.4 (1.6)$^{†-}$
Children in HH, age 0–1	−2.1 (1.3)	−.05 (1.1)	1.4 (4.7)
Children in HH, age 2–4	1.4* (.8)	−1.6 (1.0)	−4.2 (2.6)
Children in HH, age 5–10	1.6 (1.1)	−.1 (.9)	1.8 (2.2)
Children in HH, age 11–15	1.0 (1.1)	−1.2 (.8)	.9 (1.2)
Children in HH, age 16+	−.01 (.4)	.4 (.3)	.04 (.4)
Own children in HH, age 0–1	1.5** (.7)	.3 (.7)	−1.3 (4.6)
Own children in HH, age 2–4	−.1 (.8)	1.2 (1.0)	3.3 (2.6)
Own children in HH, age 5–10	−1.6 (1.0)	−.6 (.8)	−1.3 (2.1)
Own children in HH, age 11–15	−1.5 (1.0)	.5 (.7)	−.5 (1.1)
Own children in HH, age 16+		−.4 (.3)	.5 (.4)
Political Interest$_{t-1}$	.03** (.01)	.04*** (.01)	.03** (.01)
Political Interest$_{t-2}$	.01 (.01)	.01 (.01)	
Required instruments	$\Delta PI_{i,t-2}$	$\Delta PI_{i,t-m}$ for $m = 2,3,4$	$\Delta PI_{i,t-2}$
Optional instruments	$\Delta PI_{i,t-m}$ for $m = 3,4,5$	None	$\Delta PI_{i,t-m}$ for $m = 3,\ldots,6$
AB test for AR(1)	−38.0, $p < .001$	−57.8, $p < .001$	−34.8, $p < .001$
AB test for AR(2)	.8, $p = .42$	−.7, $p = .48$	−.9, $p = .39$
Sargan test	$\chi^2(2) = 1.3$, $p = .53$	$\chi^2(3) = .3$, $p = .97$	$\chi^2(4) = 3.4$, $p = .50$
Hansen test	$\chi^2(2) = .9$, $p = .63$	$\chi^2(3) = .2$, $p = .98$	$\chi^2(4) = 2.1$, $p = .72$
No. of panelists	24,493	18,143	6,882
No. of observations	81,477	159,725	42,644

*** $p < .01$, ** $p < .05$, * $p < .10$. Cell entries are long-run multipliers with robust standard errors in parentheses. Counts of children include only one lag because age coding implies longer lags. Three lags of all other variables are included except for variables in the SHP marked "a)", which were not asked in the first wave and therefore use two lags. Economic Worry is treated as predetermined and uses one lag only. All other independent variables are treated as exogenous. Models also include quartic age polynomials and measures of interestingness defined in Chapter 6. Cells in italics are based on reestimating the model with a subset of available waves.

† Lagged coefficients all equal to zero is rejected at $p < .10$
$^+$ Coefficients of contemporaneous short-run effect is positive at $p < .05$
$^-$ Coefficients of contemporaneous short-run effect is negative at $p < .05$

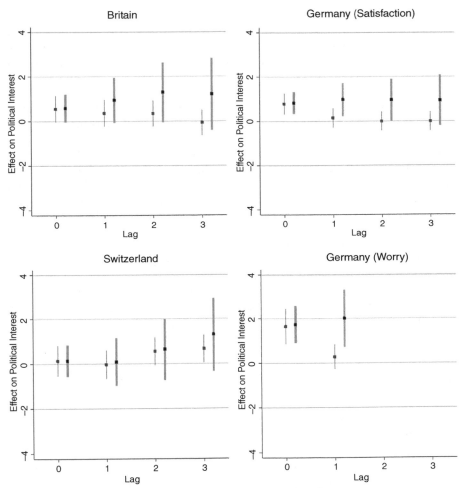

FIGURE 12.4 The Effect of Financial Satisfaction on Political Interest

Note: Graphs plot estimates of γ_k (lighter squares symbols) and long-run multipliers (larger black squares) as a function of lag length k (the horizontal axis). 95-percent confidence intervals shown. Political interest is 0–100. Financial satisfaction is measured in quarter-within-subject standard deviations. Economic worry is measured in quarter-within-subject standard deviations and treated as predetermined.

satisfaction on political interest over time. The lighter square markers show the yearly effects. The black squares show the cumulative effect over time. The independent variable is divided by quarter-within-subject standard deviations, so the graph plots the impact that results from a change at the high end of the observed year-to-year variation in financial satisfaction.

While the effect of financial satisfaction in Germany happens right away and remains constant for the next three years, it builds gradually in Britain, so the long-run effect grows for two more years to reach marginal significance at $t = 2$. In Switzerland, finally, the impact occurs with a delay. Separate, statistically significant yearly effects occur at $t = 2$ and $t = 3$ (with $p = .09$ and $p = .04$, respectively).

Greater satisfaction with their own financial situation raises Germans' political interest – but so does concern about the economic future. Only the German study permits separate measurement of how much people worry about the economy. The measure averages two strongly correlated items asking panelists how worried they are about economic development in the country and their own economic situation. As Figure 12.4 shows, greater economic worry has an immediate and significant positive effect on political interest (also see Kroh 2006). Satisfaction with one's finances and worries about the economy might seem to have effects at odds with each other, but they are in fact largely independent. Anxiety about people's current financial situation rarely changes at the same time as concern about the economic future. (The two measures do correlate at –.38 in levels, but only modestly in differences, at –.13.) And the two variables retain much of their effect when estimated separately.[21] Political interest, it turns out, can be generated by both a reduction in anxiety about one's current finances and an increase in concerns about the economic future.

THE IMPACT OF HEALTH AND WELL-BEING ON POLITICAL
INTEREST

Like economic adversity, health concerns may also preoccupy people to an extent that politics no longer seems as interesting to them (see Brody and Sniderman 1977). Indeed, Schwartz et al. (1975, 100, 113) expected that "health difficulty should lead to low or diminished sociopolitical interest and participation." "Surprisingly," however, they found the reverse in a sample of American high-school students, as health and political interest correlated negatively.

The British and Swiss studies include detailed measures of physical health conditions – based on self-reported accidents, hospitalizations, and sick days – and psychological distress and anxiety. The German study only asks panelists how satisfied they are with their overall health. Online Supplementary

---

[21] Without Economic Worry, the effect of Financial Satisfaction at $t = 0$ is .62 ($p = .007$) and the 3-year long-run effect .82 with a p value of .13. Without Financial Satisfaction, the effect of Economic Worry at $t = 0$ is 1.68 ($p < .001$) and its cumulative effect one year later (the LRM at $k = 1$ shown in Table 12.2) is 1.91 ($p < .001$).

Materials provide measurement details. All variables shown in Table 12.2 are again scaled so they estimate the effect of a change at the high end of actually occurring year-to-year variation. After accounting for lagged political interest, all measures of health meet the test for exogeneity.

Physical health has a clear effect on political interest. In both Britain and Switzerland, injuries and sickness raise political interest. The effect is statistically significant right away, but continues to grow for a year or two after the deterioration in health, as depicted in Figure 12.5. Mental health, on the other hand, has at best a temporary effect. At least in Britain, psychological distress causes a temporary drop in political interest. Mental health in Switzerland and subjective satisfaction with one's health in Germany leave interest unchanged, however. These results offer limited support for the prediction derived from Brody and Sniderman's argument about economic adversity. Only the temporary effect of mental health in Britain is consistent with the crowding out of political interest by more personal preoccupations. Instead, reminders of physical limits or contact with the health care system prompted by physical health problems might be more central mechanisms, causing a lasting increase in political interest.

All studies also regularly include a survey question asking respondents how satisfied they are with their life in general. Life satisfaction is exogenous with or without a lagged dependent variable in the model. As Table 12.2 shows, it has about the same statistically significant long-run effect in Germany and Switzerland. Within three years, an increase in life satisfaction by four within standard deviations raises political interest by about 2 points. In Britain, the effect after three years is also positive, but just misses statistical significance. The "+" superscript next to the long-run estimate indicates that the contemporaneous impact of life satisfaction is statistically significant at $p < .05$ and positive, so a change in life satisfaction is associated with an immediate change in political interest in all three countries.

Figure 12.6 shows how life satisfaction affects political interest in the three years after an initial change. In Germany, life satisfaction has statistically significant effects at both t and $t-1$ (that is, a change between two years and one year before the interview). As a result, the long-run effect increases from $k = 0$ to $k = 1$. A specification that ignores the possibility of non-constant effects would have missed this (which would have resulted in different biases in the FE and FD estimators). This kind of gradual build-up is weaker and not statistically precise in Switzerland and absent in Britain, where the full effect manifests itself immediately.

For technical reasons, the analysis can shed little light on whether the effects of subjective economic assessments and general well-being are different for young people. Because inclusion of a lagged dependent variable requires additional lags as instruments, the earliest age at which the model in Table 12.2 can detect effects is 19 in Britain, 21 in Germany, and 17 in

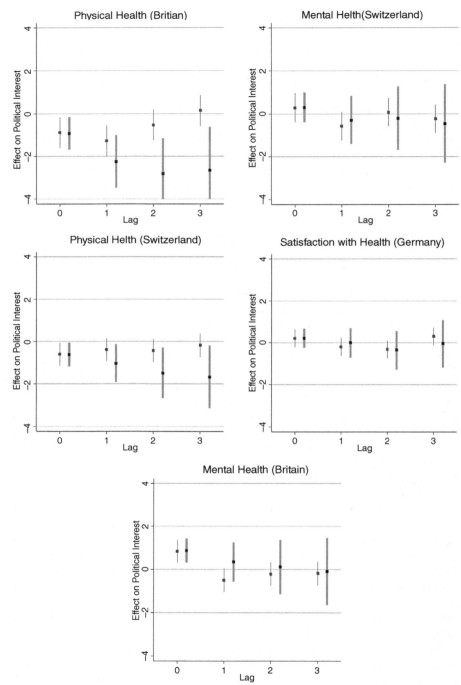

FIGURE 12.5 The Effect of Objective and Subjective Health on Political Interest

Note: Graphs plot estimates of γ_k (lighter squares, triangles, and circles symbols) and long-run multipliers (larger black squares) as a function of lag length k (the horizontal axis). 95-percent confidence intervals shown. Political interest is 0–100. Satisfaction with health is measured in within-subject standard deviations.

Switzerland. (The BHPS youth sample did not ask about health or economic assessments, so Table 12.2 uses only the adult interviews.) That is why the estimates of schooling effects shown in this table are largely uninformative: At that age, most panelists have left school, providing little data to estimate its impact. Other variables, especially physical health, are not as relevant at a young age. Estimating the model in Table 12.2 for panelists under the age of 40 yields mostly coefficients too imprecise to diagnose differences to the full age range.[22]

A Closer Look at Free Time

Do busy people have too little time to be interested in politics? Logically, an interest does not require time to pursue the interest. It is entirely consistent to feel keen political interest, but rarely have time to follow politics, talk about it with others, or participate in it. Verba et al. (1995) and Putnam (2000) conclude that lack of time is not a big factor in explaining political participation. In a study of political interest using the GSOEP, Kroh (2006) measures leisure time as hours per day not devoted to job, education, housework, childcare, and chores. In light of the difficulty of accurately reporting time use, the variable may be colored by the respondent's subjective sense of time constraints. In Kroh's study, a positive bivariate relationship between logged leisure time and political interest turns negative in a multivariate analysis that controls for factors like education and employment status.

All three studies include similar measures of self-reported time use (see Online Supplementary Materials). Adding measures of free time to the models in Table 12.2 produces no evidence that lack of time lowers political interest. In the German and Swiss data, coefficients are quite precisely estimated but tiny. In Britain, lack of free time – or people's sense of having little of it – actually causes a small, temporary increase in political interest.

It turns out that people's satisfaction with their free time, not the (self-reported) amount of it, affects political interest. Available in the German and

---

[22] In the GSOEP, the effect of financial satisfaction and life satisfaction are slightly smaller, the effect of economic worries is almost 50 percent larger, and satisfaction with one's health significantly lowers political interest (with a 2-year LRM of −1.3, p = .06). In the SHP, the effects of life satisfaction and physical health are noticeably smaller and indistinguishable from zero. Financial satisfaction has a similar effect, and satisfaction with free time has a significant positive short-term effect on interest. In the BHPS, financial satisfaction and mental health have slightly smaller effects, and life satisfaction only affects older people.

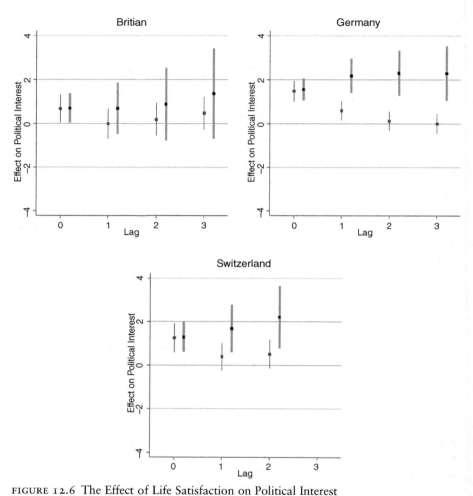

FIGURE 12.6 The Effect of Life Satisfaction on Political Interest
Note: Graphs plot estimates of γ_k (lighter squares symbols) and long-run multipliers (larger black squares) as a function of lag length k (the horizontal axis). 95-percent confidence intervals shown. Political interest is 0–100. Life satisfaction is scaled in quarter-within-subject standard deviations.

Swiss data, satisfaction with free time raises political interest (see Figure 12.7), although this effect lasts over time only in Germany.[23]

---

[23] The question is not included in all GSOEP waves, so results in Table 12.2 and Figure 12.7 are based on reestimating the original model for a subset of waves and reported estimates for life satisfaction do not control for satisfaction with free time. The two variables do not account for the same variance, however. If anything, the effect of life satisfaction is even larger when satisfaction with free time is included in the model.

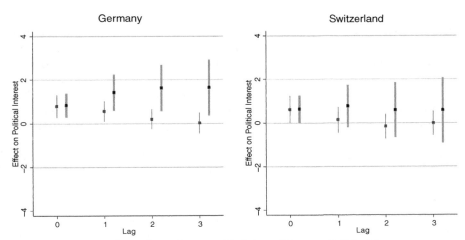

FIGURE 12.7 The Effect of Satisfaction with Leisure Time on Political Interest

Note: Graphs plot estimates of γ_k (lighter squares symbols) and long-run multipliers (larger black squares) as a function of lag length k (the horizontal axis). 95-percent confidence intervals shown. Political interest is 0–100. Satisfaction with leisure time is measured in within-subject standard deviations. It is treated as predetermined in the GSOEP, exogenous in the SHP.

CONCLUSION

Economic inequality does not feed inequality in political interest. While people with higher incomes and higher-status occupations are more interested in politics, there is little evidence that economic resources such as income, occupational status, or home ownership causally affect political interest. After accounting for educational attainment, other components of socioeconomic status, including income and type of employment, do little to explain political interest. Employment actually lowers political interest by a small amount. Raising poor people's income, making sure they have jobs, and seeing them move into high-status occupations would reduce their economic hardship – but it would do nothing to make them more interested in politics. These findings provide no support for the resource model when it comes to political interest and are more consistent with the psychological model of interest, in which material resources play no direct role.

If political interest has little to do with material resources, then reductions in socioeconomic inequality, while desirable for other reasons, would leave motivational inequality in place. A reduction in socioeconomic inequality might remove some economic obstacles to participation (being able to take time off from work, pay for transportation, hire childcare), but would not raise the motivation to participate. Better off economically, many citizens would still not get involved in politics.

Beyond material economic resources, the analysis in this chapter shows that adversity does not depress political interest, as a more general resource perspective might suggest according to which hardship of any kind lowers interest. Parental unemployment or divorce do not affect people's political interest, and single parenthood reduces it only in one of the three countries. Unemployment has a small positive effect on political interest (especially when it happens later in life). And health problems, too, make people more politically interested. These last two findings in particular point to the role that encounters with politics and policy – in this case through the healthcare system and unemployment benefits – may play in explaining the development of political interest. The next chapter probes this idea more comprehensively.

Although there is thus some evidence for objective conditions affecting people's interest, subjective satisfaction with life and particular aspects of life produce more consistent results. There is a causal connection between personal finances and political interest, but it appears to involve a subjective sense of financial security, not economic resources per se. Holding constant the effects of income and other resource variables, it is people's satisfaction with their financial situation that raises political interest. (Although this finding apparently does not imply that economic worries lower interest – I find the opposite in the German data, the only study that permits this test.)

Making people happy more generally promises to increase their interest in politics. In addition to satisfaction with personal finances, satisfaction with free time and life in general also raise interest. The magnitude of each of these effects is modest. The corresponding long-run increase in interest from about the largest happiness boost that we see in these countries is about 2 points. But the different dimensions of happiness combined raise political interest by 3–5 points, almost as much as education and much more than economic resources.

13

Encounters with Politics

Our daily lives offer a variety of chances to encounter politics. If you earn your living in the legal profession, as a journalist, or in a public-sector job, politics surrounds you at work. If you are a member of a political organization, its meetings and communications will frequently cover political topics. If you are married to a politically interested person, you will see and hear plenty of news coverage and discussion of politics in your household. But would encounters with politics such as these lead you to become more politically interested yourself?

At first blush, this seems like an easy question to answer. There is a lot of variation in the extent to which people encounter politics, and those who encounter it often are much more interested in politics. Active party members are a lot more politically interested than non-members. The difference in Switzerland is 28 points on the 0–100 political interest scale. In Britain, it is 34 points. Journalists and writers are 26, 16, and 24 points more interested than other members of the workforce in Britain, Germany, and Switzerland, respectively.

Yet there are powerful alternative explanations for these large cross-sectional differences. They may arise not because encounters with politics make people more interested, but because more interested people are more likely to encounter politics. Many political experiences happen because we seek them out, often based on our level of political interest and the expectation that its political nature will make the experience rewarding. While not the only motivation, political interest is a key factor in explaining why people join political parties or civic organizations. It affects whether individuals choose jobs that regularly deal with politics, such as journalism or work in government. Potential partners with matching political interest might be more likely to begin a relationship. People with little interest in politics are less likely to show up at the meetings of a political party, volunteer for a civic organization, work for a newspaper, or marry a politically interested person. In short, many encounters with politics are selective.

The **Selectivity Hypothesis** expresses the most extreme version of this alternative explanation: Selective encounters with politics will have no effect on political interest because people will select into the encounter only to the extent that it matches their level of political interest. When a political experience is voluntary, the people who volunteer are usually already politically interested. The people whose interest might be increased by the political experience rarely volunteer. If true, this casts doubt on claims that membership or participation in many types of organizations strengthens civic involvement. The "joiners" are good citizens not because they joined, but because they were politically interested to begin with.

Life is rarely as clean as the Selectivity Hypothesis makes it sound, however. For a number of reasons, we cannot always select our political encounters to perfectly match our existing political interest. First, some encounters are imposed on us because they are mandatory or because we select them for reasons other than their political nature. No examples of strictly mandatory political encounters appear in this chapter, but required civics classes, discussed in Chapter 9, come close. An example more pertinent to this chapter is someone with little political interest who is asked by a friend to attend a party meeting. Or someone who takes a job with connections to politics because it pays well or offers attractive hours. And in finding a spouse, matching political interest may be far down the list of reasons to move in together.

Second, the certainty we have about an encounter's political nature also constrains selectivity. A party organization is widely understood to involve politics, so there should be little uncertainty that joiners will encounter politics. Many non-political organizations, however, do not invoke the same sure expectation of encountering politics, but might still expose its members to self-governance, organization, and regulation. You may join a community organization to keep your neighborhood playground open – and be surprised that meetings are often about zoning laws and local taxes. Mutz and Martin (2001) and Huckfeldt et al. (e.g., Huckfeldt et al. 2004), for example, have argued that people who are not looking for exposure to politics often experience some of it in various social and work environments.

Third, we may be right about the political nature of an encounter, but wrong about how interesting it turns out to be. In this case, selection into the encounter works as predicted by the Selection Hypothesis, but the encounter could still lead us to update our political interest. Party meetings and the rights and responsibilities that come with membership may be so rewarding that even a politically interested individual who joined a party becomes still more interested.

Together, these reasons give rise to the **Inadvertent Political Encounters Hypothesis**, according to which political experiences have the potential to change political interest when they are difficult to avoid, inadvertent, or unexpected in their interestingness.

This chapter examines how different ways of encountering politics affect political interest. The panel data only contain information about the type of organization or event panelists report joining or participating in, not why they did or how much politics they expected to encounter. The following analysis can therefore only compare selection into, and effects of, a range of organizations and activities that typically vary in the extent to which they involve politics and emphasize their political nature.

Selection effects should dominate most clearly for obvious political encounters that people rarely seek out for reasons other than their political nature. Party organizations and participation in electoral politics fit this description. The political nature of employment in sectors related to politics is probably also well known to people looking for a job, but other aspects of employment (availability, job security, required skills) may dilute selection based on political interest. As union membership is no longer an automatic feature of taking a job, it might work similarly, known to feature politics but selected for a variety of reasons.

Selection effects should be largely absent for many non-political organizations (cultural groups, sports clubs). I explain later in the chapter why organizational involvement that clearly entails no political encounters might still raise political interest according to some political theories. Predictions are most difficult for organizations in which politics can "sneak up" on members. The distinction between political and non-political is fuzzy (see Zukin et al. 2006, 191–200). Not all civic involvement is overtly political. Some civic activities are aimed at influencing public life and expressing opinions, but not through the political or electoral process. Volunteer groups, charitable organizations, and perhaps churches fit here. (The certainty of political encounters in single-issue groups may be the most challenging to classify. An environmental organization, for example, is obviously political to many and quite certain to involve environmental policy. But some people may join a volunteer organization tending community gardens because they like gardening and unexpectedly encounter environmental policy.)

A politically interested spouse, finally, can amount to a political encounter that is hard to avoid. Because the household panel studies only begin to follow couples when they live in the same household, the following analysis cannot address the role of political interest in the early stages of a relationship. The focus will be on the impact of one partner's changes in political interest on the other partner. Due to the stability of political interest, such changes will be rare, but where they occur, they are normally unexpected and difficult for the partner to fully avoid. A sudden burst of spousal political interest is not easily neutralized by selecting out of it. These conditions should facilitate spousal influence.

It is important to appreciate that logically cause and consequence are not either/or propositions. Political interest can be both a cause of a political encounter and a consequence of it. With annual observations of both variables, it is possible, within limits, to understand which, if any, causal direction dominates. The limits are imposed by the speed of the causal effects relative to the interval between panel interviews (see Chapter 9). To gauge the plausibility of causal impact in either direction, analyses in this chapter plot the data, using the now familiar format. To isolate, as best as possible, causal effects of political encounters on political interest and provide more precise summary estimates, I also extend the panel model introduced in previous chapters. The two analytic approaches offer different strengths and weaknesses.

Graphical exploration of causal effects on political interest has the advantage of transparency but does not provide information about statistical precision. It avoids modeling assumptions but does require a decision about how many panel waves a panelist needs to complete in order to be included – a decision that is somewhat arbitrary and reduces statistical efficiency. The graphical displays do not account for the influences of other variables (except for age) and deal awkwardly with predictors that are not binary.

Estimating the effects of political encounters on political interest with a model-based approach can remedy these shortcomings. It will not always yield unambiguous answers, however, because critical assumptions cannot be directly verified and the data do not always permit the implementation of the optimal statistical solutions, so the principal value of a model-based approach is not to supersede but complement the graphical analyses. To the extent that both approaches converge on the same answer, conclusions become more confident.

This chapter uses the group of estimators introduced in Chapter 9 and already employed in Part III. The predictors of political interest examined in this chapter vary in the extent to which they are threatened by reciprocal causation, and the optimal model is not known in advance. When specification tests show no signs that a predictor violates the critical exogeneity assumption and when that is theoretically conceivable (because the feedback, if any, could plausibly operate slowly enough to support weak exogeneity), I rely on the more efficient results from simpler estimators. For many predictors, reverse causation is a strong possibility and calls for more robust estimators – which also impose greater, sometimes impossible, demands on the data. They require even more careful attention to several different specification tests and often yield multiple empirically sound estimates because the large number of panel waves makes it possible to build the necessary "scaffolding" (see Chapter 9) in many, slightly different ways. Add to that the fact that many predictors are not available in all panel waves, and the consequence is a fairly large set of plausible models that offer trade-offs between statistical efficiency, protection from endogeneity bias, and accounting for other time-varying predictors. To maintain transparency without overloading the chapter with details about instrument design and model fit, I report key results in the text (sometimes more than one, when several different modeling approaches are informative), present summaries of all models in the chapter appendix, and provide detailed estimation output in the Online Supplementary Materials.

ENCOUNTERING POLITICS THROUGH WORK

We find politically engaged employees more often in "politically impinged" jobs (Luskin 1990) – jobs related to politics or dependent on policy. State and local government employees in the United States, for example, turn out at higher rates (Rosenstone 1982). If politically interested people deliberately take such jobs, the resulting exposure to politics should not do much to change their political interest. Less interested people who select political jobs for reasons unrelated to the political aspect, on the other hand, might become more interested in politics as their job exposes them to politics regularly. Over longer periods of time, "politically impinged" jobs could conceivably sustain political interest.[1]

People with politically impinged jobs tend to be more interested in politics, sometimes considerably so. Luskin (1990, fn.19) coded 1976 American National Election Study respondents based on 1970 U.S. Census Occupation Codes and derived a "dichotomous distinction between more and less politically impinged occupations" (p. 340). Applying his coding scheme to the household panels, the top section of Table 13.1 compares political interest for respondents in politically impinged jobs and all other jobs. The difference is about 10 points in all three countries.

The midsection of Table 13.1 lists political interest specifically in the most obviously political jobs, government work, journalism, and social science. For most of them, occupants have considerably higher political interest than the average for people in politically-impinged jobs. In some cases, the differences are as large as we have seen: Journalists stand out for their high political interest, and so do government employees in Switzerland and Britain. Work in government in Germany, where it makes up a larger share of the overall workforce, bears remarkably little association with political interest.

For each country, the bottom of Table 13.1 presents the types of jobs associated with the highest political interest from the set of other employment categories that Luskin considered to be politically impinged. Religious and legal professionals make it into the top 5 in all countries and include the highest interest level in a country.

If there is a relationship between political interest and employment in politically impinged jobs, it is unlikely to be driven by quick dynamics. Deciding which sector to work in, or changing to another sector, usually requires some planning and often happens only after considerable consideration. The graphs in the left column of Figure 13.1 explore the impact of politically impinged jobs using the same template as earlier chapters. The dark line with square markers shows political interest among panelists who initially did not hold politically impinged jobs and then took such a job at $t = 0$. To the right of $t = 0$, the this line graphs political interest among these panelists in the years after taking the

---

[1] The effect of employment on participation is complex because working people have less free time, which is another necessary resource for political activity. Without a measure of free time, the effect of employment status is thus theoretically not determined. In explaining political interest, free time is less important (see Chapter 12). Moreover, the type of job can be used to distinguish the effects of time displacement and political exposure.

TABLE 13.1 *Political Interest, by Employment Sector*

	Britain		Germany		Switzerland	
	Mean	N	Mean	N	Mean	N
All Politically-Impinged Jobs	52	45,869	52	44,864	62	19,827
All Other Jobs	41	78,885	43	86,864	55	30,827
Involve Politics Most Directly						
Works in government	58	1,996	50	4,152	70	764
Journalists, writers	69	611	61	548	79	336
Social scientists, economists	53	164	58	614	65	699
Top 5 of Rest						
Religious professionals	74	234	63	263	65	311
Legal professionals	57	282	70	859	73	349
Natural scientists			57	364	69	240
Architects, engineers, urban planners	53	287	57	1,642	65	205
General managers, CEOs					65	2,231
Law enforcement, military			58	2,451		
Teaching professionals	56	6,479				
Business professionals	53	5,114				

Note: Table lists mean political interest among full- or part-time employed between ages 30 and 60. N refers to number of measurements.

politically impinged job. The empty squares to the left of $t = 0$ show their interest levels before this transition. The dark line using diamond-shaped markers defines the reverse of the first line, following panelists who were initially employed in politically impinged jobs and later left. One reference group is represented by the dashed line with all open circles. It graphs political interest for panelists who completed the same minimum number of waves as panelists summarized by the line with square markers, but never reported politically impinged employment. (They include individuals who held other jobs or were not part of the workforce.) Lastly, the dashed line with all filled circles plots political interest among panelists who completed the minimum number of waves and reported holding a politically impinged job each time they were interviewed. (When the number of always-members is too small to show the trend in their political interest, the graph's legend shows their average interest over all periods.)[2]

---

[2] Unlike other change graphs, the graphs for politically impinged jobs cannot balance age very well. By necessity, they compare younger people who tend to take jobs to older people who tend to leave jobs. The age difference between these two groups is about 20 years. The graph balances on the average age distribution of these two groups, so the stable lines are made up of panelists who are, on average, about ten years older than the job takers and ten years younger than the job leavers.

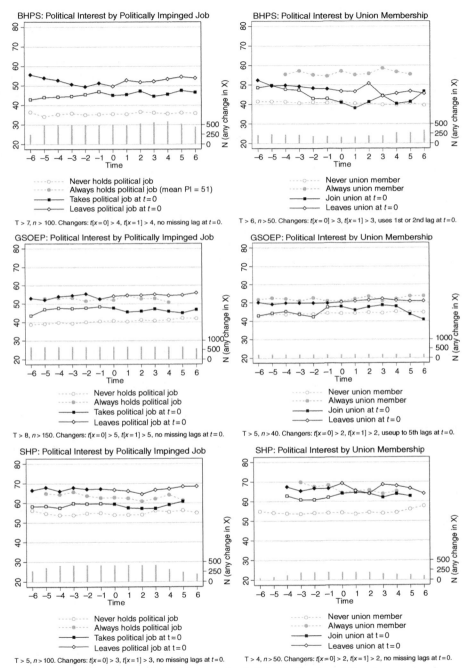

FIGURE 13.1 Change in Political Interest by Politically Impinged Employment and Union Membership

Note: Union membership based on binary question except in SHP where it pools "active" and "passive" members. Politically-impinged jobs are explained in the text. For details on graphs, see Book Appendix B.

All graphs for politically impinged jobs have one thing in common: The dashed line with open circles, summarizing panelists who never held these jobs, is always the lowest. It is about 10–15 points below the other dashed line and the filled in diamonds – political interest levels of panelists in politically impinged jobs. This is roughly the cross-sectional difference evident in Table 13.1. But did taking the politically impinged job *cause* the people represented by these lines to be considerably more interested?

No, according to several pieces of evidence in Figure 13.1. First, the dark line with squares shows higher political interest among panelists who eventually take a politically impinged job for years before they do (empty squares). Second, after they start their politically impinged job (filled squares), these individuals' political interest does not noticeably increase and they do not catch up with the filled diamonds or circles. Instead, those lines are roughly parallel, indicating that political interest levels remained about the same in each group even though one switched into a politically impinged job (squares), while the other switched out of it (diamonds).

Third, there are some suggestions that causality flows in the opposite direction: In Britain and Germany, political interest declines among people in politically impinged jobs *before they quit* and interest increases among those who eventually take a politically impinged job *before* they start. The solid lines narrow before $t = 0$ (gradually over as many as five years in Britain; between $t - 2$ and $t - 1$ in Germany). Fourth, if anything, politically impinged employment marginally reduces political interest. In Britain and Germany, the solid lines diverge again after $t = 0$ as political interest levels of panelists who just took a politically impinged job drop relative to those who just quit one.

On balance, graphical analysis suggests that political interest may lead people to take politically impinged jobs, but that these jobs do nothing to raise political interest and may possibly lower it a bit. This result is consistent with the Selection Hypothesis. Although the changes over time in Figure 13.1 are subtle, they hint at the disappointment of politically relevant jobs: They attract the politically interested, but do not make them more interested.

The influence of the work environment may extend beyond politically impinged jobs. Union members in Britain are more politically interested (Denny and Doyle 2008), but it is not clear if this is an effect of union membership. Union membership dropped in all three countries during the period of data collection. The drop in East Germany was especially steep just after reunification. In the first wave of the East German sample in 1990, 65 percent of East Germans reported union membership. By 1993, the next time the question was asked, the percentage had dropped to 26 percent (still 10 points higher than in the West). By 1998, East and West had the same unionization rates.[3]

---

[3] Other survey estimates confirm this decline, both among young people and in the population as a whole. Between 1992 and 1997, union membership dropped from 22 to 8 percent in the East and from 15 to 7 percent in the West among Germans between ages 16 and 29, according to Gaiser and de Rijke (2000). Analysis in this chapter omits the 1990 wave of the East German sample.

The right-hand column of graphs in Figure 13.1 shows that union members are more politically interested than non-members, but union membership does not generally make people more interested. In Britain, eventual joiners lose considerable political interest over several years before they join. If this is a selection effect, it is in the direction opposite to the Selection Hypothesis, which would predict selection into unions by more politically interested individuals. Results for Germany do suggest this more expected selection effect as panelists who will later join a union gain political interest in advance of that decision. A caveat applies: Union membership is only measured every few years in the GSOEP, and in order to have enough cases, the graph has to include some panelists who are first observed with changed membership status at $t = 0$, but were last interviewed five years earlier. This obfuscates the relative timing of changes in interest and membership much more than in other graphs. (All graphs note the longest lag at $t = 0$ at the bottom.)

Only the results for Switzerland show even a hint of causal effects of membership on interest – but they are temporary: In the years after leaving the union, former members' interest drops by a few points. New members' interest increases between $t - 1$ and t (so this could be selection or a membership effect). A year or two later, however, political interest among the two sets of panelists is back to where it was several years before the membership change.

Model-based analysis confirms the conclusion that politically-impinged jobs and public-sector employment do not affect political interest. Across different estimators and different handling of the endogeneity threat, detailed in the chapter appendix, results yield a set of fairly precise null effects. Just like the graphical analyses, model results show no impact of union membership on political interest. (The variable appears in too few waves of the German study to provide a meaningful estimate.)

The one exception to this conclusion is stark, unexpected, and not subject to the most rigorous probing: Legal or religious employment has a substantial negative effect on political interest in Britain and Germany. I only separated out these two professions because they were marked by noticeably *higher* political interest in the descriptive data in Table 13.1. This higher interest among legal or religious professionals is clearly not a consequence of their employment. Instead, these professions appear to attract more politically interested individuals and then deplete them of some of this interest. There are too few individuals in these two job categories to allow the variable to violate the exogeneity assumption, but in both Britain and Germany, the lagged coefficients are jointly significant and negative, so the relative timing of changes supports a slowly developing causal effect on political interest. (Data are too scarce to say for sure whether legal or religious professions are responsible for this effect. Both appear to depress political interest, but the negative effect may be especially pronounced among lawyers.[4])

ENCOUNTERING POLITICS THROUGH VOLUNTEER ACTIVITY AND ORGANIZATIONAL INVOLVEMENT

Ascribing good things to joining – joining organizations, associations, volunteer groups – has been almost irresistible recently for many observers. Does it also generate political interest? Membership in many groups, volunteering, and some extracurricular activities are associated with a host of desirable behaviors, including tolerance for opposing viewpoints, concern for the public good, and civic and political participation (e.g., Sherrod et al. 2002; Flanagan 2004). Individuals who are involved in organizations early in life, during their time in high school, are more likely to be members as adults, by then in different organizations, including civic groups, and to participate in politics by turning out to vote or even work for political campaigns (e.g., Smith 1999; Stolle and Hooghe 2004; McFarland and Thomas 2006). Group membership, community service, and extracurricular activities "may be a developmental foundation for later civic engagement because it is in such experiences that youth develop an affection for the polity" (Flanagan 2004, 725).

Some of the proposed mechanisms for these relationships do not require the organizations to involve politics at all. Organizational membership may teach people to participate effectively, strengthen their self-esteem or sense of efficacy (Verba et al. 1995), and inculcate norms of reciprocity and trust (Putnam 2000; Stolle and Hooghe 2004). Brady, Verba, and Schlozman (1995; Verba et al. 1995) argue that people learn civic skills, such as addressing groups of people or planning meetings, at work, in church, and in voluntary organizations. These skills help people in their political participation, directly and because they instill a sense of political efficacy.

How important the political nature of groups is in promoting political participation and civic engagement has remained ambiguous. Verba et al. (1995, 369) refer to work, church, and many voluntary associations as "nonpolitical" environments where people engage in "activities having no demonstrable political content." But they also argue that work and organizational involvement "nurture political engagement" by exposing people to political conversations, information, and mobilization.[5]

---

[4] The three-year multipliers are large and negative for both legal and religious professions in Britain and Germany, but only legal profession in Germany is statistically significant at $p < .05$. In the Swiss data, legal profession also has a sizable and marginally significant negative effect (-5.8 points, $p = .15$), while religious profession has a non-significant positive effect.

[5] According to Verba et al.'s (1995) results, involvement in "non-political" organizations (which correlates with political interest and participation) is higher among people who were engaged in civic activities in high school and discussed politics at home. As civic engagement at home and in

For the more political groups and activities, causal impact of organizational involvement may be limited or entirely absent, as the Selection Hypothesis looms large. Selection makes it critical to account for the impact of political interest on participation in voluntary programs in the first place. A relatively small fraction of organizational involvement in high school and college, for example, is related to politics, school government, or civics more generally; sports and musical groups are much more popular (Eccles and Barber 1999; Zukin et al. 2006, 139–41). If participants in community service or extracurricular activities with political or social elements were more interested even before they took up these activities – and began to participate because they had become more interested for other, unrelated reasons – then what looks like an effect of youth participation is in fact a consequence of preexisting political interest. As Zaff, Malanchuck, and Eccles (2008, 38) observe, "the available research findings are subject to self-selection bias, and experimental research has not produced consistently positive results." The key question is not whether these students continue to participate in politics as a result, but why they decided to join high-school government or the Model UN in the first place – and not (only) the band.

People maintain their tendency to be organizationally involved even as the pertinent groups change when they get older or the environment changes. Students with high self-esteem and social trust are significantly more likely to participate in politics and civic organizations as adults (Stolle and Hooghe 2004; McFarland and Thomas 2006). But as the tendency to join membership organizations and groups persists over time, so do the reasons for joining. And selection is reinforced by organizations focusing their recruitment on people who are already organizationally involved, so organizational involvement is partly the result of members being asked to join more groups (Brady et al. 1999).

Among the most plausible reasons for joining political and civic organizations is a preexisting interest in politics. Analyzing the Youth-Parent Socialization Panel (Jennings et al. 2004), Shani (2009b, ch.4) shows that Americans who reported participating in protests and demonstrations in the 1973 interview expressed greater political interest than non-participants in subsequent panel waves (9 and 24 years later) – but they were already more interested as high-school students in 1965 by almost precisely the same margin. For military service during the Vietnam era, Shani finds changes more consistent with a motivating effect of political encounters (or their anticipation): Relative to those who did not serve, the change in political interest between 1965 and 1973 is about 10 points greater among those who did. Shani's two findings are consistent with the Selectivity Hypothesis according to which changes in

---

school was reported retrospectively and could well be influenced by current political involvement, the precise origins of political motivations remain unclear in their analysis.

political interest from exposure to politics should be smaller when exposure is subject to selection (as in the case of protest behavior) than when it is not (as most who served were drafted). Even the possible impact of military service did not last: In their mid-30s and early 50s, the political interest difference between those who served and those who did not reverted back to what it was in high school.

Obviously Political Encounters

According to the Selection Hypothesis, selection effects should dominate the relationship between political interest and involvement in the most obviously political organizations and activities. It is not inconceivable, however, for this involvement to also have an effect on interest if some people participate for reasons unrelated to their political interest or find politics more (or less) interesting than expected.

Figure 13.2 applies the now familiar graphical template to follow panelists before and after they report joining or leaving a political party (in Switzerland), a party or other civic organization (in Britain), participating in political grassroots activities (in Germany), or going to the polls (in Britain and Switzerland).[6] The very strong association of political involvement and political interest is evident by comparing panelists who never report the respective behavior (dashed line with open circles) and those who do consistently over many years (dashed lines with filled circles).

Political interest of long-time party or civic-group members exceeds interest among never-members by well over 40 points in Britain and by about 30 points in Switzerland. Differences between consistent (self-proclaimed) voters and non-voters in those two countries are about 30 points. German panelists who regularly report at least weekly "involvement in a citizens' group, political party, [or] local government" are close to 50 points more politically interested than those who never report this kind of involvement. By any yardstick, these are very large differences.

Figure 13.2 provides clear evidence that politically involved individuals are more involved because they have greater interest in politics – and much less so the other way around. Panelists who join party/civic organizations or start participating in politics (shown by the squared markers) were already

---

[6] The BHPS asks separately about membership in a political party and, at the end of the list of organizations, any "other community or civic group." Too few panelists report being a member of a party to provide informative estimates, so I pool these two types of political organizations. The Online Supplementary Materials include full wording and reported frequencies of all available group membership and attendance items. The GSOEP only asks about party activity, not party membership, and included a question about turnout in only three of its panel waves, so equivalent analyses for Germany are not feasible.

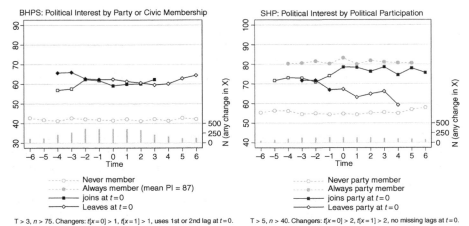

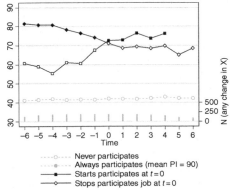

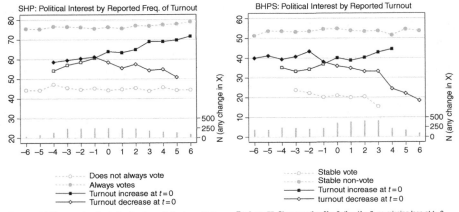

FIGURE 13.2 Change in Political Interest by Political Activity

Note: BHPS measures are based on binary questions. SHP party membership pools "active" and "passive" members. SHP turnout is based on an 11-point scale treating changes of 3 or more categories as change. GSOEP participation is based on a categorical scale treating "monthly" or more frequent as participation. For details on graphs, see Book Appendix B.

gaining political interest in the years before they first reported membership or participation. And participants begin to lose political interest before they leave the organization or stop participating (except for Swiss panelists whose turnout drops at $t = 0$).

The cleanest illustration of political interest as cause of political involvement appears in the graph examining political participation in Germany: Half a decade before participants stop participating and non-participants get involved, political interest among the former is over 20 points higher. One year before the change in involvement, at $t = -1$, this difference is already down by more than half. Similar if smaller results are evident for political/civic membership in Britain and Switzerland and reported turnout in Britain. In all of these cases, political interest begins to change more than a year before the change in political participation.

Changes in political interest that occur between $t = -1$ and $t = 0$ are typically causally ambiguous, consistent with interest either as cause or effect. We know that the other variable (here, participation) changed by $t = 0$, but not when in this interval the change occurred. Hence, the change in interest during this interval could precede or follow the change in the other variable. The turnout graph for Switzerland (lower right in Figure 13.2) is a good example: During the same interval, habitual voters became non-voters and less interested in politics (and infrequent voters both started voting and gained interest). By this logic, the change in political interest in the year before $t = 0$ evident in the graph for participation in Germany, party membership in Switzerland, and turnout in Britain is causally ambiguous, too. But in each of these three cases, the change in interest continues a trend that started at least a year earlier. Cautiously put, this pattern appears more indicative of political interest as cause of participation in the interval between $t = -1$ and $t = 0$.

What about the other causal direction, participation as a cause of political interest? Several graphs in Figure 13.2 suggest modest effects in this direction as the difference between the solid lines continues to widen after $t = 0$, most notably for turnout in Switzerland and, starting with a remarkable delay, in Britain. Not all of these effects last, and their magnitude tends to be smaller than the selection effects before $t = 0$, however. Moreover, in some cases (most notably participation in Germany and turnout in Britain) we would expect some widening after $t = 0$ based on the continuation of the "pre-treatment" trend alone even if participation had no causal effect. People stop participating because they are losing interest, and the end of participation neither stops this decline nor accelerates it.[7]

---

[7] The number of panelists who change political membership (in BHPS and SHP) is too low to focus on effects among young people specifically. For turnout (SHP, BHPS; starting at age 18) and political participation (GSOEP), limiting the sample to young people makes little obvious difference.

Even if the causal direction from interest to political activity dominates, Figure 13.2 suggests that political activity can also cause political interest. Model-based analysis confirms this suggestion in fairly unambiguous terms. The most robust modeling approach yields significant and positive effects on political interest for four of the five available variables. Only in the case of membership in a political party or civic group in Britain do the model-based results indicate a clear null finding. These results are summarized in Appendix Table A13.1.[8] Of the various political encounters examined here, these are among the most vulnerable to concerns about endogeneity. Results from the FE estimator in the first column of the table confirm this suspicion, showing clearly that it is a poor choice to get an unbiased answer to this question because even the slow-moving selection suggested in Figure 13.2 can violate the strong exogeneity assumption it requires. Reciprocal causation leads to violations of exogeneity for three of the five available variables. The other columns present the results of models that make weaker assumptions. The chapter appendix describes in greater detail the practical challenges and trade-offs this involves. I focus here mainly on the fourth column, which shows the results most robust to violations of exogeneity.

Estimates for different variables differ in the extent to which they address the challenge from reciprocal causation. For turnout in the BHPS and political participation in the GSOEP, the instruments are sufficiently strong to treat turnout as an endogenous predictor, identifying its effect based only on survey reports given at $t - 2$ and earlier. The approach requires dropping all lags from the second stage, but the models in the previous columns, which include three lags, give no indication of lagged impact. The contemporaneous effects of both variables on political interest are sizable and clearly statistically significant. The smaller Swiss dataset only permits treating self-reported turnout and party membership as predetermined. For party membership, the first lag has a statistically significant effect of its own, strengthening the case for membership as a cause based on temporal ordering.

Put together, these results constitute consistent evidence that (self-reported) political engagement raises political interest even though it is an activity most common among already politically interested individuals. The key conclusion is thus not that political participation never raises political interest, but that the reverse causal direction is usually much more powerful, as shown in Figure 13.2. But even if obviously political activity, such as party membership or political participation, is predominantly a consequence of political interest, eyeballing the graphs leaves open the possibility that political activity also has some effect on interest, and the model-based approach clearly confirms this suggestion in several instances.

---

[8] Because some waves do not include these predictors and I drop them, the estimates for Britain and Germany in this section no longer refer to annual reinterviews, but a mix of annual and biennial intervals (see chapter appendix).

Political participation and group membership are measured by self-reports which do not always reflect behavior accurately (e.g., Silver et al. 1986; Belli et al. 2001; Vavreck 2007). It is possible that the results presented here reflect not the impact of a change in behavior but self-image or other psychological factors that explain misreporting. This concern might appear particularly acute in the BHPS because its turnout question refers to the same parliamentary election in successive panel waves, so the difference score is at least partly a measure of self-report reliability (as turnout by the same individual in the same election is by design a constant). The same concern is not present in the Swiss study, however, because the SHP asks about referenda, a number of which are held in Switzerland every year. The similarity of the results for Britain and Switzerland indicates that the specific way of measuring turnout is not the primary driver of the results.

To the extent that the turnout findings speak to behavior, they offer a new perspective on the literature on turnout as a habit (e.g., Green and Shachar 2000; Plutzer 2002; Gerber et al. 2003; Franklin 2004; Meredith 2009), which argues that voting in the first election(s) for which people are eligible fashions a routine for future participation. Proponents of this view have not always been clear about the mechanism underlying this empirical regularity. Meredith (2009, 189), in fact, questioned the use of the term habit, pointing out that "because persistence in political participation may occur for non-psychological reasons ... the term state dependence better reflects the phenomenon than habit." The finding here that turnout can raise political interest pushes back against the common interpretation of habit as a routine, even mindless repetition based on the "muscle memory" instilled by performing the behavior for the first time. Instead, it looks like "voting may alter psychological orientations to favor future participation," as Meredith (2009, 206) speculated. If turnout inspires a rise in political interest, which in turn makes future turnout more likely, acquired taste looks like a more appropriate metaphor for the underlying mechanism than habit.

Ambiguously Political Encounters

For organizations of a less obviously political nature, but which still touch on political topics regularly, selection effects should be weaker than for parties and political activities. Figure 13.3 bears out this expectation for membership in environmental organizations, repeatedly measured in all three panel studies. The cross-sectional association between membership and political interest is smaller but still clearly positive, with members about 15–25 points more interested. Yet it would be an analytical mistake to attribute these differences to the causal power of political participation. The graphs make it very clear that much of this cross-sectional association is not, in fact, due to an underlying causal relationship. Even though political interest may change slightly among

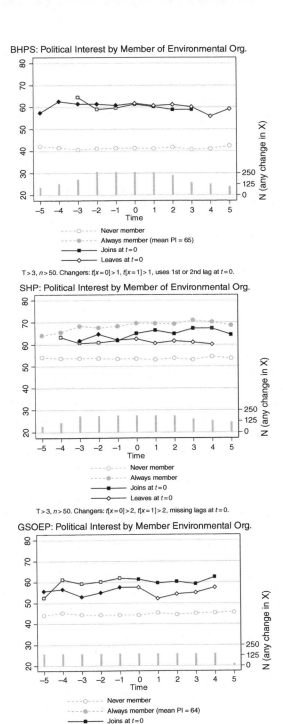

FIGURE 13.3 Change in Political Interest by Membership in Environmental Organizations

Note: Membership based on binary question except in SHP where it pools "active" and "passive" members. For details on graphs, see Book Appendix B.

people who join or leave these organizations, the magnitude of these changes is much smaller than the association between levels.[9]

In two out of three cases, the graphical analysis points to small effects of group membership on political interest. In both Germany and Switzerland, the interest difference between members and non-members widens in the years after $t = 0$, by something close to 5 points. In Germany, this effect is temporary, whereas in Switzerland it appears to develop gradually over several years. Model-based analysis confirms this result for Switzerland (see Appendix Table A13.1). The German study included the question too infrequently to permit an equivalent analysis. If there is an effect of membership in an environmental group in Britain, it is negative, but the data are too sparse to say with any confidence.

Membership or activity in volunteer groups or charitable organizations is measured in all three panel studies. According to the loose theoretical expectations for this chapter, these groups should not be subject to selection effects because they are not explicitly devoted to political issues. Whether we should expect them to affect political interest is ambiguous because "volunteer groups" cover a range of areas spanning political and non-political causes. The groups respondents include when they are asked about volunteering may not be political enough to raise political interest. I present empirical results here using this broad definition of volunteering because past research has often been satisfied with generalizations about this rather heterogeneous set of group activity.

Graphical analyses in Figure 13.4 indeed show signs of both selection effects and effects of membership on political interest. In all four graphs, joiners (dark lines with square markers) are less interested than leavers (dark lines with diamond markers) before their participation changes, but their political interest levels already converge prior to $t = -1$ (sometimes smoothly, sometimes in a noisy way), indicating selection effects. The two left-hand graphs suggest a small positive effect of membership on political interest after $t = 0$, but model-based estimates do not confirm it. Political interest makes people volunteer, and volunteering can occasionally raise interest – but any such effects are both rare and small.[10]

A few other groups included in the household panel studies probably cover politics unexpectedly and are included in the model-based analysis. (The full lists and reported membership frequencies appear in the Supplementary Online Materials, Tables OL13.1 to OL13.3.) On the whole, organizational involvement or activity in groups that are not overtly political has little effect on political interest. The only exception is a pooled indicator of membership in "local or parents'," "women's," or "tenants' rights associations" in

---

[9] Selection effects are largely absent for environmental groups. Only the Swiss study reveals even a hint of selection in the year after $t - 2$. The trends in Britain and Germany do not fit the Selection Hypothesis as members become slightly *more* interested before they leave the organization (in Germany) and non-members' interest drops several years *before* they join (in Britain).

[10] Appendix Table A13.1 does show a significant but small effect of the self-reported extent of volunteering in Switzerland, a continuous variable not examined graphically.

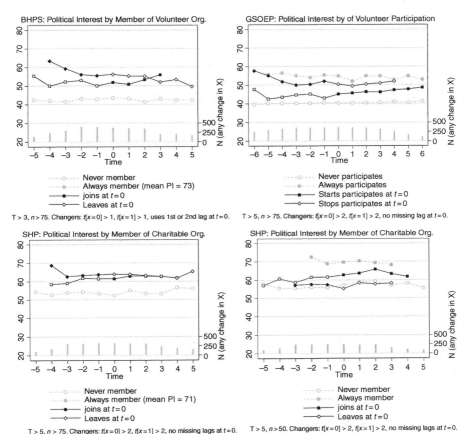

FIGURE 13.4 Change in Political Interest by Membership/Activity in Volunteer
Organizations

Note: BHPS measure is based on a binary question. SHP membership pools "active" and "passive"
members. SHP volunteer activity is based on reported hours per month treating changes of 25 or
more as change. GSOEP participation is based on a categorical scale treating "monthly" or more
frequent as participation. For details on graphs, see Book Appendix B.

Switzerland, which raises political interest. The corresponding graph, in the
lower right of Figure 13.4, also suggests a positive, small, and possibly temporary effect of membership on political interest.

Non-Political Encounters

For several groups and activities, politics is clearly not involved. These are
important empirical tests because positive effects on political interest would

show that the benefits of membership for political interest development do not depend on an organization's political mission and thematic focus and might involve mechanisms emphasized in the social capital literature, such as social interactions, trust formation, or acquisition of skills. Figure 13.5 displays the results for membership in a "social club/working men's club" in Britain, membership in a Swiss "organization involved in cultural activities, music, or education," and frequent attendance of either "high-brow" or more common cultural events in Germany (the former including classical music, theater, lectures, the latter movies, popular music, and sports events).

Involvement in these clearly non-political activities is still associated with political interest, and quite strongly so for "high-brow" cultural events with an interest gap between participants and non-participants of about 20 points. There is little evidence, however, that this type of organizational involvement has much to do with generation of political interest. Selection can still occur, as when people join social clubs in Britain after a rise in political interest (and leave them after a drop). But the effect of membership actually appears to be negative, at least temporarily, for cultural organizations in Switzerland and social clubs in Britain. In both cases, model-based analyses indicate null effects.

The graph for (high-brow) cultural activities in Germany is difficult to interpret because of a temporary convergence of future joiners and leavers at $t = -1$, just before they join or leave. But it does suggest a positive effect on political interest, and the modeling results in Appendix Table A13.1 confirm it. Even popular culture appears to raise interest in Germany, according to the statistical results. Thanks to its large sample size and categorical measurement of activity, the German study can detect even small effects. Like all other non-binary variables, attendance of cultural events is scored in quarter standard deviations, so the coefficients represent the effect of something close to the largest over-time increase observed in the data. At slightly more than half a point on the 0–100 interest scale, the impact is small.[11]

The final type of involvement examined here is membership in religious organizations and attendance of religious services. Verba et al. (1995, 434) show a significant association between church attendance and political interest in the United States. Figure 13.6 corroborates the positive relationship in

---

[11] Another type of activity, the self-reported frequency of playing sports, has the opposite effect in Germany, lowering political interest a bit (even though those who play are still somewhat more politically interested). The corresponding graph, shown in Figure OL13.1 in the Supplementary Online Materials, suggests that this effect might not last. Either way, it is also small, and the other two studies, which ask about membership in a "sports club" (BHPS) or "sports or leisure association" (SHP), produce no additional evidence that this type of organizational involvement affects political interest.

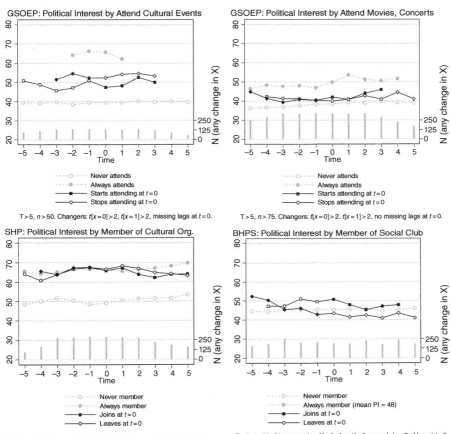

FIGURE 13.5 Change in Political Interest by Membership/Activity in Cultural Organizations, Social Clubs

Note: BHPS measure is based on a binary question. SHP membership pools "active" and "passive" members. GSOEP attendance is based on categorical scales treating "monthly" or more frequent as attendance. For details on graphs, see Book Appendix B.

Britain, but not in Germany or Switzerland. Verba et al. (1995, 436) describe the cross-sectional association in unequivocally causal language, claiming that "church attendance increases political interest." This chapter has already raised doubts about the causal effect of non-political organizations. For church attendance, the impact on political interest may even be negative.

As the top row of graphs in Figure 13.6 shows, British people who at some point report joining religious organizations or attending church more often are decidedly more politically interested *before* this change occurs than those who

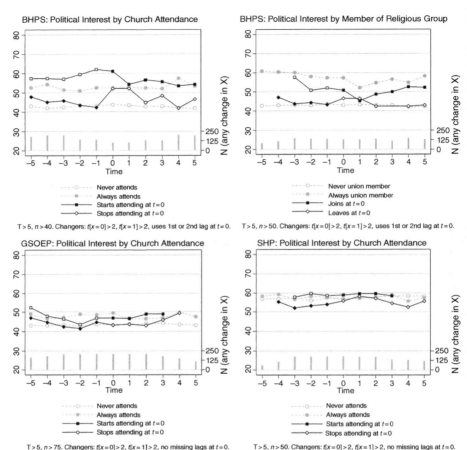

FIGURE 13.6 Change in Political Interest by Church Attendance and Religious Activity
Note: Church attendance items are based on categorical scales treating "monthly" or more frequent as attendance. BHPS membership item is based on binary question. For details on graphs, see Book Appendix B.

eventually leave. In the year after the reported change in religious participation, however, this difference is gone. Religious participation in Britain, in other words, depresses political interest, at least for a while. Long-term, it appears not to matter, one way or another, and the model-based estimate of the impact of religious membership in Britain is close to zero. (Church attendance in the BHPS is measured too infrequently to include in a model.)

For Germany, the model most robust to violations of exogeneity also shows a significant negative effect of church attendance, a finding not evident in the graph. In Switzerland, finally, people who stop attending church temporarily gain political interest, but the magnitude of this effect is lower than in Britain, and it remains ambiguous if they attend church less because they became more politically interested or if they become more interested because they stopped going to church. Either way, church attendance in Switzerland does not contribute to the development of political interest, a conclusion confirmed by the statistical models.[12]

In all three countries, the present analysis thus fails to back up the claim by Verba at al. that "church attendance increases political interest." It is not impossible that causal impact is positive in the United States, but more likely Verba et al. mistook correlation in cross-sectional data for evidence of causation. Across the board, the effect of non-political organizations is best summarized as somewhere between minor and absent.

ENCOUNTERING POLITICS THROUGH SPOUSES

The more politically interested his or her spouse, the more likely an individual should be to encounter politics at home. Influence through a spouse's political interest and the engagement with politics brought about by that political interest operates differently at different stages of a relationship. As people get to know each other, they learn the extent of the other's political interest, but political interest is probably not a particularly important factor in determining the length and closeness of a relationship. During an established relationship, couples with different levels of political interest might not discuss politics much, but a more interested spouse is still bound to present an individual with more political encounters than she would seek out on her own. The end of a relationship removes a close confidante with possibly different political interest, but the end rarely comes about because of a couple's match or mismatch of political interest levels.

Because of the way the household panel studies are designed, we have little information about couples before they live in the same household. The sample design in all three countries is based on recruiting all members of randomly selected households and following them even after they move out. This generates independent data on both members of a couple starting from the time they live with each other (whether they are married or not) or from the time they joined the panel (for existing couples recruited into the panel together).

---

[12] The SHP also asks about the frequency of prayer (see Figure OL13.2 in the Online Supplementary Materials). This item produces the only instance of an activity sharing a (weak) negative cross-sectional relationship with political interest. As an activity that can be performed privately and individually, praying is not organizational involvement. The graphical analysis suggests a positive effect (albeit small and temporary) of praying on political interest. A model assuming exogeneity confirms the positive effect (Appendix Table A13.1), but the data fail to yield an informative estimate when exogeneity is relaxed.

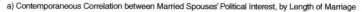

a) Contemporaneous Correlation between Married Spouses' Political Interest, by Length of Marriage

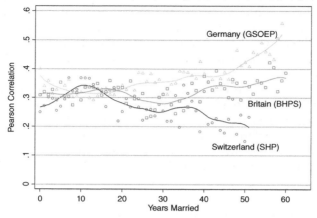

b) Correlation between Current Politicial Interest and Spouse's Frist Interest Report, by Measurement Interval

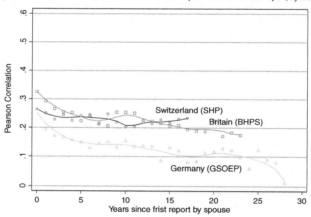

FIGURE 13.7 Association between Spouses' Political Interest
Note: Markers are Pearson correlations. Lines apply mean smoothing. Top graph includes only married couples living in the same household. Bottom graphs based on any cohabitating partners living in the same household (see Online Supplementary Materials for details).

The available data can thus only examine the role of spousal political interest during (and after) a couple has already established their relationship.[13]

---

[13] Stoker and Jennings (1995) face a similar problem in their panel data, but rely on retrospective reports of political participation to suggest that the effect of marriage on participation is large and negative when the spouse has low participation rates, but marginally positive for marriage to a politically active spouse.

Spouses often resemble each other as far as their party identification, ideology, and vote choice are concerned (Stoker and Jennings 2005; Zuckerman et al. 2007; Alford et al. 2011). This is true for political interest as well: The top graph in Figure 13.7 shows positive contemporaneous correlations of moderate magnitude between political interest levels of people who are married to each other.[14]

Over the course of a marriage, the similarity of partisan leanings increases, but growing resemblance appears not to extend to many other political and social attitudes (Stoker and Jennings 2005; Alford et al. 2011). Neither Stoker and Jennings nor Alford et al. examine political interest, however. Figure 13.7 reveals that spousal similarity of political interest does not depend either on how long people have been married except for very long marriages. In the Swiss data, correlations increase early on, but then drop again. Only for marriages longer than 30 or 40 years does the graph show divergence between studies. In the SHP, the drop continues. In the German data, spousal similarity is noticeably greater among couples who have been married for 40 years or longer.

Several aspects of the top graph limit how much we can infer from it. It determines length of marriage based on the panelists' reported wedding dates. Spouses who lived together before marriage cannot be included because cohabitation periods are not consistently known. Although the graph can describe spousal similarity after many decades of marriage, none of the studies is remotely long enough to follow the same couple for a half-century. This makes it more difficult to interpret the changing correlations for long marriages. These couples married decades before data collection began, so we cannot know if their political interest levels became more similar over the course of the marriage or were more similar to begin with. The graph, in other words, combines within-couple and between-couple changes – with unclear implications for what actually happens in a marriage.

The bottom graph in Figure 13.7 provides further insights. It plots correlations between a panelist's political interest in a given panel wave and his or her spouse's first reported interest. The horizontal axis marks the interval between these two measurements. This way of slicing the data comes closer to following couples through their marriages. It still combines marriages of different age for different lengths of time, but that appears to be relatively unimportant: Limiting the analysis to panelists who provided at least five interest reports essentially reproduces the graph. Separate plots based on shorter (under 20 years) and longer marriages (at least 20 years) are also very similar. Because it is based on joint household residence, which is measured in each wave, the analysis can

---

[14] Correlations are not much attenuated by measurement error. Correlations between average interest reports given by each partner while the panelist was between 30 and 60 years old are only marginally higher than average correlations for individual panel waves over the same period: .32 versus .26 in the BHPS; .27 versus .24 in the GSOEP; and .25 versus .21 in the SHP.

now include unmarried couples living together as well. (I will continue to use the terms "wife," "husband," and "spouse" out of convenience.)

The bottom graph in Figure 13.7 strongly suggests that the increase in correlations with length of marriage in Germany and the drop in Switzerland (in the top graph) are compositional effects, not effects of marriage. This conclusion is reinforced because the mild downward slope in the bottom graph replicated when only marriages over at least 20 years are included in the calculations. Most likely, Germans who have been married for a long time have more similar political interest because they married more similar people.

The main conclusion from Figure 13.7 is thus that similarity of spouses' political interest changes rather little over the course of a marriage. Similar political interest among household members does not necessarily indicate inter-personal influence (see Nickerson 2008, 50–1). People may be more likely to move in, or stay with, someone who shares their interest in politics. Likewise, stable correlations over time do not imply the absence of influence between spouses. Changes in political interest by one member of a couple might quickly be followed by corresponding changes of the other member, thus leaving the correlation unchanged. Similar experiences and concerns that arise in a rela-tionship can also change both partners' political interest without affecting how similar they are. Even with longitudinal data, distinguishing between the impact of shared environments and reciprocal influences between spouses is tricky. Nickerson (2008) does find that mobilization of one household member of (randomly selected) two-person households also increased turnout of the other member. Without the benefit of randomly changing one spouse's interest, the household panel data can best address the question of spousal influence by tracing a panelist's political interest during the years when his or her spouse's interest changes.

Figure 13.8 uses the same graphical tool as before to examine the effect of spousal political interest. Change is defined in the most straightforward way for Britain and Germany, taking the top two categories as "high" political interest, the other two categories as "low" interest, and movement between "high" and "low" as "change." For Switzerland, the cutpoint between "high" and "low" is between 50 and 60 on the 0-to-100 scale. (The model-based approach again avoids the arbitrariness of this cutoff by estimating the impact of changes between all of the underlying response categories.) Graphs on the left plot husbands' political interest as a function of the wife's interest. Graphs on the right show the reverse, following wives' interest as the husband does or does not change.[15]

---

[15] Figure 13.8 uses the political interest of the spouse living in the respondent's household at the time of the interview and thus includes the effect of differences in interest levels between successive spouses. The graphs look almost the same if the analysis is limited to only a panelist's first spouse and includes interest reports by that spouse when s/he does not live in the same household. This is mostly due to the relatively small number of divorces, separations, and spousal deaths in the data.

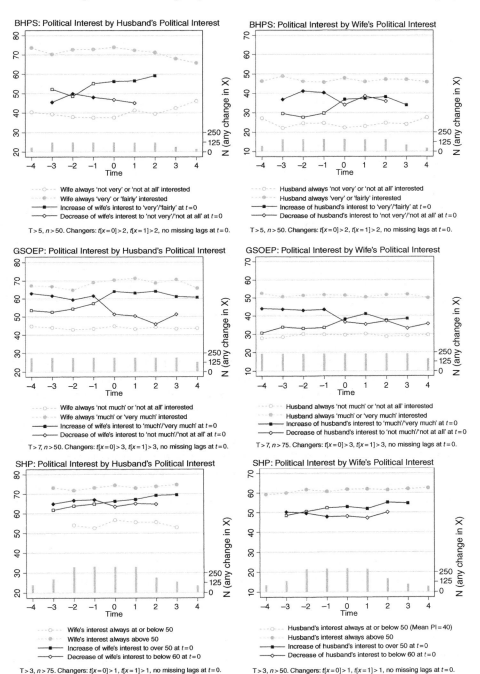

FIGURE 13.8 Change in Political Interest after Change in Spouse's Political Interest
Note: Definition of change explained in the text. For details on graphs, see Book Appendix B.

Figure 13.8 shows that changes in political interest happen among both spouses, but these changes are not of the same magnitude and do not occur entirely at the same time. First, the change at $t = 0$ is defined as one category or more – that is, at least 33 points in the BHPS and GSOEP. None of the associated changes of the other spouse are as big, and many are much smaller. When one partner experiences a change in political interest, the other does *not* experience change of the same magnitude. This makes it less likely that a third variable affecting both partners similarly explains the patterns we see. (Although a third variable that disproportionately affects one partner could underlie the patterns. The model-based analysis that follows controls for at least some such influences.) Second, and more importantly, the changes among both spouses are to some extent sequential occurring in succession over several years. This makes household-level causes less likely and permits some disentangling of who influences whom.

The sequence of changes in husbands' and wives' political interest evident in Figure 13.8 points to husbands as the starting point in Britain and perhaps also Germany. In the British data, the lines depicting interest of the average husband whose wife's interest changes between $t - 1$ and t already move in the years before $t - 1$. In graphs for wives' interest on the right of Figure 13.8, the reverse is not true, as wives exhibit rather constant interest levels in the years before $t - 1$, the onset of their husband's change. Put more simply, husbands change between $t - 2$ and $t - 1$, wives follow a year later.

The model-based estimates detailed in the chapter appendix also support the conclusion that husbands in Britain have greater impact on their spouses than wives. Appendix Table A13.2 summarizes the results of different specifications that successively relax the exogeneity assumption by employing more demanding instrumenting strategies. In all specifications, the coefficients measuring the impact of the husband's political interest exceed the equivalent coefficients for the wife, by more than a 100 percent in the most plausible models.

The same sequence of change may be evident, less clearly, in Germany as well. The husband's political interest already increases for a year or two *before* his wife gains interest between $t - 1$ and t. For husbands, the solid lines already converge before $t - 1$; for wives, they remain parallel. Moreover, a wife's political interest increases further after t – and thus unambiguously *after* the increase in her husband's interest. The reverse for husbands is not as evident (and not at all between t and $t + 1$). Unlike for the British data, model-based estimates do not support an asymmetry of causal direction for Germany, however. In all specifications, coefficients for husbands and wives indicate statistically significant effects of similar magnitude.

In Switzerland, the dominant causal direction may be reversed. Here it is the wife's political interest that moves first, as seen by the divergence between the solid lines in the interval between $t - 2$ and $t - 1$ in the lower right-hand graph, and remains largely unchanged subsequently. Her husband's interest moves between $t - 1$ and t (and, to add more weight to this causal direction, a bit more between $t+1$ and $t+2$, unambiguously after the wife became more interested). The model-based estimates confirm the graphical analysis only partially. When spousal interest is treated as predetermined, only the effect of wives' political interest is statistically significant. Spousal interest as endogenous, which requires dropping all lags to get informative estimates, produces statistically significant estimates that are almost identical in both directions. (Overall, Figure 13.8 seems to indicate a weaker association between changes in spousal interest in Switzerland compared to the other two countries, but this is likely an artifact of unceremoniously cutting the 11-point scale at the midpoint to define "change." The models, which do not require a cutpoint, show roughly similar magnitudes as in Britain.)

In any case, asymmetric spousal impact does not mean unidirectional impact. British wives still influence their husbands – but the causal direction from husband to wife is stronger or more common in Britain. Likewise, Swiss husbands have a sizable impact on their spouses as well, according to the estimates that are most robust to violations of exogeneity. These model estimates, which guard against endogeneity bias by building "scaffolding" from information about the spouse collected at least two years earlier, provide the most compelling influence for causal impact among spouses. Pushing the data to the limit, they reassuringly yield quite similar estimates for all three countries even if the estimates for Britain are so noisy they just miss statistical significance. Asymmetric or not, both graphical and model-based analyses indicate mutual influence between spouses when it comes to the development of political interest.

CONCLUSION

Some political encounters come to people. Part I of the book covered salient political events, a few of which may have been momentous enough to constitute almost universal political encounters. Their effects were statistically detectable but substantively small. The focus of this chapter was on people coming, for one reason or another, to political encounters. In many instances, this reason is political interest.

Interest-based selection into political encounters received a lot of support in this chapter. For encounters with politics, including politically impinged jobs and employment in the public sector, volunteering, political participation, and membership in political parties, the graphical evidence shows repeatedly that political interest governs whether people seek out these political experiences. These results confirm the large amount of research (reviewed in Chapter 1) that shows political interest to encourage behavioral outcomes associated with good citizenship.

The Selectivity Hypothesis is stronger, however, predicting that people succeed in calibrating their political encounters so accurately based on their pre-existing political interest that these encounters do not modify interest, only confirm the expectation. This turns out to be correct for politically-impinged and public-sector jobs, but not for possibly more transitory political encounters that require less of a commitment, such as turnout or participation in political organizations. Even though political interest is a very strong determinant of such behaviors, this chapter also finds causal impact of these selective political experiences on political interest.

It is easy to overstate these effects on political interest. Although some are among the strongest causes of political interest identified in this book, they explain only a fraction of the cross-sectional difference in political interest between those who do and do not report these encounters. The magnitude of even clearly significant causal effects is always much smaller than the corresponding cross-sectional association.

Nonetheless, the evidence is quite clear that even obvious encounters with politics can still increase political interest among those who seek them out, perhaps because other factors contribute to the decision. A moderately interested person may go to the polls out of a sense of duty or because someone else asked her to come. A political meeting may attract some people for social or instrumental reasons, not because they enjoy politics. Or people may simply get the calibration wrong and end up surprised by how interesting politics can be.

In the panel household studies, we do not observe the reasons that led panelists to obvious encounters with politics, but some these considerations suggest support for the Inadvertent Political Encounters Hypothesis. Reasons unrelated to the appeal of politics may have made obviously political encounters inadvertent for some people. This explanation is particularly likely to account for the significant influence of one spouse's political interest on that of the other. The extent to which marital life amounts to political encounters will quickly be well known to both spouses, but selecting out of it is bound to remain difficult.

This chapter also examined a different mechanism that could give rise to inadvertent political experiences: involvement in groups that deal with politics but conceal their political nature by nominally focusing on specific causes or broad "volunteer" efforts. Membership or activity in groups that fit this description raised politics only in a few (3 out of 9) cases.

The analysis of cultural organizations and athletic clubs serves as a useful placebo test for the Inadvertent Political Encounters Hypothesis. Even though political experiences in these kinds of groups would indeed be inadvertent, they are probably rare. There are few good reasons why membership in organizations that have nothing to do with politics *should* have an effect on political interest. And despite the fact that even for these types of activities, participants are often more politically interested than non-participants, the analysis shows mostly absence of causal effects (5 out of 7 tests, including one negative estimate) or (in two cases in the higher-powered German study) significant but substantively small effects. Joiners are politically interested people – even joiners of sports teams! – but that has little to do with their participation in these non-political groups.

The results regarding religious attendance and involvement are surprising in this context, in part because previous research has made strong claims about them, but also because religion can easily have political undertones. Yet the empirical analysis of religious participation uncovers two of the strongest negative effects on political interest (along with two null findings). Religious involvement may still facilitate good citizenship by directly encouraging political participation, but at least in several European democracies, it is more likely to dampen than cultivate political interest.

To sum up, for encounters with politics to raise political interest, these encounters apparently have to be quite obviously political. If serendipity plays a role, it does so by exposing moderately interested people to overtly political experiences rather than by sneaking politics into ostensibly non-political encounters. These results are important as a counterpoint to strong claims about the benefits of joining that appear in the literature. At least when it comes to political interest, membership, participation, and group activities fail to make much of a difference when the groups and activities have nothing to do with politics. Possible content-independent mechanisms such as formation of social ties and interpersonal trust are apparently not sufficient on their own to generate political interest.

The concept of social capital has received considerable attention by scholars interested in understanding the functioning of political institutions and the capacity for effective self-governance. Organizational involvement is at the heart of the social capital literature (e.g., Smith 1999; Putnam 2000; Stolle and Hooghe 2004; McFarland and Thomas 2006). Institutions are more effective in areas with many voluntary associations, and members of those associations exhibit many characteristics of good citizenship, among them social trust and political involvement.

Arguments about social capital rarely invoke political interest. This seems at best half right. Whatever other outcomes are produced by involvement in non-political groups, political interest is indeed not among them. But as a precursor to such group involvement, political interest is clearly of some importance. As Part II of this book demonstrated, political interest begins to develop and crystallize before people become eligible to vote and is possibly already in place when students make decisions about extracurricular activities and other forms of early group involvement. The graphical analyses in this chapter point to political interest as a starting point for the formation of social capital because it leads people to join many types of organizations.

The same logic applies somewhat differently to arguments about turnout as a habit. Voting in one election makes voting in subsequent elections more likely (e.g., Green and Shachar 2000; Plutzer 2002; Gerber et al. 2003; Franklin 2004; Meredith 2009). Research designs used in these studies typically make sure that initial voters and non-voters do not differ in terms of their political interest, so political interest cannot explain the initial turnout difference. It can, however, explain (some of) the effect of voting once on voting again in the future, as shown in this chapter's analysis. And even though the habit studies use samples or statistical techniques that make initial voters and non-voters indistinguishable with respect to political interest, a typical voter is considerably more interested than a typical non-voter, in all likelihood the result of a causal effect of political interest. Hence, while there is persistence in voter turnout, political interest is critical in both starting and sustaining this behavioral regularity in a mutually reinforcing dynamic. Interest encourages voting, and voting raises interest. It is less mindless habit and more an acquired taste for politics that leads people to continue their political engagement over time.

While political interest is also an impetus for joining non-political groups, its role in perpetuating behavioral involvement is different for those groups because there is no reinforcement through participation. Membership is higher among politically interested individuals and sometimes quite obviously the consequence of pre-existing interest. But political interest does not rise as a result of group involvement unless the groups are obviously political. Political interest sustains social capital formation not through positive feedback loops, but because it is stable and keeps sending people back to organizational meetings and activities.

Appendix to Chapter 13

MODEL-BASED ESTIMATES OF THE IMPACT OF POLITICAL ENCOUNTERS ON POLITICAL INTEREST

Table A13.1 presents results from different estimators that make successively weaker assumptions regarding exogeneity. (The independent variables from Chapter 12 initially remain in the model, but their effects are not reported again. The first three columns include two or three lags of them, as noted in the table note.) Cells in brackets indicate that the exogeneity assumption for the respective estimator is not met so the results are biased. The FE estimator in the leftmost column requires strict exogeneity, so the error term must not be correlated with the independent variable throughout the whole panel (see Chapter 9). The FD estimator in the second column only requires weak exogeneity, the independence of error and covariate at $t - 1$, t, and $t + 1$.

Column (3) adds lagged political interest. When selection and reverse causation occur slowly, as the graphical analyses suggest for some employment and group membership effects, controlling for lagged political interest can effectively remove reciprocal influences of an unexpected rise in political interest leading someone to take a politically impinged job or join a civic organization, or of an unexpected drop in interest leading someone to quit that job or leave that organization. (Practically, this effect is muted by the small coefficient on the lagged dependent variable which is significant in most specifications but substantively close to zero. This explains why the results in columns (2) and (3) are typically similar.)

If selection occurs over long periods of time, it is not implausible that that the FD estimator in column (2) and the dynamic panel model in column (3) that treats covariates as exogenous pass the specification tests. For the FD model in column (2) and the dynamic panel model in column (3), the relevant test of (weak) exogeneity is test of $E(w_{i,t}\ \varepsilon_{it}) = 0$. In most models, this test is

TABLE A13.1 *The Impact of Political Encounters on Political Interest*

		(1) FE	(2) FD	(3) LDV, exogenous covariates	(4) LDV, instrumenting covariates
Encounters through Work					
Works in government	(BHPS)	-.9 (1.6)	-.1 (2.7)	-.1 (2.1)	
	(GSOEP)	-.9 (1.0)†	-.8 (1.6)	-1.2 (1.3)	
	(SHP)	[1.6 (2.0)]	2.0 (3.2)	2.0 (2.2)	
Journalist, writer, social scientist, economist	(BHPS)	.4 (3.1)	-.6 (4.6)	-.5 (4.1)	
	(GSOEP)	[-2.9 (2.1)]	.9 (2.7)	1.0 (2.1)	
	(SHP)	.9 (1.7)	1.5 (2.8)	1.7 (2.4)	
Legal or religious professional	(BHPS)	-6.8** (2.8)†	-5.4 (5.0)	-5.4 (3.7)†	
	(GSOEP)	[-.6 (2.5)]	-7.3* (3.7)†	-8.2*** (3.0)†	
	(SHP)	-1.7 (1.8)	-.1 (4.0)	-.02 (2.7)	
Other politically-impinged job	(BHPS)	-.9* (.5)	-.3 (.9)	.3 (.8)	
	(GSOEP)	-.3 (.4)	-.6 (.7)	-.4 (.6)	
	(SHP)	-.2 (.6)	.8 (1.0)	.8 (.8)	
Any politically-impinged job	(BHPS)			.2 (.7)	.5 (1.3)
	(GSOEP)			-.6 (.6)	-.3 (.7)
	(SHP)			.8 (.8)	-.1 (1.3)
Public-sector employment	(GSOEP)	[.9** (.4)†]	1.1 (.7)	1.2* (.6)†	.04 (.7)
	(SHP)	.3 (.5)	-.7 (.9)⁻	-.8 (.7)⁻	.7 (.8)
Civil-service employment	(GSOEP)	-.2 (.9)	-.3 (1.7)	-.2 (1.3)	.7 (2.2)
Full-time employment	(BHPS)	-2.1*** (.7)⁻	-1.6 (1.3)⁻	-1.7 (1.1)⁻	.9 (2.5)
	(GSOEP)	-1.5*** (.4)⁻	-1.4* (.8)⁻	-1.4** (.6)⁻	-.3 (.9)
	(SHP)	-1.2* (.7)†	-2.8*** (1.2)†	-2.9*** (.9)†	-1.4 (1.5)
Union membership	(BHPS)	1.5* (.8)†	.1 (1.2)	-.9 (1.3)	-.6 (2.5)
	(SHP)	.6 (.9)	.4 (1.4)	.4 (1.2)	e)

Political Membership/Activity

Party/civic group membership	(BHPS) [a]	2.4** (1.2)+	.6 (1.7)	1.1 (1.9)	-.7 (2.5)
Party membership	(SHP)	2.6** (1.0)+	2.7 (1.8)+	2.7* (1.5)+	6.9*** (2.0)+
Political participation	(GSOEP) [b]	[1.7*** (.1)+]	.8*** (.2)+	.8*** (.2)+	1.8*** (.5) [d]
Self-reported turnout	(BHPS) [a]	[4.3*** (.7)+]	4.0*** (.9)+	4.0*** (.8)+	8.7*** (2.8) [d]
	(SHP) [b]	[10.4*** (1.1)+]	8.3*** (1.8)+	7.9*** (1.4)+	8.3*** (2.4)+

Inadvertently Political Membership/Activity

Environmental organization	(BHPS) [a]	[.03 (1.5]]	-1.2 (1.9)	-3.5* (2.0)	-3.4 (3.3)+
	(SHP)	1.4* (.8)+	1.6 (1.4)	1.7 (1.2)	2.9** (1.4)+
Voluntary organization	(BHPS) [a]	.4 (1.1)	-.3 (1.7)	-1.1 (1.8)	.03 (2.9)
Volunteer work	(GSOEP) [b]	[.3** (.1)+]	.2 (2.2)+	.2 (2.2)+	-.5 (.3)+
Charitable organization	(SHP)	.6 (.7)	.3 (1.0)	.3 (.9)	-.2 (.8)
Reported volunteering (log hrs)	(SHP) [b]	.1 (.3)	.2 (.5)	.2 (.4)	.9* (.5)
Parents/school association	(BHPS) [a]	2.8** (1.1)+	1.1 (1.7)	1.9 (1.9)	1.2 (3.0)
Residents' organization	(BHPS) [a]	2.0** (1.0)+	3.5** (1.3)+	5.0*** (1.5)+	-.7 (2.2)
Various issue groups [c]	(SHP)	-.4 (.7)	-.7 (1.2)	-.9 (1.0)+	2.9** (1.2)+

Non-Political Membership/Activity

Attendance of cultural events	(GSOEP) [b]	.7 (.1)+	.5** (.2)+	.5*** (.2)+	.6** (.2)+
Attendance of popular culture	(GSOEP) [b]	[.05 (.1)+]	.3 (.2)+	.3 (.2)+	.7*** (.2)+
Cultural organization	(SHP)	-.1 (.7)	.6 (1.1)	.8 (1.0)	-1.3 (1.0)
Social club	(BHPS) [a]	2.4*** (.9)+	1.1 (1.3)+	.6 (1.4)	.6 (2.3)
Sports club	(BHPS) [a]	.6 (.8)	-1.6 (1.0)	-.4 (1.2)	.1 (1.8)

(continued)

TABLE A13.1 *(continued)*

		(1) FE	(2) FD	(3) LDV, exogenous covariates	(4) LDV, instrumenting covariates
Sports activity	(GSOEP)[b]	[.1 (.1)]†	[-.05 (.2)]	-.04 (.2)	-.6** (.3)†
Sports/leisure association	(SHP)	[-1.3** (.7)]†	-1.5 (1.1)	-1.6* (.9)	.7 (1.0)
Religious Membership/Activity					
Religious organization	(BHPS)[a]	.7 (1.3)	1.9 (1.7)	1.6 (2.1)	-1.1 (3.6)
Church attendance	(GSOEP)[b]	[.5* (.3)†]	-.5 (.5)†+	-.2 (.2)†+	-3.2*** (.7)[d]
Religious attendance	(SHP)[b]	[.7 (.9)]	.2 (1.5)	.04 (1.4)	-.2 (1.4)
Frequency of prayer	(SHP)[b]	.8 (.9)	2.0 (1.4)	2.2* (1.3)	[e]

*** $p < .01$, ** $p < .05$, * $p < .10$. Cell entries are long-run multipliers with robust standard errors in parentheses. Unless otherwise noted, long-run multipliers for columns (1) to (3) are calculated over $t = 0, -1, -2, -3$ using the same waves for each estimator. Long-run multipliers in column (4) use only $t = 0, -1$ unless otherwise noted. Estimates in brackets violate exogeneity.

a) Long-run multipliers for columns (1) to (3) calculated over $t = 0, -1, -2$.
b) Categorical variable, scored in quarter-within-subject standard deviations.
c) Membership in any of the following associations "local or parents'," "women's," "tenants' rights" (see Table OL13.2 in the Online Supplementary Materials for details).
d) no lags, treated as endogenous
e) predetermined violates specification test; instruments too weak to treat as endogenous
† Lagged coefficients all equal to zero is rejected at $p < .10$
+ Coefficients of contemporaneous short-run effect is positive at $p < .05$
- Coefficients of contemporaneous short-run effect is negative at $p < .05$

comfortably rejected, indicating that the contemporaneous term of the variable and the error term are independent, justifying their treatment as exogenous. For politically impinged jobs, for example, this is plausible in light of the very slow moving selection process revealed in the graphs. Feedback may be present but operate beyond $t + 1$ and hence not challenge the weak exogeneity assumption necessary for these estimators.

Assuming only weak exogeneity generates no violations here. To verify that this result is not due to weak specification tests, models reported in column (4) treat predictors as predetermined or, when possible, endogenous regardless. This involves a practical trade-off in specifying the models because instruments become stronger with fewer lags in the second-stage equation, but fewer lags might exacerbate misspecification. Dropping lags and using them as excluded instruments instead therefore risks trading one kind of bias for another. While columns (1)–(3) use two or three lags of the independent variables, column (4) uses only one lag or, for endogenous specifications, only the contemporaneous term. For some variables, even that is not enough to obtain sufficiently strong instruments. The estimates for party/civic membership in both Britain and Switzerland, for example, have uninformatively large standard errors because excluded lags turn out to be weak instruments.

In interpreting null findings, it is useful to keep in mind the limitations of the modeling approach. The efficiency of model-based estimates, and thus the smallest possible detectable effect, varies widely across datasets. Several design differences have implications for efficiency, including sample size and number of waves that include a given independent variable, frequency and rate of change of a particular encounter, and the measurement scale. Panel design explains the large, sometimes uninformative standard errors for BHPS estimates of group membership effects: Membership is usually asked every other year, and political interest was omitted for five years in the late 1990s – a combination that not only reduces the amount of data but also limits the number of lags by effectively cutting the panel in half. For some stretches, the GSOEP also includes many of the predictors only every other year (see Tables OL13.1 and OL13.3 in the Online Supplementary Material for details). I address this problem by calculating the lagged two-year average of political interest, dropping waves that omit a predictor, and using the two-year interest averages as additional instruments. The resulting combination of one- and two-year intervals between measurements of the predictors creates some imprecision about the discount rate implied by lags. Because the coefficient on the lagged dependent variable is very close to zero, distortions from fuzzily modeled dynamics should be minimal. The SHP uses a stretch of the panel with annual measurement of all variables.

The GSOEP allows for endogenous estimates in part because, unlike group membership in Britain and Switzerland, group activity is measured on a four-point scale. Unlike the graphs, a model-based approach deals easily with such non-binary predictors. For the graphs, I defined "change" as any transition between the upper and the lower two categories, but this cutpoint is arbitrary and throws away some information. Including the full scale as an independent variable in a regression model treats all transitions between categories as change. (Dichotomizing non-binary measures is even more awkward on the 11-point scale used in the SHP for some variables, such as spousal interest, because it treats many more changes between categories as stability.)

Depending on the dynamics of an independent variable, some instrument sets are stronger than others. Sets can vary by the number of instruments and by whether levels or differences (or both) are used. As long as the instrument set does not include information collected at t or later (for predetermined variables) or $t-1$ or later (for endogenous variables), it is appropriate to select the set that maximizes instrument strength and meets the specification tests for dynamic panel models introduced in Chapter 9.

Weak tests are another reason why columns (2) and (3) may not detect violations of exogeneity, however. For a more robust approach, column (4) relaxes the exogeneity assumption by allowing predictors to be predetermined or endogenous. The most difficult challenge is to account for reciprocal influences that operate quickly, so they are not absorbed by political interest at $t-1$. The models reported in column (4) aim to remove these influences by not using information about the independent variable at $t=0$ because it could be subject to feedback from political interest. As explained in Chapter 9, the feasibility of this technique is not guaranteed but depends on the strength of the "scaffolding" that can be built from earlier observations of the independent variable.

All panel waves include the employment variables so the results for encounters at work (except for union membership) reported in the table are from models that add these variables to the models estimated in Chapter 12. The most credible results, treating the various employment measures as predetermined with one lag in the second-stage equation, yield no significant estimates and coefficients very close to zero. I therefore drop these variables from subsequent models along with part-time employment, occupational prestige, parental employment, and, because it is a rare event, parental divorce. (I retain unemployed status because it produced a few suggestive effects in Chapter 12.) Dropping these variables risks omitted variable bias, whereas keeping them as predetermined requires instrumenting and risks greater finite sample bias. Given the consistent null findings, the former risk appears smaller. In the Swiss data, the impact of full-time employment unfolds more slowly, so the estimate in Table A13.1 understates its full impact. (The long-run multiplier over three lags, still treating the variable as endogenous, is −4.2 with a standard error of 2.1. Lags at $t-1$ and $t-2$ are statistically significant and negative.) There is no sign of such gradual employment effects in the larger British and German studies, so I opt for simplicity by removing all employment variables in all three datasets from here on.

MODEL-BASED ESTIMATES OF THE SPOUSAL IMPACT ON POLITICAL INTEREST

For each of the three household panel studies, Table A13.2 presents the results of four different specifications to estimate the impact of one spouse's political interest on that of the other. Estimation includes panelists whether or not they had a spouse or the spouse reported his or her political interest in a given panel wave. Observations without a measure of spousal interest are set to zero and a dummy variable is included to account for these instances of missing data. This indicator for missingness is modeled the same way as spousal interest (so spousal interest and missingness are both instrumented in predetermined and endogenous specifications).

All results in Table A13.2 come from models that include lagged political interest as well as the same list of covariates as the models in the previous section (giving the model the structure of Equation 9.6). From top to bottom, specifications successively relax the exogeneity assumption for spousal interest (and its missingness). The top two models assume exogeneity. For the influence of spousal political interest, this assumption is not very plausible. The third model therefore treats spousal interest as predetermined. Difference-in-Hansen tests of $E(w_{i,t-1} \varepsilon_{it}) = 0$ show no clear violations of this assumption. The last row presents estimates that treat spousal interest variables as endogenous, using only values at $t-2$ and earlier as instruments. Instrument sets are chosen to minimize standard errors while meeting the specification tests of the Arellano-Bond difference estimator (see Chapter 9). This approach leads to slightly different instrument sets for different models in Table A13.2.

Other things equal, more lags in the second-stage equation weaken the efficiency of the estimation. This trade-off limits the number of lags that can be included in the third and fourth specifications. In order to generate sufficiently strong instrument sets, lags 2 and 3 have to be dropped when spousal interest is treated as predetermined. For the endogenous specification, even one lag leads to standard errors that are essentially uninformative. (Retaining one lag in the endogenous model increases the standard error of the long-run multiplier for t and $t-1$ by close to 50 percent in most cases, and as much as 75 percent for the effect of husbands' interest in the BHPS.)

Even after dropping lags, standard errors increase noticeably for predetermined and endogenous specifications. Going from the second exogenous to the predetermined specification roughly triples them. Moving to the endogenous model doubles or triples them once again even after dropping one more lag. This pattern well illustrates the demands instrumenting puts on the data.

With one exception, the models summarized in Table A13.2 meet the specification tests of the assumptions they require. Given the theoretical implausibility of spousal interest as an exogenous variable, this is surprising. (The FE estimator rejects exogeneity for the 3-lag model of wife's impact in BHPS and GSOEP and of husband's impact in the SHP.) Technically, it may be the result

TABLE AI3.2 *The Impact of Spousal Political Interest*

	Britain (BHPS)	Germany (GSOEP)	Switzerland (SHP)
Effect of Husband on Wife			
3 lags, exogenous			
t	.080*** (.007)	.145*** (.006)	.037*** (.011)
$t-1$	.010 (.007)	−.002 (.005)	.012 (.011)
$t-2$	−.007 (.007)	−.007 (.005)	.012 (.011)
$t-3$	.003 (.006)	.003 (.005)	−.010 (.011)
LRM(3)	.098*** (.018)	.145*** (.012)	.052* (.028)
AB test for AR(2)	−.5, $p=.63$	−.4, $p=.71$	−1.0, $p=.33$
Sargan test	$\chi^2(2)=.5, p=.80$	$\chi^2(1)=.3, p=.57$	$\chi^2(4)=4.2, p=.38$
No. of panelists	13,833	9,529	3,830
1 lag, exogenous			
t	.082*** (.007)	.147*** (.006)	.034*** (.011)
$t-1$	.014** (.007)	.002 (.005)	.006 (.010)
LRM(1)	.099*** (.011)	.154*** (.009)	.040** (.017)
AB test for AR(2)	−.5, $p=.64$	−.1, $p=.92$	−1.0, $p=.32$
Sargan test	$\chi^2(2)=.5, p=.79$	$\chi^2(1)=.3, p=.59$	$\chi^2(4)=4.2, p=.38$
No. of panelists	13,833	9,529	3,830
1 lag, predetermined			
t	.116*** (.025)	.178*** (.018)	.015 (.031)
$t-1$	.029** (.014)	.017* (.010)	−.001 (.017)
LRM(1)	.149*** (.039)	.200*** (.029)	.014 (.047)
AB test for AR(2)	−.6, $p=.57$	−.5, $p=.65$	−1.0, $p=.31$
Sargan test	$\chi^2(2)=4, p=.81$	$\chi^2(1)=.3, p=.59$	$\chi^2(6)=7.0, p=-.32$
No. of panelists	13,833	9,529	3,830
No lags, endogenous			
t	.283 (.173)	.103** (.041)	.171* (.092)
AB test for AR(2)	−.3, $p=.79$	.03, $p=.97$	−1.1, $p=.28$
Sargan test	$\chi^2(6)=6.5, p=.37$	$\chi^2(5)=5.5, p=.36$	$\chi^2(12)=15, p=.27$
No. of panelists	13,833	9,529	3,830

Effect of Wife on Husband

3 lags, exogenous			
t	.071*** (.008)	.164*** (.007)	.037*** (.010)
$t-1$	-.019** (.008)	-.010* (.006)	.019* (.010)
$t-2$	.002 (.008)	-.010* (.006)	.005 (.009)
$t-3$	-.003 (.007)	.0002 (.006)	.008 (.009)
$LRM(3)$	.054** (.022)	.156*** (.016)	.071*** (.026)
AB test for AR(2)	-6, $p=.56$	-1.1, $p=.29$	-.2, $p=.81$
Sargan test	$\chi^2(2)=.2, p=.93$	$\chi^2(1)=1.1, p=.30$	$\chi^2(4)=6.1, p=.19$
No. of panelists	10,871	8,872	3,062
1 lag, exogenous			
t	.070*** (.008)	.167*** (.007)	[.036*** (.010)]
$t-1$	-.021*** (.008)	-.004 (.006)	[.017 (.011)]
$LRM(1)$	.052*** (.013)	.177*** (.011)	[.054** (.017)]
AB test for AR(2)	-6, $p=.54$	-.8, $p=.45$	-.3, $p=.80$
Sargan test	$\chi^2(2)=.2, p=.93$	$\chi^2(1)=1.0, p=.31$	$\chi^2(4)=6.2, p=.19$
No. of panelists	10,871	8,872	3,062
1 lag, predetermined			
t	.076*** (.017)	.175*** (.010)	.037* (.021)
$t-1$	-.016 (.011)	-.002 (.007)	.017 (.014)
$LRM(1)$	.064** (.029)	.186*** (.016)	.055* (.033)
AB test for AR(2)	-6, $p=.57$	-.6, $p=.56$	-.3, $p=.78$
Sargan test	$\chi^2(10)=8.5, p=.59$	$\chi^2(5)=3.8, p=.58$	$\chi^2(8)=7.8, p=.45$
No. of panelists	10,871	8,872	3,062
No lags, endogenous			
t	.138 (.094)	.116* (.065)	.171* (.095)
AB test for AR(2)	-7, $p=.48$	-6, $p=.52$	-3, $p=.79$
Sargan test	$\chi^2(40)=43, p=.32$	$\chi^2(5)=2.7, p=.75$	$\chi^2(12)=14, p=.32$
No. of panelists	10,871	8,872	3,062

*** $p < .01$, ** $p < .05$, * $p < .10$. Cell entries are coefficients and long-run multipliers (LRM) with robust standard errors in parentheses. Estimates in brackets violate exogeneity at $p < .10$.

of weak specification tests. (As another illustration of the relative inefficiency of these estimators, the difference between estimates from different specifications for the same dataset and gender is never significant at $p < .05$. In other words, it is not possible to conclude that treating spousal interest as predetermined or endogenous leads to a different answer regarding spousal impact. As best as the data can tell, the answer is quite robust to different modeling assumptions.) Substantively, it could indicate that the causal process between spouses operates relatively slowly so that reverse causation occurs only outside the window for weak exogeneity between $t - 1$ and $t + 1$ that the FD and Arellano-Bond estimators require.

14

The Impact of Political Attitudes and Identities

Among the most important findings in the previous chapter stands the strong impact on political interest of squarely political encounters, through parties, turnout, and other forms of political participation. If the politics we encounter in our daily lives matters, perhaps so does the politics in our minds. There is great variation in the extent to which people think about politics and identify as political. Chapter 2 already presented evidence on the close association between political interest and subjective importance of politics. The goal of this chapter's analysis is to understand if political salience can causally precede political interest.

Political identities, often through attachment to a political party or ideological grouping, are among the most powerful influences on people's political thinking and behavior (e.g., Campbell et al. 1960; Bartels 2002; Green et al. 2002; Taber and Lodge 2006). Whether they also affect political interest is not well known. According to some psychological models of interest, identity is a precursor or component of subjective value and thus makes political identity a prime candidate for explanations of interest in the domain of politics.

This chapter also looks more closely at the effects of another prominent variable in psychological explanations of interest formation, efficacy, the sense that actions and engagement in the domain of interest have the potential to make a difference, by influencing an outcome or even just understanding the domain better.

Perhaps more than for any other variables examined in this book, rapid feedback poses a severe challenge when it comes to the effects of political salience, identity, and efficacy. The threat of reverse causation was clearly present in the previous chapter about political encounters, but taking jobs or joining organizations is a slow process by comparison to the speed with which the concepts examined in this chapter might operate. Theoretically at least, a strengthening of party identification or a rise in the importance of politics could right away raise political interest. Indeed, the graphical presentations repeatedly show change in political interest concentrated in the interval between $t-1$ and t, the last interview before a change in identification or salience had occurred and the next interview, when this change is first measured. When change in one variable occurs over the same year as change in the other variable, it is important to remember the inherent causal ambiguity. But the pattern does *not* constitute evidence *against* causal impact. And in some instances in this chapter, earlier or later changes help with the diagnosis of causal direction. In others, statistical models contribute important additional evidence for or against causal effects on political interest.

IMPORTANCE OF POLITICS

People for whom politics is important are much more likely to take an interest in it. This association, already shown once in Chapter 2 and reported by Westle (2006) for school-age children in Germany as well, is confirmed in the German and Swiss household panels, which contain questions suitable for examining the relationship. The GSOEP measure, developed by Arnold et al. (2015), is based on three different questions, used in different waves, that all ask about the importance of political engagement.[1] The study also frequently includes a series of questions about public concerns, another way to gauge political salience.

In the Swiss study, importance of politics is measured differently, as opinionation, by counting the number of opinions respondents give on a series of issues that are queried in most panel waves (as opposed to answering "Don't know"). Opinionation is at best a rough proxy for political salience and attentiveness, and also picks up cognitive dimensions of political sophistication, such as political knowledge (Baum 2003, 133–7, 154; Neuman 1986, 57–61). It is the closest measure available in the SHP, however. Using Jennings' panel data for the United States (Jennings et al. 2004), Shani (2009b) finds that young people who voice strong political opinions are still more interested many years later (see also Merelman and King 1986).

The differences in Figure 14.1 between political interest levels of panelists who consistently[2] find politics important and those who do not are very large, reaching 50 points in the German data and 40 points in the Swiss data. But does the subjective value of politics affect political interest? Figure 14.1 shows that political interest changes when importance does. While much of this happens in the interval between $t=-1$ and $t=0$, where we cannot determine which variable changed first, the graphs offer suggestive evidence for a causal effect of importance on interest. German panelists who cease to find politics important between

---

[1] Book Appendix A provides details about questions and construction of all variables used in this chapter's analyses.

[2] How many waves of giving the same answer count as "consistent" depends on availability of data and is noted at the bottom of each graph.

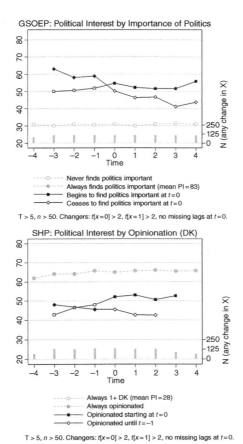

FIGURE 14.1 Political Interest after Change in Importance of Politics
Note: Importance of Politics is described in detail in the Online Supplementary Materials.
Opinionation is based on six issue questions using the difference between no Don't Know responses
and at least one as the cutoff. For details on graphs, see Book Appendix B.

$t = -1$ and $t = 0$ were not already dropping in interest in the year before and
continue to lose political interest in the years after.

Model-based analysis, described in greater detail in the chapter appendix,
confirms that considering politics important raises interest in it. The results
from different models that successively relax the assumption of exogeneity
indicate a large effect of 10 or more points (see Table A14.1). The GSOEP data
make it possible to treat political importance as an endogenous variable.
Although the necessary scaffolding increases the standard error considerably,
the large effect size retains statistical significance. Graphical analysis and the

most robust statistical treatment thus both support political importance as a cause of political interest.

In the Swiss data, a trend in political interest is already evident before importance of politics changes, so the case for importance as a cause is more ambiguous, but the difference between the two groups of panelists who changed at $t = 0$ continues to widen for at least another year. Model-based analysis, which uses a count of Don't Know responses instead of the binary variable employed in the graphs, does not show a lasting effect of opinionation on political interest, however.

Public concerns are another manifestation of subjective value. Every year, the German study asks panelists how worried they are about conditions in the country, including the economy, the environment, and crime. Figure 14.2 displays the connection between these concerns and political interest for six different issues included in the GSOEP sufficiently often.

The graphs in Figure 14.2 for the most part support the conclusion that public concerns raise political interest. For several issues, the effects are moderate in size and fairly unambiguous in terms of causal order. On crime and preserving peace, political interest changes only after $t = 0$, and thus clearly after these issues became more salient for respondents. For concerns about the economy and the environment, change in interest begins earlier, so the reverse causal direction remains more plausible. Only for worries about immigration does the effect look merely temporary.

Comparing the different types of concern covered by Figure 14.2 emphasizes another important point. The people who tend to worry about issues are not always decidedly more politically interested. Less interested Germans are more worried about crime, for example. Yet starting to worry about crime still clearly increases political interest (and ceasing to worry about it lowers it). Concern about crime, in other words, is negatively associated with political interest, but has a positive causal effect on it. This seeming contradiction is reconciled by noting that those who worry about crime are less politically interested *for other reasons*, reasons that must be so strong that they more than counter the positive impact of worrying about crime. A cross-sectional comparison of different individuals would most likely have missed this evidence and been in acute danger of concluding that concerns about "law and order" issues lead to alienation from politics and tuning out. That is clearly not the case, but we only see it when we follow the same individuals over time.[3]

---

[3] The instrument for Inglehart's (1971) measure of post-materialism permits another test. Those who prioritize "maintaining order in the nation" are just as politically interested as those who rank another one of four goals ("giving people more say," "fighting rising prices," and "protecting freedom of speech") as more important. The correlation with interest does not exceed .1 for levels or differences in either the BHPS or the GSOEP, each of which included the instrument in five waves.

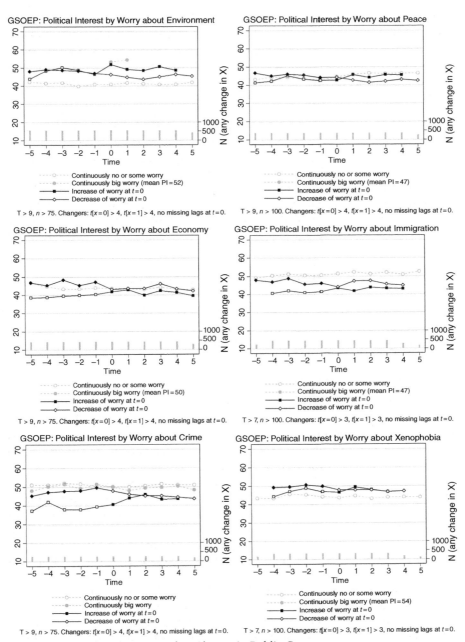

FIGURE 14.2 Political Interest after Change in Public Concerns

Note: Questions about public concerns use a four-point response scale, with a cutoff between the top and bottom two in this figure. For question wording, see Online Supplementary Materials. For details on graphs, see Book Appendix B.

For model-based analyses, the similar results across areas of concern justify pooling the items into one index. A three-item scale available in all waves is sufficiently correlated (.79 in differences) with a scale made up of all six items when they are available to use the former in the model. Political salience as measured by this scale has a large effect on political interest. All specifications of the dynamic panel model confirm this conclusion, including the most robust treatment of salience as endogenous that only uses information panelists gave two or more years prior to the measurement of the dependent variable. What is more, the contribution of the first lag of salience is significant in its own right, further strengthening causal inference by showing that earlier change in salience relates to subsequent change in political interest.

No matter how the model is specified, the long-run impact of political concerns, scored as usual in quarter-within-standard deviations, is at least 10 points, a large magnitude by the standards of both other effects documented in this book and the average change in political interest over the course of people's lives.

Overall, evidence that political importance causally affects political interest is limited by data availability – the BHPS lacks appropriate measures entirely; opinionation measured in the Swiss study may pick up something other than importance – but for the most direct and nuanced available measures, all in the GSOEP, the evidence is clear: An increase in the importance of politics or concerns about matters of public policy heightens political interest.

PARTY IDENTIFICATION AND OTHER POLITICAL IDENTITIES

Attachment to a political party is another path to political interest, according to the Partisan Identity Hypothesis, because topics or domains related to our identity have greater subjective value to us. Social identity has been defined as deriving from an individual's "knowledge of his membership of a social group (or groups) together with the value and emotional significance attached to that membership" (Tajfel 1981, 255). It has been shown repeatedly that the more strongly people identify with a political party, the more interested in politics they are (Campbell et al. 1960, 144; Bennett 1986, 80; Verba et al. 1995, 348 fn.29; Martin 2008; Wolak 2009). In one of the early survey-based studies of elections, Berelson et al. (1954, 26–8) find a clear relationship between strength of partisanship and campaign interest that strengthens between June and October of 1948.

Allowing for a thorough test, the British and German household panels include annual questions about partisan attachment and the strength with which panelists hold them. The SHP does not offer an equivalent measure of party identification, but panelists are asked every year which party they would vote for in a National Council election. To measure salience of partisanship in Switzerland, I distinguish respondents who name a party from those who say they don't know, would not vote, or would "not vote for a party."

Not surprisingly, people who identify strongly with a political party year in, year out are dramatically more interested in politics than people with weaker or no party identification. As Figure 14.3 shows, the difference is more than 50 points in Britain, over 40 points in Germany, and still over 30 points for the measure of party salience in Switzerland. It has been speculated that rising political interest (or political knowledge, one of its behavioral manifestations) makes people more partisan (e.g., Campbell et al. 1960, 144; Palfrey and Poole 1987), and Figure 14.3 provides a good deal of evidence for it. The solid lines clearly narrow in the years before $t - 1$ in all three studies, demonstrating that people gain (lose) political interest before their partisan identity strengthens (weakens). But what about the impact of identity on interest, the subject of the Partisan Identity Hypothesis?

Strong evidence that partisan attachments make people more interested in politics comes from the British study, which shows increasing divergence in political interest in the years after the change in party attachment at $t = 0$. The immediate change associated with becoming a strong party supporter is already close to 10 points. In the years that follow, it more than doubles, making it one of the biggest effects in this book. The patterns for Germany and Switzerland are more difficult to interpret. Among German panelists transitioning from strong to weaker partisanship, the largest change in political interest occurs in the ambiguous period before $t = 0$, but some additional change happens later. In the SHP, the clear evidence for political interest as a cause of party salience obscures evidence regarding the reverse direction. The increase in political interest begins years earlier among people who eventually report that they would cast their vote based on partisan considerations, and so does the decrease among people for whom the salience of party later drops. But the solid lines continue to narrow after $t = 0$, and at least for the diamond markers, the rate of change picks up again.

Model-based analysis, which checks for additional impact of partisan identity after holding constant an individual's level of political interest before the change in identity, handsomely confirms the causal impact of identity. In all three studies, bias in the fixed-effects estimates illustrates the inappropriateness of this estimator in the presence of reciprocal causation. Switching to a first-difference approach and including lagged political interest yields small, but still clearly statistically significant estimates. They hardly buckle when partisan identity is treated as predetermined. But the graphical analysis already indicated that most of the change occurs fast, between $t - 1$ and t, calling for a specification that treats identity as endogenous. Thanks to the categorical measurement of partisan attachment and its inclusion in all panel waves, this specification yields informative estimates, as shown in the right-most column of Table A14.1. In all three studies, they clearly support the conclusion that the strength of partisan identity causes political interest. In all three studies, the magnitude of the estimates increases over the predetermined specification (in the German and Swiss data, these increases in the long-run multiplier are statistically

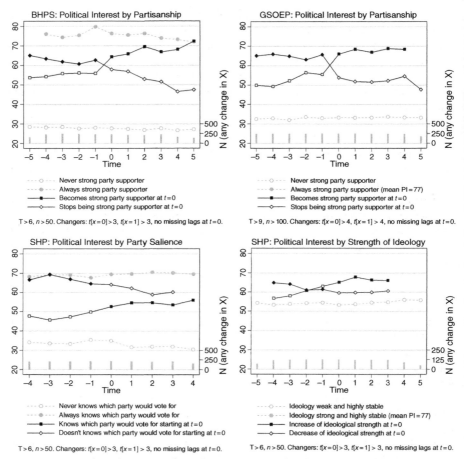

FIGURE 14.3 Political Interest after Change in Strength of Partisan or Ideological Identity

Note: BHPS and GSOEP identify strong party supporters based on a branching sequence of items (see Online Supplementary Materials). Party salience in the SHP is described in the text. Strength of ideological leanings is a folded 11-point measure with the cutpoint between the top and bottom three categories. For details on graphs, see Book Appendix B.

significant). In all three countries, the magnitude of the impact exceeds that of any other predictor examined for this book.

The Swiss data permit a second test, using the strength of ideological identity. In the Swiss multi-party, consensus-based system, some people's primary political identification might not be with a party but with a particular ideological stance. The SHP asks respondents to place themselves on an 11-point ideology scale. The strength of respondents' ideology is calculated by folding the ideology scale at the midpoint. As seen in Figure 14.3, the difference between people who consistently report strong ideological views and those who do not is only a little over 20 points, about half of what it is for party salience.[4] The graph suggests a causal impact of strength of ideological identity on political interest, and model-based analysis reported in the chapter appendix confirms this conclusion. Additional analyses reported there indicate that party salience and strength of ideology are (weakly) related and pick up some of the same effect. Without party salience in the model, the impact of ideological identity is larger. This pattern of results is consistent with the notion that different types of political identities affect political interest.[5]

EFFICACY, CONFIDENCE IN GOVERNMENT, AND SUPPORT FOR DEMOCRACY

The review of a well-known question wording experiment and its many replications in Chapter 2 already indicated support for the Efficacy Hypothesis according to which a subjective sense of being able to understand and influence politics raises political interest. A series of difficult factual questions about politics lowered subsequent reports of political interest, especially among respondents who could not answer the questions (Bishop et al. 1982, 1984b; Bishop 1987; Schwarz and Schuman 1997; Lasorsa 2003, 2009; Robison 2015). The result has strong validity because it has been replicated so many times and is based on randomly varying the position of the knowledge questions – so respondents in the control group, who saw the knowledge questions later, were on average just as knowledgeable but did not receive a demonstration of the limits of their knowledge just before they reported their political interest. Observational research has also repeatedly shown correlations between political efficacy and political interest (Bennett 1986, 81; Craig et al. 1990; Verba et al. 1995, 348 fn.29; Gille et al. 2000; Westle 2006).

Other research casts doubt on the Efficacy Hypothesis, however. In her study of youths in Germany in the two years after reunification, Ingrisch (1997) finds political interest to be higher in the East in 1990. By 1991–2, however, interest among youths in the East had dropped and was now indistinguishable from West Germans' level of interest. Asked in open-ended questions to explain the reasons for their interest, East German youth in 1990 were significantly less likely to mention (than West Germans of similar age at the same time) that

---

[4] Dichotomizing the underlying 6-point scale may understate the magnitude of the difference between people with different levels of consistent ideological identification.

[5] As Appendix Figure A14.1 shows, effects look very similar among young people. With the possible exception of Britain, its magnitude is not larger among adolescents and young adults, suggesting that political identity can modify people's political interest trajectories equally powerfully at any point in the life cycle.

politics was boring or that they did not understand politics. A year and half later, their view of politics as boring had gone up, but the East-West difference in political efficacy remained (in closed-ended questions). In other words, political efficacy remained higher in the East even two years after reunification, but political interest did not. Political efficacy was not enough to sustain political interest.

The question order experiments and Ingrisch's study focus on *internal* political efficacy specifically, the sense of possessing the necessary political competence to understand and influence politics. Psychologists have also used a domain-independent version of internal efficacy, the sense of having the capacity to manage life and accomplish goals generally (e.g., Bandura 1997). The GSOEP confirms Ingrisch's result using a high-quality population sample and a measure of general internal efficacy. Among residents of East Germany, political interest fell by 13 points between 1990 and 1992, the largest aggregate shift observed in any of the household panel studies (see Figure 5.5). Over the same period, general internal efficacy *increased* modestly but significantly among the same respondents.

The first graph in Figure 14.4 examines the relationship between changes in this measure of general internal efficacy and political interest in Germany over all waves in which efficacy was asked. The disadvantage of using general efficacy is that an individual might have different levels of efficacy when it comes to politics specifically. The advantage of a general measure, however, is the reduced possibility of reciprocal causation because it is unlikely that lack of political interest is important enough to affect someone's overall sense of efficacy. Condon and Holleque (2013) show self-reported turnout to be higher among young people with a general sense of efficacy even when the (positive) association with political efficacy is controlled.[6] Blais and St-Vincent (2011), on the other hand, find no relationship between political interest and a trait measure of efficacy that does not reference the political domain. The graphical analysis shows that consistently efficacious people are about 10 points more interested in politics, but there is no evidence in either the graphs or the model-based analysis (see Table A14.1) that general internal efficacy is causally related to political interest.[7]

The three household panel studies have also occasionally included questions about specifically political efficacy asking respondents how much influence

---

[6] Self-esteem is similar but distinct from self-efficacy, as the former involves feelings about self-worth. Examining predictors of adult political participation, McFarland and Thomas (2006) show a significant relationship in two different panel datasets with self-esteem measured in high school.

[7] Condon and Holleque (2013) find a stronger association between efficacy and turnout for children of mothers who lack education. Omitting panelists whose mother or father have an upper-secondary schooling degree leaves the graphical patterns in Figure 14.4 almost exactly unchanged.

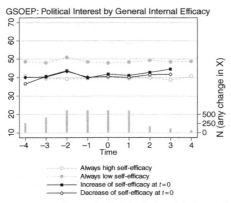

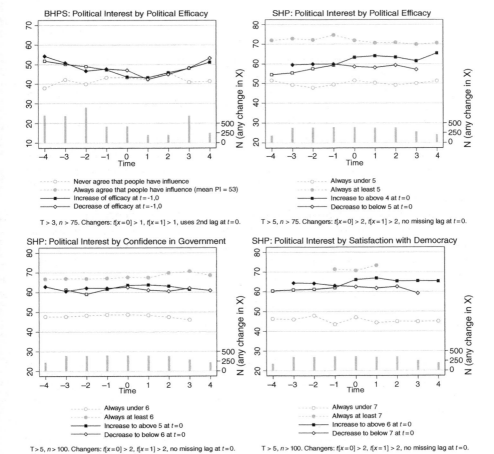

FIGURE 14.4 Political Interest after Change in Efficacy

Note: All independent variables dichotomize categorical scales as described in the legends and, in more detail, the Online Supplementary Materials. For details on graphs, see Book Appendix B.

"ordinary people" or "someone like you" have over government policy or societal conditions. These items combine elements of internal and external political efficacy, that is, beliefs about one's abilities to exert influence and the extent to which political representatives respond to citizens' preferences and concerns.

These items correlate only modestly with political interest (.09 in Britain, .20 in Germany, .27 in Switzerland).[8] Measurement error does not attenuate these correlations all that much: When repeated responses are averaged before calculating the correlations for panelists who answered the questions at least four times, the correlations become only moderately stronger (.19 in Britain and .36 in Switzerland).[9] What is more, correlations between changes in interest and changes in political efficacy are close to zero (.01 in Britain over a two-year interval, .01 in Germany over a five-year interval, .10 in Switzerland over a one-year interval).

The middle row of Figure 14.4 probes for graphical evidence of causal impact in Britain and Switzerland, the two countries with enough data to carry out the analysis. Only the Swiss study asked about political efficacy every year. It shows clearly that people who develop a stronger sense of efficacy also develop greater political interest compared to people whose efficacy drops. The change in political interest begins several years before $t = -1$ among people who eventually cross the cutoff between low and high efficacy, but it appears to accelerate after $t = -1$, and the line with diamond markers dips slightly at $t = 0$ and $t = 1$. Hence, while efficacy is partly a consequence of earlier interest change, there is also evidence that efficacy raises political interest. Model-based analysis (in Table A14.1) shows a sizable effect of political efficacy when it is treated as predetermined. (Instruments are too weak to provide an informative estimate when efficacy is treated as endogenous.)

While the results for Switzerland are in line with the independent evidence from the question wording experiments, the British data cast more doubt that political efficacy and political interest are causally related. Even though people with consistently high political efficacy are about 12 points more politically interested than those with consistently low efficacy, a change in efficacy does not correspond to a change in interest. If anything, people who gain efficacy temporarily lose interest. (The BHPS never included the efficacy question in successive waves, so these conclusions pertain to a two-year interval. Because of

---

[8] For respondents under the age of 25, the correlations are larger in Germany (.30), lower in Switzerland (.22), and about the same in Britain (.10). In the GSOEP, the political efficacy question was only included in two waves and never appeared in the same wave as general internal efficacy. Taking the average of the two responses panelists gave to the political efficacy question and relating it to the average across two general efficacy responses in adjacent waves yields a surprisingly low correlation of .11. (All of these waves occurred between 2008 and 2013.)

[9] The GSOEP included the political efficacy item in only two waves. First averaging those two responses per panelist in the GSOEP changes the correlation between political efficacy and interest to .25.

the omission of political interest between 1997 and 2000, it is not possible to estimate a dynamic panel model even for two-year intervals.)

The external element of political efficacy is practically difficult to separate from trust in institutions and satisfaction with the way they operate. People who believe that elected officials, or the political system more abstractly, are responsive to voters' wishes will also be inclined to view incumbents and the existing form of government positively (e.g., Craig et al. 1990). Answers by Swiss respondents' to a question about "confidence in the Federal Government (in Bern)" may thus reflect a mix of external political efficacy and support for the Swiss system of government. Another item, about their satisfaction with Swiss democracy veers more clearly toward measuring system support, but questions such as these correlate strongly in Switzerland and elsewhere (Zmerli and Newton 2008). Although I present these two items as (the only available) tests of the System Support Hypothesis, they also round out the analysis of political efficacy.

The System Support Hypothesis holds that trust in government and satisfaction with democracy increase political interest because reengagement is more rewarding with an object that "works well" and operates as intended. These attitudes toward politics could affect political interest even if many people have limited experience with government. Politics has a way of making it into headlines and conversations, and people pick up statements by their friends, relatives, and co-workers about the functioning of government.

The positive version of the System Support Hypothesis is pretty close to the Efficacy Hypothesis, which derives from the prominent role of coping potential in psychological models of interest development – things tend to be more interesting to us if we can understand them and "cope with" them. A negative effect of evaluations of the political system on political interest is not implausible either. If public concern about specific issues and conditions can generate political interest, as this chapter has already shown, perhaps concern about the political system more generally or skepticism toward elected representatives stimulates or sustains political interest. (A negative effect of efficacy seems more remote but could theoretically occur if politics lacks the complexity to keep people intrigued.)

Past research findings reflect this theoretical elusiveness. Valence assessments of government or the political system are sometimes negatively, sometimes positively, and sometimes not at all associated with political interest. Bennett (1986, 81–6, 171) finds no clear pattern for trust in government. In Britain, Clarke et al. (2004, 306) find a strong negative association between political interest and satisfaction with democracy. Zukin et al. (2006, 113, 130–1) show that some negative attitudes toward politics are positively related to political engagement.

Albeit limited to Switzerland, the analysis here indicates a positive relationship between system support and political interest, and a stronger role for satisfaction with democracy than confidence/external efficacy. The graph for satisfaction with democracy in the lower right of Figure 14.4 suggests that most of the change occurs in the interval between $t-1$ and t, which leaves causal direction ambiguous. Treating satisfaction as a predetermined variable in a dynamic panel model does indicate a statistically significant effect on political interest (see chapter appendix). At 2.5 points over two years, it is fairly small, but longer lags in an exogenous model suggest a gradual build-up of this effect starting a year or two earlier.[10] Confidence in government, on the other hand, has no statistically discernable effect on political interest (regardless of specification) and the graphical evidence in Figure 14.4 shows very modest change that could just as well be the consequence of political interest than its cause.[11]

The result for confidence in government pours more cold water on the Efficacy Hypothesis. Psychologists have stressed the importance of efficacy in the development of interest, and the question order experiments discussed above appeared to provide clear evidence for the idea that we lose interest in politics when we are made to believe that we cannot cope with its difficulty. But the household panels provide one finding that clearly supports the Efficacy Hypothesis, the impact of political efficacy in Switzerland. The BHPS does not even show an association in levels between efficacy and political interest, and the correlations between change in one and change in the other is close to zero in four out of five tests (general internal efficacy in the GSOEP; political efficacy in BHPS and GSOEP; confidence in government in Switzerland).

---

[10] The LRM for satisfaction with democracy is larger in column (2) of Table A14.1, which calculates it over four years. The coefficients for $t-2$ and $t-3$, with standard errors in parentheses, are .8 (.6) and 1.0 (.5), respectively, so in this case moving to a two-year LRM in column (3) is at least partly responsible for the reduced magnitude.

[11] Trust in people could also make politics more interesting, perhaps because it makes self-governance and cooperation seem more promising as "trust between people makes it easier, less risky and more rewarding for them to participate in community and civic affairs" (Zmerli and Newton 2008, 706–7). Although the relationship between social trust and political confidence is low in some studies, Zmerli and Newton find solid correlations around .3 (across a series of institutions). The correlation between the two 11-point scales in the SHP is .28. Figure OL14.1 in the Online Supplementary Materials shows clear associations – consistently trusting individuals are about 20 points more interested in politics in Britain and Switzerland – and support for a causal effect on political interest. After a change in social trust, political interest moves in the same direction. To the extent that we can rule out feedback on theoretical grounds because social trust is very likely not the subject of feedback from political interest, even the movement between $t=-1$ and 0 would be a causal effect of social trust. What is more, the causal process operates slowly, with interest continuing to react over several more years. With or without the assumption that social trust is exogenous, the graphical analysis thus provides evidence for social trust as a systematic if weak cause of political interest in both Britain and Switzerland. Model-based analysis is only feasible for the SHP. Results confirm the effect of social trust on political interest regardless of model specification, thus confirming that exogenous treatment of this variable appears to be well justified. In a model that adds social trust to the baseline specification without the employment-related variables (see chapter appendix), the two-year LRM is 2.6 (1.0) when treated as predetermined, 3.6 (4.9) when treated as exogenous.

Given the strong theoretical grounding and some robust existing support for the Efficacy Hypothesis, the present analysis should not reject the proposition altogether that a feeling of politics as too complicated affects the development of political interest. Rather, future research will have to establish more carefully if these effects are limited to some components of efficacy (domain-specific internal efficacy, but not general efficacy or beliefs about system responsiveness) or so fleeting that they operate over the course of a short survey, but have long attenuated by the time of the next panel interview, a year on.

CONCLUSION

Political identities and attitudes toward politics matter for political interest. The causal impact of partisan identity exceeds that of any other variable examined for this book. Considering politics important is a close second, but less consistently measured in the three studies. Long ago, the authors of *The American Voter* speculated that "[t]he individual who has a strong and continuing involvement in politics is more likely to develop a commitment to one or the other of the major parties. And the individual who has such a commitment is likely to have his interest and concern with politics sustained at a higher level" (Campbell et al. 1960, 144). But they were careful to note that it was "by no means clear what causal interpretation should be given to the association between strength of partisanship and degree of political involvement." The analysis here has strengthened the case for reciprocal causation. Over the course of years, both variables causally affect each other. These kinds of reciprocal relationships are notoriously difficult to disentangle with observational data, but graphical examination and panel models that permitted the treatment of predictors as endogenous confirm the impact on political interest.

At first blush, it is perhaps not surprising that people with a stake in politics or a sense that it matters find it interesting. But the path to political interest through political identity and salience is an important counterpoint to other dominant paths. People don't need a particular personality, the right kinds of parents, or years of education to become politically interested. All it takes to develop political interest is the realization that politics matters and is part of who we are.

Appendix to Chapter 14

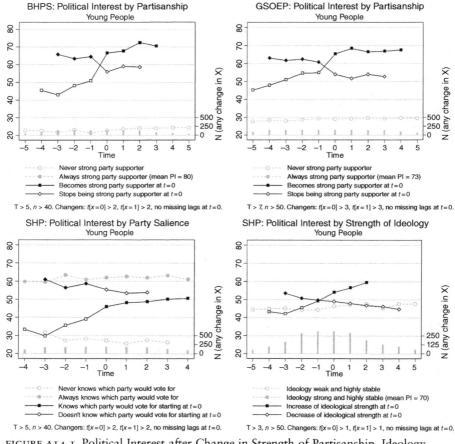

FIGURE A14.1 Political Interest after Change in Strength of Partisanship, Ideology (Young People only)

Note: Graphs use the same variables as Figure 14.3 for sample of young people defined to include panelists with an average age across all completed panel waves under 30 or panelists who were under 25 at the time of their first interview. See Figure OL14.2 in the Online Supplementary Material for results when a different measure of partisanship available in the BHPS youth interviews is used to also include panelists between 11 and 16 years of age. For details on graphs, see Book Appendix B.

MODEL-BASED ESTIMATES OF THE IMPACT OF ATTITUDES
ON POLITICAL INTEREST

Table A14.1 presents results from different estimators that make successively weaker assumptions regarding exogeneity. The FE estimator in the leftmost column requires strict exogeneity. Column (2) adds lagged political interest. It continues to treat covariates as exogenous and retains the same number of lags – three unless otherwise noted – as column (1). Models reported in column (3) use only one lag and treat predictors as predetermined. Column (4) reports results from an endogenous specification of predictors when instrument strength permits it. Unless otherwise noted, these models retain one lag of the covariate in addition to the contemporaneous term.

The modeling strategy and the approach to building instruments using earlier lags is the same as in Chapter 13 for group membership and activities. The baseline specification of independent variables is the same as in Chapter 13 after dropping the employment-related variables. Most variables tested in this chapter (and the membership/activity variables in Chapter 13) are only available for different subsets of waves. As a result, it is not possible to control for the impact of all variables simultaneously, but I estimate the impact of different predictors in the same model when possible. The Online Supplementary Materials provide exact model specifications for each estimate shown in Table A14.1. For variables that are more likely to be correlated in differences (so that the timing of changes in one variable coincides with changes in other variables), I examined both conditional and (partially) unconditional estimates.

Measures of strength of partisan and ideological identity are available in all years in all studies. For them, Table A14.1 reports partial effects when these variables are added to the baseline specification. For the SHP, both party salience and strength of ideological identity are included. The two variables are correlated at .29 in levels, but only .06 in differences. Without ideological identity in the model, the effect of partisan salience remains similar [5.0 (.9) in column 3, 14.7 (4.5) in column 4]. Without party salience in the model, the effect of strength of ideological identity increases for the endogenous specification, but not when treated as predetermined [2.9 (1.0) in column 3, 12.8 (5.1) in column 4].

Extent of Public Concern in the GSOEP is also available in all waves and included together with strength of partisanship. (Dropping Extent leaves the impact of partisan strength little changed.) GSOEP variables Importance of Politics (1990, 1992–5, 1998–9) and General Efficacy (1992, 1993, 1995–7) are separately added to this model, estimating effects for the years in which they are available and dropping other years (see chapter appendix to Chapter 13 for an explanation of how dropped waves are handled). Dropping strength of partisanship leaves estimates for Importance of Politics and Extent of Public Concern as predetermined essentially the same. The endogenous specification generates somewhat larger estimates than appear in Table A14.1 (but the large standard errors caution against making much out of this difference).

TABLE A14.1 *The Impact of Political Attitudes and Identities on Political Interest*

		(1) FE	(2) LDV, covariate as exogenous	(3) LDV, covariate as predetermined	(4) LDV, covariate as endogenous
Importance of Politics	(GSOEP)	[11.7*** (1.4)]^+	9.4*** (1.6)^+	10.1*** (1.7)^†+	16.5** (5.9)^†+
Opinionation	(SHP)	1.8*** (1.2)^+	-.6 (1.7)	-1.0 (1.4)^†	d)
Extent of Public Concern	(GSOEP)	[4.8*** (.4)]^†+	3.9*** (.5)^†+	2.4*** (.8)^+	5.2* (2.9)
Strength of Partisanship	(BHPS)	[18.9*** (.6)]^†+	12.1*** (.9)^+	12.2*** (1.0)^+	14.3*** (5.1)^+
Strength of Partisanship	(GSOEP)	[13.2*** (.4^+]†	10.6*** (.5)^†+	9.1*** (.8)^+	20.3*** (2.4)^+
Party Salience	(SHP)	[6.3*** (.7^+]†	3.4*** (1.0)^+c)	3.6** (1.5)^+c)	19.1*** (5.6)^b)c)
Strength of Ideological Identity	(SHP)	3.9*** (.7)^†+	2.9*** (.9)^+c)	2.4 (1.4)^+c)	3.0 (6.1)^b)c)
General Efficacy	(GSOEP)	-.1 (2.0)^a)	-.2 (1.3)^a)	-1.8 (1.7)	d)
Political Efficacy	(SHP)	[4.7*** (1.1)^+]†	4.0*** (1.5)^+	7.3*** (1.5)^†+	d)
Confidence in Government	(SHP)	-.6 (1.0)	-1.3 (1.5)	1.8 (1.6)	d)
Satisfaction with Democracy	(SHP)	[7.0*** (1.1)^+]†	7.6*** (1.7)^†+	2.6* (1.5)^+	d)

*** $p < .01$, ** $p < .05$, * $p < .10$. Cell entries are long-run multipliers with robust standard errors in parentheses. Unless otherwise noted, long-run multipliers for columns (1) and (2) are calculated over $t = 0, -1, -2, -3$ using the same waves for each estimator. Long-run multipliers in columns (3) and (4) use only $t = 0, -1$ unless otherwise noted. Estimates in brackets violate exogeneity. Independent variables are categorical and scored in quarter-within-subject standard deviations.

a) Long-run multipliers for columns (1) to (3) calculated over $t = 0, -1, -2$.
b) no lags, treated as endogenous
c) violates AR(2) test at $p < .05$
d) insufficient instruments
† Lagged coefficients all equal to zero is rejected at $p < .10$
+ Coefficients of contemporaneous short-run effect is positive at $p < .05$
- Coefficients of contemporaneous short-run effect is negative at $p < .05$

The remaining SHP variables in Table A14.1 (Opinionation, Political Efficacy, Confidence in Government, Satisfaction with Democracy) are available without gaps for 1999–2009. I estimate their impact in one joint model. The global specification tests for columns (3) and (4) indicate a better fit with (instrumented) strength of partisan and ideological identity, and results come from a model that exclude those. When they remain in the model, the substantive results are highly similar. Political Efficacy, Confidence in Government, and Satisfaction with Democracy are correlated, the latter two most strongly (.61 in levels, .30 in differences), and when their effects are estimated without the other variables in the model, all LRM estimates corresponding to column (3) are significant at $p < .001$ and about 2 points larger than in the table.

15

Conclusion

Even though the 2016 presidential campaign in the United States was unusual and controversial, it should not be surprising that the share of Americans expressing interest in politics and turning out to vote was about the same as usual. The grotesque candidacy of Donald Trump may have uprooted the logic (and soul) of American politics in ways not seen in many decades, yet as hard as it was for some to look away, many Americans did look away, as they always do, and expressed little or no interest in politics, as they always do (Prior and Bougher 2018).

Political interest is key to the civic foundation of a country because it encourages good citizenship. The immense individual-level stability of political interest makes this foundation as hard to strengthen as to destroy. As demonstrated, it is largely impervious to political events or economic fluctuations. A new head of government, a controversial bill before the legislature, or a big drop in the markets does little to capture people's general interest in politics. This is perhaps unfortunate because we cannot count on the foundation becoming stronger when needed, in times of critical controversy. But our civic foundation, middling as it is, endures even when politics is unappealing. For the most part, it is not eroded by negative campaigns, horserace coverage, or obfuscating candidates.

There is no doubt that political interest in the Western democracies examined in this book – and thus their civic foundation – is lower than it could be. Average political interest among citizens is typically around the midpoint of the scale on which it is measured. Its distribution is centered on intermediate interest levels. The unexceptional average and the shining example of some, but not too many, extraordinarily interested individuals give this diagnosis a sense of glass-half-empty/glass-half-full. It is important to appreciate what's in the glass. This is the stuff of textbook democracy and self-governance at its best. It is also important to understand better why so many people lack political interest – and in particular the extent to which inferences about what is interesting and what isn't reflects structural disadvantage.

THE SELF-GOVERNING CLASS

Political interest is a predisposition based on affective, often positive, reactions to political stimuli that congeal because interested individuals look forward to the gratification of more political content. The high individual-level stability of interest responses over time and limited impact of events and elections demonstrate that it is more than a series of situational interest experiences. Political interest is not primarily motivated by the expectation of material rewards, nor is it purely instrumental.

If political interest is, first, the sense that politics is fun and gripping and worth one's time, then it amounts to a huge subsidy for democracy. A material cost-benefit analysis would counsel against voting or becoming informed. Famously, the chance of getting hit by lightning on the way to the polls is higher than the chance of casting the deciding ballot in a large electorate. Collective action problems challenge systems of governance in many ways. We benefit from informed decisions, but are better off when others bear the cost of learning about the choice. How convenient, then, that politically interested people enjoy spending time following politics, learning about it, and developing informed opinions about political choices! Their hobby provides the civic foundation we all draw on.

As easy and convenient as it sounds, political interest as a subsidy for democracy also has its risk. While the link between political interest and good citizenship is strong and likely causal, it is not automatic. Even though there is little evidence that Donald Trump benefited from an unusual swell of interest among those predisposed toward him in 2016 (Prior and Bougher 2018), interest and populism have the potential to combine in unhealthy ways. Not all consequences of political interest may be good, and the good consequences don't always happen, sometimes due to obstacles that keep people from making the most of their political interest, sometimes because other interesting things can get in the way, even for people with a strong interest in politics.

Even if the consequences of political interest are mostly desirable and even if lack of political interest does not reflect structural disadvantages, the idea of a happy division of labor between politically interested citizens who gladly subsidize democracy because it's so much fun and politically uninterested citizens who do not pay a price for exercising their right to abstention may still be too sanguine.

High inequality in the distribution of political interest, combined with its potent effects, creates a de-facto self-governing class. Thanks to their political interest, this class of people contributes disproportionately to political decision-making by voting at higher rates and providing more structured, perhaps more actionable input, by putting in the time necessary to make policy, and by taking jobs related to politics or even running for elective office.

Decision-making in democratic systems will predominantly reflect the preferences of the self-governing class. And it is well known that the preferences of politically knowledgeable individuals differ from those who are less well-informed (Bartels 1996; Althaus 1998; Gilens 2001). Insofar as political knowledge follows political interest, that research points to the limits of the self-governing class as an even-handed collective representative of all. If politically interested people get an amplified voice in decision-making and their preferences differ from the less interested, a critical question arises: What does it take to join the self-governing class?

An empirical question at first, explaining lack of political interest soon leads to normative concerns: When people who have the opportunity to become involved abstain because they have concluded that politics is not interesting to them, should researchers second-guess the wisdom of their choice? Abstention from political participation for simple lack of interest is rarely seen as a cause for concern. Yet, as Verba, Schlozman, and Brady (1995, 27–8) point out, lack of political engagement may not reflect a thorough and deliberate judgment if "citizen preference to be active in politics ... is itself the result of social processes and social learning." What looks like voluntary abstention, in other words, may turn out to be the consequence of past resource constraints or lack of opportunity, so "even cases in which lack of activity appears to reflect a lack of motivation might require closer scrutiny of the source of the lack of motivation." Much of this book has been devoted to just this scrutiny.

THE ORIGINS OF POLITICAL INTEREST

Over the course of thirteen empirical chapters, analysis has clarified many of political interest's key features and begun to tackle the puzzle of its development. Some pieces turn out to be at the center of the puzzle: The pace of motivational development which opens up a short window for interest formation in adolescence and early adulthood; the role of parents during this time; an open personality; and cognitive skills, perhaps enhanced by secondary education. Other pieces are not part of this puzzle despite their prominence in the literature on public opinion and participation: Elections and events; aging beyond early adulthood; education beyond secondary level; socioeconomic resources; and involvement in many social organizations and activities. For several puzzle pieces, only the careful use of the methodological toolkit reveals how they fit together: The role of aging is poorly estimated when data are collected at only one point in time. The dynamics of parental influence only become evident when we can compare the link between parent and child repeatedly as the child gets older. Many variables are correlated with political interest cross-sectionally, but they often turn out not to causally affect it. Other variables only reveal their impact when we build statistical scaffolding for them that breaks the rapid succession of cause-and-effect that relates them to political interest.

Despite different political systems and histories, different survey procedures, and different questions to measure political interest, getting older has remarkably similar effects on political interest in all three countries examined here. The analysis took advantage of several European household panel studies that have reinterviewed large samples of respondents every year for several decades. Thanks to over two dozen observations for some panelists, I could describe individual-level development of political interest in unprecedented detail and precision. Although some panelists have participated in annual interviews for decades, there is remarkably little evidence for panel effects in the estimation of aging trajectory.

In their respective importance for political interest development, the life cycle clearly outstrips the electoral cycle. As far as political interest is concerned, campaigns are mostly "sound and fury, signifying nothing." The key predictor of political engagement during elections is not the campaign or the amount of hoopla and controversy it generates, but the dispositional interest people have in politics. Most people do not become interested when an election approaches. They are either already interested long before the campaign starts, or they have decided that politics is not for them. Political interest is little affected by day-to-day politics – or even year-to-year politics. A breezy ride through 60 years of history from the perspective of aggregate political interest at the end of Part I showed many parallel lines. Events that matter for political interest are the rare exception, not the rule. The size of the self-governing class does not wax and wane much.

Political interest begins to crystalize early, before people become eligible to vote and before they make many decisions about other ways to get involved politically or socially. Stability correlations that are corrected for measurement error already reach levels above .8 (over a two-year period) before age 18 (see Chapter 7). Among adults, membership in the self-governing class changes rarely and slowly.

The analysis in Part II demonstrated how political interest develops differently for different individuals. The panel data allowed me to distinguish aging from cohort differences when cross-sectional data produce misleading conclusions about the effect of age on political interest. Age trajectories take different shapes depending on stable, or nearly stable, individual characteristics such as family background, personality, cognitive ability, and gender. Subgroups of people that develop political interest more rapidly still mostly do so before they reach their thirties.

Among the most important findings in Part III is the conclusion that the self-governing class does not have a literal price of admission, so people with limited means are not systematically kept out. Contrary to much cross-sectional research on political participation, resources do not affect political interest, income has no effect on political interest, and some forms of economic and health-related hardship even generate interest. Socioeconomic inequality does not translate into inequality in political interest.

But there are obstacles to joining the self-governing class that reproduce existing structures. The two most commonly mentioned socializing influences in the socialization literature, parents and education, appear to affect political interest, but important caveats emerge in both cases. Children of educated parents develop political interest to a greater extent as teenagers. And children's political interest can eventually match their parents' levels quite closely, although it does so neither automatically nor in every family. When parental political interest fluctuates or when mother and father display markedly different levels of interest, a child's interest development is more autonomous. Still, the upshot is a considerable degree of propagation of interest – and thus self-governing class membership – from generation to generation.

Education can interrupt this generational replication, but its impact is smaller than expected based on cross-sectional association and the conventional wisdom about its benefits. Only secondary schooling raises political interest, and the mechanism by which it does so remains unclear. The absence of university-level effects fits the general conclusion that selectivity of political encounters – in this case the choice of politics-related fields of study – often blunts their impact. For this reason, it is unlikely that offering young people *the option* of taking more civics coursework would do much to raise their political interest. What about requiring civics classes? The one direct test – assessing the impact of lower-secondary education in Britain before and after reforms made civics instruction mandatory – produces no evidence that teaching politics is responsible for the effect of secondary schooling. This study thus joins a considerable amount of existing research that tried and failed to compellingly demonstrate an impact of civics education.

If it is not civics coursework specifically that generates political interest, why does secondary schooling have an effect? A mechanism rooted in the acquisition of general cognitive skills is a possibility. The analysis in Chapter 8 showed that individuals with greater cognitive skills develop higher political interest. In their study of political participation, Brady et al. (1995) find that education ceases to be a significant predictor when they include careful measures of non-political skills. And the psychology of interest gives a prominent role to coping potential and feelings of efficacy: We tend to find things more interesting that we understand (or believe we could understand). That subjective sense of mastery is in turn affected by objective ability. There is one problem with this account, however. It implies that efficacy (general or specific to politics) should increase political interest, a hypothesis for which this study could supply only rather mixed evidence. The precise causal connections between education, skills, efficacy, and political involvement remain murky.

Losing one's job and getting sick may raise political interest precisely because they cannot easily be avoided and constitute inadvertent encounters with politics and policy. The same presumably goes for the impact of a spouse's political interest. When it comes to encounters with politics over which individuals have more control, non-political or sneakily political involvement leaves political interest largely unchanged.

While material resources constitute no clear direct obstacle to developing political interest, satisfaction with different aspects of one's life plays a role. Happiness and life satisfaction raise political interest. Worries about political issues and areas of public policy (in the German data, the only one to measure the concept) do, too. Put together with the positive effects of unemployment and health problems, these findings show that encounters with, and attitudes about, politics do not have to be pleasant to raise interest. Subjective personal security, challenges to security that involve the state, and societal concerns all generate political interest.

More important than general education, inadvertent political encounters, and life satisfaction are overtly political factors. Stronger political identities, engagement in politics, and a recognition of politics as important all foster political interest and push people into the self-governing class. They rarely just happen out of the blue, so in some ways these findings kick the can down the road – when and why does politics come to play a greater role in some people's lives? – but they do document a clear counterpoint to a self-governing class that self-perpetuates from generation to generation. The empirical results clearly indicate that holding opinions on political issues and identifying enthusiastically with political parties raises interest in politics. Dispassionate, middle-of-the-road political views may be attractive for many other reasons but appear to be counterproductive when it comes to stimulating greater political involvement.

Four Countries, a Unified Account

A striking feature of many results in this book is the degree of resemblance among Western democracies. Even though the analysis covers four different countries with different political systems and different political cultures, it is the similarities across countries that dominate. The United States, Britain, Germany, and Switzerland all share a high level of stability in aggregate political interest. The three European countries, for which decade-long annual panels are available, reveal very similar age-interest relationships and patterns of individual stability. By the end of Part II, it is patently obvious that explanations are unlikely to be specific to any one country.

Analysis in Part III identifies many instances where influences operate in a comparable way across the three countries examined. Life satisfaction, employment status, political participation, strength of political identity, and spousal political interest explain why some people have greater interest in politics than others in Britain, Germany, and Switzerland. Employment in politically relevant or public-sector jobs, income, home ownership, and self-reported amount of free time do not matter in any country.

The cross-country similarities are all the more remarkable as the three European countries and the United States, while all developed democracies, feature rather different political systems and cultures. Yet political interest appears to develop similarly in the federal systems of Germany, Switzerland, and the United States and the more centralized British system. Differences are minimal among the American presidential system, the British parliamentary system with single-member districts, the dual electoral system of Germany, and Switzerland with its strong tradition of direct democracy. The few country differences that do occur – a shock to political interest in Germany when East and West re-unified at the end of the Cold War; the utter absence of election effects in Switzerland where elections are much less consequential than referenda and initiatives – neatly illustrate that overall country similarity is not due to insensitive methodology, but to common human development.

Another country difference hides in plain sight in the analysis of age and aging. The main accomplishment of Chapter 6 was to distinguish the impact of getting older from associations between age and political interest that arise for other reasons, most notably differences between cohorts of people born at different times (who thus came of age in different political environments). For the purpose of clarifying the effect of aging, cohort differences are distortions that need to be stripped away because they do not contribute to our understanding of how getting older affects political interest. Yet, to get a sense of why people's interest differs at any point in time cohort differences provide substantive insights.

Sometimes, cohort differences are consistent across countries. People born in the 1940s, who reached early adulthood and became eligible to vote in the 1960s, have the highest levels of political interest in all three countries. Sometimes they are not. The "long civic generation" that Putnam (2000) diagnosed in the United States – Americans who were born in the first decades of the 20th century and reached adulthood in the 1930s and 40s – finds a (shorter) counterpart only in Britain when it comes to political interest. In Germany, the same generation grew up guilty and hungry and does not display a similar upsurge of civic sentiment. Germans born in the first two decades of the 20th century, who came of age in the Weimar Republic or during World War II, are noticeable for their low levels of political interest (when the GSOEP interviewed them, starting in the 1980s).

An important finding in Chapter 6 is that allowing cohorts to have different long-term interest averages is sufficient to make cohort trajectories indistinguishable. So different experiences of distinct cohorts matter, but mostly for the starting point of their trajectories.[1] Some cohorts have somewhat higher or

---

[1] Cohort differences, of course, need not be present from early on in a cohort. We know that post-WWII cohorts have higher political interest than earlier or later cohorts, but with data collection beginning only in the mid-1980s, there is no telling whether the cohort-level boost occurred soon after the war or later, perhaps during the 1960s, which could have been a disruptive experience for people coming of age in conservative, orderly post-war Europe.

lower interest levels than other cohorts across the board, but their aging trajectories still have about the same shape over the life cycle. It is this finding in particular that encourages the generalization of political interest trajectories across countries and generations to an apparently common feature of human development (with the obvious caveat that the generalization is still based on only three countries and data collected over no more than three decades).

Young People's Problem?

Decline in civic engagement is often explained by pointing to lower levels of engagement among young people. Distinguishing aging and cohort differences helps adjudicate those claims. Young people often get blamed for the wrong reasons. The more consequential difference between young people and old people in recent decades seems to be that young people are still young, not that they will be systematically less interested than previous generations. Using the interest levels of those born earlier as a reference point, the youths of the 1980s and 1990s mostly caught up as they grew up. In Britain, political interest in the 1980s birth cohort is 2 points lower than in the 1970s birth cohort and dropped by another 1.5 points among those born since 1990. But in Germany, the 1990s cohort is more interested than the 1980s cohort and as interested as the 1970s cohort. In Switzerland, the 1990s cohort is the least interested, but people born in the 1980s are more interested than those born in the 1970s. Even if younger cohorts tend to have slightly lower political interest than the post-war cohorts, there is no clear evidence, and no logical reason, for a continuing downward trend.

Data for recent U.S. presidential elections are not consistent with continuing decline of youth engagement either. The 2008 election retains the recent record for youth turnout, but both 2004 and 2016 also saw levels above the average of recent decades (Kirby and Kawashima-Ginsberg 2009; estimates by Michael McDonald discussed in Prior and Bougher 2018). Turnout estimates for people over 60 years of age are flat in this period, so the age gap in turnout has been reduced in several recent elections. In the run-up to the 2016 election, starting in the year before the election, political interest among young Americans also picked up in absolute terms and relative to older age segments (Prior and Bougher 2018). There is no good reason why these descriptive statistics would mark the beginning of a shrinking age gap in political involvement, but they help dismiss the notion that the only way is down for interest and engagement among today's and tomorrow's young people.

POLITICAL INTEREST AND POLITICAL BEHAVIOR

The internal motivation of politically interested people makes a critical difference for continuous and multifaceted political involvement. If largely stable political interest underlies much continuous political involvement, that does not imply, however, that political interest and involvement *always* go together. It is not the case that less interested individuals are incapable of getting involved, monitoring elected officials, and participating in the political process. At election time, for instance, political parties often rent buses to give people a ride to the polls. Some of them are probably quite interested but simply unable to get to the polls without help. For others, the reduction in opportunity costs provides just the little push needed to make them participate in the election (Arceneaux and Nickerson 2009). In another example, when we gave survey respondents a full day to find answers to a series of political knowledge questions and a reward for getting them right, quite a few more did – especially respondents with lower political interest (Prior and Lupia 2008). The most interested respondents did relatively better on the spot, without the extra time, because they carry political information around with them regardless.

The electoral behavior of African Americans in recent U.S. presidential elections gives a third illustration of the difference between political involvement based on deep-seated interest versus occasional participation by less interested individuals. Among African Americans, election-specific indicators of short-term political involvement – campaign interest, cognitive engagement with the election, and turnout – were unusually high in 2008 and 2012. In fact, relative to 2004 and 2016, the race gap on these metrics flipped: For two elections, African Americans' election involvement surged beyond that of whites. In 2016, it dropped back to the historical average (including for turnout based on both self-reports and voter files; for details, see Prior and Bougher 2018). On a measure of general political interest, in contrast, observed periodically over this period, the difference between white and African American respondents is very stable. Whites expressed greater general political interest than Blacks throughout. This example is unusual and illustrates the impact of enduring general interest by its absence: Barack Obama's draw as the first Black nominee and incumbent was strong enough to raise turnout and campaign-specific interest among African Americans, but not more general political interest – and so their amplified contribution to the Democrats' voting coalition did not outlast the Obama presidency.

The point, then, is not that citizens who lack political interest will never contribute to democratic self-governance; they will, occasionally, under the right circumstances. What makes generally and predispositionally politically interested people particularly valuable is that for them to get involved politically, we do not need to hope for extra time, extra buses, or Barack Obama on the ballot.

THE CASE FOR POLITICAL INTEREST AS A CIVIC FOUNDATION

It is advantageous to characterize the civic foundation of a country based on people's general political interest, not their civic behavior, even when, in rare situations – such as African American turnout in 2008 and 2012 – the two diverge. At any given moment, a thorough accounting of actual behavior would provide a helpful diagnosis of civic involvement. But there are practical and conceptual reasons to give more weight to people's expressed motivations than their reported or observed actions.

A lot of political behavior follows from an interest in politics, so, practically speaking, behavioral involvement and political interest will lead to the same answer most of the time, but behavioral involvement is much harder to assess. Turnout is fairly well measured by drawing on official voter files. Campaign donations are well measured above a certain threshold that requires reporting, but small donations are missed. Volunteering and involvement in political or civic organizations defy easy measurement. Because different civic behaviors such as these may be substitutes for each other, not complements, it is problematic to think of them as "behavioral indicators of interest." Inferring interest from well-measured turnout reports while ignoring volunteering, for example, mischaracterizes the underlying interest of volunteers, and especially volunteers who do not vote. Drawing on campaign contributions without considering volunteering is bound to understate political interest and overall political involvement of individuals with more time to give than money.

Political interest correlates with (self-reported) electoral and non-electoral forms of participation, but the strengths of these correlations differ by age and generation. The underlying civic foundation can thus manifest in different types of political and civic behavior at different times. Because different ways of participating in political and civic life are to a considerable extent (age- or perhaps lifestyle-specific) substitutes, looking at particular behaviors in isolation can lead to contradictory, incomplete conclusions, as when young people are deemed non-participatory because they vote at low rates, or old people because they rarely attend demonstrations and are less likely than younger people to boycott consumer products (Gaiser and Rijke 2000; Keeter et al. 2002; Martin 2012, 91–4).

Following politics in the news, itself just one component of behavioral involvement with politics, illustrates the enormous challenge in characterizing the civic foundation by behavioral indicators. Tracking of print media use, online consumption of newspaper websites and other news outlets, radio listening, and television viewing is not inconceivable even if it is done today by different entities using different technologies. But anything beyond adding up "unique users" on different media and platforms quickly runs into roadblocks. How would we combine sales data for newspaper subscriptions with tracking of TV news exposure and metrics of social media use to derive a continuous behavioral measure of civic involvement? And while different ways of following the news most likely all correlate positively with underlying interest, many of them are substitutes for each other. (Newspapers are read by disproportionately interested people. Newspaper websites receive more visits from politically interested people. But an interested individual will most likely read an article at most once, either in print or online.) Information about all behavioral substitutes is required to characterize civic involvement. When data on even just a few substitutes are missing or unavailable in a comparable metric, over time trends and comparisons of different groups are easily distorted.

But there is another reason to interpret behavioral involvement in politics and civic life with caution, a reason that has nothing to do with measurement. Perhaps it will be feasible one day to track political involvement across platforms and modes of participation. Even then, understanding and forecasting a country's civic foundation beyond momentary snapshots will require an assessment of the underlying motivation, not just its behavioral manifestations for the simple reason that context distorts the translation of motivation into behavior, and does so differently over time and for different people. When the two diverge, it can easily be the behavior, not the underlying motivation, that is distorted by the political system. As Verba et al. (1978, 71) explain, "psychological involvement in politics ought to differ from political activity in that it should be less susceptible to the intervening effects of institutions. Institutions may prevent some people with the appropriate resources and motivation from converting them into political activity. But it is more difficult to prevent the individual from converting resources and motivation into political interest and political concern."

Predicting the future development of the civic foundation requires disentangling the impact of internal predispositions from the impact of constraints imposed by context (including, but not limited to, institutions). Barack Obama, the first Black candidate for president, apparently increased political activity among African Americans, but the reason was idiosyncratic to the candidate. Hence, for the purpose of understanding African Americans' electoral participation in 2016, their general political interest turned out to be a better predictor than their turnout in 2008 and 2012 precisely because general interest was not affected by Obama's candidacy. Obama, it seems, managed to raise excitement among African Americans for two election cycles – but not to strengthen their political involvement in a lasting fashion.

In a similar vein, Get out the vote (GOTV) can change electoral participation without changing interest. Picture two states with equal levels of political interest in the population, but only one state has a close election: Campaign workers give people a ride to the polls only in the competitive state, so turnout is higher there. With equal levels of interest, turnout rates in the two states might have been about the same in the absence of GOTV. Just because institutional features – a first-past-the-post electoral system paired with party resources – generate higher turnout in one of the states, we should not conclude that the civic foundation is all of a sudden higher there. Remove the temporary efforts to turn out more people, and self-governance after the election – policy-making, the implementation of new and existing rules, the monitoring of representatives – has to rely on those whose involvement persists without GOTV. The day-to-day civic foundation is usually provided by the politically interested.

LIMITATIONS AND FUTURE RESEARCH

For better and worse, this project has painted with a broad brush on a very large canvas. There are white patches. And there are many areas that could use more subtle painting. The obvious example is variables that were not, or only infrequently, included in the household panel studies. Most importantly, the BHPS, which started in 1991, decided to omit the political interest question between 1997 and 2000, creating an ugly hole in the data that complicates the application of standard panel analysis. Maddeningly, the BHPS youth questionnaire, given to household members under 16 years of age, uses three response options for its political interest question whereas the adult questionnaire offers four. (At least the question is the same.)

Further down on the list of regrets is the use of a single item to measure political interest. Chapters 3 and 4 offered considerable evidence that political interest is well approximated as a one-dimensional concept. Nonetheless, measuring political interest with more than one question would still be desirable. Any individual survey item is measured with error, and political interest is no exception. There was plenty of evidence for measurement error in my analysis, including response order effects of 5–6 points and much stronger correlations between different interest questions when random error was accounted for (also see Prior 2010). A multi-item measure of political interest would raise measurement reliability. Based on the evidence presented here, it would not, however, much increase the validity of a single question measuring general political interest.

The occasional spikes in the time series of political interest – triggered by German reunification, the two military interventions in Iraq, several U.S. elections – raise the possibility that political interest can be more situational. Psychological accounts have situational interest subside in a matter of minutes or seconds when environmental stimulation does not sustain it. The spikes in the data here are consistent with the notion that dramatic political events and the intense coverage they received from news media sustained situational political interest as long as the stimulation lasted, but without generating dispositional interest. An analytical challenge arises because we do not have different measures of situational and dispositional political interest – the distinction becomes evident through repeated use of the same survey question. Independent measurement of situational political interest – probably through frequent monitoring of interest responses – would be useful. Not only would it permit more focused study of the crucial transition from situational to dispositional interest, but researchers could better understand if situational political interest affects political reasoning or behavior even though it is transitory. To date, evidence for the (often desirable) effects of political interest is, by nature of the research designs on which it is based, evidence that dispositional political interest matters.

There was no obvious evidence for the theoretically plausible argument that "issue publics" are not interested in politics generally, but derive gratification or material gain from issue-specific interest. A number of analyses of datasets with questions about interest in different areas of politics in Chapter 3 showed typically rather strong correlations between areas and a dominant first dimension. In the German household panel, concerns with different areas of public policy raised general political interest in fairly similar ways (Chapter 14). None of these analyses can directly assess the extent to which interest in specific issues serves as a starting point for more general interest, however, and it is possible that survey questions about other areas of politics could unearth interests that do not line up neatly with the dominant general interest dimension.

Beyond measurement of the dependent variable, many theoretically relevant predictors in all three household panel studies are not included in every wave, making it more challenging to check if political interest changes when they change. These shortcomings were particularly acute in Chapter 14 for the analysis of efficacy as an explanation for political interest. Despite the prominent place in the psychological literature on interest, efficacy and coping potential produced few systematic effects there, but that may be partly due to the low number of panel waves that included appropriate measures.

Many more theoretically relevant variables were not included at all: The three studies are not primarily designed by, or for the purpose of, political scientists. Measures of many of the concepts that would obviously be included in election studies and political socialization panels are thus not available. (And yet, I still feel a large debt of gratitude to their principal investigators and funding agencies for including political questions at all, a sentiment that only grows with the realization that the Panel Study of Income Dynamics, the U.S. equivalent and role model to these household surveys, recoiled from politics entirely.)

As far as theoretical gaps are concerned, perhaps the biggest and most foundational one is the vanilla problem, which got its name from Verba et al.'s (1995, 527) contention that "political interest is, unlike an individual's preference for chocolate or vanilla, not simply a matter of taste." Although perhaps true in a biological sense, the resemblance of interest in politics and a taste for politics leaves a rather large theoretical indeterminacy at the heart of not only this study, but existing psychological models of interest formation. Something in the environment can trigger situational interest and the simple hope of experiencing that gratifying sensation again in the future can be enough to build dispositional interest. Why that is politics for some, but painting or pottery for others, remains theoretically vague.

A different challenge, combining research design and theory, focuses on the incomplete explanation of mechanisms by which early between-subject factors influence political socialization. Much advanced socialization research has this flavor. It commendably uses panel data, often with early observations at a younger age than the household panel studies in this book. But the proposed starting point, chronologically speaking, for the development of an attitude, a skill, or a behavioral tendency is often a variable that does not vary for a given individual. Explanations of political involvement deriving from education as class status (e.g., Nie et al. 1996), personality (e.g., Chapter 8), and the catch-up version of parental influence (e.g., Chapter 11) have in common that a constant is predicted to explain individual change over time. Methodologically, such accounts are subject to strong alternative explanations. A more precise analysis would need to show that class status, personality, and early parental interest serve as moderators for some other time-varying variable that translates into political outcomes to a greater extent among people with higher class status, certain personality types, and children of interested parents.

Another future refinement is only seemingly of a less theoretical nature: dynamically mindful data collection. How long do processes take? The answer of course depends on the type of process. But it's always (about) one year to the next interview in the household panel studies analyzed here. This book, and Part III in particular, demonstrates the need for continued methodological innovation with regard to dynamic processes. At first blush, it may go entirely without saying that the development of attitudes, beliefs, and other, more complex sentiments such as political interest, is a longitudinal phenomenon. What that means for the appropriate analytical approach is anything but obvious, however. In trying to disentangle causes of political interest from its consequences, neither the graphical analyses of change nor the statistical models yield unambiguous answers. Different interpretations of pre-treatment trends can make it difficult to understand the graphs. Using a unit effect and a lagged dependent variable, statistical models aim to hold constant the past – but there are other ways of doing so. The instrumenting approach used by the Arellano-Bond estimator represents a theoretically sound if practically messy and empirically demanding way of addressing one problem of causal inference, but the selection of prior observations as instruments makes its own (unstated and poorly understood) assumptions about the dynamic process. The speed of the dynamics should affect the choice (and specification) of models more explicitly than my analysis was able to implement. For fast-moving, reciprocal processes, a multi-year pre-treatment trend is likely unnecessary. Distinguishing pre-treatment trends from spirals of reciprocal causation is a tricky question conceptually and for the Arellano-Bond estimator employed here.

What may sound like a technical issue is in fact the tip of a large conceptual iceberg and unlikely to be solved by improvement of analytical tools alone. The appropriate specification of panel models, including pre-treatment trends, is difficult to conceptualize without some sense of the underlying developmental dynamic and the half-life of prior processes. To understand development of political interest, annual reinterviews are not a bad place to start. But some of the potential causes examined here probably operate too fast for annual data to catch. Different types of processes require different panel designs. Although methodological innovation is needed, it is critical for applied researchers to also do their part. Dynamics are not primarily a statistical challenge. Understanding the speed of politics requires theoretical innovation and data collection mindful of how politically relevant processes unfold over time.

SLOW POLITICS

In politics as elsewhere, discrete events tend to be a lot more visible than gradually unfolding actions, but are often a sideshow that distracts from the slow churn of persistent forces shaping human development. Focusing on long-term development has proven to be helpful when it comes to understanding partisan politics. Party identification rarely changes abruptly and strongly affects voting behavior, thus linking series of elections over many years and jurisdictions. This continuity of partisan politics seems to enter the public discourse more often these days, helped by, among other things, the success of election forecasting and pockets of more data-driven journalism. But the continuity perspective is up against the allure of day-to-day, and increasingly hour-to-hour, unfolding of events and pseudo-events, which serves journalists' first need, for news, and fuels political junkies' addiction, for more news.

In the case of political interest, this sort of "short-terminism" tries to push into the picture, too, especially during election campaigns and around the more salient political events. Debates, ads, rapid response teams, and tweets around the clock all make it hard to resist the rash inference that this much brouhaha must somehow trigger people's interest, more so than long-past parental influence, years in education, and mostly stable political identities. Most of the findings in this book caution against the quick view.

The point is not that all politics is slow. Clearly, some processes happen very fast. Psychologists have demonstrated what a few milliseconds can do to us (e.g., Zajonc 1980; Kahneman 2011). Political scientists studying physiological responses demonstrate their relevance for politics (e.g., Lodge and Taber 2000; Mutz and Reeves 2005; Valentino et al. 2011). In fact, activation of situational political interest is a very fast process.

Fast is often fleeting, however. If situational political interest arises, it often does not develop into predispositional interest. Many other fast processes may not add up to anything much or dissipate quickly. What is needed is greater understanding of the appropriate time horizon of different psychological processes (or the same processes under different circumstances) and the accumulation of fast processes into lasting sentiments.

This study has tried to examine political interest with tools that are sensitive to different time scales (daily measurements in Chapter 4; political interest over 60 years in Chapter 5; annual reinterviews in Part III), but even with respect to just this one specific variable, many questions about time horizons remain. By the end of the empirical analysis, it is clear, however, that important features of political interest take years to develop and then often remain impervious to change for long periods, sometimes decades.

It is easier logistically to study fast processes, if only because it takes less time to collect data. At a minimum, this book aims to emphasize that slowly unfolding processes and resistance to short-term forces must not be cast aside just because they are more cumbersome to examine. Taking dynamics seriously may produce new insights beyond the variable of political interest and the area of political involvement. A Slow Politics Movement would ask not only if one variable affects another, but (as do, for example, Iyengar and Kinder 1987; Gerber et al. 2011) if the effect is still evident at a later time. It would ask not only if an effect persists, but also (as do, for example, Chong and Druckman 2010) how the residue of the early effect conditions the impact of the next stimulus. It would examine the effect of stimuli at different intensities, different times, and different ordering. It would more carefully measure the strength of prior beliefs to understand how new influences erode them. There are of course a good number of existing studies that build some of these elements into their designs. A Slow Politics Movement would expand these efforts and consider more explicitly the possibility that it is "turtles all the way down."

A Slow Politics Movement can benefit the practice of self-governance, too. It would shift the focus from studying moments to understanding people's lives. One of the clearest results of this study is the entrenched nature of political inequality. People differ immensely in their level of political interest, and this variation is very persistent over time. For better or worse, many people are resolute in their judgment that politics is not interesting. Quick practical fixes – an inspiring candidate here, a new political cause there – cannot easily overcome this inequality in our civic foundation. The challenge for those wanting to change the civic foundation is to understand better how situational interest – plentiful, but fleeting and, literally, all over the place – develops into a predisposition. One thing we know: It happens slowly.

Book Appendices

Appendix A: Household Panel Studies

This appendix introduces the main data source for analyzing the development of political interest over the course of individuals' lives, the three household panel studies conducted in Britain, Germany, and Switzerland. A more detailed description and information about other data sets used in this book are available in the Online Supplementary Materials.

The samples for each household study include all members of randomly selected households of eligible age (which varies from study to study). Interviews with sampled individuals are conducted annually.

British Household Panel Survey (BHPS), 1991–2013. The BHPS is an annual panel study of all adults (age 16 and over) in a representative sample of British households. The study began with a sample of over 5,000 households in 1991. The BHPS became part of the larger Understanding Society panel survey in 2009. Each year between 1991 and 1996 and between 2001 and 2012, respondents were asked, "How interested would you say you are in politics? Would you say you are very interested, fairly interested, not very interested, or not at all interested?" Unlike the adult interviews, youth interviews asked about political interest in the waves between 1997 and 2000 as well. The political interest question in the BHPS youth interviews ("How interested are you in politics?") uses only three response categories: "very interested," "fairly interested," and "not interested." In all, 71,961 BHPS/USoc respondents provided a combined 359,531 political interest reports. (There were 259 cases of item non-response.)

German Socio-Economic Panel Study (GSOEP), 1984–2013. The GSOEP is the longest-running annual household survey in Europe. An initial sample of West German households has been interviewed since 1984. Now in its third decade, the GSOEP also includes several refreshment samples and a new sample of East German households. All household members aged 16 and older are eligible for interviews. Each year since the second wave in 1985, respondents have been asked, "Generally speaking, how strongly interested are you in politics: Very strongly, strongly, not so strongly, or not at all?" In the listed samples combined, 44,730 respondents provided a combined 377,743 political interest reports. (In addition, 1,182 instances of item non-response occurred.)

Swiss Household Panel (SHP), 1999–2015. The SHP is an ongoing annual household survey with an eligibility age of 14 that started in 1999. Each year, respondents were asked, "Generally, how interested are you in politics, if 0 means 'not at all interested' and 10 'very interested'?" A total of 21,803 respondents provided a combined 125,645 political interest reports. ("Don't Know" or no answer were recorded in 171 instances.)

COMBINING DIFFERENT SAMPLES

Household panels use precisely specified follow-up rules to guide the tracking of initial panel members and the addition of new ones to their sample. The most restrictive sample consists of all members in the initially selected households old enough to be eligible for interviews. In addition to household members who were interviewed in the first panel wave, this sample also includes eligible respondents who were first interviewed successfully in a later wave. With this sample definition, the *core sample*, the population being represented is individuals (above a certain age, which differs across studies) living in private households in the first year of the panel. Members of the core sample are being tracked if they leave their original household (unless they move abroad), but new household members are not added to the sample.

As the panel grows, the core sample ages and declines in size because some panelists die, but no new panelists are added. A second sample definition, the *rolling core sample*, includes the core sample as well as children of the original respondents and other individuals who become members of their household. Children were either not old enough to be interviewed in the first wave or not yet born. New household members become part of the sample either when they move into an eligible household or when an original panel respondent moves into their household. The rolling core sample thus follows the population of individuals living in private households *over time*, that is, with generational and mobility-related replacement. All of the households in this sample contain at least one member of an originally selected household (or a child born to an originally selected panelist). When all originally selected panelists leave a household, other members who were not initially part of the panel are no longer included in the rolling core sample.

Unless otherwise noted, analyses use the rolling core sample. Using this sample definition, the number of panelists who provide at least one valid political interest response is 71,182 in the BHPS/USoc, 21,547 in the SHP, and 42,893 in the GSOEP.

Appendix B: Constructing Change Graphs

The purpose of Change Graphs used throughout Part III of this book is to visualize trends in political interest for groups of panelists defined by their transitions on another variable (the "transition variable.") Chapter 9 introduces Change Graphs and provides an extended description of their creation. Either naturally or after appropriate recoding, the transition variable is always binary ("high" or "low") with up to four possible transitions between panel waves: decrease (high to low), increase (low to high), constant low, and constant high. Graphs aim to plot political interest levels for up to four groups: panelists who are constantly low, who are constantly high, who experience an increase on the transition variable, and who experience a decrease. Because most panelists participate for more than two waves, they can experience more than a single type of transition.

"Constant high" and "constant low" groups (shown in the graphs by black and light grey lines, respectively) are defined as panelists who only experience one state of the transition variable. Panelists who experience exactly one transition during their panel tenure map straightforwardly into the "decrease" or "increase" groups based on that transition. For panelists with more than one transition, the graphing algorithm identifies the highest number of panel waves without change surrounding a transition and drops other observations for the panelists. In order to be included in the graph, stretches on both sides of the transition must last for at least the minimum number of panel waves specified. The graphs also specify the length of the gap between $t=0$ and the preceding observation. These requirements are noted below each graph. This selection ensures that each panelist contributes as much data as possible to the graph, but only data for a single transition. Constant panelists also require a minimum number of completed panel waves to be included in the calculations.

Some transition variables are created by dichotomizing an underlying categorical or continuous measure. The legend for a graph provides information about the dichotomization. Chapter 11 discusses this procedure in detail for the case of parental interest.

The bars at the bottom of a Change Graph indicate the total number of increases and decreases at a particular value of t. Estimates for each graph and time t are plotted only when they are based on a minimum number of observations, as noted at the bottom of a graph.

References

Achen, Christopher H. 1992. "Social Psychology, Demographic Variables, and Linear Regression: Breaking the Iron Triangle in Voting Research." *Political Behavior* 14(3): 195–211.

———. 2002. "Parental Socialization and Rational Party Identification." *Political Behavior* 24(2): 151–70.

Adman, Per. 2008. "Does Workplace Experience Enhance Political Participation? A Critical Test of a Venerable Hypothesis." *Political Behavior* 30(1): 115–38.

Advisory Group on Citizenship. 1998. *Education for Citizenship and the Teaching of Democracy in Schools*. London: Qualifications and Curriculum Authority.

Albert, Mathias, Klaus Hurrelmann, and Gudrun Quenzel. 2010. *16. Shell Jugendstudie. Jugend 2010*. Frankfurt/Main: Fischer Taschenbuch Verlag.

Alford, John R., Peter K. Hatemi, John R. Hibbing, Nicholas G. Martin, and Lindon J. Eaves. 2011. "The Politics of Mate Choice." *Journal of Politics* 73(2): 362–79.

Allport, Gordon W. 1946. "Effect: A Secondary Principle of Learning." *Psychological Review* 53(6): 335–47.

Almond, Gabriel A., and Sidney Verba. 1963. *Civic Culture*. Princeton, NJ: Princeton University Press.

Althaus, Scott L. 1998. "Information Effects in Collective Preferences." *American Political Science Review* 92: 545–58.

Alwin, Duane F. 1994. "Aging, Personality and Social Change: The Stability of Individual Differences over the Adult Life-Span." In *Life-Span Development and Behavior*, edited by David L. Featherman, Richard M. Lerner, and Marion Perlmuter (pp. 135–85). Hillsdale, NJ: Lawrence Erlbaum.

Alwin, Duane F., and Jon A. Krosnick. 1991. "Aging, Cohorts, and the Stability of Sociopolitical Orientations Over the Life Span." *American Journal of Sociology* 97(1): 169–95.

Anderson, T. W., and Cheng Hsiao. 1981. "Estimation of Dynamic Models with Error Components." *Journal of the American Statistical Association* 76(375): 598–606.

Anger, Silke, and Guido Heineck. 2010. "Do Smart Parents Raise Smart Children? The Intergenerational Transmission of Cognitive Abilities." *Journal of Population Economics* 23(3): 1105–32.

Ansolabehere, Stephen, and Eitan Hersh. 2012. "Validation: What Big Data Reveal about Survey Misreporting and the Real Electorate." *Political Analysis* 20(4): 437–59.

Ansolabehere, Stephen, Jonathan Rodden, and James M. Snyder, Jr. 2008. "The Strength of Issues: Using Multiple Measures to Gauge Preference Stability, Ideological Constraint, and Issue Voting." *American Political Science Review* 102(2): 215–32.

Anusic, Ivana, Richard E. Lucas, and M. Brent Donnellan. 2012. "Cross-Sectional Age Differences in Personality: Evidence from Nationally Representative Samples from Switzerland and the United States." *Journal of Research in Personality* 46(1): 116–20.

Arceneaux, Kevin, and David W. Nickerson. 2009. "Who Is Mobilized to Vote? A Re-Analysis of 11 Field Experiments." *American Journal of Political Science* 53(1): 1–16.

Arellano, Manuel, and Stephen Bond. 1991. "Some Tests of Specification for Panel Data: Monte Carlo Evidence and an Application to Employment Equations." *Review of Economic Studies* 58(2): 277–97.

Arellano, Manuel, and O. Bover. 1995. "Another Look at the Instrumental Variable Estimation of Error-Components Models." *Journal of Econometrics* 68(1): 29–51.

Arnold, Felix, Ronny Freier, and Martin Kroh. 2015. "Political Culture Still Divided 25 Years After Reunification?" *DIW Economic Bulletin* 37(5): 481–91.

Atkin, Charles K. 1973. "Instrumental Utilities and Information Seeking." In *New Models for Mass Communication Research*, edited by Peter Clarke (pp. 205–42). Oxford: Sage.

Atkin, Charles K., John Galloway, and Oguz B. Nayman. 1976. "News Media Exposure, Political Knowledge and Campaign Interest." *Journalism Quarterly* 53(2): 231–7.

Atkin, Charles K., and Walter Gantz. 1978. "Television News and Political Socialization." *Public Opinion Quarterly* 42(2): 183–94.

Baldassarri, Delia, and Andrew Gelman. 2008. "Partisans without Constraint: Political Polarization and Trends in American Public Opinion." *American Journal of Sociology* 114(2): 408–46.

Bandura, Albert. 1969. "Social-Learning Theory of Identificatory Processes." In *Handbook of Socialization Theory and Research*, edited by David A. Goslin (pp. 213–62). Chicago: Rand McNally.

1997. *Self-Efficacy: The Exercise of Control.* New York: Freeman.

Bartels, Larry M. 1993. "Messages Received: The Political Impact of Media Exposure." *American Political Science Review* 87: 267–85.

1996. "Uninformed Votes: Information Effects in Presidential Elections." *American Journal of Political Science* 40(1): 177–207.

2002. "Beyond the Running Tally: Partisan Bias in Political Perceptions." *Political Behavior* 24(2): 117–50.

2008. *Unequal Democracy: The Political Economy of the New Gilded Age.* Princeton: Princeton University Press.

Baum, Christopher F., Mark E. Schaffer, and Steven Stillman. 2007. "Enhanced Routines for Instrumental Variables/Generalized Method of Moments Estimation and Testing." *The Stata Journal* 7(4): 465–506.

Baum, Matthew A. 2003. *Soft News Goes to War*. Princeton: Princeton University Press.

Belli, Robert F., Michael W. Traugott, and Matthew N. Beckmann. 2001. "What Leads to Voting Overreports? Contrasts of Overreporters to Validated Voters and Admitted Nonvoters in the American National Election Studies." *Journal of Official Statistics* 17(4): 479–98.

Bennett, Stephen Earl. 1986. *Apathy in America, 1960–1984: Causes and Consequences of Citizen Political Indifference*. Dobbs Ferry, NY: Transnational Publishers.

1998. "Young Americans' Indifference to Media Coverage of Public Affairs." *PS: Political Science and Politics* 31(3): 535–41.

Bennett, Stephen Earl, and Eric W. Rademacher. 1997. "The 'Age of Indifference' Revisited: Patterns of Political Interest, Media Exposure, and Knowledge Among Generation X." In *After the Boom: The Politics of Generation X*, edited by Stephen C. Craig and Stephen Earl Bennett (pp. 21–42). Lanham, MD: Rowman & Littlefield.

Berelson, Bernard R., Paul F. Lazarsfeld, and William N. McPhee. 1954. *Voting: A Study of Opinion Formation in a Presidential Campaign*. Chicago: University of Chicago Press.

Berinsky, Adam J., and Gabriel S. Lenz. 2011. "Education and Political Participation: Exploring the Causal Link." *Political Behavior* 33(3): 357–73.

Berti, Anna Emilia, and Alessandra Andriolo. 2001. "Third Graders' Understanding of Core Political Concepts (Law, Nation-State, Government) Before and After Teaching." *Genetic, Social, and General Psychology Monographs* 127(4): 346–77.

Bishop, George. 1987. "Context Effects on Self-Perceptions of Interest in Government and Public Affairs." In *Social Information Processing and Survey Methodology*, edited by Hans-J. Hippler, Norbert Schwarz, and Seymour Sudman (pp. 179–99). New York: Springer Verlag.

Bishop, George F., Robert W. Oldendick, and Alfred J. Tuchfarber. 1982. "Political Information Processing: Question Order and Context Effects." *Political Behavior* 4(2): 177–200.

1984a. "Interest in Political Campaigns: The Influence of Question Order and Electoral Context." *Political Behavior* 6(2): 159–69.

1984b. "What Must My Interest in Politics Be If I Just Told You 'I Don't Know?'" *Public Opinion Quarterly* 48(2): 510–19.

Blais, André. 2016. *Do I Wish to Vote?* Unpublished manuscript, Université de Montréal.

Blais, André, and Christopher H. Achen. 2018. "Civic Duty and Voter Turnout."

Blais, André, Carol Galais, and Shaun Bowler. 2014. *Is Political Interest Absolute or Relative?* Unpublished manuscript, Université de Montréal.

Blais, André, and Simon Labbé St-Vincent. 2011. "Personality Traits, Political Attitudes and the Propensity to Vote." *European Journal of Political Research* 50(3): 395–417.

Blanden, Jo, Franz Buscha, Patrick Sturgis, and Peter Urwin. 2012. "Measuring the Earnings Returns to Lifelong Learning in the Uk." *Economics of Education Review* 31(4): 501–14.

Blundell, Richard W., and Stephen R. Bond. 1998. "Initial Conditions and Moment Restrictions in Dynamic Panel Data Models." *Journal of Econometrics* 87(1): 115–43.

Bollen, Kenneth A., and Patrick J. Curran. 2006. *Latent Curve Models: A Structural Equation Approach*. Hoboken, NJ: Wiley.

Bond, Stephen R. 2002. "Dynamic Panel Data Models: A Guide to Micro Data Methods and Practice." *Portuguese Economic Journal* 1(2): 141–62.

Boulianne, Shelley. 2011. "Stimulating or Reinforcing Political Interest: Using Panel Data to Examine Reciprocal Effects Between News Media and Political Interest." *Political Communication* 28(2): 147–62.

Brady, Henry E., Kay Lehman Schlozman, and Sidney Verba. 1999. "Prospecting for Participants: Rational Expectations and the Recruitment of Political Activists." *American Political Science Review* 93(1): 153–68.

Brady, Henry E., Sidney Verba, and Kay Lehman Schlozman. 1995. "Beyond Ses: A Resource Model of Political Participation." *American Political Science Review* 89(2): 271–94.

Brody, Richard A., and Paul M. Sniderman. 1977. "From Life Space to Polling Place: The Relevance of Personal Concerns for Voting Behavior." *British Journal of Political Science* 7(3): 337–60.

Burton, Scot, and Edward Blair. 1991. "Task Conditions, Response Formulation Processes, and Response Accuracy for Behavioral Frequency Questions in Surveys." *Public Opinion Quarterly* 55(1): 50–79.

Butler, Daniel M., and Ana L. De La O. 2011. "The Causal Effect of Media-Driven Political Interest on Political Attitudes and Behavior." *Quarterly Journal of Political Science* 5(4): 321–37.

Butler, David, and Dennis Kavanagh. 1997. *The British General Election of 1997*. London: Palgrave MacMillan.

    2002. *The British General Election of 2001*. London: Palgrave MacMillan.

Cacioppo, John T., and Richard E. Petty. 1982. "The Need for Cognition." *Journal of Personality and Social Psychology* 42(1): 116–31.

Cacioppo, John T., Richard E. Petty, Jeffrey A. Feinstein, and W. Blair G. Jarvis. 1996. "Dispositional Differences in Cognitive Motivation: The Life and Times of Individuals Varying in Need for Cognition." *Psychological Bulletin* 119(2): 197–253.

Campbell, Andrea Louise. 2003. *How Policies Make Citizens: Senior Political Activism and the American Welfare State*. Princeton: Princeton University Press.

Campbell, Angus, Philip Converse, Warren E. Miller, and Donald Stokes. 1960. *The American Voter*. New York: Wiley.

Campbell, David E. 2006. *Why We Vote: How Schools and Communities Shape Our Civic Life*. Princeton: Princeton University Press.

    2008. "Voice in the Classroom: How an Open Classroom Climate Fosters Political Engagement Among Adolescents." *Political Behavior* 30(4): 437–54.

    2009. "Civic Engagement and Education: An Empirical Test of the Sorting Model." *American Journal of Political Science* 53(4): 771–86.

Campbell, Rosie, and Kristi Winters. 2008. "Understanding Men's and Women's Political Interests: Evidence from a Study of Gendered Political Attitudes." *Journal of Elections, Public Opinion and Parties* 18(1): 53–74.

Caspi, Avshalom, Brent W. Roberts, and Rebecca L. Shiner. 2005. "Personality Development: Stability and Change." *Annual Review of Psychology* 56: 453–84.

Cesarini, David, Magnus Johannesson, and Sven Oskarsson. 2014. "Pre-Birth Factors, Post-Birth Factors, and Voting: Evidence from Swedish Adoption Data." *American Political Science Review* 108(1): 71–87.

Chaffee, Steven H., and Seung-Mock Yang. 1990. "Communication and Political Socialization." In *Political Socialization, Citizenship Education, and Democracy*, edited by Orit Ichilov (pp. 137–57). New York: Teachers College Press.

Chong, Dennis, and James N. Druckman. 2010. "Dynamic Public Opinion: Communication Effects over Time." *American Political Science Review* 104(4): 663–80.

Clarke, Harold D., David Sanders, Marianne C. Stewart, and Paul Whiteley. 2004. *Political Choice in Britain*. Oxford: Oxford University Press.

Condon, Meghan, and Matthew Holleque. 2013. "Entering Politics: General Self-Efficacy and Voting Behavior Among Young People." *Political Psychology* 34(2): 167–81.

Condra, Mollie B. 1992. "The Link Between Need for Cognition and Political Interest, Involvement, and Media Usage." *Psychology: A Journal of Human Behavior* 29(304): 13–18.

Converse, Philip E. 1964. "The Nature of Belief Systems in Mass Publics." In *Ideology and Discontent*, edited by David E. Apter (pp. 206–61). New York: Free Press.

1972. "A Change in the American Electorate." In *The Human Meaning of Social Change*, edited by Angus Campbell and Philip E. Converse (pp. 263–338). New York: Russell Sage Foundation.

Conway, M. Margaret, Mikel L. Wyckoff, Eleanor Feldbaum, and David Ahern. 1981. "The News Media in Children's Political Socialization." *Public Opinion Quarterly* 45(2): 164–78.

Craig, Stephen C., Richard G. Niemi, and Glenn E. Silver. 1990. "Political Efficacy and Trust: A Report on the Nes Pilot Study Items." *Political Behavior* 12(3): 289–314.

David, Clarissa C. 2009. "Learning Political Information from the News: A Closer Look at the Role of Motivation." *Journal of Communication* 59(2): 243–61.

De Boef, Suzanna, and Luke Keele. 2008. "Taking Time Seriously." *American Journal of Political Science* 52(1): 184–200.

Deary, Ian J., G. David Batty, and Catharine R. Gale. 2008. "Childhood Intelligence Predicts Voter Turnout, Voting Preferences, and Political Involvement in Adulthood: The 1970 British Cohort Study." *Intelligence* 36(6): 548–55.

Dee, Thomas S. 2004. "Are There Civic Returns to Education?" *Journal of Public Economics* 88(9–10): 1697–720.

Delli Carpini, Michael X., and Scott Keeter. 1996. *What Americans Know about Politics and Why It Matters*. New Haven: Yale University Press.

Denny, Kevin, and Orla Doyle. 2008. "Political Interest, Cognitive Ability and Personality: Determinants of Voter Turnout in Britain." *British Journal of Political Science* 38: 291–310.

Dimitrova, Daniela V., Adam Shehata, Jesper Strömbäck, and Lars W. Nord. 2011. "The Effects of Digital Media on Political Knowledge and Participation in Election Campaigns: Evidence from Panel Data." *Communication Research* 41(1): 95–118.

Dinas, Elias. 2014. "Why Does the Apple Fall Far from the Tree? How Early Political Socialization Prompts Parent-Child Dissimilarity." *British Journal of Political Science* 44(4): 827–52.

Dostie-Goulet, Eugénie. 2009. "Social Networks and the Development of Political Interest." *Journal of Youth Studies* 12(4): 405–21.

Easton, David, and Jack Dennis. 1969. *Children in the Political System: Origins of Political Legitimacy*. New York: McGraw-Hill.

Eccles, Jacquelynne S. 2009. "Who Am I and What Am I Going to Do with My Life? Personal and Collective Identities as Motivators of Action." *Educational Psychologist* 44(2): 78–89.

Eccles, Jacquelynne S., and Bonnie L. Barber. 1999. "Student Council, Volunteering, Basketball, or Marching Band: What Kind of Extracurricular Involvement Matters?" *Journal of Adolescent Research* 14(1): 10–43.

Eccles, Jacquelynne S., and Allan L. Wigfield. 2002. "Motivational Beliefs, Values, and Goals." *Annual Review of Psychology* 53: 109–32.

Emmenegger, Patrick, Paul Marx, and Dominik Schraff. 2017. "Off to a Bad Start: Unemployment and Political Interest During Early Adulthood." *Journal of Politics* 79(1): 315–28.

Enos, Ryan D., Anthony Fowler, and Lynn Vavreck. 2014. "Increasing Inequality: The Effect of Gotv Mobilization on the Composition of the Electorate." *Journal of Politics* 76(1): 273–88.

Erikson, Robert, and John H. Goldthorpe. 2002. "Intergenerational Inequality: A Sociological Perspective." *Journal of Economic Perspectives* 16(3): 31–44.

Evans, Geoffrey. 1992. "Testing the Validity of the Goldthorpe Class Schema." *European Sociological Review* 8(3): 211–32.

Eveland, William P. Jr., Andrew F. Hayes, Dhavan V. Shah, and Nojin Kwak. 2005. "Understanding the Relationship between Communication and Political Knowledge: A Model Comparison Approach Using Panel Data." *Political Communication* 22(4): 423–46.

Feldman, Lauren, Josh Pasek, Daniel Romer, and Kathleen Hall Jamieson. 2007. "Identifying Best Practices in Civic Education: Lessons from the Student Voices Program." *American Journal of Education* 114(1): 75–100.

Feldman, Stanley. 1989. "Measuring Issue Preferences: The Problem of Response Instability." *Political Analysis* 1(1): 25–60.

Finkel, Steven E. 2002. "Civic Education and the Mobilization of Political Participation in Developing Democracies." *Journal of Politics* 64(4): 994–1020.

Fitzgerald, Jennifer. 2013. "What Does 'Political' Mean to You?" *Political Behavior* 35(3): 453–79.

Flanagan, Constance A. 2004. "Volunteerism, Leadership, Political Socialization, and Civic Engagement." In *Handbook of Adolescent Psychology*, edited by Richard M. Lerner and Laurence Steinberg (pp. 721–45). Hoboken, NJ: John Wiley & Sons.

Franklin, Mark. 2004. *Voter Turnout and the Dynamics of Electoral Competition in Established Democracies Since 1945*. New York: Cambridge University Press.

Gaiser, Wolfgang, and Johann de Rijke. 2000. "Partizipation Und Politisches Engagement." In *Unzufriedene Demokraten. Politische Orientierungen Der 16- Bis 29jährigen Im Vereinigten Deutschland*, edited by Martina Gille and Winfried Krüger (pp. 267–323). Opladen: Verlag Leske und Budrich.

Gallego, Aina, Franz Buscha, Patrick Sturgis, and Daniel Oberski. 2016. "Places and Preferences: A Longitudinal Analysis of Self-Selection and Contextual Effects." *British Journal of Political Science* 46(3): 529-550.

Ganzeboom, Harry B. G., and Donald J. Treiman. 1996. "Internationally Comparable Measures of Occupational Status for the 1988 International Standard Classification of Occupations." *Social Science Research* 25(3): 201-39.

Garcia-Albacete, Gema. 2013. "Promoting Political Interest in School: The Role of Civic Education." In *Growing into Politics: Contexts and Timing of Political Socialisation*, edited by Simone Abenschön (pp. 91–113). Colchester: ECPR Press.

Geer, John G., Richard R. Lau, Lynn Vavreck, and David Nickerson. 2014. *Changing Times: Political Advertising and Information Seeking in the 21st Century.* Unpublished.

Gerber, Alan S., James G. Gimpel, Donald P. Green, and Daron R. Shaw. 2011. "How Large and Long-Lasting Are the Persuasive Effects of Televised Campaign Ads? Results from a Randomized Field Experiment." *American Political Science Review* 105(1): 135–50.

Gerber, Alan S., and Donald P. Green. 1998. "Rational Learning and Partisan Attitudes" *American Journal of Political Science* 42(3): 794–818.

Gerber, Alan S., Donald P. Green, and Ron Shachar. 2003. "Voting May Be Habit-Forming: Evidence from a Randomized Field Experiment." *American Journal of Political Science* 47(3): 540–50.

Gerber, Alan S., Gregory A. Huber, David Doherty, and Conor M. Dowling. 2011. "The Big Five Personality Traits in the Political Arena." *Annual Review of Political Science* 14: 265–87.

Gidengil, Elisabeth, Elizabeth Goodyear-Grant, Neil Nevitte, and Andre Blais. 2006. "Gender, Knowledge and Social Capital." In *Gender and Social Capital*, New York: Routledge.

Gilens, Martin. 2001. "Political Ignorance and Collective Policy Preferences." *American Political Science Review* 95(2): 379–396.

2012. *Affluence and Influence: Economic Inequality and Political Power in America.* New York and Princeton: Russell Sage Foundation and Princeton University Press.

Gille, Martina, Winfried Krüger, and Johann de Rijke. 2000. "Politische Orientierungen." In *Unzufriedene Demokraten. Politische Orientierungen Der 16- Bis 29jährigen Im Vereinigten Deutschland*, edited by Martina Gille and Winfried Krüger (pp. 205–65). Opladen: Verlag Leske und Budrich.

Glenn, Norval D. 1976. "Cohort Analysts' Futile Quest." *American Sociological Review* 41(5): 900–4.

Glenn, Norval D., and Michael Grimes. 1968. "Aging, Voting, and Political Interest." *American Sociological Review* 33(4): 563–75.

Goldberg, Lewis R. 1990. "An Alternative 'Description of Personality': The Big-Five Factor Structure." *Journal of Personality and Social Psychology* 59(6): 1216–29.

Goldthorpe, John H. 1999. "Modelling the Pattern of Class Voting in British Elections, 1964 to 1992." In *The End of Class Politics?: Class Voting in Comparative Context*, edited by Geoffrey Evans (pp. 59–82). Oxford: Oxford University Press.

Green, Donald P., and Ron Shachar. 2000. "Habit Formation and Political Behaviour: Evidence of Consuetude in Voter Turnout." *British Journal of Political Science* 30(4): 561–73.

Green, Donald, Bradley Palmquist, and Eric Schickler. 2002. *Partisan Hearts and Minds*. New Haven: Yale University Press.

Halaby, Charles N. 2003. "Panel Models for the Analysis of Change and Growth in Life Course Studies." In *Handbook of the Life Course*, edited by Jeylan T. Mortimer and Michael J. Shanahan (pp. 503–27). New York: Kluwer Academic Publishers.

Hall, Bronwyn H., Jacques Mairesse, and Laure Turner. 2007. "Identifying Age, Cohort and Period Effects in Scientific Research Productivity: Discussion and Illustration Using Simulated and Actual Data on French Physicists." *Economics of Innovation and New Technology* 16(2): 159–77.

Han, Hahrie C. 2009. *Moved to Action. Motivation, Participation, and Inequality in American Politics*. Stanford: Stanford University Press.

Hartry, Ardice, and Kristie Porter. 2004. *"We the People Curriculum: Results of Pilot Test."* MPR Associates, Inc.

Haug, Lena. 2013. "A Picture Paints a Thousand Words: Children's Drawings as a Medium to Study Early Political Socialisation." In *Growing into Politics: Contexts and Timing of Political Socialisation*, edited by Simone Abendschön (pp. 231–71). Colchester, UK: European Consortium for Political Research Press.

Hedeker, Donald, and Robert D. Gibbons. 2006. *Longitudinal Data Analysis*. Hoboken, NJ: John Wiley & Sons.

Heise, David R. 1969. "Separating Reliability and Stability in Test-Retest-Correlations." *American Sociological Review* 34(1): 93–101.

Henderson, Michael. 2014. "Issue Publics, Campaigns, and Political Knowledge." *Political Behavior* 36(3): 631–57.

Hener, Timo, Helmut Rainer, and Thomas Siedler. 2016. "Political Socialization in Flux? Linking Family Non-Intactness During Childhood to Adult Civic Engagement." *Journal of the Royal Statistical Society: Series A* 179(3): 633-56.

Hersh, Eitan D. 2015. *Hacking the Electorate: How Campaigns Perceive Voters*. New York: Cambridge University Press.

Hess, Robert D., and Judith V. Torney. 1967. *The Development of Political Attitudes in Children*. Chicago: Aldine.

Hidi, Suzanne. 2000. "An Interest Researcher's Perspective: The Effect of Intrinsic and Extrinsic Factors on Motivation." In *Intrinsic and Extrinsic Motivation: The Search for Optimal Motivation and Performance*, edited by Carol Sansone and Judith M. Harackiewicz (pp. 309–39). San Diego: Academic Press.

Hidi, Suzanne, and K. Ann Renninger. 2006. "The Four-Phase Model of Interest Development." *Educational Psychologist* 41(2): 111–27.

Highton, Benjamin. 2009. "Revisiting the Relationship between Educational Attainment and Political Sophistication." *Journal of Politics* 71(4): 1564–76.

Highton, Benjamin, and Raymond E. Wolfinger. 2001. "The First Seven Years of the Political Life Cycle." *American Journal of Political Science* 45(1): 202–9.

Hobbs, William R., Nicholas A. Christakis, and James H. Fowler. 2014. "Widowhood Effects in Voter Participation." *American Journal of Political Science* 58(1): 1–16.

Holtz-Eakin, Douglas, Whitney Newey, and Harvey S. Rosen. 1988. "Estimating Vector Autoregressions with Panel Data." *Econometrica* 56(6): 1371–95.

Hout, Michael, Clem Brooks, and Jeff Manza. 1995. "The Democratic Class Struggle in the United States, 1948–1992." *American Sociological Review* 60(6): 805–28.

Howe, Paul. 2010. *Citizens Adrift. The Political Disengagement of Young Canadians.* Vancouver: UBC Press.

Huckfeldt, Robert, Paul E. Johnson, and John Sprague. 2004. *Political Disagreement. The Survival of Diverse Opinions within Communication Networks.* New York: Cambridge University Press.

Hutchings, Vincent. 2001. "Political Context, Issue Salience, and Selective Attentiveness: Constituent Knowledge of the Clarence Thomas Confirmation Vote." *Journal of Politics* 63(3): 846–68.

Inglehart, Ronald. 1971. "The Silent Revolution in Europe: Intergenerational Change in Post-Industrial Societies." *American Political Science Review* 65(4): 991–1017.

Ingrisch, Michaela. 1997. *Politisches Wissen, Politisches Interesse Und Politische Handlungsbereitschaft Bei Jugendlichen Aus Den Alten Und Neuen Bundesländern.* Regensburg: Roderer.

Iyengar, Shanto, and Donald R. Kinder. 1987. *News That Matters: Television and American Opinion.* Chicago: University of Chicago Press.

Izard, Carroll E., and Brian P. Ackerman. 2000. "Motivational, Organizational, and Regulatory Functions of Discrete Emotions." In *Handbook of Emotions*, edited by Michael Lewis and Jeannette M. Haviland-Jones (pp. 253–64). Guilford Publications.

Jarvis, W. Blair G., and Richard E. Petty. 1996. "The Need to Evaluate." *Journal of Personality and Social Psychology* 70(1): 172–94.

Jennings, M. Kent. 1996. "Political Knowledge Over Time and across Generations." *Public Opinion Quarterly* 60(2): 228–52.

Jennings, M. Kent, and Gregory B. Markus. 1984. "Partisan Orientations Over the Long Haul: Results from the Three-Wave Political Socialization Panel Study." *American Political Science Review* 78(4): 1000–18.

Jennings, M. Kent, Gregory B. Markus, Richard G. Niemi, and Laura Stoker. 2004. *Youth-Parent Socialization Panel Study, 1965–1997, Four Waves Combined [Computer File].* Ann Arbor, MI: University of Michigan, Center for Political Studies/ Survey Research Center [producer].

Jennings, M. Kent, and Richard G. Niemi. 1968. "The Transmission of Political Values from Parent to Child." *American Political Science Review* 62(1): 169–84.

1981. *Generations and Politics.* Princeton: Princeton University Press.

Jennings, M. Kent, Laura Stoker, and Jake Bowers. 2009. "Politics across Generations: Family Transmission Reexamined." *Journal of Politics* 71(3): 782–99.

John, Oliver P., and Sanjay Srivastava. 1999. "The Big Five Trait Taxonomy: History, Measurement, and Theoretical Perspectives." In *Handbook of Personality: Theory and Research (Vol. 2)*, edited by Lawrence A. Pervin and Oliver P. John (pp. 102–38). New York: Guilford Press.

Kahneman, Daniel. 2011. *Thinking, Fast and Slow.* New York: Farrar, Straus & Giroux.

Kashdan, Todd B., Paul Rose, and Frank D. Fincham. 2004. "Curiosity and Exploration: Facilitating Positive Subjective Experiences and Personal Growth Opportunities." *Journal of Personality Assessment* 82(3): 291–305.

Keating, Avril, David Kerr, Joana Lopes, Gill Featherstone, and Thomas Benton. 2009. "Embedding Citizenship Education in Secondary Schools in England (2002–08)." National Foundation for Educational Research.

Keeter, Scott, Courtney Kennedy, Michael Dimock, Jonathan Best, and Peyton Craighill. 2006. "Gauging the Impact of Growing Nonresponse on Estimates from a National RDD Telephone Survey." *Public Opinion Quarterly* 70(5): 759–79.

Keeter, Scott, Cliff Zukin, Molly Andolina, and Krista Jenkins. 2002. "The Civic and Political Health of the Nation: A Generational Portrait." Center for Information and Research on Civic Learning and Education.

Kirby, Emily Hoban, and Kei Kawashima-Ginsberg. 2009. "The Youth Vote in 2008." Center for Information and Learning on Civic Learning and Engagement.

Kisby, Ben, and James Sloam. 2012. "Citizenship, Democracy and Education in the UK: Towards a Common Framework for Citizenship Lessons in the Four Home Nations." *Parliamentary Affairs* 65(1): 68–89.

Kleibergen, Frank, and Richard Paap. 2006. "Generalized Reduced Rank Tests Using the Singular Value Decomposition." *Journal of Econometrics* 133(1): 97–126.

Kohler, Ulrich. 2005. "Changing Class Locations and Partisanship in Germany." In *The Social Logic of Politics: Personal Networks as Contexts for Political Behavior*, edited by Alan S. Zuckerman (pp. 117–31). Philadelphia: Temple University Press.

Krapp, Andreas. 2002. "Structural and Dynamic Aspects of Interest Development: Theoretical Considerations from an Ontogenetic Perspective." *Learning and Instruction* 12(4): 383–409.

Kroh, Martin. 2006. "Das Politische Interesse Jugendlicher: Stabilität Oder Wandel?" In *Jugend Und Politik: "Voll Normal!"* edited by Edeltraud Roller, Frank Brettschneider, and Jan W. van Deth (pp. 185–208). Wiesbaden: VS Verlag.

Kroh, Martin, and Christian Könnecke. 2014. "Poor, Unemployed, and Politically Inactive?" *DIW Economic Bulletin* 4(1): 3–14.

Lafferty, William M. 1989. "Work as a Source of Political Learning Among Wage-Laborers and Lower-Level Employees." In *Political Learning in Adulthood. A Sourcebook of Theory and Research*, edited by Roberta S. Sigel (pp. 102–42). Chicago: University of Chicago Press.

Lane, Robert Edwards. 1959. *Political Life: Why People Get Involved in Politics*. Glencoe, Il: Free Press.

Laporte, Audrey, and Frank Windmeijer. 2005. "Estimation of Panel Data Models with Binary Indicators When Treatment Effects Are Not Constant over Time." *Economics Letters* 88(3): 389–96.

Lasorsa, Dominic L. 2003. "Question-Order Effects in Surveys: The Case of Political Interest, News Attention, and Knowledge." *Journalism and Mass Communication Quarterly* 80(3): 499 – 512.

2009. "Political Interest, Political Knowledge, and Evaluations of Political News Sources: Their Interplay in Producing Context Effects." *Journalism and Mass Communication Quarterly* 86(3): 533–44.

Lazarsfeld, Paul F., Bernard Berelson, and Hazel Gaudet. 1948 [1944]. *The People's Choice*. 2nd ed. New York: Columbia University Press.

Levy, Brett L. M., Benjamin G. Solomon, and Lauren Collet-Gildard. 2016. "Fostering Political Interest among Youth During the 2012 Presidential Election." *Educational Researcher* 45(9): 483–95.

Lipsitz, Keena. 2011. *Competitive Elections and the American Voter*. Philadelphia: University of Pennsylvania Press.

Litman, Jordan A. 2005. "Curiosity and the Pleasures of Learning: Wanting and Liking New Information." *Cognition and Emotion* 19(6): 793–814.

———. 2010. "Relationships between Measures of I- and D-Type Curiosity, Ambiguity Tolerance, and Need for Closure: An Initial Test of the Wanting-Liking Model of Information-Seeking." *Personality and Individual Differences* 48(4): 397–402.

Litman, Jordan A., Tiffany L. Hutchins, and Ryan K. Russon. 2005. "Epistemic Curiosity, Feeling-of-Knowing, and Exploratory Behaviour." *Cognition and Emotion* 19(4): 559–82.

Lodge, Milton, and Charles Taber. 2000. "Three Steps Toward a Theory of Motivated Political Reasoning." In *Elements of Reason: Cognition, Choice, and the Bounds of Rationality*, edited by Arthur Lupia, Mathew D. McCubbins, and Samuel L. Popkin (pp. 183–213). Cambridge; New York: Cambridge University Press.

Lupia, Arthur, and Tasha S. Philpot. 2005. "Views from inside the Net: How Websites Affect Young Adults Political Interest." *Journal of Politics* 67(4): 1122–42.

Luskin, Robert C. 1990. "Explaining Political Sophistication." *Political Behavior* 12(4): 331–61.

Macedo, Stephen. 2005. *Democracy at Risk. How Political Choices Undermine Citizen Participation, and What We Can Do about It.* Washington, DC: Brookings Institution Press.

Manning, Nathan, and Kathy Edwards. 2014. "Does Civic Education for Young People Increase Political Participation? A Systematic Review." *Educational Review* 66(1): 22–45.

Marcus, George E., and Michael B. MacKuen. 1993. "Anxiety, Enthusiasm, and the Vote: The Emotional Underpinnings of Learning and Involvement during Presidential Campaigns." *American Political Science Review* 87(3): 672–85.

Marcus, George E., W. Russell Neuman, and Michael MacKuen. 2000. *Affective Intelligence and Political Judgment.* Chicago: University of Chicago Press.

Martin, Aaron J. 2012. *Young People and Politics: Political Engagement in the Anglo-American Democracies.* New York: Routledge.

Martín, Irene. 2005. *Contending Explanations about Interest in Politics in Two New Democracies: Greece and Spain.* Working Paper, Universidad Autonoma de Madrid.

Martin, Paul S. 2008. "The Mass Media as Sentinel: Why Bad News about Issues Is Good News for Participation." *Political Communication* 25(2): 180–93.

Mason, Karen O., William M. Mason, H. H. Winsborough, and W. Kenneth Poole. 1973. "Some Methodological Issues in Cohort Analysis of Archival Data." *American Sociological Review* 38(2): 242–58.

Masten, Ann S., Glenn I. Roisman, Jeffrey D. Long, Keith B. Burt, Jelena Obradović, Jennifer R. Riley, Kristen Boelcke-Stennes, and Auke Tellegen. 2005. "Developmental Cascades: Linking Academic Achievement, Externalizing and Internalizing Symptoms over 20 Years." *Developmental Psychology* 41(5): 733–46.

McCrae, Robert R., and Paul T. Costa. 1987. "Validation of the Five-Factor Model of Personality across Instruments and Observers." *Journal of Personality and Social Psychology* 52(1): 81–90.

McDevitt, Michael, and Steven Chaffee. 2002. "From Top-Down to Trickle-up Influence: Revisiting Assumptions about the Family in Political Socialization." *Political Communication* 19(3): 281–301.

References

McDevitt, Michael, and Steven H. Chaffee. 2000. "Closing Gaps in Political Communication and Knowledge: Effects of a School Intervention." *Communication Research* 27(3): 259–92.

McDevitt, Michael, and Spiro Kiousis. 2004. "Education for Deliberative Democracy: The Long-Term Influence of Kids Voting USA." Circle Working Paper 22.

McFarland, Daniel A., and Reuben J. Thomas. 2006. "Bowling Young: How Youth Voluntary Associations Influence Adult Political Participation." *American Sociological Review* 71(3): 401–25.

McIntosh, Hugh, Daniel Hart, and James Youniss. 2007. "The Influence of Family Political Discussion on Youth Civic Development: Which Parent Qualities Matter?" *PS: Political Science and Politics* 40(3): 495–99.

McLeod, Jack M. 2000. "Media and Civic Socialization of Youth." *Journal of Adolescent Health* 27(2): 45–51.

Meirick, Patrick C., and Daniel B. Wackman. 2004. "Kids Voting and Political Knowledge: Narrowing Gaps, Informing Votes." *Social Science Quarterly* 85(5): 1161–77.

Meredith, Marc. 2009. "Persistence in Political Participation." *Quarterly Journal of Political Science* 4(3): 187–209.

Merelman, Richard, and Gary King. 1986. "The Development of Political Activists: A Model of Early Learning." *Social Science Quarterly* 67(3): 473–90.

Milligan, Kevin, Enrico Moretti, and Philip Oreopoulos. 2004. "Does Education Improve Citizenship? Evidence from the United States and the United Kingdom." *Journal of Public Economics* 88(9–10): 1667–95.

Mondak, Jeffery J., Matthew V. Hibbing, Damarys Canache, Mitchell A. Seligson, and Mary R. Anderson. 2010. "Personality and Civic Engagement: An Integrative Framework for the Study of Trait Effects on Political Behavior." *American Political Science Review* 104(1): 85–110.

Moore, Stanley W., James Lare, and Kenneth A. Wagner. 1985. *The Child's Political World.* New York: Praeger.

Müssig, Stephanie, and Susanne Worbs. 2012. *Politische Einstellungen Und Politische Partizipation Von Migranten in Deutschland.* Nürnberg: Bundesamt für Migration und Flüchtlinge.

Mutz, Diana C., and Paul S. Martin. 2001. "Facilitating Communication across Lines of Political Difference: The Role of Mass Media." *American Political Science Review* 95(1): 97–114.

Mutz, Diana C., and Byron Reeves. 2005. "The New Videomalaise: Effects of Televised Incivility on Political Trust." *American Political Science Review* 99(1): 1–15.

Neuman, W. Russell. 1986. *The Paradox of Mass Politics: Knowledge and Opinion in the American Electorate.* Cambridge, MA: Harvard University Press.

Neundorf, Anja, Kaat Smets, and Gema M. Garcia-Albacete. 2013. "Homemade Citizens: The Development of Political Interest During Adolescence and Young Adulthood." *Acta Politica* 48(1): 92–116.

Nickerson, David W. 2008. "Is Voting Contagious? Evidence from Two Field Experiments." *American Political Science Review* 102(1): 49–57.

Nie, Norman H., Jane Junn, and Kenneth Stehlik-Barry. 1996. *Education and Democratic Citizenship in America.* Chicago: University of Chicago Press.

Niemi, Richard G., and Chris Chapman. 1998. *The Civic Development of 9th- through 12th-Grade Students in the United States: 1996*. Washington, D.C.: U.S. Department of Education, National Center for Education Statistics.

Niemi, Richard G., and M. Kent Jennings. 1991. "Issues and Inheritance in the Formation of Party Identification." *American Journal of Political Science* 35(4): 970–88.

Niemi, Richard G., and Jane Junn. 1998. *Civic Education: What Makes Students Learn*. New Haven: Yale University Press.

Obradović, Jelena, and Ann S. Masten. 2007. "Developmental Antecedents of Young Adult Civic Engagement." *Applied Developmental Science* 11(1): 2–19.

Ojeda, Christopher, and Peter Hatemi. 2015a. *The Transmission of Political Preferences from Parents to Children: Perception then Adoption*. Paper presented at the 111th Annual Meeting of the American Political Science Association, San Francisco.

Ojeda, Christopher, and Peter K. Hatemi. 2015b. "Accounting for the Child in the Transmission of Party Identification." *American Sociological Review* 80(6): 1150–74.

Pacheco, Julianna S. 2008. "Political Socialization in Context: The Effect of Political Competition on Youth Voter Turnout." *Political Behavior* 30(4): 415–36.

Pacheco, Julianna S., and Eric Plutzer. 2008. "Political Participation and Cumulative Disadvantage: The Impact of Economic and Social Hardship on Young Citizens." *Journal of Social Issues* 64(3): 571–93.

Pacheco, Julianna Sandell, and Eric Plutzer. 2007. "Stay in School, Don't Become a Parent: Teen Life Transitions and Cumulative Disadvantages for Voter Turnout." *American Politics Research* 35(1): 32–56.

Palfrey, Thomas R., and Keith T. Poole. 1987. "The Relationship between Information, Ideology, and Voting Behavior." *American Journal of Political Science* 31(3): 511–30.

Pasek, Josh, Lauren Feldman, Daniel Romer, and Kathleen Hall Jamieson. 2008. "Schools as Incubators of Democratic Participation: Building Long-Term Political Efficacy with Civic Education." *Applied Developmental Science* 12(1): 26–37.

Pateman, Carole. 1970. *Participation and Democratic Theory*. Cambridge: Cambridge University Press.

Patrick, John J. 1970. *The Impact of an Experimental Course, American Political Behavior, on the Knowledge of Secondary School Students*. Paper presented at the Annual Meeting of the American Political Science Association, Los Angeles.

Pew Research Center. 2012. *"Assessing the Representativeness of Public Opinion Surveys."* Washington, DC.

Plutzer, Eric. 2002. "Becoming a Habitual Voter: Inertia, Resources, and Growth in Young Adulthood." *American Political Science Review* 96(1): 41–56.

Powell, G. Bingham. 1986. "American Voter Turnout in Comparative Perspective." *American Political Science Review* 80(1): 17–43.

Preacher, Kristopher J., Aaron L. Wichman, Robert C. MacCallum, and Nancy E. Briggs. 2008. *Latent Growth Curve Modeling*. Los Angeles: SAGE.

Prior, Markus. 2003. "Any Good News in Soft News? The Impact of Soft News Preference on Political Knowledge." *Political Communication* 20(2): 149–72.

2005. "News V. Entertainment: How Increasing Media Choice Widens Gaps in Political Knowledge and Turnout." *American Journal of Political Science* 49(3): 577–92.

2007. *Post-Broadcast Democracy: How Media Choice Increases Inequality in Political Involvement and Polarizes Elections.* New York: Cambridge University Press.

2009a. "The Immensely Inflated News Audience: Assessing Bias in Self-Reported News Exposure." *Public Opinion Quarterly* 73(1): 130–43.

2009b. "Improving Media Effects Research through Better Measurement of News Exposure." *Journal of Politics* 71(3): 893–908.

2010. "You've Either Got It or You Don't? The Stability of Political Interest over the Life Cycle." *Journal of Politics* 72(3): 747–66.

2012. "Who Watches Presidential Debates? Measurement Problems in Campaign Effects Research." *Public Opinion Quarterly* 76(2): 350–63.

2013. "Media and Political Polarization." *Annual Review of Political Science* 16: 101–27.

2014. "Visual Political Knowledge: A Different Road to Competence?" *Journal of Politics* 76(1): 41–57.

Prior, Markus, and Lori D. Bougher. 2018. "'Like They've Never, Ever Seen in This Country'? Political Interest and Voter Engagement in 2016." *Public Opinion Quarterly* 82(S1): 236–256.

Prior, Markus, and Arthur Lupia. 2008. "Money, Time, and Political Knowledge: Distinguishing Quick Recall and Political Learning Skills." *American Journal of Political Science* 52(1): 168–82.

Putnam, Robert D. 2000. *Bowling Alone. The Collapse and Revival of American Community.* New York: Simon & Schuster.

Quintelier, Ellen, and Jan W. van Deth. 2014. "Supporting Democracy: Political Participation and Political Attitudes. Exploring Causality Using Panel Data." *Political Studies* 62(S1): 153–71.

Rabe-Hesketh, Sophia, and Anders Skrondal. 2008. *Multilevel and Longitudinal Modeling Using Stata.* 2nd ed. College Station: Stata Press.

Renninger, K. Ann, and Suzanne Hidi. 2011. "Revisiting the Conceptualization, Measurement, and Generation of Interest." *Educational Psychologist* 46(3): 168–84.

Roberts, Brent W., and Wendy F. DelVecchio. 2000. "The Rank-Order Consistency of Personality Traits from Childhood to Old Age: A Quantitative Review of Longitudinal Studies." *Psychological Bulletin* 126(1): 3–25.

Robison, Joshua. 2015. "Gaps in Political Interest: Following Public Affairs in Surveys from Gallup, Pew, and the Anes." *International Journal of Public Opinion Research* 27(3): 406–16.

2017. "The Social Rewards of Engagement: Appealing to Social Motivations to Stimulate Political Interest at High and Low Levels of External Efficacy." *Political Studies* 65(1): 24–41.

Roisman, Glenn I., Ann S. Masten, J. Douglas Coatsworth, and Auke Tellegen. 2004. "Salient and Emerging Developmental Tasks in the Transition to Adulthood." *Child Development* 75(1): 123–33.

Roodman, David. 2009a. "How to Do Xtabond2: An Introduction to Difference and System Gmm in Stata." *The Stata Journal* 9(1): 86–136.

2009b. "A Note on the Theme of Too Many Instruments." *Oxford Bulletin of Economics and Statistics* 71(1): 135–58.

Rose, David, and David J. Pevalin. 2003. *A Researcher's Guide to the National Statistics Socio-Economic Classification.* London: Sage.

Rosenstone, Steven J. 1982. "Economic Adversity and Voter Turnout." *American Journal of Political Science* 26(1): 25–46.

Russo, Silvia, and Håkan Stattin. 2016. "Stability and Change in Youths' Political Interest." *Social Indicators Research* 127.

Sandell, Julianna, and Eric Plutzer. 2005. "Families, Divorce, and Voter Turnout." *Political Behavior* 27(2): 133–62.

Sansone, Carol, and Jessi L. Smith. 2000. "Interest and Self-Regulation: The Relation between Having to and Wanting To." In *Intrinsic and Extrinsic Motivation: The Search for Optimal Motivation and Performance*, edited by Carol Sansone and Judith M. Harackiewicz (pp. 341–72). San Diego: Academic Press.

Saphir, Melissa Nicholas, and Steven H. Chaffee. 2002. "Adolescents' Contributions to Family Communication Patterns." *Human Communication Research* 28(1): 86–108.

Sapiro, Virginia. 1994. "Political Socialization During Adulthood: Clarifying the Political Time of Our Lives." In *Research in Micropolitics: New Directions in Political Psychology*, edited by Michael X. Delli Carpini, Leonie Huddy, and Robert Y. Shapiro (pp. 197–223). Greenwich, CT: JAI Press.

Schneider, Silke L., ed. 2008. *The International Standard Classification of Education (Isced-97): An Evaluation of Content and Criterion Validity for 15 European Countries*. Mannheim: Mannheim Centre for European Social Research.

Schraw, Gregory, and Stephen Lehman. 2001. "Situational Interest: A Review of the Literature and Directions for Future Research." *Educational Psychology Review* 13(1): 23–52.

Schwartz, David C., Joseph Garrison, and James Alouf. 1975. "Health, Body Images, and Political Socialization." In *New Directions in Political Socialization*, edited by David C. Schwartz and Sandra Kenyon Schwartz (pp. 96–126). New York: The Free Press.

Schwarz, Norbert, and Howard Schuman. 1997. "Political Knowledge, Attribution, and Inferred Interest in Politics: The Operation of Buffer Items." *International Journal of Public Opinion Research* 9(2): 191–5.

Sears, David O. 1983. "The Persistence of Early Political Predispositions: The Roles of Attitude Object and Life Stage." In *Review of Personality and Social Psychology*, edited by Ladd Wheeler and Phillip R. Shaver (pp. 79–116). Beverly Hills: Sage.

Sears, David O., and Carolyn L. Funk. 1991. "The Role of Self-Interest in Social and Political Attitudes." *Advances in Experimental Social Psychology* 24: 1–91.

1999. "Evidence of the Long-Term Persistence of Adults' Political Predispositions." *Journal of Politics* 61(1): 1–28.

Sears, David O., and Sheri Levy. 2003. "Childhood and Adult Political Development." In *Oxford Handbook of Political Psychology*, edited by David O. Sears, Leonie Huddy, and Robert Jervis (pp. 60–109). New York: Oxford University Press.

Sears, David O., and Nicholas A. Valentino. 1997. "Politics Matters: Political Events as Catalysts for Preadult Socialization." *American Political Science Review* 91(1): 45–65.

Seitz, Hans, Christoph Metzger, and Christoph Kobler. 2005. "Vocational Education in Switzerland – Characteristics, Challenges and Strategies. Some Reflections on Structures, Transitions, Supply and Demand, and Normative Aspects." *Berufsbildung in Wissenschaft und Praxis* 7: 1–25.

Shani, Danielle. 2009a. "Measuring Political Interest." In *Improving Public Opinion Surveys*, edited by John H. Aldrich and Kathleen M. McGraw (pp. 137–57). Princeton: Princeton University Press.

2009b. On the Origins of Political Interest. Ph.D. dissertation, Princeton University, Princeton.

Sherrod, Lonnie R., Constance A. Flanagan, and James Youniss. 2002. "Dimensions of Citizenship and Opportunities for Youth Development: The What, Why, When, Where, and Who of Citizenship Development." *Applied Developmental Science* 6(4): 264–72.

Shiner, Rebecca L., Ann S. Masten, and Jennifer M. Roberts. 2003. "Childhood Personality Foreshadows Adult Personality and Life Outcomes Two Decades Later." *Journal of Personality* 71(6): 1145–70.

Sides, John, and Lynn Vavreck. 2013. *The Gamble: Choice and Chance in the 2012 Presidential Election*. Princeton: Princeton University Press.

Siedler, Thomas. 2010. "Schooling and Citizenship in a Young Democracy: Evidence from Postwar Germany." *Scandinavian Journal of Economics* 112(2): 315–38.

Sigel, Roberta S., ed. 1989. *Political Learning in Adulthood. A Sourcebook of Theory and Research*. Chicago: University of Chicago Press.

Silver, Brian D., Barbara A. Anderson, and Paul R. Abramson. 1986. "Who Overreports Voting?" *American Political Science Review* 80(2): 613–24.

Silvia, Paul J. 2005. "What Is Interesting? Exploring the Appraisal Structure of Interest." *Emotion* 5(1): 89–102.

Silvia, Paul J. 2006. *Exploring the Psychology of Interest*. Oxford; New York: Oxford University Press.

2008. "Interest – The Curious Emotion." *Current Directions in Psychological Science,* 17(1): 57–60.

Singer, Judith D., and John B. Willett. 2003. *Applied Longitudinal Data Analysis: Modeling Change and Event Occurrence*. New York: Oxford University Press.

Smith, Elizabeth S. 1999. "The Effects of Investments in the Social Capital of Youth on Political and Civic Behavior in Young Adulthood: A Longitudinal Analysis." *Political Psychology* 20(3): 553–80.

Smith, Eric R. A. N. 1989. *The Unchanging American Voter*. Berkeley: University of California Press.

Snell, Patricia. 2010. "Emerging Adult Civic and Political Disengagement: A Longitudinal Analysis of Lack of Involvement with Politics." *Journal of Adolescent Research* 25(2): 258–87.

Sohlberg, Jacob. 2015. "Thinking Matters: The Validity and Political Relevance of Need for Cognition." *International Journal of Public Opinion Research* 28 (3): 428–39.

Solvak, Mihkel. 2009. "Events and Reliability of Measures: The Effect of Elections on Measures of Interest in Politics." *International Journal of Public Opinion Research* 21(3): 316–32.

Sondheimer, Rachel M., and Donald P. Green. 2010. "Using Experiments to Estimate the Effects of Education on Voter Turnout." *American Journal of Political Science* 54(1): 174–89.

Srivastava, Sanjay, Oliver P. John, Samuel D. Gosling, and Jeff Potter. 2003. "Development of Personality in Early and Middle Adulthood: Set Like Plaster or Persistent Change?" *Journal of Personality and Social Psychology* 84(5): 1041–53.

Stattin, Håkan, Oula Hussein, Metin Özdemir, and Silvia Russo. 2017. "Why Do Some Adolescents Encounter Everyday Events That Increase Their Civic Interest Whereas Others Do Not?" *Developmental Psychology* 53(2): 306–18.

Stoker, Laura, and M. Kent Jennings. 1995. "Life-Cycle Transitions and Political Participation: The Case of Marriage." *American Political Science Review* 89: 421–33.

2005. "Political Similarity and Influence between Husbands and Wives." In *Social Logic of Politics: Personal Networks as Contexts*, edited by Alan S. Zuckerman (pp. 51–74). Philadelphia: Temple University Press.

Stolle, Dietlind, and Marc Hooghe. 2004. "The Roots of Social Capital: Attitudinal and Network Mechanisms in the Relation between Youth and Adult Indicators of Social Capital." *Acta Politica* 39(4): 422–41.

Strömbäck, Jesper, and Bengt Johansson. 2007. "Electoral Cycles and the Mobilizing Effects of Elections: A Longitudinal Study of the Swedish Case." *Journal of Elections, Public Opinion and Parties* 17(1): 79–99.

Strömbäck, Jesper, and Adam Shehata. 2010. "Media Malaise or a Virtuous Circle? Exploring the Causal Relationships between News Media Exposure, Political News Attention, and Political Interest." *European Journal of Political Research* 49: 575–97.

Syvertsen, Amy K., Laura Wray-Lake, Constance A. Flanagan, D. Wayne Osgood, and Laine Briddell. 2011. "Thirty-Year Trends in U.S. Adolescents' Civic Engagement: A Story of Changing Participation and Educational Differences." *Journal of Research on Adolescence* 21(3): 586–94.

Taber, Charles S., and Milton Lodge. 2006. "Motivated Skepticism in the Evaluation of Political Beliefs." *American Journal of Political Science* 50(3): 755–69.

Tajfel, Henri. 1981. *Human Groups and Social Categories*. Cambridge: Cambridge University Press.

Valentino, Nicholas A., Ted Brader, Eric W. Groenendyk, Krysha Gregorowicz, and Vincent L. Hutchings. 2011. "Election Night's Alright for Fighting: The Role of Emotions in Political Participation." *Journal of Politics* 73(1): 156–70.

Valentino, Nicholas A., Vincent L. Hutchings, Antoine J. Banks, and Anne K. Davis. 2008. "Is a Worried Citizen a Good Citizen? Emotions, Political Information Seeking, and Learning Via the Internet." *Political Psychology* 29(2): 247–73.

Valentino, Nicholas A., and David O. Sears. 1998. "Event-Driven Political Communication and the Preadult Socialization of Partisanship." *Political Behavior* 20(2): 127–55.

van Deth, Jan W. 1990. "Interest in Politics." In *Continuities in Political Action: A Longitudinal Study of Political Orientations in Three Western Democracies*, edited by M. Kent Jennings and Jan W. van Deth (pp. 275–312). Berlin: Walter De Gruyter.

van Deth, Jan W., Simone Abendschön, Julia Rathke, and Maike Vollmar. 2007. *Kinder Und Politik. Politische Einstellungen Von Jungen Kindern Im Ersten Grundschuljahr*. Wiesbaden: VS Verlag für Sozialwissenschaften.

van Ingen, Erik, and Tom van der Meer. 2016. "Schools or Pools of Democracy? A Longitudinal Test of the Relation between Civic Participation and Political Socialization." *Political Behavior* 38(1): 83–103.

Vavreck, Lynn. 2007. "The Exaggerated Effects of Advertising on Turnout: The Dangers of Self-Reports." *Quarterly Journal of Political Science* 2(4): 287–305.

Verba, Sidney, Nancy Burns, and Kay Lehman Schlozman. 1997. "Knowing and Caring about Politics: Gender and Political Engagement." *Journal of Politics* 59(4): 1051–72.

Verba, Sidney, and Norman H. Nie. 1972. *Participation in America: Political Democracy and Social Equality*. New York: Harper and Row.

Verba, Sidney, Norman H. Nie, and Jae-on Kim. 1978. *Participation and Political Equality: A Seven-Nation Comparison*. New York: Cambridge University Press.

Verba, Sidney, Kay Lehman Schlozman, and Henry E. Brady. 1995. *Voice and Equality: Civic Voluntarism in American Politics*. Cambridge, MA: Harvard University Press.

Verba, Sidney, Kay Lehman Schlozman, and Nancy Burns. 2005. "Family Ties: Understanding the Intergenerational Transmission of Participation." In *The Social Logic of Politics*, edited by Alan S. Zuckerman (pp. 95–114). Philadelphia: Temple University Press.

Walsh, Katherine Cramer. 2004. *Talking about Politics: Informal Groups and Social Identity in American Life*. Chicago: University of Chicago Press.

Wawro, Gregory. 2002. "Estimating Dynamic Panel Data Models in Political Science." *Political Analysis* 10(1): 25–48.

Weiss, Robert E. 2005. *Modeling Longitudinal Data*. New York: Springer.

Westle, Bettina. 2006. "Politisches Interesse, Subjektive Politische Kompetenz Und Politisches Wissen – Eine Fallstudie Mit Jugendlichen Im Nürnberger Raum." In *Jugend Und Politik:"Voll Normal!"*, edited by Edeltraud Roller, Frank Brettschneider and Jan W. van Deth (pp. 209–40). Wiesbaden: VS Verlag.

White, Clarissa, Sara Bruce, and Jane Ritchie. 2000. *Young People's Politics: Political Interest and Engagement Amongst 14–24 Year Olds*. London: National Centre for Social Research.

Wiley, David E., and James A. Wiley. 1970. "The Estimation of Measurement Error in Panel Data." *American Sociological Review* 35(1): 112–17.

Wolak, Jennifer. 2009. "Explaining Change in Party Identification in Adolescence." *Electoral Studies* 28(4): 573–83.

Wooldridge, Jeffrey M. 2002. *Econometric Analysis of Cross Section and Panel Data*. Cambridge, MA: MIT Press.

2009. *Introductory Econometrics: A Modern Approach*. 4th ed. Mason, OH: South-Western Cengage Learning.

Yang, Yang, and Kenneth C. Land. 2013. *Age-Period-Cohort Analysis: New Models, Methods, and Empirical Applications*. Boca Raton: Chapman and Hall/CRC.

Zaff, Jonathan F., Oksana Malanchuk, and Jacquelynne S. Eccles. 2008. "Predicting Positive Citizenship from Adolescence to Young Adulthood: The Effects of a Civic Context." *Applied Developmental Science* 12(1): 38–53.

Zajonc, Robert B. 1980. "Feeling and Thinking: Preferences Need No Inferences." *American Psychologist* 35(2): 151–75.

Zaller, John. 1992. *The Nature and Origins of Mass Opinion*. New York: Cambridge University Press.

Zmerli, Sonja, and Ken Newton. 2008. "Social Trust and Attitudes Toward Democracy." *Public Opinion Quarterly* 72(4): 706–24.

Zuckerman, Alan S., Jennifer Fitzgerald, and Josip Dasovic. 2007. *Partisan Families: The Social Logic of Bounded Partisanship in Germany and Britain*. New York: Cambridge University Press.

Zukin, Cliff, Scott Keeter, Molly Andolina, Krista Jenkins, and Michael X. Delli Carpini. 2006. *A New Engagement? Political Participation, Civic Life, and the Changing American Citizen*. Oxford: Oxford University Press.

Index